STUDIES IN IMPERIALISM

General editors: Andrew S. Thompson an
Founding editor: John M. MacKe

C000093119

When the 'Studies in Imperialism' series was iounucu
by Professor John M. MacKenzie more than thirty years
ago, emphasis was laid upon the conviction that
'imperialism as a cultural phenomenon had as significant an
effect on the dominant as on the subordinate societies'.
With well over a hundred titles now published, this
remains the prime concern of the series. Cross-disciplinary
work has indeed appeared covering the full spectrum of
cultural phenomena, as well as examining aspects of
gender and sex, frontiers and law, science and the
environment, language and literature, migration and
patriotic societies and much else. Moreover, the series has
always wished to present comparative work on European
and American imperialism, and particularly welcomes the
submission of books in these areas. The fascination with
imperialism, in all its aspects, shows no sign of abating
and this series will continue to lead the way in
encouraging the widest possible range of studies in the
field. 'Studies in Imperialism' is fully organic in its
development, always seeking to be at the cutting edge,
responding to the latest interests of scholars and the needs
of this ever-expanding area of scholarship.

Class, work and whiteness

Manchester University Press

Class, work and whiteness

RACE AND SETTLER COLONIALISM IN SOUTHERN RHODESIA, 1919–79

Nicola Ginsburgh

MANCHESTER UNIVERSITY PRESS

Published by Manchester University Press
Oxford Road, Manchester M13 9PL
www.manchesteruniversitypress.co.uk

British Library Cataloguing-in-Publication Data
A catalogue record for this book is available from the British Library

ISBN   978 1 5261 4387 7   hardback
ISBN   978 1 5261 6709 5   paperback

First published 2020
Paperback published 2023

Typeset by Newgen Publishing UK

CONTENTS

FIGURES

GRAPHS

TABLES

FOUNDING EDITOR'S INTRODUCTION

Since the era of violent conquest of the Shona and Ndebele peoples in the 1890s, Rhodesia/Zimbabwe has always been a country of paradoxes. Intended as the 'Second Rand' by Cecil Rhodes (who felt he had missed out on the wealth to be made in the Transvaal), it became merely a territory of small and scattered mines, quite unlike the larger-scale capitalism of the Rand. It was soon considered to be primarily an agricultural country, with significant developments in tobacco and sugar growing, maize production, as well as in cattle ranching. The relatively slow growth in the economy was nonetheless intended to pull in British settlers and it rapidly came to be regarded as a supremely British colony. It was this supposed adherence to Britishness that seemed to lead the settlers to guard their autonomy by voting in 1922 for responsible government and against incorporation in South Africa. In 1953, however, they were generally active participants in the Central African Federation (with Northern Rhodesia and Nyasaland), eager to extend their power in Central Africa. Yet, the reality was that the composition of the white settler group turned out to be highly cosmopolitan, particularly as time went on. Moreover, the great majority of the settlers, as in other territories of settlement, headed for the towns rather than the rural areas. Most significantly, the expected explosion of capitalist enterprise did not materialise. Capitalist formations in the territory tended to be relatively small scale, including the development of manufacturing that took place during and after the Second World War.

But small scale did not mean lacking in complexity, particularly in respect of labour supply, its ethnic and class composition and the resulting labour relations. Moreover, despite the scattered and relatively fragmentary nature of much employment, trade unionisation did take place, particularly after the First World War, and this forms a key focus of this book.

This was particularly true of the railways, with employment concentrated in Bulawayo and Salisbury (Harare), embracing a striking hierarchy of different trades and services. It was on the railways that the full intricacy of racial, class, ethnic and even gender issues abounded. It was railway employment that stimulated the liveliest trade union activity, created club affiliations and even influenced the significant spatial layout of the two main centres of Bulawayo and Salisbury. Ginsburgh's book is the first to examine the dynamics of labour, both in the railways and elsewhere, over a longer timescale from the early twentieth century to the arrival of majority rule after the tiny white minority (never more than 5 per cent of the entire population) had attempted to hold out in the face of the great wave of acts of decolonisation in Africa in the 1950s and 1960s. Using a Marxist framework, she rightly points out that capitalism is a highly dynamic phenomenon, subject to the booms and busts of the world economy and producing constant changes even on the smaller-scale framework of Rhodesia. By taking the long view, Ginsburgh reveals the highly diverse interactions of class, race and gender in strikingly illuminating ways, including the ups and downs of African participation and the interaction between the desire for fresh white settlement and the constant settler fear of the alleged degeneration of 'poor whiteism'. She charts the creation of 'emotional communities' and the manner in which they 'variously cohered and fractured'. Her approach is greatly favoured by the use of a remarkable range of sources, drawing insights from various publications, including trade union magazines, letters, poems, cartoons and other illustrations, as well as biographies and novels. In these ways she demonstrates that the composition and relationships of labour forces in different capitalist settings can be analysed from materials well beyond official reports, censuses and newspaper commentaries. The result is a blend of public, official and seemingly informal materials (combined with scholarly accounts), which unveil the range of attitudes that activated labour relations and approaches to policy coming both from above and from below.

Among her most illuminating sources are the novels, autobiography and other writings of the Nobel Prize winner, Doris Lessing (1919–2013). All historians of Rhodesia/Zimbabwe owe a great debt to the remarkably acute insights of this distinguished writer. In her early work, *The Grass Is Singing* (which Ginsburgh briefly quotes in her final chapter), she perfectly captures the relationship between town and country for settlers. Mary Turner, her leading character, finds fulfilment in clerical employment in town (and female clerical employment is carefully charted in this book). When she marries a farmer who is reluctant to follow the insensitivities of most of his type, for example in his approach to the environment and his attitudes to his African labourers, he is unable to find success. The neighbouring farmer, Charlie Slatter, becomes rich by following all the policies that Dick Turner avoids. Slatter is also a local imperialist, eager to take over the Turner farm. Mary's loss of any self-respect leads her to descend into a combination of ennui and antipathy that sinks into a form of nihilism. Most horrifying of all, she becomes dependent on a black servant who even helps to dress her before murdering her, an outcome she seems to expect. This book repeatedly came to mind as

I read key phrases in Ginsburgh's introduction, such as the privileges and limitations of being white, the settler efforts to erase the indigenous presence, while of course being entirely dependent on it, and the settlers' emotional disengagement from Africans, leading them into the fantasy that they could do without them. All the while, they suffer from the psychological distress of expectant failure to live up to white expectations and standards. These often bleak problems of the settler condition run through all of Lessing's writings and do indeed present the paradoxes of the settler condition. In this book Ginsburgh superbly develops them into a notable academic study, soundly based on the widest range of sources yet used by any historian of the country. It is a remarkable achievement.

John M. MacKenzie
Lancaster University

ACKNOWLEDGEMENTS

This book was made possible by the support, encouragement and kindness of many people. I was able to pursue this research with funding provided by the ESRC White Rose scholarship. Some of the material in Chapter 4 has previously appeared in a modified form in 'Labour and Mobility on Rhodesia's Railways: The 1954 firemen's Strike' in *Rethinking White Societies in Southern Africa, 1930s–1990s*, edited by Duncan Money and Danelle van Zyl-Hermann. My thanks to Duncan and Danelle for allowing this material to appear in this book and for their feedback on my work. I am incredibly grateful to Will Jackson and Shane Doyle who have both inspired and supported me since my undergraduate years at the University of Leeds. Their encouragement and understanding enabled me to develop and articulate my ideas with confidence and overcome a seemingly relentless multiplicity of personal and intellectual crises. I was helped by numerous people during my fieldwork in Zimbabwe and South Africa. I would have been completely out of my depth without their advice and generosity. In particular the Blakes, the Bassons, the Elliots, the Jacks, Wendy, Munya and Tafadzwa, Ushe, Nicky Brown, Elliot and Judith Todd, as well as the staff at the Bulawayo National Railway Museum and the Zimbabwe Amalgamated Railwaymen's Union. In my time in the International Studies Group I have hugely benefited from the expertise and guidance of Ian Phimister. It has been wonderful to be able to discuss various ideas with all of my amazing colleagues at the ISG at the University of the Free State. I am particularly grateful to my office buddy Rebecca Swartz for comments on a draft, but also for the multiple pictures of cats. Anna Hájková, Maria Reyes Baztán and Dan Branch have also gone out of their way to support me in my early career. I'd also like to thank Donal Lowry for his enthusiasm and understanding as well as Jeremy Krikler, Neil Roos and Emma Brennan for their advice and encouragement in turning this research into a book.

It would have been impossible for me to complete this book without the support of my family and friends, particularly John Nott, Joshy Doble and Dan Edmonds. My sister, Lesley, to whom I owe a lot of money, helped me often without hesitation or qualification whenever I was in need. The boy, for his help with numbers, and Dad for his various anecdotes and critiques. And to Dan, Jen, Roy, Emily, Paz,

ACKNOWLEDGEMENTS

Marcus and Tom who have provided ample sources of love, booze and memes.

My mother was born in Bulawayo in 1951. One of six children, her father was employed as a works foreman on Rhodesia Railways while her mother was a housewife (and in later life a purveyor of delicious shortbread). After attending school in Gweru she was employed as a customs officer and eventually moved to Grays, Essex in the late 1980s. My own passion for this research emerged from my curiosity about her life. She never tired of answering my incessant questions, she read my drafts and I was lucky enough to have her accompany me on some of my research trips across Zimbabwe and South Africa. She was my greatest champion and best friend. This book is dedicated to her.

ABBREVIATIONS

Organisations, political parties

AEU	Amalgamated Engineering Union
AMWR	Associated Mine Workers of Rhodesia
AWB	Afrikaner Weerstandsbeweging
BSAC	British South Africa Company
BSAP	British South Africa Police
CID	Criminal Investigation Department
ICA	Industrial Conciliation Act
ICU	Industrial and Commercial Workers' Union
ILO	International Labour Organisation
MDC	Movement for Democratic Change
NIC	National Industrial Council
RALE	Railway Association of Locomotive Employees
RAP	Rhodesian Action Party
RAWU	Railway African Workers' Union
RF	Rhodesian Front
RICU	Reformed Industrial and Commercial Workers' Union
RLI	Rhodesian Light Infantry
RLP	Rhodesia Labour Party
RMGWA	Rhodesia Mine and General Workers' Association
RNA	Rhodesia Nurses Association
RRAEA	Rhodesian Railways African Employees' Association
RRWU	Rhodesia Railways Workers' Union
SRLP	Southern Rhodesia Labour Party
TUC	Trades Union Congress
UDI	Unilateral Declaration of Independence
UFP	United Federal Party
UNIP	United National Independence Party
ZANU	Zimbabwe African National Union
ZANU PF	Zimbabwe African National Union – Patriotic Front
ZAPU	Zimbabwe African People's Union

Archives and journals

BRMA	Bulawayo Railway Museum Archives
ICOMM	Institute of Commonwealth Studies Collection
JSAS	*Journal of Southern African Studies*

ABBREVIATIONS

NASA	National Archives of South Africa
NAZ	National Archives of Zimbabwe
RNN	*Rhodesian Nurses Newsletter*
RRM	*Rhodesia Railways Magazine*
RRR	*Rhodesian Railways Review*
TNA	National Archives of the United Kingdom

A NOTE ON TERMS

In Rhodesia the codification of race by the state in various laws and proclamations existed in dialectical tension with its everyday uses across homes, workplaces and social clubs. Racial categories were predicated on the language of differentiation and dehumanisation and settlers used a number of derogatory terms to describe racial others. In this book I have opted to use the terms 'black' and 'African' interchangeably. I have also used 'white' and 'European' – the most common terms used by settlers to describe themselves. In using these terms myself, my intention is to convey as clearly as possible how people in the past understood race. In what follows, I hope I have made it clear as to where I am writing about representations of race in the past and where I am using descriptive or analytical terminology of my own.

Outside of southern Africa, 'Coloured' has been generally used as a derogatory slur for non-whites. Here, however, Coloured refers to a racial category that emerged in the late nineteenth-century western Cape and sought to group together a diverse range of persons of mixed African and European heritage, but also to a number of Asian persons, Cape slaves and the Khoisan population. In its Rhodesian expression, the term Coloured was used to describe some mixed-race persons whose very existence threatened colonial binaries. This argument, developed by Christopher Lee in *Unreasonable Histories*, is explored in Chapters 1 and 3 of this book.

INTRODUCTION

In 2015 BBC Radio 4 broadcast a programme consisting of a series of interviews with Zimbabweans – some black, some white – which set out to illustrate 'the reality of life in Rhodesia before 1980'.[1] The lives of two white women, Celia and her daughter Mary Jane, were highlighted by the BBC introducer as particularly unusual. Like many other whites in Rhodesia they had holidayed in South Africa, attended segregated schools and relocated to the United Kingdom in the 1970s as Rhodesian repression and African resistance to white rule intensified. Yet Celia's life had significantly deviated from a common image of Rhodesian housewives as ladies of leisure whose sole work consisted of overseeing African domestic labour in the home. Born in Bulawayo in 1915, Celia had attended university at fifteen, worked as a headmistress and continued to work after she was married. She had been a founding member of the Interracial Association, a liberal organisation opposed to apartheid-style segregation and dedicated to fostering multiracial partnership. During the interview she described the anger she felt as a child when she witnessed a white man chasing a black man from the pavement, going on to recall 'the terrible attitude of the people'. As she explained: 'Most of them let me tell you, were people who came from the UK. And when they came from the UK you know they were the lowest of the low. But suddenly because of their colour they would become so important that they could chase the black people away.' Her daughter Mary Jane, born in Bulawayo in 1942, agreed that

> there was a distinct difference ... There were the people who had been born there, the settlers if you like, and they were the people who actually bothered to learn an African language and bothered to actually attempt to have some cohesion and respect for races. Then, I think it was after the war, the Second World War, there were a lot of people who came from

[1]

poor, cold places in normally the north of England and suddenly they
were of the upper classes and they were ... the most disgustingly behaved
arrogant lot of people that gave most Rhodesians a bad name.

The discussion between these two women conveys a vivid picture of a
white society fractured between 'old settlers' and newcomers; a society
in which white skin secured an individual upper-class status, even if
that status proved ephemeral and superficial. Working-class whites
were seen by many middle-class and established settlers as interlopers
in elite spaces who claimed undeserved privileges. Particular accents
and blue-collar jobs betrayed their lowly origins, classlessness and
pretensions to unearned status and these 'low' whites were often
deemed unable to wield power in ways befitting of a respectable and
civilised society. The disdain felt towards the ways in which particular
social groups performed – or failed to perform – their identities as
'white' was as much a reflection of class antagonism and ethnic and
national prejudice as it was the failure of settler society to socialise its
members into a set of standardised 'white' behaviours.

This book challenges the idea that white settlers in Rhodesia
conformed to a uniform set of outlooks and behaviours. Rhodesians
were not homogenous. There was no typical 'white settler'. Ideas
about race, empire and 'civilisation' varied across the social spectrum
and changed dramatically over time. The continual flow of people,
ideas and cultures across national borders frustrated attempts to create
a cohesive Rhodesian or British imperial identity and many individuals who left Britain and South Africa in search of greener pastures
were also often unable to transcend the barriers of class and status they
were trying to leave behind. Class was not displaced by race in British
settler colonies. Instead, precisely because dominant racial ideologies
demanded a set of unifying characteristics and visible signifiers of the
'natural' superiority of white settlers, class took on novel yet pressing
dimensions.

Scholarship that has analysed how racial categories were variously
produced, policed and transgressed in the colonies has focused on
domestic social and cultural spaces – what Ann Laura Stoler has called
the 'intimate frontiers' of empire.[2] Yet the worlds of work were equally,
if not more, important than the domestic realm in forging race. Many
male settlers spent most of their waking lives at work. Work shaped
the material limits and cultural horizons of settlers' daily lives, their
opportunities and their social status. The workplace also brought a
wide range of different people, ideas and cultures into contact with one
another, which itself led to the formation of new identities, ideas and
organisations. Workplaces often had multiracial workforces and were
key sites of interracial encounters. Wage labour became increasingly

important for white women from the Second World War onwards, but even before their entrance into wage labour on a wide scale the formal labour of the men they depended on was crucial to the character of their domestic lives and their immediate communities. Despite its neglect by historians of settler colonialism, work was a central and dynamic element of settler life.

Class, however, has become increasingly unfashionable in recent decades.[3] Generally speaking, when it appears in historical analysis it tends to be descriptive and under-theorised.[4] This book contributes to the ongoing attempts to reinstate class as an essential analytical tool in understanding social identities, power and inequality.[5] It explores the self-activity of men and women in the worlds of work in which race, gender and class were produced and remoulded, shaped both by changes in material production, dominant ideologies and the struggles of men and women at the point of production as well as at the cultural level in people's daily lives. In doing so it emphasises that racial categories were often highly ambiguous – even to the most ardent proselytisers of racial difference – and that class and the worlds of work had a significant bearing on how race and the settler colonial structure were experienced and reproduced.

The demystification of class, moreover, has become an increasingly important task in debunking essentialist notions of race and nationality. Paul Gilroy has argued that the lived experience of anxiety in an increasingly austere and precarious world in which cultures are ossified and race and national borders are fetishised and objectified as transhistorical entities, has provided fertile ground for the rise of xenophobia, nationalism, racism and neo-fascism.[6] Internationally, the insidious effects of race and nationalism increasingly appear with egregious intensity: the militarisation of state borders proceeds apace while thousands of people die every year trying to cross the Mediterranean and the US–Mexico border, people who have lived in the United Kingdom for decades are forcibly deported, others face indefinite detention in 'immigration removal centres'. These have occurred alongside the rise of a specific form of racialised class politics. In Europe and the United States, popular commentary on the 'white working-class' or blue-collar, 'ordinary' men and women has variously been used to articulate a sense of imperial loss, bolster nationalism and attack multiculturalism. In post-apartheid South Africa white poverty has been weaponised to bolster myths of a white genocide, rally whites against affirmative action policies and frame whites as the new oppressed minority. Whites in Zimbabwe have also been increasingly portrayed as a structurally disadvantaged and unfairly targeted group. Neither the instrumentalisation of white poverty nor the active

[3]

role of white workers in racism and segregation are new phenomena. Examining the historical antecedents of these processes is essential if we are to understand how class has been racialised to justify inequality and strengthen white supremacy and nationalism.

Despite illuminating work by Jon Lunn and Ian Phimister,[7] research into lower-class whites, the worlds of white labour and poor whites in African settler states has been dominated by a geographical focus on South Africa, Algeria and to a lesser extent Mozambique and Angola.[8] The particularities of the racialised class structure in Southern Rhodesia prove especially valuable for understanding the relationship between class and race formation and the ideological constructions of white poverty. Whites never made up more than 5 per cent of the total population; positioning white workers as essential, albeit subordinate, allies in the settler colonial structure. It was precisely the intersection of class exploitation and racial empowerment among white workers in a demographically weak settler state that gave their roles in the reproduction and defence of Rhodesian settler colonialism its forceful and idiosyncratic character.

A brief overview of Rhodesian settler colonialism

Celia and Mary Jane's perceptions of liberal white middle classes struggling to control the visceral racist excesses of the naturally intolerant lower classes has much in common with how racism has been represented and understood globally. Racism has often been portrayed as a problem confined to a rabid, insular and illiterate white working class; whether white trash or rednecks in the United States, chavs in the United Kingdom or poor whites in South Africa. Of course, lower-class whites have not been passive bearers of elite constructions of race, but this focus often deliberately obscures the role of capitalism, the state and the rich in perpetuating racist inequalities. Despite the existence of some middle-class liberals in Rhodesia, middle-class whites benefited from Rhodesian settler colonialism and overwhelmingly supported and reinforced racial inequalities. It was the particularly brutal character of capitalist exploitation, the authoritarian settler state and the actions of Rhodesians writ large that 'gave Rhodesians a bad name'. The specific character of Rhodesian settler colonialism, its prevailing ideologies and wider historical trajectory in turn were shaped by the struggles between different sections of capital and of oppressed and exploited groups within broader processes of capital accumulation.

Fuelled by a toxic blend of financial imperialism and Cape colonial expansion, the annexation of Rhodesia can broadly be traced back to the

[4]

discovery of gold on the Witwatersrand in 1886. European missionaries, hunters and traders had been present in the Ndebele kingdom from the late 1850s. Yet it was not until gold speculation heightened in the late 1880s that competition for control over mining rights in the area intensified. Driven by a mixture of greed and imperial fervour, mining magnate Cecil Rhodes sought to bring the area under British control and sent his emissaries to negotiate with Lobengula Khumalo, the Ndebele king. The Rudd Concession, secured in 1888 under conditions of duplicity, granted all metals and mineral rights in the Ndebele kingdom and Mashonaland to Rhodes. With the Rudd Concession in hand, Rhodes secured a royal charter from Britain the following year, which enabled his British South Africa Company (BSAC) to make laws and treaties, undertake public works and create a police force in the territory. Soon after, a white militia known as the Pioneer Column was recruited in South Africa. Promised over 3,000 acres of farmland and gold claims in this anticipated 'Second Rand', their entrance into the territory in 1890 marked the beginning of white settlement. Lobengula desperately attempted to repudiate the Concession once it became clear he had been tricked, but to little avail.[9]

The first waves of settler occupation were concentrated in Mashonaland. Fresh speculative capital followed on the heels of white expansion and Rhodes relied on a number of investors on the Rand and in the City of London to prop up the BSAC.[10] Yet capital flows dried up as the poverty of local gold fields were quickly established; the BSAC's finances looked poor and the Ndebele still posed a formidable barrier to the company's consolidation of power in the region.[11] In 1893, an Ndebele raid near Fort Victoria (now Masvingo) provided Rhodes and Leander Starr Jameson the excuse to enter Matabeleland under the auspices of a retributive war. The war itself was short and violent; the Ndebele were successfully subordinated and settlers were enabled to move into Matabeleland.[12] By the mid-1890s, in conditions of vast over-speculation and the failure to find a major gold field, both the BSAC and settlers turned to looting cattle from the Ndebele to accumulate wealth. Cattle theft coupled with the increased use of forced labour led to a series of African uprisings across Matabeleland and Mashonaland from 1896–97. Some 10 per cent of settlers were killed before the uprisings were crushed by local settler volunteers and imperial reinforcements from South Africa.[13] The risings had a disastrous effect on speculative capital and in turn the BSAC belatedly encouraged industrial capital in mining and agriculture in order to ensure returns on investments. Gold production gradually rose and after the turn of the century settler agriculture slowly expanded as peasant competition was stifled by the state.[14]

[5]

Through a combination of shareholding in foreign companies and direct control, the BSAC controlled the railways, a large proportion of gold production and most of the land used for cattle, maize and tobacco production, as well as the local Rhodesian press. The BSAC generally favoured mining capital and bestowed rights to miners over farmers on privately owned land, much to the annoyance of the domestic bourgeoisie who were concentrated in agriculture.[15] Yet for all their divergent interests, in the early years international and domestic capital were united in their desire to create the conditions necessary for profitability, which rested on the super-exploitation and oppression of Africans. Mining and agricultural industries both favoured migrant labour systems, which meant that the bulk of the cost of the reproduction of labour was shifted to the reserves. Yet the uneven development of capitalism in the region frustrated African labour recruitment. In 1903 mine owners set up the Rhodesia Native Labour Bureau in order to secure a consistent supply of coerced African labour. This forced *Chibaro* labour was also diverted to work on settler farms.[16]

The state implemented numerous measures to keep Africans uneducated, poorly paid and tightly controlled. A highly restrictive franchise prevented the majority of Africans from voting, hut taxes were levied to speed up processes of land alienation and proletarianisation and pass laws and the Masters and Servants Act was implemented to control the black workforce and curtail African mobility. While during the preliminary stages of colonisation African agricultural production was relatively strong and settler development depended on the existence of African produce, by 1908 white commercial agriculture had developed to the extent that the BSAC was emboldened to marginalise African production. In 1914, 2,040 white farmers were cultivating 183,000 acres of land.[17]

Early historians weaved the extension of British rule north of the Limpopo into a narrative of the unrelenting spread of civilisation under the aegis of British imperialism.[18] Settlers depicted themselves as the direct bearers of the white man's burden, enlightening and educating Africans, developing industry, agriculture and extracting mineral wealth.[19] Settler identity was created in reference to a host of external others and a set of unifying foundational mythologies. The cult of Rhodes and an emphasis on the struggle and hardships of pioneer society were coupled with a loudly proclaimed Britishness in opposition to both Afrikaners and Africans.[20] Rhodesian authorities put particular effort into manufacturing the 'right type' of white settler. They implemented discriminatory immigration stipulations to ensure both the British character of the country and the socio-economic standing of its settlers.

However, they regularly failed to secure white immigrants with these desired traits.[21] Doubt plagued early Rhodesian settlers regarding the future of white presence in Africa. Anxieties over settlers' ability to successfully live and thrive in the African environment – perceived simultaneously as bountifully fertile and menacingly hostile – were compounded by fresh memories of African rebellion. Lower-class whites also provoked concern from settler authorities. White workers had been recruited from Britain and South Africa in order to fill skilled positions on expanding mines and railways, yet many who arrived lacked basic necessary skills.[22] The position of white labour gradually improved in the late 1910s and effective white worker organisation and militancy reached its height. Nevertheless by the mid-1920s white worker militancy had been brutally smashed by employers and a settler government fearful of white worker challenges to state power and potential alliances with black workers.

Moreover, the rising importance of settler agriculture and the stabilisation of a class of white workers significantly contributed to increasing demands for autonomy and an end to chartered rule.[23] Relations between the BSAC and settlers had considerably deteriorated; settlers complained of high railway rates and accused the BSAC of being more interested in satisfying their shareholders than meeting responsibilities to the Europeans in the colony. After increasing agitation against the BSAC, 59 per cent of settlers voted for responsible government and Rhodesia gained control over its legislative affairs in 1923. Rhodesian settlers saw this as the first step towards the much-coveted dominion status held by other territories in the British Empire such as South Africa, Canada and Australia. However, London retained the right to intervene in Rhodesian legislative matters and the assembly's powers were circumscribed by imperial interests.[24]

Southern Rhodesia's already precarious economy was put under increasing strain as the effects of the Great Depression reverberated across the world. The profitability of white agriculture and impoverishment of lower-class whites became pressing concerns and interventionist policies aimed at securing the position of the European population were given renewed support. Public works were initiated to absorb the white unemployed, Industrial Conciliation Acts in 1934 and 1937 were enforced to protect the informal white monopoly of skilled jobs and the Land Apportionment Act of 1930 intensified previous alienation processes and formalised racial land segregation. White farmers received the best land, a series of subsidies, relief and loans, while African farmers were restricted to the least fertile areas and faced a series of discriminatory marketing boards and fees. Elected in 1933, Godfrey Huggins's Reform Party committed themselves to this segregationist ideology by

[7]

implementing a 'two-pyramid' policy in which different races would supposedly develop in their own separate spheres of influence. Despite Whitehall's power to intervene to protect African interests, such legislation went ahead unimpeded. African resistance to these measures and the fledgling political and trade union activity were ruthlessly suppressed by the state, which simultaneously bolstered the power of traditional African authorities to secure white power.

The ascendancy of the two-pyramid policy was short-lived, however, as the Second World War encouraged the growth of secondary industry that favoured a stabilised and increasingly skilled African workforce. Africans were propelled into urban areas and into competition with white workers. As the 1940s came to an end, the triumphalism of previous settler historiography was tempered by the dual challenges of decolonisation and African nationalism. Yet across southern Africa these threats to settler power coincided with the consolidation of white rule.[25] A year after the decolonisation process signalled its beginning with Indian independence in 1947, nationalist rule in South Africa was reaching its apogee with the implementation of apartheid. While Kenyan settlers united in a violent counterinsurgency campaign against Mau Mau nationalists, Southern Rhodesia found temporary reprieve from the pressures of decolonisation in the short-lived Central African Federation that joined together the Rhodesias and Nyasaland.[26] White immigration soared while limited reforms, such as ending the prohibition on Africans purchasing liquor, were made to prove the Federation's multiracial credentials. These largely tokenistic gestures did little to satisfy rising African nationalist movements and by the early 1960s the Federation had dissolved. While former British colonies such as Ghana, Kenya, Zambia and Malawi emerged as independent states, Britain refused to grant independence to Southern Rhodesia so long as its constitution prevented African majority rule. Dropping the 'Southern' prefix, Rhodesia reacted violently to the growing African resistance to settler rule. The Rhodesian Front (RF) was voted in by the predominantly white electorate in 1962. The RF promised to defend minority rule and their leader Ian Smith, prime minister of Rhodesia from 1964 to 1979, became a symbol of settler defiance and white supremacy. The RF capitalised upon a sense of British betrayal to cement support for the Unilateral Declaration of Independence (UDI) in 1965 and declared themselves an autonomous state, becoming an international pariah in the process.[27]

During this period Rhodesian settlers portrayed themselves as the bearers of traditional British values, while the metropole was invariably considered to be a site of moral degeneration that was prepared to sell out kith and kin for the sake of political expediency.[28] Ian Smith

[8]

described mutual interests and ideals of Rhodesians including loyalty to the queen and the British Empire and a dedication to the national sports of cricket and rugby.[29] Under the RF this imagined community was presented as a classless bastion of civilisation on the front lines against barbarism and communism. A guerrilla war between African nationalists and Rhodesian counterinsurgent forces intensified in the 1970s, ultimately rendering white rule untenable. Minority rule was overturned in 1980 and Robert Mugabe was elected prime minister of the newly independent Zimbabwe.

Settler self-valorisation was widely challenged. The intransigence of the white community fighting bitterly to uphold racist minority rule in the face of a popular nationalist movement and international criticism generated a body of research from a generation of scholars in solidarity with the liberation movement.[30] However, in rightly drawing attention to the oppression and inequality at the heart of white minority rule, nationalist historiography tended towards teleo-logical narratives and romantic exaggeration. By plastering over divisions within both the colonised and colonising population, much of this scholarship replicated homogenising patterns emblematic of the previous settler and Whig historiographies.[31] Thus James Alfred Mutambirwa argued that Europeans 'were united and their attitudes and behaviour toward the Africans were the same'.[32] Yet this image of a white ruling class and a black working class, of, as Henri Rolins describes, 'two separate communities, one superimposed on the other, an aristocracy composed of white landowners and entrepreneurs, and a black proletariat',[33] insufficiently explains the extent of fragmentation within both the colonising and colonised population. Certainly, this dualism often tells us much more about imperial and colonial ideolo-gies than the reality of Rhodesian settler colonialism.[34]

As optimism for the nationalist narrative retreated, a rich body of literature emerged that challenged the existence of cohesive anti-colonial and settler nationalist movements.[35] State-sponsored violence in Matabeleland in the early 1980s and student and worker protests against the postcolonial state in the late 1980s and 1990s, saw increasing critiques of the one-party state and the entrenched democratic deficits of the Zimbabwe African National Union – Patriotic Front (ZANU PF).[36] Other scholars sought to critically evaluate ZANU PF's associ-ation with Marxism–Leninism and the potential of socialist transform-ation within Zimbabwe. Acknowledging that there had been little change to the socio-economic structure, many of these critiques were nonetheless bound by a limited conception of socialist transformation, which focused on revolution 'from above' – i.e. the ability of the ruling party, petty bourgeois elements and the state to enact socialist change.[37]

Moreover, by the early 2000s a series of struggles over land and power prompted a renewed focus on the legacies of settler colonialism and the place of whites in contemporary Zimbabwe. Yet both popular and state-sanctioned history in Zimbabwe has seen the persistence of earlier Manichaean narratives. In 2004 Terence Ranger coined the term 'patriotic history': a hyper-nationalist narrow version of the past that had been instrumentalised by the ruling party, ZANU PF, to legitimise its own authoritarian actions. In this highly selective account of the past, Zimbabweans have been divided into revolutionaries and sell-outs. The opposition party, the Movement for Democratic Change (MDC) has been portrayed as little more than a cloak for remaining whites and imperial powers to reassert control.[38] Yet, as Ian Phimister has pointed out, many of the defining features of patriotic history have their roots in previous nationalist iterations.[39] Elsewhere scholars have combined anti-imperialist rhetoric with mechanical interpretations of political economy to defend Mugabe's land interventions as an act of radical redistribution despite the wider context of repressive class policies, human rights abuses and the suppression of political opposition. As Brian Raftopoulos has argued, authoritarian politics in the independent state have been infused with anti-colonial and pan-Africanist rhetoric and 'with great intensity in Zimbabwe, but with increasing frequency in South Africa, the mobilisation of race as a legitimising force has been used to justify the battle against historical inequities, while attempting to conceal the structures that increase such inequality'.[40]

The (mis)uses of history, continuing state violence and racialised inequalities in independent Zimbabwe and beyond can only be understood within historical genealogies of class, race, gender and power rooted in the broader political economy. This book is heavily indebted to labour and social historians of Zimbabwe who have explored multiple struggles against exploitation and oppression, unearthed the complex relationships between class, gender, race, ethnicity and nationalism and examined the processes of capital accumulation and state power.[41] This work hopes to further illuminate these subjects through synthesising insights on whiteness, emotions, space, gender and imperial and settler colonial studies within a materialist class analysis of white workers. In doing so it hopes to overcome 'the twin problems of economism and culturalism' by recuperating a Marxist framework that allows for complexity and places human agency at the heart of historical processes.[42]

Defining white workers

The convergence of racial supremacy and class exploitation among white workers across southern Africa caused problems of definition for

[10]

generations of activists and scholars alike. In South Africa three major positions on the structural position of the white working class came to the fore. The first was the idea that white wage earners were all members of the working class, albeit divided by ideological constraints of race, a position propagated by the early South African Communist Party.[43] The second position utilised the conceptual framework developed by Nicos Poulantzas and proposed that no white working class existed; this contended that white workers lived off the surplus value created by productive non-white labourers and were essentially parasitical upon the value created in exploitation.[44] The third was a position formulated by Harold Wolpe, which demonstrated a multiplicity of class positions held by various groups of white workers, influenced by Erik Olin Wright and Guglielmo Carchedi's theorisation of the 'new middle class'.[45] Wright identified the new middle class as occupying 'contradictory class locations' in which wage earners combined elements of both the proletariat and the bourgeoisie. These workers performed the functions of the collective worker as well as the functions of capital. A function of capital 'corresponds to the maintenance of economic exploitation and oppression' and involves the work of supervision, control or surveillance.[46] Using this analysis, Wolpe was able to differentiate between employees such as white miners, who took on supervisory and coercive functions that generally lessened the productive element of their employment, and other types of white wage labourers who did not play the function of global capital.

This book bridges the gap between structuralist and consciousness-centred accounts of white workers through using the category of class experience. The notion of class experience was developed and popularised by British Marxist historians in reaction to the reductive and mechanical Marxist models influenced by Althusserian ideas of history as a process without a subject. Experience, because it incorporates how meaning is contested and cognised by subjects experiencing material processes, contains the potential to mediate between structure and consciousness. This relationship between material process and human subjectivity was articulated by Russian linguists in the early twentieth century who saw language as part of 'social being'. In particular, Valentin Volosinov's sophisticated conception of language grounded the discursive in the material and postulated that different social actors use language in different ways and this is subject to change. As a result of numerous social classes using the same language, 'differently oriented accents intersect every ideological sign. Sign becomes an arena of the class struggle'.[47] This 'multi-accentuality' of the sign refers to the struggle over meaning in language. Language does not simply reflect immediate reality, but *refracts* social being: 'Every sign ... is a construct between socially organised persons in the process of their interaction. Therefore, the forms of signs are conditioned above all by the social organisation of the participants involved and also by the immediate conditions of their interaction.'[48] In other words, class structure does not automatically produce an unmediated class consciousness, but through the category of experience, structure and consciousness are organically linked through the contestation over the meanings attached to particular signs. By looking at the language of various white workers we can identify varying 'class experiences' and the struggle over meaning therein: whether that be the meaning over racial identity, status or refractions of hegemonic gender roles. Competing notions of whiteness, Britishness, masculinity and femininity were rooted in broader class divisions across the settler community. For white workers, manliness was achieved and performed through blue-collar employment and the monopoly of skilled work, 'Britishness' was regularly attached to socialist reform and whiteness was understood through notions of free labour, productivity and the dignity of work.

In its popular usage, class categorises people into different social groups on the basis of a set of shared common characteristics.[49] At the level of appearance it seems self-evident that a white miner who worked as a shift boss and a white train steward who attended to railway passengers were part of the same social class in Rhodesia. However, with regards to South Africa, Alexander has argued that the different attitudes of miners and mechanics towards 'officials', the former claiming that as supervisors they should be considered in the same bracket, while the latter recognised a difference between the 'men' who worked as mechanics and the 'gentlemen' who worked as foremen, etc., 'surely reflected a different "experience"'. They concluded that white miners located a contradictory class position, as opposed to white mechanics, whom they defined as being part of 'a racialised dual working class'.[50]

Jon Lunn and Ian Phimister have both provided revealing analyses of white workers in Southern Rhodesia. Lunn's work is instructive in its achievements in 'plac[ing] culture and identity back at the heart of analysis' by exploring the 'hidden abode' of white workers on Rhodesia Railways. Yet for all its strengths there is no definition of class offered in his work.[51] Ian Phimister, on the other hand, in his examination of white miners has defined white workers in Rhodesia as an 'aristocracy of labour' in the classic sense of the phrase, taking Eric Hobsbawm's formulation of an upper strata of the working class, who were in receipt of better wages and were more politically moderate and 'respectable' than the ordinary proletariat.[52] He has characterised the position of white miners as one of relative strength, but also 'one of great insecurity'; as

[12]

dependent partners in a white cross-class coalition who were acutely aware of their vulnerability of being undercut by the large numbers of lower paid African workers. White workers' privileges were conditional; they were never fully incorporated into the settler community and were ruthlessly disciplined by employers and the settler state if they overstepped established boundaries or challenged their place as subordinate members of the ruling racial elite.[53] Notions of contradictory class locations, the racialised dual working class and class experience stands to build upon this analysis, and should be utilised to elucidate differences *between* white workers, as well as their relationship to white employers and African employees.

In Rhodesia, white nurses, typists, engineers, mechanics and miners were all workers in a broad sense. They were simultaneously vulnerable to being undercut or replaced by African workers yet privileged through higher wages and wider skilled employment opportunities afforded to settlers. But they did not necessarily share the same class experience. White miners had a vested interest in maximising the productivity of the black workers they supervised and their jobs were dependent on the super-exploitation of Africans workers: 'the very existence of the highly paid white mineworkers depended on ... exploitation colour bars'.[54] This brought them into contact with African workers in specific ways that cannot be generalised to other white workers. For example, the employment of white nurses did not *rely* on a colour bar. White nurses' day-to-day interactions with African orderlies and nurses in conditions of perpetual staff shortages were generally characterised by degrees of dependence rather than coercion.[55] Neither does grouping workers by occupation necessarily grasp the specifics of class relations. Chapter 4 demonstrates that white railwaymen on Rhodesia Railways attempted to remove white supervisory workers from holding positions of power in their trade union on the basis that the functions these workers played as inspectors and instructors effectively made them part of management. What follows is a modest attempt to situate white workers within a critical synthesis of work on class and race and gender in the settler colonial context.

Whiteness in Rhodesia

Whiteness studies has been increasingly utilised to conceptualise whites in Rhodesia and Zimbabwe.[56] The best of this work has been attentive to the complex processes in the creation of white racial identity, yet, due to the centrality of white farmers in the struggles over land during the early 2000s, this research has disproportionately centred on the rural white population.[57] Moreover, much of this work has presented a monolithic white community and class divisions have often been entirely erased.[58] Analyses of race and class in southern Africa stand to benefit from a critical engagement with whiteness scholarship developed in the United States. Recent research on colonial anxieties provides a useful framework to probe the Janus-faced nature of David Roediger's 'psychological wage' and to provide an understanding of whiteness that reflects its complexities yet restores its utility.[59] Noel Ignatiev's work on the Irish in the United States also provides a useful comparison with non-British whites in Rhodesia. Moreover, Theodore Allen's argument that the modern notion of the 'white race' emerged as a ruling class policy of social control remains the most convincing explication of the rise of race.[60] Allen used a Marxist conception of class, which has also been adopted here.[61] The best exposition of this definition is provided by Geoffrey de Ste Croix, who posits that class '(essentially a relationship) is the collective social expression of the fact of exploitation, the way in which exploitation is embodied in a social structure'.[62]

This formulation requires the exploitation of one class by another. Because this relationship between exploiter and exploited is necessarily antagonistic, distinct interests emerge in the struggle over surplus value, although those interests may not be consciously recognised by the members of each given class. While class struggle gives rise to class consciousness, the former's existence is not conditional on being able to identify explicit formulations of the latter. This notion of exploitation necessarily produced an understanding of class predicated on the relationship between exploiter and exploited. Yet numerous social groups exist that do not easily fit within this paradigm. Ste Croix's formulation shines light on a way out of this dichotomous abstraction; the relationship of a class to *other classes*. Ste Croix argues that, while the relationship to the means of production is fundamental to understanding class, it is not the only concern and its overemphasis has led to a narrow definition of class; class should be understood as a relationship between people. From a dichotomous perspective of class, white workers in southern Africa simply appear as members of the working class. However, if we take into account their relationship to other classes, in particular the African workforce, we can see how particular groups of white wage earners cannot be defined as being part of the working class, but rather fall into various intermediate strata.

This means that Allen's work on the United States requires some adaptation in the settler colonial context of Rhodesia. The ideological function of the 'white race' was to provide justification for Empire in general and minority rule in particular. It was central to the settler colonial project in that race offered a means through which settlers could claim that they had better right to land, to employment, indeed more right to exist, than any indigenous inhabitant. White workers occupied different class positions from the majority of African workers; race operated here not to divide a multiracial working class as such. It sought to influence the conflation of skin colour with class and succeeded in creating a racialised occupational and class structure. However, its success was muted by white poverty, African struggle and uneven class development. The wealth, status and power of the settler colonial project was not equally shared; being white came with privileges but these privileges came with more limitations and provisos the further down the socio-economic scale an individual came.

White workers' production of race (or production of whiteness) has three meanings here. It refers to the ways in which dominant racial ideologies were internalised, subverted and experienced; the attempts to create a coherent white class identity; and the struggles to lay claim to particular rights or privileges for white workers through appeals to ideas of innate racial difference and the need to possess a degree of skill, education, wealth and status that remained above the general level of the African population.

The logic of elimination

In their heart of hearts the white Rhodesians bear a wordless wish – that the Africans would disappear.[63]

White workers' ideas about race were conditioned by their specific experience of settler colonialism. Often conflated with colonialism and imperialism, the settler colonial structure must be understood as a specific formation in its own right. While colonialism is tradition-ally understood as a relationship premised upon the exploitation of an indigenous majority by a foreign minority, Patrick Wolfe has argued that settler colonialism is centred upon a logic of elimination and that 'whatever settlers may say – and they generally have a lot to say – the primary motive for elimination is not race (or religion, ethnicity, grade of civilisation, etc.) but access to territory. Territoriality is settler colonialism's specific, irreducible element'.[64] Dialectically opposed, colonialism seeks to reproduce itself to enable continued exploit-ation, while settler colonialism is geared towards its own annihila-tion; to erase indigenous presence altogether. What this 'going away' meant, as Veracini has argued, differed among settlers: 'being phys-ically eliminated or displaced, having one's cultural practices erased, being "absorbed", "assimilated" or "amalgamated" in the wider popu-lation, but the list could go on'.[65] In an attempt to nuance how scholars

[15]

utilise the multifaceted notion of 'elimination' in the Australian context, A. Dirk Moses has argued that it is perhaps better to understand settler colonisation as 'a dynamic process with genocidal potential that could be released in circumstances of crisis', but nevertheless a process that was 'objectively and inherently "ethnocidal" (i.e., the attack of Aboriginal cultures) and fatal for many Aborigines, and potentially genocidal'.[66]

Settler societies in Africa have tended to combine both colonialism and settler colonialism as defined here. Reliance on indigenous labour characterised settler states whose inhabitants remained acutely aware that their high living standards were only enabled through the super-exploitation and oppression of the indigenous majority (although this is not to say that genocidal episodes were entirely absent from settler colonies in Africa).[67] Settlers may well have wanted the indigenous population to 'go away' to realise their fantasies of white supremacy and secure unchallenged sovereignty – but then who would fulfil the domestic role in the house? Who would work down the mines? Or labour on commercial farms? Likewise cultural assimilation provoked intense distaste from most settlers. That the indigenous population were essentially different was a key reasoning behind the justification for their differential treatment. Across central and southern Africa the idea that Africans were inherently rural and tribal was central in legitimising migrant systems of labour that allowed Africans to be paid a single man's wages. Settlers urged Africans to stay 'traditional', while simultaneously pursuing economic and political policies that disrupted the very foundations of traditional indigenous society. Subject to an array of legal, political and economic sanctions that rendered them outside of the settler body politic, Africans were routinely imagined as living beyond the boundaries of white civilisation.

However, the presence of Africans at work, in urban areas and in settlers' very homes could not be completely denied. Dane Kennedy has demonstrated how settlers kept distinctive racialised identities as 'prestige served as a psychological substitute for the physical separation of the races, an attempt at emotional disengagement from the indigenous peoples encountered in daily life'.[68] Racial theories worked not just to legitimise the oppression of indigenous people, but as an apparatus to control and regulate the white population. Yet, white prestige could never be boiled down to a particular set of rigidly defined rituals and appropriate behaviours; prestige and the ideas of racial difference that underpinned it were understood and performed differentially across sections of the settler community.

It is contended here that white workers not only performed their racial identities in idiosyncratic ways in order to differentiate themselves from Africans, but they also imagined the erasure or elimination of the indigenous population in ways that reflected their position in the settler community. White workers faced a unique challenge from Africans who threatened to displace them in the labour process. Periodically white labour organisations would outline a vision of an entirely white labour force; these fantasies sprung from the desire to eliminate Africans from the world of work in which white workers made their identity. This desire expressed itself in proposals for white labour schemes, in struggles over the delineating lines of 'black' and 'white' work, over the labour process itself, in vocal resentment and violence towards Africans and in attempts to create white classed spaces. 'Territoriality' therefore must be modified here to include these struggles to make the workplace white as well as the cognitive dissonance involved in the perpetual disavowal of the importance and productivity of African labour.

Who was white?

The specific character of Rhodesian settler colonialism has important consequences for understanding who was white. The social, political and economic context in which race is made is fundamental to the ways in which racial difference and racial identities are expressed. Formerly oppressed groups can become part of the privileged racial group while new racialised others emerge. Noel Ignatiev's *How the Irish Became White* sought to elucidate how the Irish were transformed from an oppressed racial group in Britain to violent oppressors of African Americans in the United States. By detailing the discrimination the Irish faced in the United States, Ignatiev observed that this metamorphosis was not a simple process; 'it was by no means obvious who was "white"'.[69]

In many settler societies the difference between indigenous and settler, freeman and slave was paramount, both of which were delineated through skin colour. Colour had such an overbearing structuring effect on Rhodesia that European minority groups, although discriminated against, could be united under the homogenising language of whiteness in order to oppose African interests. Stereotypes and prejudices against non-British whites did not erect insurmountable barriers to their inclusion in the Rhodesian community, nor to claiming the privileges and power that white skin conferred. Those who were most successful in this regard were arguably those who professed loyalty to Britain and her empire. Roy Welensky, who rose from railwayman to the premiership, famously described himself as 'half Jewish, half-Afrikaner, but 'a hundred per cent British' in what

Donal Lowry has described as a phenomenon of 'non-British loyalism' to empire that occurred throughout the white dominions.[70]

Yet poor whites, non-British whites and mixed-race groups disrupted attempts to fix an uncomplicated colonial binary. White workers' physical, structural and conceptual proximity to these racialised groups meant that their reactions towards them were characterised by a particular intensity. Certainly, there was considerable doubt over the racial purity of many workers who claimed European heritage. The boundaries that delineated desirable and undesirable social groups expanded and retracted over the period of minority rule. Non-British whites were not unilaterally or consistently regarded as undesirable and there was considerable confusion over racial categorisation and the precise way this internal hierarchy of Europeans should work in practice, particularly in relation to the employment of the Coloured population and white women.

Wages of whiteness and the dynamics of pride, anxiety and shame

In order to maintain the racial boundaries fundamental to settler rule, white workers had to *feel* superior to Africans. As well as receiving better job opportunities, wages, housing, education and health care than the African population, white workers manufactured a pride in their white skin to proclaim racial difference so that even poor, unskilled and uneducated whites could feel distinguished. These shared feelings of superiority among white workers have much in common with the notion of psychological wages formulated by W. E. B. Du Bois and reinterpreted by David Roediger in his book *Wages of Whiteness*. Roediger argued that in the context of the United States, while the white working class may have not always been materially better off than African Americans and both were exploited by capital, white workers were paid a psychological wage in which 'status and privileges conferred by race could be used to make up for alienating and exploitative class relationships'.[71]

Following Deborah Posel, in this book I argue that the psychological wage is better understood as 'a mix of costs and benefits, pleasures and pains'. During South African apartheid, the government provided employment to whites who were unable to compete in private labour markets. However, it was generally considered that this recruitment policy coupled with perpetual labour shortages within the apartheid bureaucratic behemoth had created a workforce plagued by mediocrity, or worse, ineptitude. Consequently many white civil servants were treated with contempt; there was an element of shame in taking these jobs that had been safeguarded for white 'factory rejects'. Posel argued therefore that ' "the status and privileges" attached to whiteness could themselves be the source of some indignity and humiliation in the workplace and beyond'.[72]

In Rhodesia, white workers were berated by middle-class settlers who criticised their demands for high pay and status, which it was considered they did not deserve. The fact that some whites secured status and employment on account of their skin colour was periodically highlighted to shame and discipline white workers. The Rhodesian state repeatedly intervened to restrain white workers and remind them of their subordinate status. As the century progressed increasing numbers of Africans also publicly argued that lower-class whites were inadequate and unworthy of the wages they received. Such assertions infuriated white workers who struggled to make Africans behave in ways that supported racial hierarchies. That the most vocal Africans who castigated white workers as delusional tended to be wealthier, more educated or more skilled than the majority of the white lower classes proved especially troubling.

More generally poor whites were often presented as an aberration of the white race. Chapter 2 shows that, while relief during the Great Depression was made available to whites, accepting assistance from the state involved a significant element of shame. Employment camps in particular reveal how the state tried to hide these whites away.[73] While relief can be seen as a privilege denied to Africans, it is harder to reconcile the idea that such camps would confer status or a psychological wage as defined by Roediger. The tensions between self-identification as inherently superior and the reality of low-paid work and relative poverty were a source of intense dislocation. White skin could offer a sense of pride and status, but also profound anxiety over racial status; over the feared removal of privileges attached to race. The failure to live up to the standards demanded of the master race often resulted in psychological distress rather than pride.

These insecurities and anxieties both propelled and structured the ongoing production of settler identity.[74] Such anxieties reflected the perceived and actual vulnerabilities of white workers: their tenuous access to power, the questionable racial status of some who self-identified as white workers, their proximity to poor whites and the existence of poor whites among their number. For white workers anxieties were regulated through dynamics of pride and shame. The shame of poverty was transformed through pride in work, in trade unionism and the struggle against unscrupulous capitalists and employers. These in turn were reified as the essence of what it meant to be white. Pride was also engendered through defining the white male worker in

[19]

relation to several white social groups that could be used to emphasise white vulnerability: the youth, the elderly, women and impoverished whites. These groups were often portrayed as virtuous embodiments of the white race unable to defend themselves from the self-interested actions of the white elite, the settler government, global capitalism and Africans. In turn, white male workers positioned themselves as the protectors of the weak and the harbingers of civilisation.[75]

Gender and white women

Racial anxieties were felt in highly gendered ways but they also took on a particular forcefulness when gender norms were threatened or transgressed. White women's role in biological reproduction and the racial socialisation of children, bourgeois ideals of family life and ideas about masculinity and femininity existed in uneasy tension with continuing labour shortages and settler commitment to the colour bar. When white women did take employment, it was seen as a temporary or extraordinary measure; a stop gap for young women on the route towards their 'natural' life's work of marriage and childbirth or a necessary sacrifice in times of war or male absence. This book argues that white women were central to white working-class communities and played important roles in white workers' struggles against employers and racialised others. In doing so it seeks to complement existing research on white women in Southern Rhodesia, which has predominately focused on the experiences of the middle classes.[76]

Hegemonic notions of white femininity and masculinity were fiercely rearticulated, challenged and ultimately remade as a result of white women's wage labour. As Ava Baron has argued, 'in learning to work and in working, in struggles between workers and employers over the nature and meaning of work, both sides construct and contest definitions of masculinity and femininity'.[77] In industrial Britain, male skilled workers were active agents in gendered segregation across the workforce and skilled work itself was intricately linked to these workers' own identities as men. Yet these skilled workers did not only unite to oppose women's entrance into their trades, they also rallied against unskilled men who challenged their monopoly.[78] In Rhodesia, unskilled men were invariably African. White male struggles around skilled work were struggles of differentiation from both white women and African men. Their demands were framed not only with reference to race and nation, but were gendered claims over the 'rights' of men to exist as sources of provision within the idealised nuclear family unit.

White male workers generally opposed the employment of women on the basis that women represented a form of cheap labour that threatened to undercut their own wages, but also because they represented a psychological threat by undermining the ability of men to prove their manliness by being the sole breadwinner. In South Africa, white women's entrance into wage labour has been linked to cultural crises of masculinity as well as outbreaks of Black Peril.[79] Likewise, in Rhodesia anxieties provoked by the disintegration of gender roles, the breakdown of the nuclear family unit and the increased independence of white women were experienced and articulated through ideologies that linked white women's presence in the home to white racial health and the future of settler rule, as well as ideologies that routinely pathologised the colonised population and framed Africans as inherently violent, lustful and unstable.[80] Struggles over work, male unemployment and female wage labour provide unique insight into competing constructions of social identities, their reworkings and subversions; the panics and anxieties that result from perceived aberrations to normative social behaviours; and the attempts to impose or reinstate social hierarchies.

Imperial mobility and the transnational dimensions of class formation

While visiting Johannesburg in 2015 I stayed with a white man who worked on the railways in Rhodesia during the 1970s and had subsequently moved to South Africa in the 1980s. He had never travelled outside southern Africa, let alone to London, but as he spoke a variety of cockney rhyming slang punctuated his Rhodesian accent, particularly as he reminisced about 'old chinas' he used to work with.[81] A few months later while in Zimbabwe, I took the short walk from Bulawayo railway station to Raylton Club – once the heart of white lower-class social life in the city. Previously owned by the all-white railway workers' trade union and constructed in the tradition of the typical British working-man's club, today it is frequented by an African clientele who use the space to meet friends, enjoy drinks at the bar or make use of the sports facilities. Cockney rhyming slang and British working men's clubs may at first seem out of place in southern Africa. Yet, just as the movement of people from the colonies to the United Kingdom reshaped the British working class, British working-class culture was transported to the colonies, remoulded and fused with existing identities and cultures.[82]

Global processes were central to class formation and struggle across the empire and migration framed the construction and reworking of local and global social identities and transnational racial thinking.[83] In Southern Rhodesia global flows of labour as well as workers'

[21]

experiences in South Africa and Britain informed the dominant ways in which white workers articulated their grievances and conceived themselves as a racialised international working class.[84] White workers were pragmatic and drew on a range of available epistemologies and rhetorical devices in order to protect their own structural position, while framing themselves as progressive and respectable. At times, white workers' agitation was formulated through explicitly racial appeals and the language of socialism. In other periods, particular white labour organisations were at pains to dissociate themselves from any racist connotations or the ideologies of class war. Recourse to outright racist sloganeering and a heightened stress upon white skin occurred when white workers felt particularly threatened, but was also influenced by the dominant ideological justifications of settler colonialism that changed from conquest to decolonisation. The settler project was justified variously through the language of civilisation, segregation, multi-racialism and the maintenance of standards, and white workers drew upon these narratives in their own agitation. Yet the expansion of certain industries and high turnover of labour meant that new migrants, social groups, ideas and ideologies were continually introduced into the labour force. These new additions meant that the socialisation of new arrivals into normative behaviours was a continual process; but it also meant that existing white workers' identities, cultures and politics were constantly modified. Notably, the experiences of prohibited immigrant and strike leader Charles Taylor discussed in Chapter 4 demonstrate how some radical non-racialists found their way into Rhodesia.

A note on sources and historical focus

Studies of white workers have been dominated by miners, reflecting both the ubiquitous representation of mining as the archetypal working-class occupation as well as the importance of the mining sector in southern Africa more generally. Yet mining and quarrying never accounted for more than 15 per cent of total economically active Europeans in Southern Rhodesia. As early as 1926 more Europeans were employed in manufacturing than in mining and quarrying (Table 1). This book moves beyond the focus on miners. In particular, it has used the railways due to their centrality to imperialism and the contested notion of colonial railways as a vector of modernity and progress, but also because of the exceptional richness of the trade union records of Rhodesia Railways. Railways enabled settlement, influenced social identifications and created new public spaces and social relations. In colonial territories they informed racial

Table 1 Percentage of total economically active
Europeans engaged in mining and quarrying[a]

Year	Percentage (%)
1921	12.8
1926	11.7
1931	8.1
1936	14.8
1941	11.5
1956	8.8
1961	3
1969	3.2

[a] All figures in the tables throughout the book are collated from successive Southern Rhodesian censuses unless stated otherwise.

and national identities and produced hierarchies of labour in which racial status was constructed and proclaimed.[85] Rhodesia Railways consistently employed a significant proportion of the country's white population in a wide range of different types of work including skilled and unskilled, manual and clerical and boasted the strongest and largest trade union. In this regard the railways offer the opportunity to examine a multiplicity of experiences, identities and struggles over different types of work. Moreover, in the latter half of the twentieth century white trade unions were increasingly incorporated into the state machinery and the popularity of various labour parties declined, corresponding to an increase in measures designed to secure the socio-economic position of whites in the settler colony. Labour historians' attention on white workers decreased as the existence of 'traditional' class identities and industrial militancy dissipated. This book argues that class continued to divide the white population throughout the Federation and RF years, despite the erosion of what might be seen as a traditional class consciousness.[86]

This research relied upon a wide range of rich primary source material based in national archives, private homes, social clubs, trade union headquarters and museums across the United Kingdom, Zimbabwe and South Africa. Its strength lies in its use of a wide cross section of material: from Southern Rhodesian Legislative Assembly debates and parliamentary reports to British Foreign and Commonwealth Office documents as well as novels, national newspapers, a selection of white memoirs and original interviews conducted by the author. A close examination of successive Rhodesian censuses has been used to reconstruct long-term employment patterns and demographic data relating to gender and ethnicity. Print material including the *Bulawayo Chronicle* and *Rhodesia Herald*, both owned by the Argus Press, a publishing company with strong links to Johannesburg mining companies, as well as *Rhodesia Railways Magazine*, which was owned by the Rhodesia Railways administration, have offered incisive points of contrast with independent trade union journals such as the *Rhodesia Railway Review, Rhodesian Trade Union Review*, the *Granite Review* and the *Rhodesia Nurses Newsletter* and newspapers of the Rhodesia Labour Party and Southern Rhodesia Labour Party, *Labour Era* and *Labour Front*. These have been used alongside the memoirs and novels of Doris Lessing, Peter Godwin, Daphne Anderson, as well as a number of lesser-known settler autobiographies.

The ambivalences and tensions between these sources have provided insight into how meaning was constructed and contested by different social groups in Rhodesian settler society. Yet most of these sources produced by settlers do not explicitly confront the fundamental violence of the settler colonial structure. Settlers, after all, were not in the habit of presenting themselves as violently racist. Moreover, the African voices that appear in this book are predominantly male and overwhelmingly from the ranks of the petite bourgeoisie and intelligentsia. As invaluable as they are to this study, the memoirs of Lawrence Vambe, Joshua Nkomo and Ezekiel Makunike or the novels of Alexander Kanengoni, Stanley Nyamfukudza and Charles Mungoshi ultimately reflect particular classed and gendered experiences. The census was particularly unhelpful as it consistently underestimated African wage labour and tended to erase the work of African women altogether. In white trade union journals, the work of African women was recognised only when it could be instrumentalised to denounce African men as lazy and effeminate. Where possible, I have drawn upon several illuminating studies of African women that emphasise the importance and variety of African women's work in formal wage labour and informal economies, their roles in nationalist and working-class movements and their struggles against colonial and African patriarchal forces in order to counter the distorted images of African women produced in the settler accounts used here.[87]

Chapter outline

This book follows a broadly chronological structure over five chapters. It does not aim to provide a comprehensive narrative account of white workers or the historical minutiae of trade union bodies or labour parties, but outlines significant events and day-to-day activities that show the ways in which racial identity was produced.

Chapter 1 focuses on the rise of European trade unions in the wake of the First World War. The chapter outlines the major tenets of white worker identity, considers how white workers were internally fractured according to ethnicity, nationality, gender, skill and occupation and demonstrates how trade unions used notions of respectability and pride in whiteness to temper these divisions. Drawing on Barbara Rosenwein, it considers the gendered emotional communities on Rhodesia Railways, with particular emphasis on the disciplining effects of pride, shame and anger. It argues that expressed emotions were structured by race, class and gender and continued to be important markers of white worker identity throughout the period under study. This chapter also interrogates Jonathan Hyslop's notion of 'white labourism' among European workers in Rhodesia and ends by exploring the role of the 'othering' of Africans and Coloureds in the construction of white class identities in the settler colony.

Chapter 2 focuses on the Great Depression and examines the concept of poor whiteism from the perspectives of European trade unions and the Rhodesia Labour Party. It makes the case for recognising the dynamism of white worker experience by evidencing that economic crisis forced the reworking of white workers' identities and the boundaries of white, male work outlined in Chapter 1. In particular it details the entrance of white women into wage labour and shows that unskilled work, in certain circumstances, was valorised as character building. In 1934 the colour bar was formalised under the Industrial Conciliation Act. This chapter probes how white workers agitated around this important piece of legislation and argues that the Act failed to fully consolidate white worker loyalty or successfully cauterise their struggles against employers and the state.

Chapter 3 explores the struggles of white British, non-British European, Coloured and African men and white women to variously challenge or uphold racialised and gendered patterns of recruitment, wages and working and living conditions in the context of the Second World War. Part 1 explores the limitations of white workers' wartime nationalism and shows that the presence of white working-class Royal Air Force (RAF) recruits, Polish refugees and Italian internees as well as a growing number of Coloured wage labourers provoked contestation both over what it meant to be British as well as what it meant to be white. Through examining trade unionist discussions over the desirability of particular nationalities and ethnicities, Part 1 argues that racial boundaries were not always obvious. Alongside confusion over non-British whites and Coloureds, the increasing numbers of white women in wage labour provoked further consternation among trade unionists. Anxieties over white women exploited by employers, impoverished and alone, were aggravated by the relative absence of white men due to the large numbers of volunteers for the war. Black Peril and illusions to African violence became increasingly prominent in trade union journals. White working men utilised these images in their appeals to the settler state and employers for labour reforms and enhancement of their racial and gender privileges.

Anxieties around non-British whites and white women were compounded by simultaneous African urbanisation, the rise of an African middle class and increasing African militancy and organisation. These phenomena, which proved dislocating or emasculating to white male workers, form the context for Part 2. Two major outbursts of African industrial action, the 1945 Railway strike and the 1948 general strike, are used to demonstrate how white workers' ideas concerning the rights of workers and principled solidarity combined with racial supremacy to create contradictory and unexpected responses to African militancy. Part 2 also draws on research on the production of settler colonial space and the insights of W. E. B. Du Bois to explore white worker anxieties with regards to perceived encroachment on 'white' cities and the threats posed by educated, skilled and professional Africans to lower-class whites. The chapter ends with an analysis of the decline of Rhodesia's Labour parties to explore the contested racialised boundaries of white workers' socialism.

Chapter 4 covers the period in which Southern and Northern Rhodesia joined with Nyasaland in the Central African Federation from 1953 to 1963. The chapter begins with an assessment of white labour strength in the post-war years, with particular emphasis on the position of white women and non-British whites in the labour market. In response to the increasing encroachment on white male jobs, white workers agitated for a 'white labour policy' in which every job in the colony would be performed by whites despite the centrality of African labour to the economy. This proposed policy is examined as an example of mass cognitive dissonance and a collective fantasy of African elimination. The chapter turns to a strike of European firemen in 1954 to consider how the mobility of white settlers disrupted existing trade union structures and racialised practices and argues the strike points to a broader general failure of settler socialisation. The chapter ends with a consideration of the role of white workers in the turn to more segregationist and racist practice and election of the RF.

Chapter 5 looks at the last struggles of white workers as they attempted to protect their racial privileges in the context of RF rule and a brutal war. This chapter challenges the idea that white workers had a harmonious relationship with the RF and looks at the ways white trade unionists struggled against African workers, European employers as well as the Rhodesian state to retain their privileges. White men were increasingly conscripted into counterinsurgency forces; lower-class whites were the least able to evade conscription and the most likely to take on undesirable roles in the war. Conscription also intensified labour shortages, eroded the white male monopoly of skilled trades and put serious strains on family and work life. The numbers of white women in work and the types of work that white women performed significantly broadened. The chapter ends by arguing that for white men, anxieties over their racial and gendered power that had previously been expressed through Black Peril were increasingly experienced and articulated through fears of castration.

Settler experiences cannot be explained simply through reference to whiteness. Class divisions shaped racial interactions and the ways in which settler identities were produced and performed. Notions of free and coerced labour, craftsmanship, productivity, divisions of skill and the dignity of labour were all deeply racialised. Through these concepts white workers laid claim to respectability and proclaimed their difference both from white elites and racialised others. Struggles over the social composition and conditions of work were also ultimately struggles over the meanings attached to race, class, nationality and gender. This book analyses the role of white workers in the production of social identities and the settler colonial structure. In doing so it reveals white workers' tenuous access to power, their incomplete absorption into the settler community and the fundamental malleability and ambivalence of race.

Notes

1 Celia and Mary Jane were both interviewed in 2013 as part of the Listening Project www.bbc.co.uk/programmes/p02tfl9z (accessed 10 July 2019).
2 Ann Laura Stoler, 'Tense and Tender Ties: The Politics of Comparison in North American History and (Post) Colonial Studies', *Journal of American History*, 88:3 (2001), pp. 829–865.
3 Numerous individuals have proclaimed the 'death' of class, its inadequacy in understanding social relations or called for a complete overhaul of its use in historical and social analysis. See Eric Hobsbawm, 'The Forward March of Labour Halted?', *Marxism Today* (1978), pp. 279–286; Stuart Hall and Martin Jacques (eds), *New Times: The Changing Face of Politics in the 1990s* (London: Lawrence & Wishart, 1989); Jan Pakulski and Malcolm Waters, *The Death of Class* (London: Sage, 1990); Patrick Joyce, *Visions of the People: Industrial England and the Question of Class, c.1848–1914* (Cambridge, UK: Cambridge University Press, 1991); Gareth Steadman Jones, *Languages of Class: Studies in English Working-Class History, 1832–1982* (Cambridge, UK: Cambridge University Press, 1983).
4 For some debates regarding the usefulness of class in British labour history, see Katrina Navickas, 'What Happened to Class? New Histories of Labour and Collective Action in Britain', *Social History*, 36:2 (2011), pp. 192–204.
5 Neil Roos, 'South African History and Subaltern Historiography: Ideas for a Radical History of White Folk', *International Review of Social History*, 61:1 (2016), pp. 117–150.

6 Paul Gilroy, Holberg Lecture, University of Bergen, 4 June 2019, www.newframe. com/long-read-refusing-race-and-salvaging-the-human/?fbclid=IwAR1fZhvVHs_ dklFQdk5pp7MQdf3TFW7pSMO2pduEg6Pe5Ggf3ZNWoR9gFe8 (accessed 17 July 2019).
7 Ian Phimister, *An Economic and Social History of Zimbabwe, 1890–1948: Capital Accumulation and Class Struggle* (London: Longman, 1988); Jon Lunn, *Capital and Labour on the Rhodesian Railway System, 1888–1947* (Basingstoke: Macmillan in Association with St Antony's College, 1997).
8 See Timothy J. Coates, *Convicts and Orphans: Forced and State-Sponsored Colonisers in the Portuguese Empire, 1550–1755* (Stanford, CA: Stanford University Press, 2001); Antoinette Errante, 'White Skin, Many Masks: Colonial Schooling, Race and National Consciousness among White Settler Children in Mozambique, 1934–1974', *International Journal of African Historical Studies*, 36:1 (2003), pp. 7–33; Ali Yedes, 'Social Dynamics in Colonial Algeria: The Question of Pieds-Noirs Identity', in *French Civilisation and Its Discontents: Nationalism, Colonialism, Race*, ed. Tyler Stovall and Georges van den Abbeele (Plymouth, NH: Lexington Books, 2003), pp. 235–250; Jeremy Krikler, *White Rising: The 1922 Insurrection and Racial Killing in South Africa* (Manchester: Manchester University Press, 2005); Charles van Onselen, *Studies in the Social and Economic History of the Witwatersrand, 1886–1914* (Harlow: Longman, 1982).
9 Synthesis of chap. 1 in Phimister, *Economic and Social History*; and Alois Mlambo, *A History of Zimbabwe* (New York: Cambridge University Press, 2014).
10 Mlambo, *History of Zimbabwe*, pp. 30–31.
11 Lunn, *Rhodesian Railway*, p. 18.
12 Mlambo, *History of Zimbabwe*, p. 44.
13 Terence Ranger's portrayal of a coordinated singular uprising received considerable criticism from David Beach, 'Chimurenga: The Shona Rising of 1896-7', *Journal of African History*, 20 (1979), pp. 395–420; Julian Cobbing, 'The Absent Priesthood: Another Look at the Rhodesian Risings of 1896–1897', *Journal of African History*, 18:1 (1977), pp. 61–84; Ian Phimister, 'Narratives of Progress: Zimbabwean Historiography and the End of History', *Journal of Contemporary African Studies*, 30:1 (2012), pp. 27–34.
14 Phimister, *Economic and Social History*, chap. 1.
15 Elaine Lee, 'An Analysis of the Rhodesian Referendum, 1922', *Rhodesian History*, 8 (1977), pp. 71–99.
16 Charles van Onselen, *Chibaro: African Mine Labour in Southern Rhodesia, 1900–1933* (London: Pluto Press, 1976).
17 Mlambo, *History of Zimbabwe*, pp. 54–58.
18 Stephen Constantine, 'Migrants and Settlers', in *The Oxford History of the British Empire: Vol. IV, The Twentieth Century*, ed. Judith M. Brown and W. M. Roger Louis (Oxford: Oxford University Press, 1999), pp. 163–164. For such texts, see James Rochfort Maguire, *Cecil Rhodes: A Biography and Appreciation by Imperialist* London: Macmillan, 1897); Howard Hensman, *A History of Rhodesia* (Edinburgh: W. Blackwood, 1900); Percy F. Hone, *Southern Rhodesia* (London: G. Bell & Sons, 1909).
19 Robert Bickers, 'Introduction: Britains and Britons Over the Seas', in *Settlers and Expatriates: Britons Over the Seas*, ed. Robert Bickers (Oxford: Oxford University Press, 2010), p. 11. See also Lewis H. Gann and Michael Gelfand, *Huggins of Rhodesia* (London: Allen & Unwin, 1964); Lewis H. Gann, *A History of Southern Rhodesia: Early Days to 1934* (London: Chatto & Windus, 1965); Colin Leys, *European Politics in Southern Rhodesia* (Oxford: Clarendon Press, 1959).
20 Julie Bonello, 'The Development of Early Settler Identity in Southern Rhodesia: 1890–1914', *International Journal of African Historical Studies*, 43:2 (2010), pp. 341–367; Allison K. Shutt and Tony King, 'Imperial Rhodesians: The 1953 Rhodes Centenary Exhibition in Southern Rhodesia', *JSAS* (2005), 31:2, pp. 357–379.
21 Alois Mlambo, 'Building a White Man's Country: Aspects of White Immigration into Rhodesia up Until World War II', *Zambezia*, 25:2 (1998), pp. 123–146; Alois

INTRODUCTION

Mlambo, ' "Some Are More White than Others": Racial Chauvinism as a Factor in Rhodesian Immigration Policy, 1890 to 1963', *Zambezia*, 27:2 (2000), pp. 139–160.

22 Marguerite Elaine Lee, 'Politics and Pressure Groups in Southern Rhodesia, 1898–1923' (unpublished doctoral thesis, University of London, 1974), p. 169.

23 Phimister, *Economic and Social History*, pp. 100–118.

24 *Ibid*. See also Claire Palley, *The Constitutional History and Law of Southern Rhodesia, 1888–1965 with Special Reference to Imperial Control* (Oxford: Clarendon Press, 1966).

25 Shula Marks, 'Southern Africa', in *The Oxford History of the British Empire: Vol IV*, p. 565.

26 Andrew Cohen, *The Politics and Economics of Decolonisation in Africa: The Failed Experiment of the Central African Federation* (London: I. B. Taurus, 2017).

27 Tinashe Nyamunda, ' "More a Cause than a Country": Historiography, UDI and the Crisis of Decolonisation in Rhodesia', *JSAS*, 42:5 (2016), pp. 1005–1019.

28 A particularly vitriolic defence of white rule in the face of supposed British degeneracy is given by Guy van Eeden, *The Crime of Being White* (Cape Town: Nasionale, 1965).

29 Ian Smith, *The Great Betrayal: The Memoirs of Ian Douglas Smith* (London: Blake, 1998).

30 Terence Ranger, *Revolt in Southern Rhodesia, 1896–97* (London: Heinemen, 1967); Terence Ranger, *The African Voice in Southern Rhodesia, 1898–1930* (London: Heinemann Education, 1970); Eshmael Mlambo, *The Struggle for a Birthright* (London: Hurst, 1972).

31 See Brian Raftopoulos, 'Problematising Nationalism in Zimbabwe: A Historiographical Review', *Zambezia*, 26:2 (1999), pp. 115–134.

32 James Alfred Mutambirwa, *The Rise of Settler Power in Southern Rhodesia (Zimbabwe), 1898–1923* (Rutherford, NJ: Fairleigh Dickinson University Press, 1980), p. 27.

33 Henri Rolin, *Rolin's Rhodesia*, trans. Deborah Kirkwood (Bulawayo: Books of Rhodesia, 1978), p. vii.

34 Harald Fischer-Tiné and Susanne Gehrmann, 'Introduction: Empires, Boundaries and the Production of Difference', in *Empires and Boundaries: Race, Class and Gender in Colonial Settings* ed. Harald Fischer-Tiné and Susanne Gehrmann (New York: Routledge, 2009), pp. 4–5.

35 Norma Kriger, 'The Zimbabwean War of Liberation: Struggles within the Struggle', *JSAS*, 14:2 (1988), pp. 304–322; Dane Kennedy, *Islands of White: Settler Society and Culture in Kenya and Southern Rhodesia, 1890–1939* (Durham, NC: Duke University Press, 1987); Peter Godwin and Ian Hancock, *Rhodesians Never Die: The Impact of War and Political Change on White Rhodesia, 1970–1980* (Harare: Baobab Books, 1995).

36 Lloyd Sachikonye, *When a State Turns on Its Citizens: 60 Years of Institutionalised Violence in Zimbabwe* (Harare: Weaver Press, 2011); Brian Raftopoulos, 'The Zimbabwean Crisis and the Challenges for the Left', *JSAS*, 32:2 (2006), p. 206.

37 Colin Stoneman and Lionel Cliffe, *Zimbabwe: Politics, Economics and Society* (London: Pinter, 1989); Raftopoulos, 'Challenges for the Left'. For the best explication of the differences between socialism 'from above' and 'from below', see Hal Draper, 'The Two Souls of Socialism', *New Politics*, 5:1 (1966), pp. 57–84, www.marxists.org/archive/draper/1966/twosouls/ (accessed 12 November 2019).

38 Terence Ranger, 'Nationalist Historiography, Patriotic History and the History of the Nation: The Struggle Over the Past in Zimbabwe', *JSAS*, 30:2 (2004), pp. 215–234.

39 Phimister, 'Narratives of Progress'.

40 Raftopoulos, 'Challenges for the Left', p. 212.

41 Brian Raftopoulos and Alois Mlambo (eds), *Becoming Zimbabwe: A History from the Pre-Colonial Period to 2008* (Harare: Weaver Press, 2009); Brian Raftopoulos, 'Nationalism and Labour in Salisbury 1953–1965', *JSAS*, 21:1 (1995), pp. 79–93; Teresa Barnes, *'We Women Worked So Hard': Gender, Urbanisation, and Social Reproduction in Colonial Harare, Zimbabwe, 1930–1956* (Portsmouth, NH:

Heinemann, 1999); Michael West, *The Rise of an African Middle Class: Colonial Zimbabwe, 1898–1965* (Bloomington, IN: Indiana University Press, 2002); Phimister, *Economic and Social*; van Onselen, *Chibaro*.

42 Raftopoulos, 'Challenges for the Left'.
43 Alex Callinicos and John Rogers, *Southern Africa After Soweto* (London: Pluto Press, 1977), pp. 42–44.
44 Nicos Poulantzas, 'Marxism and Social Classes', *New Left Review*, 78 (1973), pp. 27–54. This was most forcefully realised in Howard Simson, 'The Myth of the White Working Class in South Africa', *African Review*, 4:2 (1974), pp. 189–203. See also Frederick A. Johnstone, *Class, Race and Gold: A Study of Class Relations and Racial Discrimination in South Africa* (London: Routledge and Kegan Paul, 1976); Robert Davies, 'The White Working Class in South Africa', *New Left Review*, 82 (1973), p. 51. Davies did modify his position in a later article, arguing that unskilled white labour positions did exist, but they were limited to apprenticeship roles that would allow for the progression into skilled work. White wage earners in all sectors became 'labour aristocrats' or part of the 'new middle class'. See Robert Davies, 'Mining Capital, the State and Unskilled White Workers in South Africa, 1901–1913', *JSAS*, 3:1 (1976), p. 56.
45 Harold Wolpe, 'The "White Working Class" in South Africa', *Economy and Society*, 5:2 (1976), pp. 197–240; Erik Olin Wright, *Classes* (London: Verso, 1985); Guglielmo Carchedi, 'On the Economic Identification of the New Middle Class', *Economy and Society*, 4:1 (1975), pp. 1–86.
46 Wright, *Classes*, pp. 43, 24.
47 Valentin Volosinov, *Marxism and the Philosophy of Language* (Cambridge, MA: Harvard University Press, [1929] 1986), p. 23.
48 *Ibid.*, p. 21.
49 See Hal Draper, *Karl Marx's Theory of Revolution: Vol. 1, State and Bureaucracy* (New York: Monthly Review Press, 1977).
50 Peter Alexander, 'Coal, Control and Class Experience in South Africa's Rand Revolt of 1922', *Comparative Studies of South Asia, Africa and the Middle East*, 19 (1999), pp. 31–45.
51 Lunn, *Rhodesian Railway*, p. 10.
52 See Eric Hobsbawm, *Labouring Men: Studies in the History of Labour* (London: Weidenfield & Nicholson, 1964), p. 272. For a critique of the labour aristocracy, see Charles Post, 'Exploring Working-Class Consciousness: A Critique of the Theory of the "Labour Aristocracy"', *Historical Materialism*, 18:4 (2010), pp. 3–38.
53 Ian Phimister, 'White Miners in Historical Perspective: Southern Rhodesia, 1890–1953', *JSAS*, 3:2 (1977), p. 187.
54 *Ibid.*, p. 203.
55 See Clement Masakure, 'On the Frontline of Caring: A History of African Nurses in Colonial and Postcolonial Zimbabwe, 1940s–1996' (unpublished doctoral thesis, University of Minnesota, 2012).
56 See Rory Pilossof, *The Unbearable Whiteness of Being: Farmers' Voices from Zimbabwe* (Harare: Weaver Press, 2012); Lea Kalaora, 'Madness, Corruption and Exile: On Zimbabwe's Remaining White Commercial Farms', *JSAS*, 37:4 (2011), pp. 747–762; Kate Law, '"Mostly We Are White and Alone": Identity, Anxiety and the Past in Some White Zimbabwean Memoirs', *Journal of Historical Sociology* (2014), pp. 297–318; Kate Law, *Gendering the Settler State: White Women, Race, Liberalism and Empire in Rhodesia, 1950–1980* (New York: Routledge, 2016).
57 David McDermott Hughes, *Whiteness in Zimbabwe: Race, Landscape, and the Problem of Belonging* (New York: Palgrave Macmillan, 2010), p. 5. J. L. Fisher, *Pioneers, Settlers, Aliens, Exiles: The Decolonisation of White Identity in Zimbabwe* (Canberra: ANU E Press, 2010) also displays homogenising tendencies in which all Europeans speak with a singular white voice.
58 Rory Pilossof, 'Reinventing Significance: Reflections on Recent Whiteness Studies in Zimbabwe', *Africa Spectrum*, 49:3 (2014), pp. 141–142. For further criticism of the

INTRODUCTION

homogenisation of whites in Zimbabwean history, see Andrew Hartnack, 'Whiteness and Shades of Grey: Erasure, Amnesia and the Ethnography of Zimbabwe's Whites', *Journal of Contemporary African Studies*, 33:2 (2014), pp. 1–15.

59 Jeremy Krikler, 'Lessons from America: The Writings of David Roediger', *JSAS*, 20:4 (1994), pp. 663–669; David Roediger, *The Wages of Whiteness: Race and the Making of the American Working Class* (London: Verso, 2007); Theodore Allen, *The Invention of the White Race* (London: Verso, 1994); Noel Ignatiev, *How the Irish Became White* (London: Routledge, 1995).

60 Allen, *Invention*.

61 The ambiguity and arguments surrounding class in the classical Marxist tradition have undoubtedly been accentuated by the fact that class was never given detailed formulation by Marx. His chapter on classes in *Capital* was left famously unfinished.

62 G. E. M. de Ste Croix, *The Class Struggle in the Ancient World: From the Archaic Age to the Arab Conquests* (Ithaca, NY: Cornell University Press, 1989), pp. 43–44.

63 Patrick Kealty, *The Politics of Partnership* (London: Penguin, 1963), p. 278.

64 Patrick Wolfe, 'Settler Colonialism and the Elimination of the Native', *Journal of Genocide Research*, 8:4 (2006), p. 388.

65 Lorenzo Veracini, 'Introducing', *Settler Colonial Studies*, 1:1 (2011), p. 2. See also Lorenzo Veracini, *Settler Colonialism: A Theoretical Overview* (Basingstoke: Palgrave Macmillan, 2010).

66 A. Dirk Moses (ed.), *Genocide and Settler Society: Frontier Violence and Stolen Indigenous Children in Australian History* (New York: Berghahn, 2004), pp. 32–33.

67 Casper W. Erichsen and David Olusoga, *The Kaiser's Holocaust: Germany's Forgotten Genocide* (London: Faber, 2011).

68 Kennedy, *Islands of White*, p. 154.

69 Noel Ignatiev, *How the Irish Became White* (New York: Routledge, 1999), p. 49. For criticism, see Andrew Hartman, 'The Rise and Fall of Whiteness Studies', *Race and Class*, 42:6 (2004), p. 34; Eric Arnesen, 'Whiteness and the Historians' Imagination', *International Labor and Working-Class History*, 60, pp. 3–32.

70 Donal Lowry, 'The Crown, Empire Loyalism and the Assimilation of Non-British White Subjects in the British White Subjects in the British World: An Argument against "Ethnic Determinism"', *Journal of Imperial and Commonwealth History*, 31:2 (2003), p. 114.

71 Roediger, *Wages of Whiteness*, p. 13. This idea of the psychological wage came from eminent African American scholar W. E. B. Du Bois, *Black Reconstruction in America: An Essay Toward a History of the Part Which Black Folk Played in the Attempt to Reconstruct Democracy in America, 1860–1880* (Oxford: Oxford University Press, [1935] 2007). For criticism, see Theodore Allen, 'On Roediger's Wages of Whiteness', http://clogic.eserver.org/4-2/allen.html#note1 (accessed 19 July 2019).

72 Deborah Posel, 'Whiteness and Power in the South African Civil Service: Paradoxes of the Apartheid State', *JSAS*, 25:1 (1999), pp. 99–119.

73 Neil Roos, 'Work Colonies and South African Historiography', *Social History*, 36:1 (2011), pp. 54–76.

74 Harald Fischer-Tiné and Christine Whyte, 'Introduction: Empires and Emotions', in *Anxieties, Fear and Panic in Colonial Settings: Empires on the Verge of a Nervous Breakdown*, ed. Harald Fischer-Tiné (Basingstoke: Palgrave Macmillan, 2016), p. 6; Bonello, 'Development of Early Settler Identity', pp. 341–367.

75 For similar tendencies in South Africa, see J. M. Krikler, 'Re-Thinking Race and Class in South Africa: Some Ways Forward', in *Wages of Whiteness*, pp. 133–160.

76 See Donal Lowry, '"Making Fresh Britains Across the Seas": Imperial Authority and Anti-Feminism in Rhodesia', in *Women's Suffrage in the British Empire: Citizenship, Nation and Race*, ed. Christopher Fletcher, Laura Nym Mayhall and Philippa Levine (London: Routledge, 2000), pp. 175–190; Donal Lowry, '"White Women's Country": Ethel Tawse Jollie and the Making of White Rhodesia', *JSAS*, 23:2 (1997), pp. 259–281. Ushehwedu Kufakurinani's work is an exception,

[31]

see *Elasticity in Domesticity: White Women in Rhodesian Zimbabwe, 1890–1979* (Leiden: Brill, 2018).

77 Ava Baron, 'Introduction', in *Work Engendered: Toward a New History of American Labour*, ed. Ava Baron (Ithaca, NY: Cornell University Press, 1991), p. 137.

78 Sonya Rose, 'Gender at Work: Sex, Class and Industrial Capitalism', *History Workshop*, 21 (1986), pp. 120–126.

79 Timothy Keegan, 'Gender, Degeneration and Sexual Danger: Imagining Race and Class in South Africa, ca.1912', *JSAS*, 27:3 (2001), p. 461.

80 Fischer-Tiné and Whyte, 'Introduction: Empires and Emotions', p. 18.

81 China plate – mate.

82 See Satnam Virdee, *Race, Class and the Racialised Outsider* (Basingstoke: Palgrave, 2014).

83 Ann Stoler and Frederick Cooper, 'Between Metropole and Colony; Rethinking a Research Agneda', in *Tensions of Empire: Colonial Cultures in a Bourgeois World*, ed. Ann Stoler and Frederick Cooper (Berkeley, CA: University of California Press, 1997), pp. 1–56; David Lambert and Alan Lester (eds), *Colonial Lives Across the British Empire: Imperial Careering in the Long Nineteenth Century* (Cambridge, UK: Cambridge University Press, 2006); Kent Fedorowich and Andrew Thompson, 'Introduction', in *Empire, Migration and Identity in the British World*, ed. Kent Fedorowich and Andrew Thompson (Manchester: Manchester University Press, 2013), pp. 1–41. See also Philip Bonner, Jonathan Hyslop and Lucien van der Walt, 'Rethinking Worlds of Labour: Southern African Labour History in International Context', *African Studies*, 66:2–3 (2007), p. 139. For flows of African labourers across national boundaries, see van Onselen, *Chibaro*; Brian Raftopoulos and Ian Phimister, *Keep on Knocking: A History of the Labour Movement in Zimbabwe* (Zimbabwe: Baobab Books, 1997).

84 See discussion of white labourism in Chapter 1.

85 Laura Bear, *Lines of the Nation: Indian Railway Workers, Bureaucracy and the Intimate Historical Self* (New York: Columbia University Press, 2007); Lunn, *Rhodesian Railway*; John Butcher, *The British in Malaya, 1880–1941: The Social History of a European Community in Colonial Southeast Asia* (Oxford: Oxford University Press, 1979).

86 See Godwin and Hancock, *Rhodesians Never Die* for an account of the sharp divisions that plagued the RF years.

87 Barnes, 'We Women'; Elisabeth Schmidt, *Peasants, Traders and Wives: Shona Women in the History of Zimbabwe, 1870–1939* (London: J. Currey, 1992); Brian Raftopoulos, 'Gender, Nationalist Politics and the Fight for the City: Harare 1940–1950s', *Southern African Feminist Review*, 1:2 (1995), pp. 30–43; Masakure, 'On the Frontline of Caring'.

CHAPTER ONE

The making of white worker identity

Prior to the First World War white industrial action and labour organisation was largely absent. For white workers conditions in early years of settlement were poor; working twelve hours a day was not uncommon, overtime was unpaid and authoritarian tactics were regularly used by employers to quell dissent and instil discipline.[1] Struggles to establish trade union organisations were met with fierce resistance from management.[2] Only in the building industry were attempts at organisation successful; the first white trade union was established in 1910 in a bid to secure uniform wages among European employees.[3] Notably, this first trade union was formed upon a racially exclusive demand that invoked an imagined standard of living determined by race and gender, which would remain a central rallying cry of white labour organisation throughout minority rule. From the outbreak of the First World War, the position of white workers altered. The cost of living rose by 59 per cent between 1914 and 1920 and an acute shortage of skilled labour put remaining white workers in a strong position to challenge employers.[4] Under conditions of skilled white labour shortage a lightning strike of firemen at Bulawayo in 1916 saw the men gain an extra shilling a day. The Rhodesia Railway Workers' Union (RRWU) was established in the same year. In 1917 five hundred men signed resignation letters in protest at their conditions, which ultimately forced the administration into arbitration in 1918. Two successful strikes in 1919 and 1920 saw railway workers secure a 25 per cent raise and an eight-hour day.[5] Although the RRWU sought to unite European men from all grades it was dominated by lower semi- and unskilled grades such as pumpers, gangers and stewards. A rival craft union, the Amalgamated Engineers Union (AEU), a branch of the South African union eager to spread their influence into Rhodesia, was successfully established in 1916 and proved more attractive to most of the skilled workers on the railways

[33]

and the mines.[6] On the mines unionisation occurred at a slower place as organisation was frustrated by the uneven distribution of white miners who worked in more disparate groups and smaller numbers than found on the railway system. In 1918 a strike at the Cam & Motor mine by white employees saw all strikers replaced by new workers. However this was followed by a successful strike of mine workers the following year and the establishment of the Rhodesia Mine and General Workers' Association (RMGWA). Other unions proliferated across the colony including the Postal Union, the Commercial Employees Association and craft unions of engineers, boilermakers, brickmakers and wood workers.[7]

This chapter explores the political and cultural identity of white workers at the height of this trade union strength and its rapid decline during the 1920s. This period has received the most sustained research into white labour and has generally focused upon questions of political economy, industrial action, trade union and parliamentary organisation and the ways in which white workers struggled to establish a privileged position, both in the labour market and within settler society more generally. Following Jon Lunn, this chapter seeks to move beyond this focus and interrogate the identity, culture and experiences of white workers.[8] White workers were a heterogeneous formation but nevertheless coagulated around particular imperial, national, ethnic, class and gendered identities. What is explored here is how this 'white worker' identity variously encompassed and sometimes excluded or gradated other identities. Lunn has fruitfully used the notion of the bailiwick – the area in which workers could assert their limited authority and independence within wider systems and boundaries – and argued this space should be understood as a fundamental area of expression for white worker identity in which gendered and racial hierarchies were enforced.[9] Yet while Lunn is attentive to portraying a self-determined culture and highlighting divisions within white labour, a sense of how this identity changed over time is absent from his analysis; the dynamism of white labour identity is lost under a series of reified markers of culture. This chapter seeks to overcome this through outlining some central tenets of white workers' identity that were variously retained, transformed or discarded as the century progressed.

This chapter is largely based on European mining and railway trade union journals. On the railways a sense of community was fostered through union publications, particularly the RRWU's *Rhodesian Railway Review*, which reported local union news, individuals and their successes, deaths, promotions and encouraged letter writing, poetry submissions, as well as boasting an entire page each issue

dedicated to jokes and personal anecdotes. It detailed news of football leagues, picnics, dinner dances and social functions organised by
railway wives. For the most part, women were absent from the *Review*.
Articles directed at white women usually reaffirmed social norms,
addressing cooking skills or giving domestic tips. Like the RRWU, the
RMGWA produced a journal during the early 1920s, the *Rhodesian
Trade Union Review*. This chapter also uses parliamentary debates
and speeches by Rhodesia Labour Party (RLP) members, which reveal
attempts to articulate a coherent white worker identity.

Clearly these views cannot be distilled into a homogenous white
worker experience. The fundamental abstractness of class means there
is not a singular identifiable and static white labour identity.[10] Any
attempt to recreate a singular representation of class is therefore rep-
licating idealised projections rather than grasping the multifarious
experiences of diverse social actors. Yet representations can give
some insight into how white worker identity was articulated. Trade
union journals are inevitably biased towards the voices of the trade
union bureaucracy. Nevertheless, letter pages allow insight into the
viewpoints of unionised or lay members of the unions and common
themes emerge. Notably, these sources reveal how respectability
became a key component of the idealised white worker. This respectability was made up of three major planks: a professed relative skill
and education; self-sufficiency, which could include the provision for
dependants; and productivity in manual labour – the process of creating tangible things – which was imagined as central to the production of civilisation. Yet many white workers failed to attain these signs
of respectability.

These trade union journals also show how shame and pride were
used to condition workers' behaviours, and, as expressed emotions,
engendered individual and collective self-esteem. Barbara Rosenwein
has argued that emotional expression is conditioned and encouraged
differently in particular social communities. Emotions result from
judgements made whether something will be pleasurable, painful,
impact upon us negatively or positively, but are also the product of
cultural practices, morals and language. Rosenwein contends that
people live and lived in 'emotional communities': social communities (whether families, neighbourhoods, churches or trade unions) with
their own 'systems of feeling' and rules for the expression of emotions.[11]
She challenges the researcher to unearth 'what these communities
(and the individuals within them) define and assess as valuable or
harmful to them; the evaluations they make about others' emotions;
the nature of the affective bonds between people that they recognise;
and the modes of emotional expression that they expect, encourage,

tolerate, and deplore'.[12] For white workers pride and shame acted to police boundaries, link individuals to group identities and create loyalty. Pride in work, in white skin and in masculinity was contrasted with the shame of fecklessness and dependency – characteristics associated with women and Africans. For men, anger was also a legitimate expression of righteousness against employers or Africans who were deemed to be a threat to their position in the racial hierarchy. Upper-class whites and Africans were cast as parasitical figures that drew upon the strength and productive capacity of the white worker. Gender was fundamental in conditioning the expression and experience of these emotions. Male-dominated trade unions anointed white women as moral guardians and encouraged them to regulate workers' behaviours.

This chapter also explores the fluctuations in attitudes towards African education, which became more hostile as pressures on white workers deepened. It argues that attitudes to Coloured workers were dictated by a combination of racism and self-interest and that white workers' racial classification was not entirely secured, as their ambiguous relationships with Coloured workers attests. The dominant rhetoric of white labour organisation during these years was wracked with complexity and contradiction. At times white workers claimed to share racial, national and imperial identity with employers and the Rhodesian state; at others they professed a shared position of exploitation with African workers. They simultaneously railed against these social groups and defined themselves in opposition to them. Although these positions appear irreconcilable, this contradiction reflected white workers' position of exploitation within a racially stratified workforce. White worker radicalism was ultimately a rhetoric of antagonism, exploitation and financial evil, which celebrated the agency of the working man and dependent woman in creation and production, but one that was mediated through white supremacy and empire. Jonathan Hyslop's notion of 'white labourism' is extended here in order to explore these contradictions.

White worker politics: white socialism and racialised radicalism

In the colonies white workers often possessed an uneasy combination of socialist and white supremacist ideas. White union politics throughout southern African history is largely characterised by its possession of contradictory ideological positions, aptly summed up by the 1922 South African Rand Strikers' slogan 'workers of the world unite for a white South Africa'.[13] Jonathan Hyslop has argued that, prior to the

First World War, the white working classes within the British Empire should not be considered as consisting of ' "nationally" discrete identities', but as an imperial working class, connected by international flows of labour and a common ideology of 'white labourism': an idiosyncratic blend of militancy and radicalism mediated through racist ideologies.[14] Yet, as Duncan Money has argued, the notion of white labourism can extend beyond the temporal parameters of Hyslop's study.[15] Across the period of minority rule the dominant white workers' identity should be understood as an evolving sum of interactions and overlaps between Southern Rhodesia and the wider British Empire. Familial and ancestral ties cemented connections to both the white South African and British working class and white trade unions zealously proclaimed their loyalty and connection to Britain and her white colonies during the 1920s. The *Review* detailed and cheered on the progress of the British Labour Party, reprinted excerpts and cartoons from British, South African, Canadian, American and Australian trade union journals and magazines. They published articles on radical movements such as the Chartists and the Minority Movement and laid claim to the heritage and moral strength of these struggles. The RMGWA's *Rhodesian Trade Union Review* paid particular attention to the large mining trade unions in the Union of South Africa and printed numerous analyses of the 1922 Rand Revolt.

The political ideologies of white trade unions were initially informed through the radical and racial ideas white workers had inherited from their experiences in Britain and South Africa. All of the men involved in the establishment of RRWU were British bar one South African, and had been involved in the 1911 national railway strike in England before moving to Rhodesia.[16] The first attempt to form a union on the railways was led by Frank Nettleton in 1912 who had been general secretary of the Amalgamated Society of Railway and Harbour Servants of South Africa. RRWU stalwart and later parliamentary representative of white workers, Jack Keller was born in London in 1885 and began work when he was nine years old. At fourteen he worked as a London street messenger and became a railwayman at nineteen. His regular editorials in the *Review* and parliamentary speeches reveal a man well versed in the language of class war with a penchant for hyperbole. Keller was a charismatic speaker, popular among railwaymen and consistently re-elected as a Member of Parliament (MP) by the Bulawayo railway constituency of Raylton from 1928 to 1958.[17] The founder of RMGWA Herbert Walsh grew up in Bradford, was apprenticed at thirteen and heavily influenced by William Morris's Socialist Society and the Socialist League. He moved to South Africa and established a boilermakers' union in 1902 before moving on to Rhodesia in 1910.[18]

[37]

Donald Macintyre, former Glaswegian apprentice and member of the British Labour Party, became a leading member of the RLP.[19] The trade union and labour movement in Rhodesia was shaped by these men's experiences of struggle and political education in the metropole and other imperial locations. But the radicalism and racism of white workers was not simply a matter of transposing ideas from one context to another; they were rooted in capitalism and engendered through their experience of the racial monopoly of higher paid, skilled work. White workers' structural location within the settler colonial labour market meant they occupied an antagonistic position both in relation to capital and to cheap African labour. The idiosyncratic political ideologies discussed below were an expression of these social relationships.

Based on its British counterpart and with a firm relationship to the RRWU trade union bureaucracy, the RLP enjoyed success as a party nationally and garnered support from lower-class whites. While in the 1920 elections there was no uniform labour party and labour candidates stood against one another in some seats, overall labour candidates received 18.6 per cent of the total vote. The first attempt to establish a coordinated labour party in 1920 failed to last beyond 1921 as the party was ripped apart over personality disputes and skill-based sectionalism. Francis Hadfield, the first leader of the party, declared open support for the AEU, which caused anger among members from the RRWU and RMGWA railway and mining unions and ultimately led to the party's decline. The following year under the direction of Jack Keller the RRWU re-established the RLP. Ten out of fifteen labour candidates contesting seats in the 1924 election were railwaymen or ex-railwaymen.[20] The RLP paid lip service to an evolutionary path to socialism, but in essence was fundamentally a thoroughly populist party that focused on the racialised redistribution of wealth to poorer whites in the colony. Keller argued that the RLP would be more accurately named if it was the 'people's' party'.[21]

White workers' organisations generally preached the virtues of racially exclusive socialism. They used a language that set themselves against 'the capitalists' and warmongering international financiers and spoke of solidarity, unity and class pride, drawing on familiar tropes and images from British trade union movements. The Review argued that 'the workers' organisations devote their time and money to the saving of widows and orphans, whilst the capitalists' organisations made them, as witness the world's war and Rand horrors'.[22] Capitalists were identified as the source of poverty, inequality and warfare in opposition to the egalitarian principles at the heart of workers' unions that strove for universal prosperity and peace. Poverty was seen as a direct result of 'the present policy of the capitalists, particularly our own railway administration [which] means the impoverishing of all'. Illustrations in the *Review* explicitly identified company directors as responsible for the increased cost of living and the death of the community (Figure 1).[23] Management and officials were portrayed as autocrats and 'sycophants'. One anecdote recalled a particularly over-zealous officer who mistook the general manager for a lay worker and attempted to dismiss him simply for asking a question.[24] Antipathy towards management was boasted about in anecdotes that celebrated confrontation with officials. Stuart McNeillie, a prominent figure in the RRWU, recalled in an interview in 1972 that when the railway administration tried to get workers to vote to join the Union of South Africa there had been some 'really rough, really rowdy meeting[s]' with employer organisations. He recalled meetings at the old Empire Theatre in Bulawayo 'where the employer representatives came on and made the great mistake of coming in with dinner suits on' and continued that 'tomatoes and things of that kind were thrown at these pompous looking gentlemen'.[25] Such skirmishes highlight the intensity of worker animosity while the union rhetoric framed management as pretentious and self-important and cheered the ordinariness and decency of the working man. Different classes were also imagined as mediums for different emotions, which in turn marked class boundaries and trade union identity. The phrase 'happiness and contentment' repeatedly appeared in the *Review* and it was stressed that for workers, this emotional state could only be achieved through trade union activity, while employers and capitalists were repeatedly presented as sources of workers' distress (Figures 1 and 2).

The language of socialism invited accusations of Bolshevism and revolutionary communism from employers, MPs and the press. The *Rhodesia Herald* decried the RMGWA leadership during the strike of 1919 as trying 'to establish a dictatorship, a sort of glorified Soviet, in Bulawayo',[26] and noted that 'every act of the Executive Council in Bulawayo savours of an autocracy worthy of the Bolsheviks'.[27] Jack Keller was nicknamed Lenin of Rhodesia by his detractors and the RMGWA and the RLP had to repeatedly state that they harboured neither communist nor Bolshevist sympathies although this did little to curb accusations of radical dissent. The rank-and-file were often portrayed as being duped by radical leaders into action. The *Herald* wrote that the men at Wankie during the 1919 strike were actually very contented with their conditions and would return to work only if the executive committee of the union would allow it.[28]

White workers represented themselves as transcending established hierarchies through detailing a racially segregated social inclusivity. In 1923 the *Review* printed its dream for Unity Hall, 'A peep into the

[39]

Who Pays ?

By the reductions which have been inflicted on the Railwaymen, the Railway **Companies** have effected a saving of over £150,000 a year, but the high rates and fares still obtain. This amount of money is no longer spent in Rhodesia, and as a result, the public, as well as the worker, "pays the piper," while others call the tune.

Figure 1 'Who pays?'

future' (Figure 3).[29] That dream reflected how the RRWU aspired to create their own social clubs independent of those dominated by the elite from which they were excluded. Mrinalini Sinha's exploration of 'clubbability' in colonial India has shown how clubs acted as elite articulations of the legitimate boundaries of race 'whose function was to mediate and distribute elite power'.[30] Moreover, Ben Cohen has demonstrated the complexity of colonial clubs in South Asia in which the exclusivity of elite clubs on the basis of race and gender led to the proliferation of different types of colonial clubs with more flex-ible membership rules. Variants of Indian participation existed in even the most exclusive of British clubs.[31] In Southern Rhodesia the wealthy ruling class would frequent exclusive institutions such as the Salisbury Club and Bulawayo Club, where white skin alone did not ensure access but membership was dependent upon wealth, fame and power. At the Bulawayo Club women were strictly prohibited, granted entrance only

THE GOOD OLD SONG.
('Two Versions).

Figure 2 'The good old song'

on specific occasions on the condition they entered and left through a side entrance and kept to the first floor.[32] In contrast, Unity Hall depicted 'a place where [the worker] can enjoy himself socially ... with his wife or friend', a club where 'wives, sisters and brothers can meet on the level of social equality'.[33] While imitating the typical gentleman's club, there is nonetheless evidence of cultivation of a more inclusive identity and the club's foundation signalled the moves towards the replication of British working-class institutional life more broadly across Southern Rhodesia. If we accept Sinha's argument that the club represented the legitimate boundaries of racial identity, Unity Hall also shows an attempt to extend the respectability and superiority associated with the imperial club to the lower classes. Unity Hall focused upon a collective advancement wherein the entire white labouring class were welcome and deserving of entrance and membership. However, African participation would remain firmly within the master–servant dynamic. African subservience was idealised, as illustrated in Figure 3, showing an African joyfully waiting upon white clientele.

[41]

A Peep into the Future.

" Unity Hall " will be a place where the worker can meet his friends and comrades. It will be a place where he can enjoy himself socially after the worries of the day, with his wife or friend, forgetting for the time being his cares and troubles. The above illustration is possible if the worker is true to himself and those dependent on him, and will put his shoulder to the wheel and assist by taking up shares.

Figure 3 'A peep into the future: "Unity Hall" '

Creating clubs and social spaces for white workers was also about attaining respectability. Robert Ross has argued that respectability in the Cape was 'manifested most clearly in material things', which included cleanliness, clothing, housing, consumption patterns and education.[34] In 'Unity Hall' workers appear in well-turned out suits. The prominent place of newspapers and the books on the shelves point to a deliberate rejection of stereotypes of an uneducated working class. This would be a space in which white worker respectability could be projected; men reading books pointed to intelligence and hard work and fed into ideologies of aspiration and self-improvement of the trade union.[35] This was a pursuit and idealisation of an identity and culture that both imitated and subverted that of colonial elites. It remained within hegemonic ideals of racialised categorisation and white supremacy but nonetheless laid a claim to control over articulations of identity. The club was eventually built to the south of Bulawayo railway station in the mid-1920s and became a hub of railway social activity in the city. Railway wives went on to organise dinners, dances and competitions for the railway community at Unity Hall. Despite its projected egalitarianism, Unity Hall would prove to be a public arena in which the role of white women as subordinate, supportive partners was reaffirmed.

To the extent that socialism was preached by these groups, it was a strictly white socialism that pushed for racially exclusive welfare measures and did not seek to transform sexist inequalities. While the pages of the *Review* contained frequent denunciations of capitalism, unless there was a particular dispute raging between the union and the administration it seems that there was an effort to externalise and globalise the greedy capitalist elite. When £3 per month was taken from each employee in 1922, the weakened RRWU declared that 'it is not the fault of the general manager that what [the workers] gained is gradually being taken away from them. It is the policy laid down by the world's capitalists'.[36] This characterisation of the ravenous capitalist boss as an abstract international figure allowed for the propagation of an anti-capitalist message that did not irreversibly compromise workers' claims to white national unity and did not expose the very real weaknesses and failures of RRWU in challenging its own administration. As demands for the £3 to be returned increased as the 1920s proceeded, railway employers once again were portrayed as fat, cigar-smoking capitalists, but the role of the general manager in the exploitation of white workers was often downplayed.

Refracted nationalism and undesirable whites

Overall the dominant internationalism celebrated by white workers was rooted in imperialism rather than international communism. The language used by white trade unions reflected a 'Britannic nationalism' in which settlers saw themselves as part of an imperial vanguard; they were not merely British, they were partners in a global empire. Settler nationalism and imperial Britishness were mutually constitutive.

British identity was depicted as being enhanced in the settler colonial context where it became more masculine, dynamic and potent.[37] Jon Lunn has pointed to railwaymen's idealisation of themselves as pioneers and builders of empire. The spread of the railways, tied up as it was with ideals of progress and civilisation, imperialism and the fact that it was the workers themselves who built and operated the railways, allowed for railway workers to create 'a place for themselves in the pantheon of pioneerism'.[38] At times the *Review* was fiercely patriotic and viciously denounced other imperial powers, encouraging workers to align with their own factories and industries rather than let other imperial powers attain dominance.[39] RRWU stressed their loyalty to nation and empire, for example claiming that the strike action of 1919 was only taken due to 'the war being over and there being no danger of a Labour stoppage jeopardising the Empire'.[40] Yet, white workers did not simply parrot dominant understandings of imperial and racial ideologies; they attached their own understandings and fused ideologies of socialism, imperialism and white superiority to produce an idiosyncratic political discourse. The concept of 'civilisation', for example, was fundamental in colonial and imperial epistemologies, but to white Rhodesian labour, being 'civilised' was often equated with achieving socialist or populist reform.[41]

Likewise, notions of what it meant to be British were strongly contested. Being subservient, apathetic and refusing to challenge the status quo was seen as inherently un-British. The *Review* decried that the spirit of the British youth was being systematically broken; that they had been taught 'not to be a man, but to be a rat ... workers of the country, are any of these kiddies to be sacrificed on this social rack? Ask yourselves. It's up to you to see that this does not happen; then, and not til then, we will be able to give voice to what was instilled into us as children: *Britons never shall be slaves'*.[42] True Britishness would involve challenging the current system and standing up to victimisation. British ideals had been contaminated by apathy and repression, but being British, the *Review* argued, meant ensuring job security and decent wages. However, patriotism was noted as sharply double edged:

> It is only a fool who is a patriot at all cost. A parrot cry, à la Rhodesia for the Rhodesians, hip hip, etc. When the country is able to guarantee a decent living, and facilities for the upbringing of children to the workers, then it will be time enough to flagwag ... A Britisher's patriotism should start when he sees those near and dear to him comfortable and not until then: that is patriotism.[43]

During the First World War the RRWU executive attempted to prevent Jack Keller from being conscripted into the army, which was seen as a direct attack on the union. In later years one trade unionist recalled the 'scare headlines' that accompanied this action 'in endeavouring to stop one man going to the slaughter poles of Flanders ... Our real intent and motives would have been obscured, and victimisation of Jack lost sight of behind a forest of waving flags'.[44] In Southern Rhodesia Lewis Gann has argued that white labour was characterised by an 'anti-military spirit' during the First World War.[45] Yet this spirit lasted beyond the war. Many white workers remained opposed to conscription measures and in 1926 the RLP and RRWU decried moves towards compulsory military training, describing the measures as an affront to British values. They asserted that British men would gladly volunteer and they did not require to be coerced into action. The *Review* predicted that it would be used to conscript union leaders or workers deemed troublesome by management.[46]

One poem used the symbol of Henry Dubb – a well-known figure seen to represent the hard-done-by and exploited worker, bamboozled by employers, apathetic and hostile to socialism – to subvert ideals of patriotism, to attack the worker who put ideas of nation before loyalty to his class:

> I stick to my boss, sir, 'cause I do love him so.
> He may sweat me and beat me, but I do love him true,
> So here's to our emblem, the Red, White and Blue.[47]

This subversion of the dominant imperial narrative attacked the idea that workers should be entirely obedient to unscrupulous bosses in the name of national unity. Nationalism was presented as conditional upon white workers' needs being met and the evening out of social differences between white Rhodesians.

Some trade unionists believed that an imperial identity could overcome ethnic and national divisions between white workers. John Stewart, an RLP member of the Legislative Council and member of RRWU, who subsequently left both organisations in 1924 over the dominance of Bulawayo in RLP affairs and personal clashes with Keller and the RMGWA's Herbert Walsh, criticised the parochialism attached to perpetuating national myths and identity and instead preached pride in empire. Individual national background was irrelevant if the individual in question enhanced the British Empire, and Stewart argued that 'a good Dutch colonial is as essential to the progress of empire as the best Scotsman who ever lived or will ever live'.[48] However, non-British whites were not easily slotted into this imperial white worker identity. As well as xenophobia and language barriers creating hostility, the presence of European 'others' presented challenges to the formation of a homogenous settler culture. Rhodesian authorities

[45]

created selective immigration policies, in a perceived need to maintain ethnic dominance.[49] Insecure European labour included Italians, Greeks, Portuguese and Spaniards who threatened to undercut skilled white labour that was predominantly comprised of British men. On the mines hiring non-British Europeans on lower wages proved particularly prevalent during periods of recession in 1902–03 and 1907–08.[50] Divisions according to skill and craft were deepened by the allocation of roles according to ethnicity. The RRWU itself crossed national boundaries, incorporated branches in Northern Rhodesia and Portuguese East Africa and had Greek, Italian and Afrikaner members. While arguing that 'in considering the workers' affairs the union knows no nationality', low rates of Portuguese membership at Beira were attributed to the fundamental temperamental differences between 'men of British stock and those of "Latin races". The former are phlegmatic; the latter volatile and passionate'. This supposed Latin passion was seen as anathema to the rationality of trade unionism.[51]

Although Afrikaners were an important part of the settler colonial project in Rhodesia, in the first half of the twentieth century the 'race question' in southern Africa most readily referred to Afrikaner–British divisions and hostilities.[52] Prejudices were acutely felt at the turn of the century during the Anglo-Boer War and the vote for responsible government. During the 1922 referendum settlers were given the choice between self-government and joining the union to be ruled as part of South Africa. Settlers voted 59 per cent in favour of self-government, which was granted in 1923, despite opposition from the Colonial Office, the BSAC, mining companies and the railway administration. Motivations to vote for union or responsible government were rooted in class divisions and reflected divergent economic interests across Rhodesia's fledging industries.[53] While artisans and mine workers generally voted for responsible government, railway workers, although supportive, changed their allegiance at the last moment after a tour from pro-union South African railway managers.[54] Many white workers in Rhodesia feared being subject to bilingualism, lower wages, longer hours and a curtailment of trade union rights.[55] The vote for self-government was also partly motivated by fears of poor white Afrikaners and what was described as their inferior language and culture. The *Review* avidly spoke out against the union with South Africa, explicitly identifying the reasoning behind their aversion as the influx of Afrikaners into Rhodesia in which 'poor whites and criminals of all kinds will not be kept out'.[56] The RMGWA argued that unregulated immigration in the event of union would see Rhodesia overrun with 'the scum of the Free State and Johannesburg'.[57] Wages in Rhodesia were 10 per cent higher than those in the Union of South Africa, and the violent response of the Smuts government to the 1922 Rand Revolt strike of white miners did little to endear workers in Southern Rhodesia to the Union.[58] But the RRWU nevertheless attempted to persuade its Afrikaner members, who were assumed to have been loyal to South Africa, to vote for responsible government. They reminded their readership of the 1922 miners' rebellion and highlighted the role of General Smuts, prime minister of South Africa, who they declared had 'shot down and hanged workers of all nationalities'.[59] Thus while warning of Afrikaner propensity towards poverty and criminality, the RRWU attempted to diffuse Afrikaner–British hostility by demonstrating the limits of Afrikaner nationalism in protecting Afrikaner workers from mining companies and the South African state.

Despite RRWU's popularity among the lower grades who were more likely to be Italian or Portuguese nationals, it cultivated a British, rather than an inclusive white Rhodesian identity able to incorporate the national and ethnic diversity of railway staff. Presumably aware of this diversity within the RRWU the *Review* regularly printed material that demonstrated friendship and shared goals between British and non-British whites, including detailing union officials attending Dutch Reformed Church events, or commenting upon the class of football 'our Portuguese friends' achieve in inter-branch railway leagues.[60] But these seem to have been largely tokenistic gestures. Vocal denunciations of the employment of non-British workers continued. The unemployment of British nationals was used to agitate around discriminatory hiring practices and RRWU pleaded railway management to give preference to British applicants.[61] The white imperial identity white workers invested in remained fundamentally British.

White trade union decline

As well as divisions of ethnicity, nationality and gender, workers were fractured by grade, skill, occupation and the changing status attached to each job. Clerks, office workers and professional groupings were unlikely to support or align themselves with lower-status manual workers. The Rhodesia Teacher's Association felt it necessary to vehemently deny that they had ever considered any affiliation to the Labour Party. They condemned the principles and actions of Labourism and argued that, particularly in South Africa, the Labour Party had 'become drunk with the poisoned vodka of Bolshevism'.[62] In railway suburbs housing was segregated among different types of workers. One early resident of Raylton recalled that 'the first two or three avenues of houses were reserved for the railway doctors, engineers, accountants and clerical staff', while the engine drivers and firemen were housed beyond these streets.[63] While the RRWU refused to handle coal produced at Wankie during the 1919 strike, the RMGWA financially assisted RRWU during the 1920 railway strike, and the Posts and Telegraphs Union refused to deliver railway messages, such unity was limited and divisions between manual workers on the basis of skill expressed itself in the formation of rival industrial and craft-based unions.[64] Certainly, the AEU was often used by management to curb the demands of the larger industrial unions.[65]

The Industrial Disputes Act of 1920 established principles of arbitration and encouraged industries to set up their own structures to deal with labour grievances. The railway administration sought to forestall widespread action by entrenching division and providing each grade and department its own court of arbitration.[66] Fissures deepened as white trade union strength dissipated. As men returned from the war and white labour shortages ebbed, employers turned to the offensive and sought to push back the gains white workers had won over the previous years. Mine proprietors combined to create the Rhodesian Mine Owners Association in order to combat white demands. After a defeat the previous year, in 1921 at the Wankie Colliery, the daily paid men, most of whom were white, were notified that their contracts had been terminated and that they had lost all medical benefits. They were replaced with black workers while overall white wages incurred a heavy reduction.[67] In 1921 the RMGWA, with support of RRWU, recommended that its members refuse to work with any member of the AEU.[68] The Rhodesian Mine Owners Association and the national newspaper the *Herald* backed the AEU in order to smash the RMGWA and a lockout was threatened if the latter went ahead with their plans.[69] In 1922 mine owners announced plans for retrenchment and a further 12 per cent reduction in shift rates, which the RMGWA failed to prevent.[70] By 1923 RMGWA had dissolved. Attempts to reform a mining union at Wankie connected with railway workers in 1929 saw management remove all privileges of European staff and warn that any colliery employee caught advocating unionisation would be considered an 'undesirable employee'.[71]

For white rail workers the 1922 management offensive saw reductions in pay and in the cost of living allowance, an increase in working hours and the removal of the eight-hour working day. This undoubted defeat was represented as evidence of railwaymen's obedience and rationality in accepting a share in the burden of hard economic times by the RRWU. Yet the union was in decline. From 1925 the RRWU consistently asked management to restore the £3 taken from them in 1922. In 1927 the Russell Court of Enquiry dismissed the propositions of both the RRWU and the AEU craft union. In 1929, in a last ditch attempt, a three-week strike took place across the railways but the administration flatly refused the union's requests. In the weeks leading up to the strike fears circulated that railwaymen would paralyse the country. On the morning the strike broke newspapers advertised for a squad of five hundred special constables made up of settler volunteers. Rawdon Hoare, a white farmer from Britain, gleefully recalled his own part in defeating the strike. Although the strike passed relatively quietly, Hoare noted some 'hostile' demonstrations and that some of the white strike breakers had been 'greeted with stones'. What is striking in Hoare's account is his repeated invocation of the First World War. White 'volunteers' were divided up into 'platoons', performed military parades and given armlets and bludgeons to patrol the strikers and defend railway lines. Men 'reported' for their 'duty' and 'people said it was like August 4th 1914'. In this narrative strike-breaking was the ultimate nationalist act; it was a war for Rhodesia, and the enemy was the white worker. Rawdon further noted how the railway workers were humiliated 'at having to put up with the indignity of the guard'.[72] Certainly the RRWU bemoaned popular hostility towards the strikers and lamented that members of the public were engaged on 'a miserable £1 per day' who they denounced as scabs.[73] During the strike foremen and apprentices carried on working, as well as 'the whole of the headquarter offices and the district offices'.[74] It was not just the ultimate failure of the strike that elicited shame; it was their treatment by wider settler society that undermined their respectability and cast them as a rowdy mob in need of discipline.

The administration was emboldened. Roy Welensky, who would later become the prime minister of the Federation, was punished for his prominent involvement in the strike by being relocated from Wankie (Hwange) to Broken Hill (Kabwe) and reinstated at a lower grade.[75] The RRWU continued to denounce the AEU as a tool for division among railwaymen and claimed it 'is useless, it is futile, it is inept ... a mockery of trade unionism'.[76] By the late 1920s internal division within RRWU threatened to break the union apart. Bulawayo branch blamed the executive committee for failing to win back the full £3. Some 165 members of Bulawayo branch resigned in February 1929 and six members were expelled from Bulawayo for factionalism. Although short-lived and lacking mass appeal, in September 1932 further challenges arose as E. J. Scherlich attempted to split the union by forming a new 'non-political' union, the Railway Employees Union of Rhodesia, which represented growing anger at Keller's involvement in politics. Factionalism and internal dissent during this period cost the RRWU over £5,000. Clerks, engine drivers and firemen all attempted to create separate organisations.[77] Management had successfully exploited divisions within white labour, and further utilised black and white workers to break strikes and redirect antagonism over pay and working conditions.

Regulating white worker behaviour

Snobberies were most pronounced between blue- and white-collar workers, one letter to the *Review* complaining that sectionalism on the railways emanated from the fact that 'the clerical staff think they are far too respectable to join a trade union'.[78] The RRWU regularly castigated the higher-paid grades for reaping the rewards of the trade unionists from the lower rungs of the system. Nevertheless, the standardising language of race and the redefinition of unskilled jobs as skilled by the lower grades acted to promote an idea of a united skilled white working class comprised predominantly of manual labourers. Lunn has described workers' sense of self-worth as higher than upper- and middle-class observers might have believed. While a ganger was categorised as semi-skilled by management, Lunn has argued that 'in his own mind he was skilled'.[79] Workers' self-understandings relied heavily on their occupations, pride of work and physical as well as moral strength. This was contrasted with African manual labour, which was seen as unskilled, repetitive work in which Africans took no care or pride. Pride in work also allowed differentiation from non-British whites. Daphne Anderson described how her father's ideals of pride in hard work enabled him to look down upon local Afrikaners. Despite being an alcoholic and poorer than the local Afrikaners her father 'never joined in any of the local functions and considered himself superior to the homesteaders and farmers who lounged around the village dancehall'.[80] This fed into wider ways in which race was articulated through ideas of industriousness, discipline and slothfulness.[81] For many white workers Africans failed to grasp the concept of work and the 'dignity of labour'. It was noted that Africans' experiences of prison and forced labour systems had devalued the honour of work in their minds.[82] This language of slavery was utilised to reject certain types of work, to uphold the colour bar and agitate around poor working conditions. The Rand Revolt was explained as 'the objection of *free* white men to being thrown out of work and reduced to destitution by the extension of the negro *slave* labour system into what had been their spheres of employment'.[83] White work was *free* labour. Despite the absence of systematic chattel slavery, there was a widely held belief that Africans were naturally indolent and had to be coerced into work. This complex interplay between slave and free; black and white labour was, as David Roediger has argued with regards to the United States, not a call to solidarity or acknowledgement of similarity. It was used to demarcate acceptable working conditions of white men; it was part of the process of defining what constituted the essence of the white worker.[84]

Within this adversarial culture that pitted bosses against workers and white workers against Africans, anger, when channelled through appropriate mediums such as the trade union, became a mark of righteousness and was tolerated and encouraged in various forms. This anger was seen as a natural reaction when the liberty or dignity of the white man was encroached upon. During strikes management expected strikers to engage in destruction of property, threats and intimidation, as well as physical violence upon areas of strategic importance, such as pumping stations and telegraph wires. Strike breakers were also targets of threats and physical violence.[85] The *Review* published descriptions and locations of strike breakers and men who had worked against the interests of the union.[86] It also printed letters from white workers in which rival unions, employers, non-British whites, Coloureds and Africans were attacked. Many white workers exerted psychological and physical violence upon African workers, which on occasion resulted in death, with little or no recourse for their actions.[87]

Expressing anger was an important demonstration of principles and was characterised as a natural reaction to exploitation and to those who were disloyal to the trade union and industrial action. Empathy was also invoked to encourage a shared experience of struggle and hardship. Workers' organisations spoke of an unrelenting poverty that workers were forced to suffer. Housing conditions were described as 'comprised of ramshackle old wood and iron buildings, infested, in cases, with bats, rats and other vermin'.[88] 'Poverty' was acknowledged as a real material condition and threat to the white labourer, who asked, 'Why ... is there such a thing as poverty, and why has the worker to fight perpetually for a bare subsistence?'[89] Letters that complained of financial struggle to 'provide' were common in the *Review*. One asked, 'Where is the money for boots, butcher, milk, vegetables, clothing?'[90] The *Review* described 'the ganger, the man who, in this country, is practically an outcast ... not permitted to leave their cottages without permission ... for any purpose, social or otherwise'. This was likened to a state of 'serfdom' and the *Review* argued that such restrictions amounted to interference to the 'liberty of a white man'.[91]

For the white worker, manual work was not something to be ashamed of, or something that only non-whites did, but something in which to take pride, even if the middle classes and white-collar workers perceived such blue-collar work as defiling. The *Review* printed a poem entitled 'The Tally' by Richard Lord, which declared:

> To wish is the play of an office boy:
> To do is the job of a man.[92]

The settler trope of masculinity rooted in the physical mastery of nature and the heroism of the pioneer, itself a rural ideal, was reworked through an industrial, urban idiom. These self-understandings were central to how white workers upheld notions of white prestige. Pride in work and being a member of the union was seen as the epitome of masculinity. 'Nons' were ridiculed and castigated as lazy and effeminate work-shy cowards. This is explicitly represented in Figure 4, in which the RRWU, represented by suited respectable men, attempt to court the unionised 'nons' who are depicted as coy women. 'Nons' were also often depicted as greedy figures benefiting from the struggles and sacrifices of others (Figure 6).

Those who failed to meet the standards expected by union officials were shamed as flaccid perversions of the white worker; inadequate effeminised imitations. Thus one article began with an assertion that

> If you haven't got manhood enough to be concerned with the comfort and welfare of your own family, then do not read this article. If you haven't got the backbone enough to be a free man in a free country, then stop reading right here, for this article is intended for the real he-men, who do not shiver in their boots when the Roadmaster passes; men who are men enough to fight their own fights; men who are not too cowardly to demand a wage sufficient to properly care for their families whether the railroad officials like it or not.[93]

Manliness was claimed through union activity and taking a stand against management; union successes were explained through the actions of 'men – white men who were not prepared to knuckle down to it'.[94] Here, it was workers' qualities as specifically *white men* that had enabled them to rally against exploitation. Robert Morrell has argued that while multiple masculinities exist, a 'hegemonic masculinity' will dominate that seeks to suppress women as well as competing masculinities.[95] White workers both borrowed from dominant constructions of white imperial masculinity and challenged and reformulated their own sense of manliness through work. This labouring ideal was positioned as the authentic expression of maleness. One letter to the *Review* explained that intimidation and the blacklist had lowered attendance at branch meetings but went on to encourage men to overcome these fears, to 'brace up ... make a firm stand and come out boldly as one solid body of workers ... In conclusion brothers,

A Coming Event

Figure 4 'A coming event'

"be white"'.[96] Here 'being white' was about bravery and the assertion of workers' rights.

The foundational story of RRWU also revolved around the rights of white men. The *Review* detailed how the organisation was created after several men had been stranded at Wankie in 1917. It described how these stranded workers had demanded that the administration

Why "Anon"?   Do it Now—You Can't Go Wrong!

Figure 5 'Why "anon"? Do it now – you can't go wrong!'

provide them with food, but that they were told that any expense they incurred would be taken out of their pay packets. The *Review* recalled that 'the men were in open rebellion ... they marched to the house of the Magistrate and demanded food and refreshment under a Statute of the country which provides that a white individual

The Way of the Non-Unionist

Figure 6 'The way of the non-unionist'

without means of subsistence must be assisted from one police camp to another'.[97]

Stories of successful strikes and their leaders were used in later editions of the *Review* to emphasise struggle and hardship and to emphasise the characteristics of strength and respectability that sought to bind railwaymen together. The man who thought that he was above joining the union was labelled 'a "Snob" with a capital S'. Railwaymen who refused to join the trade union 'should leave the common railway service and get a job in one of the government offices at Salisbury [Harare]'.[98] Such pen-pushers were not just seen as effeminate, they were labelled grandiose, self-aggrandising with an exaggerated sense of self-importance. They were noted as unfairly looking down upon the manual worker, ignorant to the supposed fact it was the latter that had built and served the country. While distancing themselves from Africans, this self-understanding simultaneously differentiated workers from the 'office boy', the weak and pathetic daydreamer, the antithesis to the manual labourer deemed to be the embodiment of masculinity and self-respect. Thus the dominant colonial image of feminised and infantilised African 'boys' that was used to legitimate segregation in the workplace was also projected on to middle-class Europeans.[99]

White women

White women, in their roles as 'incorporated wives' on the railways, were encouraged to take pride in creating homes, producing children and investing in community activities, such as organising dances or craft competitions. One poem in the *Review*, written by a white woman, described the position of railway wives in the 1920s:

We knew it when we married him
Some twenty years ago –
That he would be away a lot,
In fact he told us so,
But the real truth we didn't guess,
Not all … or even half –
…
They have no hours, these railroad men,
Their work is never done,
They just remember that it's night
When everyone goes home.
We wives and mothers learn to smile,
The young as well as old –
And keep the meat from burning up,
The beans from getting cold.
We go to church and club, alone,
To pictures, lectures too,
We rear the children, cook the meals
And pay the bills when due.
The youngsters get the whooping cough,
And measles, mumps and grippe –
We carry on both day and night,
And don't give up the ship.[100]

White women could feel pride in the labour of the home and mother-hood, by keeping a 'tight ship', in struggling through loneliness and ingenuity in stretching wages to cover household costs. As well as overseeing domestic servants in the home, emotional care was a cen-tral responsibility of white women; manufacturing an air of content-ment in order to reassure the working man. The process of investing status into these tasks of domesticity acted as a form of cognitive dis-sonance to suppress dissatisfaction. Here, women's feelings of distress were accepted as a part of their daily experience, yet it was the endur-ance of these feelings of isolation and the suppression of emotions that was valorised as a source of pride.

The RRWU also encouraged women to use familial and gender ideologies to police male workers' behaviour. Women were encouraged to wield shame in order to discipline men into correct behaviour. They were directed to humiliate men who were unable to provide, who remained un-unionised or who did not pay union fees (Figures 5 and 6). In one piece a railwayman detailed how he resisted joining RRWU until his wife had shamed him into doing so: 'She reproached me for letting other men fight her battles and the children's. We were not quarrelsome about it, but she clinched the argument when she said, hotly, one night: "Do you want me to think my husband a cad, Jim?"'[101] The RRWU also suggested women should manage their husbands' finances, making sure they did not spend too much on drink.[102] The role of the railwayman's wife, according to the *Review*, was one of support, reproduction and regulation, which enforced gendered norms.

White female wage labour remained low in the 1920s. In 1921 forty-eight white women were employed by the railways, growing to a total of fifty-nine in 1926, which represented 4 per cent of the total 1,337 white railway staff. More broadly, the number of white women in stated occupations grew from 1,949 in 1921 to 2,359 in 1926, but as a percentage of the European female population aged fifteen years and over, this actually represented very little change, decreasing from 20.6 to 20 per cent (Table 2). Nevertheless, as voters, as part of working com-munities and as political actors in their own right, white women were not entirely excluded from public life. Enfranchised in 1919, they were recognised as an important part of the electorate by the RLP and spe-cific appeals were tailored to white women during the referendum vote, which focused on the point that they would lose the vote only recently gained (South Africa did not grant white women the vote until 1930). Some 75 per cent of white women voted for responsible government.[103] In 1923, while it was argued that women were 'as yet ... unprepared to represent us in the Legislative Chamber' they were nevertheless 'powerful factor[s] in any organisation'.[104] The RLP congress in 1928

Table 2 Economically active European women as a percentage of adult European women and of total economically active European persons, 1926–69

Year	Total numbers of European women	Percentage change from previous census (%)	Total women stated economically active occupation	Women who are economically active as a percentage of the female population 15 years and over (%)	Women as percentage of total economically active persons (%)
1921	14,633	–	1,949	20.6	13.2
1926	17,366	18.7	2,359	20	14.4
1931	22,630	30.3	3,917	24.8	17.6
1936	25,683	13.5	4,630	25.1	18.8
1941	32,339	25.9	6,861	29.5	27.9
1946	38,166	18.0	7,666	28.3	23.1
1951	64,289	68.4	14,933	33.6	24.7
1956	85,596	33.1	22,023	37.7	28
1961	109,784	28.3	30,775	41.1	32
1969	113,505	3.4	33,333	43.1	33.3

cheered the presence of women, which, it was argued, 'prove[d] that not only are women prepared to assume their political responsibilities, but that the men, who elected them, realise that without their cooperation no equitable law can be passed on matters pertaining to women and children'.[105] On a few occasions the RRWU extended invitations to women to attend meetings. In 1922 lady clerks and typists were admitted as members of RRWU at half rates, but they still had no power to vote on union matters.[106]

The experience of white women in these early years also sheds light on the perceived desirability and status of particular men. In Rhodesia's early years white women had increased opportunities to raise their social status through marriage due to stark gender imbalances (see Graphs 1 and 2). The number of European females per 1,000 males steadily rose from 407 in 1907 to 989 in 1969, except for a brief dip in the 1940s as men left for the Second World War (Table 3).[107] As middle-class children growing up in the 1920s, Doris Lessing and her brother were looked after by an Irish governess, Biddy O'Halloran. Doris's mother displayed considerable class snobberies towards Biddy; disdainful that she had 'shingled hair, used make-up and smoked, and was too interested in men'. Nevertheless, Biddy was able to marry an Honourable in the

Table 3 Numbers of European females per
1,000 males, 1907–69

Year	European females per 1,000 European males
1904	407
1907	482
1911	515
1921	771
1926	796
1931	830
1936	864
1941	883
1946	863
1951	902
1956	918
1961	982
1969	989

colony and rose into the middle classes.[108] Daphne Anderson's memoir reveals that during the 1940s, despite her impoverished background, she and her sister 'ignored the invitations from the railway employees or the motor mechanics or those who did not possess a car'.[109] Likewise her father's opinion of her sister's boyfriends reflected his acknowledgement of his daughters' ability to socially surpass him through vying for the affection of wealthy males who may have been unable to find partners of similar social status. Anderson wrote that: 'If any of the gallants wore scruffy clothes, had dirty fingernails or innocently admitted they were motor mechanics or railway workers, [my father] was openly rude to them.' Such prejudices extended to non-British Whites. While Anderson describes how she fell in love with a Portuguese man with whom she freely socialised, her sister, who wished to increase her own social standing, was intolerant of their relationship that she attempted to conceal from respectable types. Likewise Anderson's middle-class aunt resented inter-European interaction. She was 'horrified' that a British woman could marry 'a dirty Greek'.[110]

Lessing's semi-autobiographical *Martha Quest* outlines a series of romantic strained relationships between English, Afrikaner, Polish and Jewish Europeans. Stella, married to a white English man, is accepted in popular white society *in spite* of her Jewishness; although her father-in-law may have objected to the marriage, she is saved the incredulity of becoming *persona non grata* by virtue of her English upper-class credentials. On the other hand, when Martha dates a lower-class

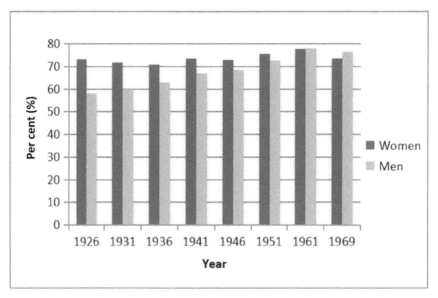

Graph 1 European women and men married at time of census as a percentage of the European male and female adult population

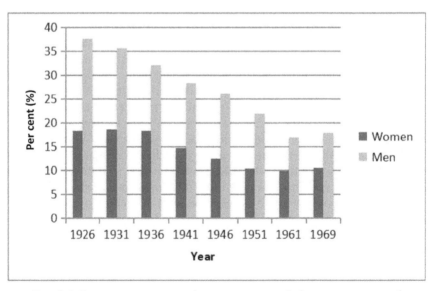

Graph 2 European women and men never married as a percentage of European male and female adult population

Polish Jew, her friends – including Stella – quickly intervene to sever the relationship and rehabilitate Martha back into respectable white society. Certainly, Martha is forgiven so rapidly for this transgression in part because of her youth, but also her desirability as an attractive, middle-class, English woman.[111] While exemplifying a route through which women could transcend their own socio-economic status, these experiences simultaneously reveal a hierarchy of suitable potential suitors, which demonstrates how white identity failed to erase prejudices and disdain for manual workers and non-British whites. Workers' self-identification as skilled and respectable citizens did little to alter external perceptions and classifications of their identity and status.

Transgressing white worker respectability

John Connell has asserted that railwaymen were 'the aristocrats of labour in Rhodesia in the 1920s. Their pay was low but their standing was high'.[112] But white workers never achieved the image of respectability, status and skill that they manufactured. In reality a substantial disjuncture existed between idealised representations of white workers and the daily experiences of a heterogeneous social group who failed to maintain 'white standards'. Lower-class whites were well aware of how they were perceived in broader settler society. Shame was not merely mobilised to discipline behaviours; it was intensely felt by individuals. Daphne Anderson experienced simultaneous ostracism and inclusion, describing that although she was always invited to community events that were supposed to foster an exclusive settler culture, she nevertheless felt out of place due to her economic circumstances. Anderson's shame of her own poverty inhibited her participation in community functions. She declared: 'The real reason I refused invitations was that I did not possess a bathing suit or the most elementary clothes for outings ... [I] was determined not to make a fool of myself again.'[113]

Yet in the eyes of the trade union bureaucracy it appeared that some were not ashamed enough of their circumstances. The desired respectable and masculine characteristics that labour organisations were attempting to project were not automatically possessed by all white workers. While there was often genuine support for industrial action, the activity of men within unions was regularly decried by its leaders as apathetic and lazy. Reports of low attendance at branch meetings and castigations of those who would prefer to spend time in the Unity Club bar rather than fighting within their union were common.[114] The trade union was having difficulty reconciling an image of respectability, of industrious and educated workers central to performances of prestige, with the reality of life on the railways.[115] Anthony Croxton's description of the 'hard-drinking sessions' and 'wild parties' that followed inter-branch football matches flew in the face of the idealised white worker propagated by RRWU. Some of these soirées resulted in visits from the police who 'occasionally had to cool off hot heads in the "calaboose" until their friends had bailed them out next morning'.[116]

Whereas the colonies had been envisioned as a site of racial renewal, prevailing ideas at the beginning of the twentieth century regarding social decline posited that dilapidated and polluted environments could engender undesirable behaviours.[117] Southern Africa was not the regenerative setting many had envisioned. For the lower classes that lived together in undesirable parts of town, close to Coloured and Indian communities, the boundaries of interaction had to be more aggressively policed. The inability of white labourers to pursue bourgeois methods of differentiation and performances of prestige stirred fear among settlers. The *Review* argued that white labour was 'entitled' to a 'standard of respect', but that a cross section of workers from different social and industrial grades were endangering the reputation of the majority: 'The term "common railway man" hurts the feelings of the great majority of railway workers, who are as respectable and noble-minded as any class in the land. If those members of our craft, who act in such a manner as to lower the status of railway men, would pause and think of the intense injury they are inflicting on themselves and all other railway workers.'[118]

The consequences of this inability to educate oneself and attain respectability were not confined to the individual violating expected standards of whiteness, but were recognised as endangering the white labouring class in its entirety. The *Review* warned of the dangerous cost of abandoning performances of prestige and means of differentiation, pointing to the Congo where 'the white worker is ousted!' Moreover, the blame lay with white workers themselves who had 'actively (and in some cases passively!) contributed to the forces which caused his "displacement"'.[119] Drunkenness, laziness and insubordination were pinpointed as the failings of Europeans in the Congo, which invited their replacement with African workers. Equally disconcerting, whites had abandoned strict adherence to preventing Africans from completing skilled jobs and had trained many African labourers to complete skilled tasks.

The *Review* laid particular stress on education and sobriety in attempts to consolidate the projection of respectability and the protestant ethic of hard work central to the prestige of the manual labourer. As Robert Ross has argued, 'the antithesis to respectability was drunkenness'.[120] The *Rhodesian Trade Union Review* published pro-prohibition articles warning of the dangers of alcoholism and intoxication.[121] Alcoholism demonstrated a lack of restraint and was increasingly associated with poor whites. White workers had to *actively* prove themselves as industrious and respectable to guard against incursion and undercutting. They had to continually project and accentuate their own worth and adhere to strict racialised behaviours. Respectability was cultivated through 'education and yet more education!'[122] Yet it is clear the progress the union bureaucracy sought was not being made. One letter to the *Review* condemned this failure of workers to self-educate, writing that railwaymen were asking for themselves to be replaced by 'new men' and that it was 'high time that some Rhodesian railwaymen realised that they have responsible jobs which implies intelligent and industrious study'.[123] Such fears concerning the level of education of white workers demonstrates that workers were acutely aware that their higher wages were not ensured by skin colour alone, but from their monopoly of skill. Thus it was noted that 'the white man has innate in him the capability of beating the black man at anything; but that innate faculty must be made available to the owner by training and education'.[124] Maintaining the informal colour bar, in part, relied upon reproducing skills and education in the white population while preventing Africans from acquiring the requisite skill and knowledge to adequately compete on the labour market.[125]

African and Coloured workers: white workers as an evolving relational formation

The lower classes of Rhodesia, as in other settler contexts, have been noted as the most reactionary layer of society, living in constant fear of their replacement by Africans and demanding more rigid segregationist policies. In 1913 the United Building Trades Trade Union formed to oppose employment of non-whites. Successful strike action during the 1910s for higher pay was also accompanied by demands for African and Coloured men to be replaced by whites in the workshops.[126] As we have seen, white labour was defined through its opposition to black, unskilled coerced labour. Frantz and Rogers have argued that manual labourers harboured stronger conservative views due to their competition with Africans in the labour market, in contrast with the relatively liberal groups in which they included architects, chemists, journalists, missionaries and teachers.[127] In the early 1920s debates surrounding African education reveal a backlash against upper-class characterisations of manual labourers as harbourers and advocates of the strictest segregation policies and instead highlight how white trade unions distinguished the labouring classes as staunch defenders of equality. The RLP, RMGWA and RRWU continually argued that

[63]

the notion that white workers were behind the most vociferous racial intolerance was a malevolent accusation made by the rich and powerful. Moreover, while we can posit that settlers were informed by ideas of white supremacy and innate racial difference, these was neither uniformly understood nor synchronically performed. The visibility and intensity of arguments against African education varied according to the particular context white labour found itself in. When white labour was confident and assured, African education was conceptualised as a humane and realistic phenomenon that would uplift both white and black workers. When white workers felt uneasy about their monopoly over white jobs or the ability for white wages to ensure a 'white' standard of living, attitudes towards African education became increasingly hostile.

In 1923 John Stewart, RLP MP for Salisbury Town, acknowledged that there was a 'commonly accepted belief ... that the wage-earner lives in daily dread of the native being educated in the arts of industry to such an extent as to threaten the welfare of the white employee'. But Stewart refuted this interpretation and argued that Africans and the white working class shared a history of oppression. Ruling-class policy towards the African, according to Stewart,

> is exactly the policy which the aristocracy advocated should be followed in the case of the British wage-earner in the not too distant past ... the wage-earner of Britain broke the bonds of repression ... We, who are descendants of those who broke the bonds, cannot in the name of justice support a policy towards the natives which when applied to us, or our forefathers, is considered unjust.

Furthermore, Stewart claimed he was not alone in his attitude, and said he had met numerous white workers who supported the need for African education.[128] Another writer for the *Review* claimed that to deny Africans education would encourage labour 'to become the tyrants and oppressors'.[129] White labour organisations laid claim to respectability and benevolence through recognition of a shared position with Africans under capitalist exploitation, while simultaneously laying considerable stress that immediate competition between black and white was unwarranted and unwanted. But a time would come when Africans' standard of living would have risen – and 'competition at that point will be on the class of work turned out, not on the cost of labour'.[130] However, that time would not be in the foreseeable future. Africans were seen as being content with receiving a low level of education and remaining 'the labourer to the white worker'.[131] Justifications of differential pay were based on the premise that Africans' 'wants are few and relatively easy to procure. He needs no house, little meat, and remains almost indifferent to the quality of his water supply. He is at home where white labourers would find it impossible to live'.[132] It was argued that Africans would eventually enter skilled positions and it was recognised that Africans' needs and wants would develop, but the role of white labour was to keep this development in check.

Arguments for social segregation were still made with ferocity. As Stewart made clear, he was 'not arguing for social equality of black and white'. That, he argued, would 'never come'. For Stewart, a social colour bar would need to be retained in order to prevent, what he called, the 'horrors of inter-marriage'.[133] One article claimed it was 'not the labourer who desires to keep the black boy back, but the employers themselves' who wanted to exploit cheap labour and use Africans against white workers. Employers wanted to see the white labourer 'eat[ing] mealie poop and liv[ing] in a location' to increase their own profit margins.[134] White workers were angered about being undercut by Africans; but importantly this anger expressed itself in disgust that they would be exploited on similar terms as Africans; to be forced to live like them and among them. In the period of trade union decline attacks upon white workers' newly won gains were interpreted to be compromising lower-class Europeans' ability to display 'white' characteristics. These attacks were responded to with pleas to not 'send us all back to the kraal'.[135] Resisting incursions of African labour into skilled positions and management's attempts to reduce wages and increase hours, white workers visualised their struggle as a battle to retain 'white standards of living' for all Europeans in the colony. These attacks upon white workers were seen as compromising workers' capabilities to perform their racialised identities, their masculinity and idealised family lifestyles.

In the face of accusations of fierce racial hatred, white workers presented themselves as defenders of all workers arguing that 'we are fighting as much for the rights of the Indian, the Coloured worker, and the native, as for ourselves'.[136] However, as white labour found itself increasingly threatened, such debates all but disappeared within the *Review*. In 1926 the *Review* declared that 'up to the present our experience leads us to the conclusion that the chief advantages gained by the native from his education are arrogance and impudence'.[137] The *Review* printed photographs of railways in chaos and claimed this was the fate that was to befall the railway administration if they allowed Africans to progress too quickly. (Figure 7).[138] White trade unions still characterised themselves as advocates of African progress, protecting other races from the evils of exploitation and capitalism, but the experiment of African education was increasingly seen as a dangerous failure.

White workers were also perceived as the most likely to transgress the appropriate boundaries of contact. In defiance of stereotypes and

A Peep into the Future

"INTELLIGENT NATIVES" ENGAGED ON "EASY" AND "IRRESPONSIBLE" JOBS!

Figure 7 'A peep into the future: "intelligent natives"
engaged on "easy" and "irresponsible" jobs'

assumptions that lower-class whites were more likely to interact in inappropriate ways with non-Europeans, white workers were at pains to publicise their detachment and distance themselves from Africans. The early experiences of gold miner H. J. Lucas show how emotional and psychological distance was maintained despite physical closeness to Africans: 'Many smallworkers did not employ an assistant and in the remote parts might not see a white man for a month or more at a stretch ... it was a lonely life for the white man. He could not sit and gossip with the Africans but often of an evening he would watch the boys laughing and gossiping around their fires and wish he could join in.'[139] Likewise the *Review* bemoaned the position of the ganger, 'practically an outcast, who knows no joy of human society'.[140] Croxton described the ganger's outposts in the 'heavy rain in the lonely forest, with lions, leopards, elephants and other wildlife as neighbours and only a momentary glimpse of the infrequent train [that] induced nerves and depression'.[141] The Africans who worked under the ganger are erased in this picture; flora and fauna appear as more appropriate companions.

Loneliness and self-imposed ostracism seemed preferable to fraternisation that could endanger the respect white workers received from their 'boys', throwing the racialised performance of labour into disarray. Here, even the possibility of the most innocuous forms of interracial interaction was denied. Of course interracial interaction could never be innocuous within the settler colonial context.

Appropriate forms of interracial interaction had to be learnt. Those who appeared to be offering support for certain non-white organisations were publicly castigated. Jack Allen, a miner from the Rand, lived beside the Coloured township and fraternised with both African and Coloured trade unionists. Allen was regularly visited by the police who attempted to intimidate him for socialising outside his race.[142] In 1927 a European railwayman signed a petition in support of an Indian-led campaign to remove a European market master from his post after he had called Indians 'Coolies'. The *Review* joked that 'our comrade must have come off a long and tiresome shift and signed the petition without realising what he signed'.[143] Solidarity on such matters was unthinkable and the European railwayman who crossed this line was publicly ridiculed in the pages of the union journal for providing support. Not only did this platform serve a function of policing white workers' behaviour, it acted as a warning to others: loyalty to other white workers was paramount.

Stereotypes levelled at white workers were projected on to the upper classes and employers. It was *they* who engaged in inappropriate contact with non-whites and threatened to erode differences between the races. One mining employer in Gwanda was accused of encouraging white unemployment by employing Africans as secretaries, storemen and timekeepers: 'While a Cape boy holds the position as compound manager ... what is your opinion of the manager, who sits side by side with these natives in the same office, carrying out his duties?'[144] The manager was accused not only of undercutting white workers, but of actually choosing to be in close proximity to Africans. He had invited Africans into the white physical space of the office and compromised racial performances of work.

Interactions with those who fell awkwardly outside of the 'native' and 'non-native' binary central to colonial classification were interacted with in more complex ways.[145] Individual encounters between white and Coloured workers were not policed in the same way as those between Africans and whites. RLP MP Harry Davies argued that white trade unions were 'prepared to receive these people into their white civilisation'. The Coloured population, he argued, was an 'offshoot of a white civilisation', but simultaneously an 'evil' that had been 'caused by the white man'.[146] Coloureds were seen as combining both the natural virtues of Europeans as well as the immutable inferiority of Africans. For white workers Coloureds also provided an important social buffer between themselves and African workers. Emphasising a sense of European–Coloured solidarity could strengthen white workers' hands against African labour. Hugh Killeen, general secretary of the RRWU, repeatedly claimed that no 'ill feeling' existed between Coloureds and white workers.[147] The RRWU hailed its paternalist and dignified approach to Coloured labour and attempted to partially incorporate Coloureds in its organisation who made representations to the union executive and on occasion joined whites in taking industrial action.[148]

Notably, by 1930 the proportion of unionised Coloured employees was much higher than the percentage of whites. When pushed to give an exact figure of Coloured membership, Keller admitted that it was 'difficult to say ... it is not stated on the record whether a man is Coloured or not. It is difficult to draw the line; a person whom one might term Coloured would be very indignant if he were called a Coloured man'.[149] There was significant ambiguity and complexity in such racial classification. Individuals' understanding of their racial status may have contradicted outside categorisation. Of course, as the complex history of racial 'passing' attests, persons with African heritage could claim white racial identities and be perceived as white by others.[150] On the railways there were clearly men living as 'white' who were precariously close to being redefined as a racial other and the RRWU appeared to be reluctant to attempt to determine the racial origin of some of its members.

This was not purely a physiognomic matter. The definition of 'native' as it appeared in the law, was sometimes seen purely as an issue of blood and heritage, as in the definition proffered in the Native Urban Locations Ordinance of 1906 and the Native Pass Ordinance of 1913, which required 'natives' to have both parents as Africans. But at times it was also defined through a combination of biological descent and lifestyle, such as was stated in the Land Apportionment Act of 1929 and local tax laws. Mixed-race individuals who lived in the style of Africans and had African blood were classified as 'native'. Yet if the same individual lived in a 'European style' they could be classified as Coloured.[151] If lifestyle was regarded as a component in codifying race, both white and mixed-race heritage employees on the railways could appeal to cultural and social markers to delineate whiteness. For RRWU executive committee member Mister Le Roux, Coloureds did not join the RRWU 'because they want to be trade unionists, it is because it brings them into the same class as us'. Le Roux admitted that he had been 'brought up amongst the Coloured man', but instead of this inviting increased familiarity, he argued for increased distance and wariness. Certainly, the existence of the Coloured population was regularly blamed upon the white lower classes. Just after the First World War the native commissioner for Umtali (Mutare) noted that interracial sex was more likely to happen in mining centres.[152] For some white workers, increasing physical and psychological distance from the Coloured population was part and parcel of deflecting accusations that the Coloured population was primarily a result of lower-class debauchery.

Nevertheless most delegates at the 1930 biannual national conference disagreed and argued that Coloureds made good trade unionists.[153] At the same conference a motion was submitted that stated that RRWU would agitate for Coloured passengers to be able to purchase second-class fares and it was agreed that by travelling with Africans in third class 'these Coloured people [were] suffering under an injustice'. The RRWU passed a motion to agitate for 'suitable accommodation' for Coloured railway employees on the trains, but only after it had received several amendments in order to prevent the motion advocating that Coloureds could share second-class compartments with whites.[154]

Additionally, because a significant proportion of Coloureds had obtained voting rights, from the RLP's point of view it made sense to attempt to court their support. However, by 1934 the RLP was furious with the Coloured population in Raylton, about 150 of whom qualified for the vote, as it came to light that most had voted for the United Party. It was claimed that Coloureds understood neither political principles nor political parties. In the final results the vote difference between the RLP and the United Party was 0.12 per cent.[155] The *Review* noted with alarm that non-Europeans could influence elections and warned that 'it means that a predominating European Labour electorate, while having to pay the piper, may have to dance to a tune called by others of an inferior culture and tradition. It is an obnoxious and intolerable position'.[156]

Contradictory attitudes to Coloured labour abounded. On the one hand it was recognised that their involvement in the union both strengthened white organisation and could be used as a barrier against African encroachment; but their social proximity remained a reminder of miscegenation and brought white workers' respectability and character into question. Perhaps those whose own racial classification was under greater scrutiny, such as Le Roux who had lived among Coloureds, were more likely to stress the importance of social and physical barriers. Discussions over the proper conduct the union should take towards Coloured workers nevertheless revealed the arbitrary nature of the lines of racial demarcation; white racial identity was something that required constant marking out. Ultimately cooperation with the Coloured community would be on terms dictated by white labour; when it acted against white workers' interests, the latter were quick to remind them of their subordinate social status and supposed inferior culture and lineage.

Conclusion

In other studies little attention has been paid to how white worker identity changed over the colonial period. White worker culture and identity thus appears reified, albeit internally differentiated, and there is no indication of how these identities were continually remade or were reflexive to other phenomenon. This chapter has complicated conceptualisations of the 'white worker' by being attentive to how changes in capitalism, labour strength and hegemonic ideologies impacted upon white workers and has set out the *production* of race as an ongoing and contested process. This chapter has also explored the extent to which workers' identities variously cohered and fractured. Being white was defined as a set of characteristics rooted in working-class traditions and culture from Britain and South Africa; it was an attitude of defiance and bravery; it was the expression of solidarity and the fight for better working conditions. Intelligence, respectability, sobriety and productiveness were regarded as both reflecting and constituting racial identity. Central to white labour notions of respectability was the idea that work made a man and a family.

What is interesting here is the inability of white workers to possess these qualities. The image of respectability that was projected was far from the reality of white workers' experiences. The tensions between the idealised white worker and the experience of white railwaymen and miners disrupted self-imaginings of an inherently superior race. Pride in work sought to overcome this tension by making manual labour a worthy and essential component of white masculinity; shame acted as its counterpart to discipline white workers who had failed or who were deemed to be not trying hard enough. The RRWU also sought to use women to shame those who had fallen below expectations. Women and men experienced and expressed emotions of pride and shame in different ways; one could perhaps speak of two mutually reinforcing gendered emotional communities. White women were greatly outnumbered in these early years yet they were acknowledged as important elements of white worker communities; their presence marked stability and progress and allowed male workers to position themselves as providers and defenders of those who physically reproduced the race.

While there were divisions among white workers the language of race sought to blur disparate groups of workers into a united mass. It had limited success in this regard as the divisions between trade unions and failure to create a coherent white worker identity attests. White male worker identity was also constituted through reference to what it was not. The invoking of difference was central; no matter how low, poverty stricken or debased individual white workers became, an inferior existed. Africans and Coloureds thus played a constitutive role in white identity through the projection of undesirable traits and characteristics on to these racialised others. However, it was never completely clear-cut where these racial boundaries lay. Attitudes to African education were not static and white workers were keen to deny their role in the restriction of education to Africans, which sat uneasily with their radical proclamations. Opposition to African education was set to intensify in the 1930s as the boundaries of white work were disrupted by the needs of capital; what little cohesion white worker identity held was about to be rocked by the onset of global economic depression.

Notes

1 Gann, A History of Southern Rhodesia, p. 226.
2 Lee, 'Politics and Pressure', p. 166.
3 Ibid., p. 165.
4 Ian Phimister, 'Gold Mining in Southern Rhodesia, 1919–1953', Rhodesian Journal of Economics, 10:1 (1976), p. 27; Lunn, Rhodesian Railway, p. 91.
5 Phimister, Economic and Social, p. 189.
6 The Amalgamated Engineering Union was initially called the ASE, but I have used AEU in order to avoid confusion.
7 Lee, 'Politics and Pressure', p. 170; Gann and Gelfand, Huggins of Rhodesia, p. 61.
8 Lunn, Rhodesian Railway.
9 Ibid., p. 85. The use of the bailiwick in this way was first used by Frank McKenna, The Railway Workers, 1840–1970 (London: Faber & Faber, 1980).
10 Peter Hitchcock, 'They Must Be Represented? Problems in Theories of Working-Class Representation', Publications of the Modern Language Association of America, 115:1 (2000), pp. 20–32.
11 Barbara Rosenwein, 'Worrying about Emotions in History', American Historical Review, 107:3 (2002), pp. 821–845.
12 Ibid., p. 842.
13 Krikler, White Rising.
14 Jonathan Hyslop, 'The Imperial Working Class Makes Itself "White": White Labourism in Britain, Australia, and South Africa Before the First World War', Journal of Historical Sociology, 12:4 (1999), pp. 398–421.
15 Duncan Money, 'The World of European Labour on the Northern Rhodesian Copperbelt, 1940–1945', International Review of Social History, 60:2 (2015), pp. 225–255.

16 Lee, 'Politics and Pressure', p. 172.
17 ' "Grand Old Man" of RRWU Passes On', *RRM*, October 1959, p. 3.
18 Lee, 'Politics and Pressure', p. 170; Gann and Gelfand, *Huggins of Rhodesia*, p. 61.
19 The best overview of Macintyre is provided by Terence Ranger in *Bulawayo Burning: The Social History of a Southern African City, 1893–1960* (Oxford: James Currey, 2010).
20 Stanlake Samkange, 'A History of the Rhodesia Labour Party, 1920–1948' (unpublished BA dissertation, Harvard, 1982), p. 12.
21 Ian Henderson, 'White Populism in Southern Rhodesia', *Society for Comparative Studies in Society and History*, 14:4 (1972), pp. 397–399; Donal Lowry, 'The Impact of Anti-Communism on White Rhodesian Political Culture, 1920s–1980', *Cold War History* 7:2 (2007), pp. 170–171.
22 J. W. Keller, 'Conciliation and Cajolery', *RRR*, August 1922, p. 1.
23 J. W. Keller, 'Who Pays?' *RRR*, March 1923, p. 19.
24 *RRR*, December 1930, p. 37.
25 Interview conducted by Ranger in *Bulawayo Burning*, p. 33.
26 'Strike Tactics', *Rhodesia Herald*, 23 December 1919, p. 13.
27 'Editorial', *Rhodesia Herald*, 30 December 1919, p. 13.
28 'The Strike Deadlock', *Rhodesia Herald*, 23 December 1919, p. 5.
29 'Unity Hall', *RRR*, November 1923, p. 11.
30 Mrinalini Sinha, 'Britishness, Clubbability, and the Colonial Public Sphere: The Genealogy of an Imperial Institution in Colonial India', *Journal of British Studies*, 40:4 (2001), p. 495.
31 See chap. 5 in Ben Cohen, *In the Club: Associational Life in Colonial South Asia* (Manchester: Manchester University Press, 2015).
32 'Bulawayo Club History', www.bulawayoclub.com/history.html (accessed 3 January 2016). Terence Ranger observed that in 2001 women were still barred from its members' bar. *Bulawayo Burning*, p. 69.
33 'Unity Hall', *RRR*, November 1923, p. 11.
34 Robert Ross, *Status and Respectability in the Cape Colony, 1750–1870* (Cambridge, UK: Cambridge University Press, 1999), p. 78.
35 For the reading culture of the British working class, see Jonathan Rose, *The Intellectual Life of the British Working Classes* (New Haven, CT: Yale University Press, 2001).
36 J. W. Keller, 'Conciliation and Cajolery', *RRR*, August 1922, p. 1.
37 John Darwin, *The Empire Project: The Rise and Fall of the British World System, 1830–1970* (New York: Cambridge University Press, 2009), p. 167.
38 Lunn, *Rhodesian Railway*, p. 87.
39 See, for example, Pro Patria, 'The Bundle of Sticks', *RRR*, January 1922, p. 23.
40 J. W. Keller, 'Profits, Parsimony and Patience', *RRR*, December 1925, p. 18.
41 P.J. Titus, 'The United Faggot', *RRR*, September 1921, pp. 15–16.
42 'Editorial: Britons Free', *RRR*, December 1924, p. 2 (original emphasis).
43 'Gwelo Branch Notes', *RRR*, June 1926, p. 29.
44 J. H. Hall, 'Reminiscences of a Rhodesian Railwayman', *RRR*, September 1923, p. 12.
45 Lewis Gann, 'The Development of Southern Rhodesia's Military System, 1890–1953', www.rhodesia.nl/gann1.htm (accessed 19 August 2017).
46 'Editorial: Germany and Rhodesia', *RRR*, November 1926, pp. 2–3.
47 Bonar Thompson, 'Ballad of a Blockhead', *RRR*, March 1923, p. 3. See also Ryan Walker, 'The Origin of Henry Dubb', *Maoriland Worker*, 17 June 1914, p. 5.
48 Mr Stewart, 'Mr Stewart and the *Rhodesia Herald*', *Rhodesia Herald*, 17 December 1920, p. 17; 'Letter from J. Stewart', *Rhodesia Herald*, 10 December 1920, p. 15.
49 Mlambo, 'White Man's Country'; Kennedy, *Islands of White*, p. 90.
50 Phimister, *Economic and Social*, pp. 189–190; van Onselen, *Chibaro*, p. 24.
51 'Trade Unionism in Portuguese Territory', *RRR*, March 1932, p. 42.
52 Donal Lowry, 'Rhodesia 1890–1980: "The Lost Dominion"', in *Settlers and Expatriates: Britons Over the Seas*, ed. Robert Bickers (Oxford: Oxford University Press, 2010), p. 124.

53 See Marguerite Elaine Lee, 'The Origins of the Rhodesian Responsible Government Movement', *Rhodesian History*, 6 (1975), pp. 33–52.
54 Lee, 'Politics and Pressure', p. 224.
55 J. W. Keller, 'Responsible Government or Union', *RRR*, May 1922, pp. 1–2; J. W. Keller, 'The Illusion in the South', *RRR*, April 1922, p. 12.
56 J. Stewart, 'Stand-to', *RRR*, August 1922, pp. 10–11.
57 'Artisan', 'After Dinner Talk', *Rhodesian Trade Union Review*, May 1922, p. 15.
58 Krikler, *White Rising*.
59 'A Warning "die Afrikaner Stem', *RRR*, November 1922, p. 2.
60 'Branch Notes and News', *RRR*, August 1922, p. 18.
61 'Salisbury Branch Notes', *RRR*, April 1928, p. 34.
62 NAZ: SR PSA *Journal of Rhodesian Services Records, Affiliated to Rhodesia Teachers' Association*, 1 September 1920, p. 10.
63 Molly P. Taylor, 'Early Recollections of Raylton', in *Down Memory Lane with Some Early Rhodesian Women* (Bulawayo: Books of Rhodesia, 1979), p. 277.
64 Lunn, *Rhodesian Railway*, p. 92.
65 See Phimister, *Economic and Social*, pp. 92–93; Lee, 'Politics and Pressure', p. 178.
66 Lunn, *Rhodesian Railway*, p. 94.
67 Ian Phimister, 'Coal, Crisis and Class Struggle: Wankie Colliery, 1918–22', *Journal of African History*, 33:1 (1992), pp. 84–85.
68 'Mr Herbert Walsh Again', *Rhodesia Herald*, 22 November 1920, p. 13; Lee, 'Politics and Pressure', p. 182.
69 'Editorial: The Acme of Folly', *Rhodesia Herald*, 25 February 1921, p. 15; 'Work at a Standstill', *Rhodesia Herald*, 25 February 1921, p. 15.
70 Lee, 'Politics and Pressure', p. 185.
71 'Wankie Colliery Notice to Employees', *RRR*, January 1929.
72 Rawdon Hoare, *Rhodesian Mosaic* (London: John Murray, 1934), pp. 190–202.
73 'Editorial', *RRR*, March 1929, pp. 8–16; Phimister, *Economic and Social History*, p. 190.
74 NAZ: S480/1460 Strikes and Labour Disputes Among Railway Employees, 1926–1929: Memorandum, 21 February 1929, p. 1.
75 Bill Schwarz, *White Man's World: Memories of Empire, Volume One* (Oxford: Oxford University Press, 2011), p. 363.
76 'Editorial', *RRR*, November 1930, p. 7.
77 Headquarters of the Zimbabwe Amalgamated Railwaymen's Union, Bulawayo, *Minutes of the 1930 RRWU Conference* (Bulawayo: RRWU, 1930), p. 47. The revenue of the RRWU fell from £6,063 in 1928 to £1,865 in 1929. *RRR*, August 1929, p. 6. See also Samkange, 'Rhodesia Labour Party', pp. 25–26.
78 'Penpusher', 'Correspondence: Salaried Association', *RRR*, December 1929, p. 11.
79 Lunn, *Rhodesian Railway*, p. 83.
80 Daphne Anderson, *The Toe-Rags: A Memoir* (London: Penguin, 1990), p. 27.
81 Ian Phimister, 'African Worker Consciousness: Origins and Aspects to 1953', in *Studies in the History of African Mine Labour in Colonial Zimbabwe*, ed. Ian Phimister and Charles van Onselen (Gwelo: Mambo Press, 1978), pp. 23–40.
82 TUK, 'Native Education', *RRR*, January 1925, pp. 16–18.
83 'The Story of a Crime', *RRR*, January 1925, p. 19 (emphasis added).
84 See chap. 4 in Roediger, *Wages of Whiteness*.
85 NAZ: S480/1460 Strikes and Labour Disputes among Railway Employees, 1926–1929: Memorandum, 21 February 1929, p. 2.
86 *RRR*, April 1929, p. 33.
87 For particularly violent outbursts, see Lunn, *Rhodesian Railway*, p. 86; van Onselen, *Chibaro*, pp. 83, 143; Phimister 'White Miners'. For letters, see below.
88 J. W. Keller 'The Truth About the Rhodesia Railwaymen', *RRR*, November 1921, p. 2.
89 Iconoclast, 'Correspondence', *RRR*, November 1921, p. 37.
90 Baldy Bent, 'Correspondence', *RRR*, March 1923, p. 10.
91 J. W. Keller, 'The Truth About the Rhodesia Railwaymen', *RRR*, November 1921, pp. 3–5.

92   Richard Lord, 'The Tally', *RRR*, August 1922, p. 7.
93   L. E. Keller, 'Solid Reasoning: Are You Helping to Starve Your Own Family?', *RRR*, April 1928, pp. 19–20.
94   *RRR*, December 1930, p. 37.
95   Robert Morrell, 'Of Boys and Men: Masculinity and Gender in Southern African Studies', *JSAS*, 24:4 (1998), pp. 607–608.
96   Dum Spiro Spero, 'Correspondence', *RRR*, December 1922, p. 10.
97   *RRR*, December 1930, p. 38.
98   A Pioneer Member, 'Correspondence, "The Non-Unionist"', *RRR*, December 1925, p. 25.
99   For discussion of the trope of African 'boys' in the colonial workplace, see Lisa A. Lindsay, *Working with Gender: Wage Labour and Social Change in Southwestern Nigeria* (Portsmouth, NH: Heinemann, 2003), p. 12.
100 J. M. Scott, 'What Every Railroad Woman Knows', *RRR*, December 1928, p. 64.
101 'Am I to Think You a Cad Jim?' *RRR*, December 1928, p. 111.
102 'Branch Notes Salisbury: What the Women Can Do', *RRR*, August 1929, p. 41.
103 Lee, 'Rhodesian Responsible Government'.
104 'The New Labour Party', *RRR*, February 1923, p. 18.
105 Helena Addis, 'Rhodesian Labour Party Congress', *RRR*, August 1928, p. 15.
106 'Lancashire Lad', 'Globe and Phoenix Branch Notes', *RRR*, September 1922, p. 19.
107 See also Deborah Kirkwood, 'Settler Wives in Southern Rhodesia: A Case Study', in *The Incorporated Wife*, ed. Shirley Ardener and Hilary Callan (London: Croom Helm, 1984), p. 146.
108 Doris Lessing, *Under My Skin: Volume 1 of My Autobiography, to 1949* (London: Flamingo, 1995), p. 46.
109 Anderson, *Toe-Rags*, p. 278.
110 *Ibid.*, pp. 241, 264, 217.
111 Doris Lessing, *Martha Quest* (London: Michael Joseph, 1952), pp. 198, 221.
112 John Connell, 'Forward: The Man and His Country', in *Welensky's 4000 Days: The Life and Death of the Federation of Rhodesia and Nyasaland*, by Sir Roy Welensky (London: Collins, 1964), p. 14.
113 *Ibid.*, p. 235.
114 'Bulawayo Branch Notes', *RRR*, June 1922, p. 11; J. W. Keller, 'Conciliation and Cajolery', *RRR*, August 1922, pp. 2–4.
115 For anger at the 'obscene' defacement of notice boards by white workers, see, 'Decency: A Proper Sense of Proportion: A Word of Warning', *RRR*, May 1922, p. 11.
116 Anthony Croxton, *Railways of Zimbabwe: The Story of the Beira, Mashonaland and Rhodesia Railways* (Newton Abbot: David & Charles, 1982), p. 140.
117 Dorothy Porter, '"Enemies of the Race": Biologism, Environmentalism, and Public Health in Edwardian England', *Victorian Studies*, 34:2 (1991), pp. 159–178.
118 Givelo, 'Musings without Method', *RRR*, April 1922, p. 18.
119 Abraham Lincoln, 'The Native Industrial Position and Problems in the Congo Belge', *RRR*, November 1922, p. 9.
120 Ross, *Status and Respectability*, p. 93.
121 'Prohibition and Labour', *Rhodesian Trade Union Review*, April 1922, p. 3.
122 Fred S. Fish, 'Wake Up!', *RRR*, June 1921, p. 7.
123 An Old Driver, 'Study and Loco. Examinations', *RRR*, November 1923, p. 25.
124 Sui Juris, 'The Crisis', *RRR*, November 1922, p. 11.
125 Carol Summers, *From Civilization to Segregation: Social Ideals and Social Control in Southern Rhodesia, 1890–1934* (Athens: Ohio University Press, 1994).
126 Lee, 'Politics and Pressure', pp. 166, 173.
127 C. Frantz, and Cyril A. Rogers, *Racial Themes in Southern Rhodesia: The Attitudes and Behaviour of the White Population* (New York: Kennikat Press, 1973), p. 124. Positioning racism as a problem of education often serves to obfuscate elite racisms and structural inequality. See Teun A. van Dijk, *Elite Discourse and Racism* (London: Sage, 1993).

128 J. Stewart, 'The Industrial Education of the Native: Does Labour Approve?', *RRR*, January 1923, pp. 6–10.
129 TUK, 'Native Education', *RRR*, January 1925, pp. 16–18.
130 J. Stewart, 'The Industrial Education of the Native: Does Labour Approve?', *RRR*, January 1923, pp. 6–8.
131 Artisan, 'After Dinner Talk', *Rhodesian Trade Union Review*, May 1922, p. 14.
132 W. Doull, 'Can we Make Northern Rhodesia White?', *RRR*, January 1922, p. 9.
133 J. Stewart, 'The Industrial Education of the Native: Does Labour Approve?', *RRR*, January 1923, p. 8.
134 TUK, 'Perpetual Subjection', *RRR*, October 1925, pp. 9–10.
135 J. Stewart, 'The Industrial Education of the Native', *RRR*, March 1923, p. 18.
136 'Editorial', *RRR*, July 1924, p. 2.
137 'Editorial: Thin of the Wedge', *RRR*, November 1925, p. 2.
138 'A Peep into the Future: "Intelligent Natives" Engaged on "Easy" and "Irresponsible" Jobs', *RRR*, August 1927 p. 17.
139 H. J. Lucas, 'Early Days on a Small Working', *Rhodesiana*, 20 (1969), pp. 14–15.
140 Jack Keller, 'The Truth about the Rhodesian Railwayman', *RRR*, November 1921, pp. 2–9.
141 Croxton, *Railways of Zimbabwe*, p. 107.
142 Lowry, 'Impact of Anti-Communism', p. 171; Lessing, *Under My Skin*, pp. 319–320.
143 'Umtali Branch Notes', *RRR*, June 1927, p. 36.
144 'How It Is Done on the Mines', *RRR*, May 1924, p. 10.
145 Christopher Lee, *Unreasonable Histories: Nativism, Multiracial Lives, and the Genealogical Imagination in British Africa* (Durham, NC: Duke University Press, 2014).
146 'The Unemployment Problem', *RRR*, June 1934, pp. 7–18.
147 Hugh Killeen, 'Our General Secretary's Organising Tour', *RRR*, September 1923, p. 10.
148 *Minutes of the 1930 RRWU Conference*, p. 287.
149 *Ibid.*, p. 288.
150 Kendrick Brown, 'Coloured and Black Relations in South Africa: The Burden of Racialized Hierarchy', *Macalester International*, 9:13 (2000), pp. 198–207.
151 Christopher Lee, '*Jus Soli* and *Jus Sanguinis* in the Colonies: The Interwar Politics of Race, Culture and Multiracial Status in British Africa', *Law and History Review*, 29:2 (2011), p. 513.
152 *Ibid.*, p. 37.
153 *Minutes of the 1930 RRWU Conference*, p. 288.
154 *Ibid.* For the Indian context on how social distinctions materialised in the division of railway carriages, see Bear, *Lines of the Nation*, p. 51.
155 Gloria C. Passmore, Margaret Mitchell and Francis Michael Glen Willson, *Source Book of Parliamentary Elections and Referenda in Southern Rhodesia, 1898–1962* (Salisbury, Rhodesia: Department of Government, University College of Rhodesia and Nyasaland, 1963).
156 'Raylton Is Predominantly Labour!', *RRR*, December 1934, p. 76.

CHAPTER TWO

The Great Depression and shifting boundaries of 'white work'

Economic crises destabilise established norms. They offer elites opportunities to pursue unpopular or unprecedented ideological agendas. Historians of southern Africa have long been attentive to the ways in which periods of economic crisis enabled state authorities to assert political and economic control over Africans, to strengthen racial boundaries and to discipline and engineer settler communities.[1] Vivian Bickford Smith has detailed the ways in which Cape Town's depression of the 1880s saw increasing support for segregation as the white poor were seen to need to be 'saved' from the racialised and damaging 'residuum'. Similarly, Susan Parnell has shown how the 1930s depression led to slum clearances in Johannesburg and paved the way for residential segregation.[2] Bogumil Jewsiewicki's work has demonstrated that economic upheaval provided an opportunity for employers to restructure the costly racialised workforce in Katanga as three-quarters of whites were laid off in the first few years of the 1930s and unemployed whites were repatriated to Europe.[3] By contrast, Neil Roos has explored how the South African state used work camps and unemployment programmes not only to uplift European populations out of poverty, but to control and discipline the settler community.[4]

Yet, while economic depression has often been recognised as pivotal in the turn towards calls for racial segregation in South Africa and Southern Rhodesia, its contribution to the socialisation of white workers and the contestation over whiteness remains underexplored. This includes wider debates about the defining boundaries and the conceptualisation of white work itself, the place of the white worker in society, the causes of unemployment and the place of white women in formal employment. Moreover, research into economic depression and white poverty in the settler colonial context has largely focused upon elite constructions of poor whiteism, the discursive formations of popular eugenicist thought and the anxieties of the colonial state.[5] While a considerable amount of literature exists on the poor white problem in South Africa, the pieds noirs of Algeria and degredados of Portuguese Africa, much less exists on the Southern Rhodesian context.[6] This is in part, as Giovanni Arrighi has argued, because white wage workers' 'settlement was a *consequence of*, and did not precede, capitalist development in the colony'.[7] While there is some important work on poor whiteism in Southern Rhodesia, the role of white fears of destitution and experiences of poverty to the process of race-making has been overlooked.[8]

Under the conditions of the Great Depression, the central tenets of white worker identity outlined in Chapter 1 had to be reworked. The first half of this chapter probes why white labour organisations reacted to the Great Depression in fatalistic hyperbole and apocalyptic prophesies of racial decline. It was argued by the RLP and RRWU that without adequate protection whites would sink into poverty, the boundaries fundamental to settler colonialism would evaporate and white civilisation itself would crumble.[9] Behind that lay a complex of ideas by which white workers articulated their group identity. This was no mere imitation or repetition of bourgeois alarmist discourse. In Southern Rhodesia white workers' self-understandings relied heavily on their occupations, pride in work and physical as well as moral strength. This was contrasted with African manual labouring, which was seen as unskilled, repetitive work in which Africans took no care. White workers laid claim to a pioneering myth that placed themselves as the driving force behind conquest and colonisation. White hands built the railroads, extracted the mineral wealth and produced commodities in narratives that were notable for the conspicuous absence of African labour. The Depression and resulting unemployment threatened to undo this identity. White labour was thrown into temporary disarray as it struggled to assert an image of respectability and to uphold its racial boundaries.

The second section of the chapter addresses how white labour organisations responded to the Depression by reformulating the ways in which white labour identity was performed. It has often been stated, both by contemporary observers and historians alike, that white workers across southern Africa refused to perform work they saw as racially degrading; work that was considered to be the sole preserve of Africans.[10] The boundaries of 'white work' were contingent on the particular confluence of racial demographics and changing economic needs across different settler states. In South Africa 'white work' always involved some lower-skilled manual positions and agricultural work. By contrast, on arrival in Kenya, one educator was told not to carry his own luggage as 'to do any work myself would mean losing all prestige with the natives'.[11] In Kenya, 'white work' disavowed manual labour. Indeed, as this passage suggests, for some settlers at least, restricting themselves to 'white work' involved an aversion to performing even the most basic personal tasks. Yet across these different settler states there has been a tendency to reify racialised occupational categories in an oversimplified dualism in which skilled work was labelled white and unskilled work was African (sometimes with reference to a mixed-race or Asian intermediate strata). These broad brushstrokes are useful generalisations in many respects, but they can also distort our understanding of how the racialised and gendered boundaries of work changed across the colonial period and how white or male work was differentially configured in particular spaces.

Changes in the labour force reflected tensions between the changing needs of capitalist development and the struggles of gendered, racial, ethnic and national groups to monopolise, defend or enter different employment spheres.[12] The capitalist crisis forced the reworking of white worker identity and the boundaries of the types of work whites should perform, as well as the gendered bodies performing the work. Unskilled work became respectable and white women's participation in wage labour became increasingly tolerated by white male workers. The concept of 'white work' or a 'white standard of living' was never static, nor universally agreed upon. Within the European community notions of what were acceptable white forms of behaviour, income, lifestyles and occupations differed along class lines. This chapter seeks to complicate the idea of a static 'white worker identity' as well as unchanging categorisations of 'black' and 'white' work within settler states by pointing to the ways in which white worker identity was constantly made and remade, responding to the dynamism of wider economic, political, cultural and social structural changes. This chapter also contends that it is precisely the proximity of white workers to the spectre of poor whiteism and their structural location – simultaneously as exploited workers and as part of a racial elite – which gives the reactions of the RLP and RRWU to the Great Depression and the machinations of the state their intensity.

Unemployment: the white male affliction

By the early 1930s the effects of the Great Depression had reverberated across the global economic system. In Southern Rhodesia mineral production slumped, maize and cattle farming were thrown into crisis, Rhodesia Railways saw its revenue halve and the country suffered a general fall in national income. Labour was put on the defensive as

[78]

capital pushed for wage cuts and retrenchment in order to restore profitability. The settler administration effectively used the African population as a shock absorber to protect Europeans from economic strife. The Maize Control Act, Cattle Levy Act, Public Service Act, Industrial Conciliation Act and Land Apportionment Act, were passed by the mid-1930s to ensure that Europeans retained economic dominance as Africans suffered the worst effects of the Great Depression. Immigration regulations were tightened and workers from outside the colony were only allowed to enter on a temporary permit if there was an essential post that could not be filled by someone already inside the colony. If a Rhodesian became available the person hired could be deported.[13]

As in South Africa, but in contrast to the non-settler Belgian Congo, white workers were singled out in state measures to protect and uplift the European community and were sheltered through a series of measures to alleviate unemployment. In South Africa as many as one in twelve white male workers were employed in public or subsidised work programmes by 1933.[14] In Southern Rhodesia a work camp was set up at Mtao Forest, about fifty miles east of Gwelo (Gweru), in 1925 and in 1931 a second camp was established at Stapleford, twenty miles north of Umtali. Isolated from populous centres, these camps hid the poorest whites away. Roadworks and afforestation programmes, as well as a police cadet corps, were also initiated to absorb the unemployed.[15] These protective measures culminated with the passing of the 1934 Industrial Conciliation Act, which effectively formalised the colour bar and protected the white monopoly of skilled jobs.

While the numbers of white registered unemployed in the early 1920s never reached 350 and the number of men employed on relief remained in double figures, by September 1931, Bulawayo district alone noted 417 unemployed men and 600 dependants.[16] Decreasing traffic on the railways saw at least 1,600 white railwaymen retrenched from 1930 to 1932 as the white workforce on the railways was reduced by around 25 per cent.[17] The *Review* estimated that up to 2,000 European jobs across Rhodesia's industries had been lost over the same period.[18] A national investigation undertaken by G. E. Wells in 1933 identified a total of 826 unemployed men, representing about 4 per cent of all adult men nationally, and an additional 1,581 dependants.[19] It also identified 406 men employed on relief schemes and around 300 older men who survived on government rations, maintenance allowance, support of friends or family and old men's homes.[20] By 1936 male unemployment had decreased to 657, representing 3 per cent of the adult male population over fifteen, most of whom were concentrated in mining, building and construction.[21]

Retrenchment on the railways was mostly targeted at African workers. The number of black workers fell from 18,492 in April 1930 to 7,898 just three years later in June 1933.[22] Yet unemployment was conceptualised as a white, and specifically male, affliction. Hegemonic ideals about the role of white men as breadwinners within the idealised nuclear family also meant white female unemployment was often dismissed as a trivial concern.[23] While white women were seen as dependants to be provided for, African men who resided in the towns were described as dangerous loafers. Wells's investigation cast unemployment as a deliberate choice on behalf of skilled white men, signalled by their refusal to work for the low wages offered by employers attempting to lower wage bills. Unskilled white men, on the other hand, were noted as 'the most difficult group of the unemployed' who suffered the most regardless of economic conditions as a result of African competition and comprised a greater proportion of the unemployed than their skilled counterparts.[24]

White trade unions were decisively weakened as the post-war slump intensified and unemployment steadily rose.[25] The only two workers' organisations to survive in any meaningful sense into the 1930s were the RRWU and the RLP. By 1926, despite the influence of Keller, the RRWU rejected formal links to the RLP.[26] Nevertheless, the RLP won three seats in 1928, secured 16 per cent of the vote and five seats in 1933 and 26.32 per cent and five seats in 1934.[27] The RRWU and RLP treated government statistics on unemployment with great suspicion. They argued that the numbers provided by unemployment registries could not be trusted as the individual pride of white workers prevented many from openly admitting that they were unemployed.[28] Men and women who sought government relief had to go through a rigorous application process that included providing statements to the unemployment officers and the Criminal Investigation Department, followed by an interview and the taking of fingerprints. In Britain fingerprinting had been used as a means of identifying criminals from 1900, but while fingerprinting welfare recipients had been entertained by the British Treasury in the 1910s in order to prevent fraud, it was never implemented as it was thought to provoke hostility and resentment from ordinary respectable citizens.[29] In Rhodesia, however, provoking lower-class resentment was of lesser concern. Keller argued that this 'criminalisation' of the poor and the 'indignity' of the process of applying for relief was so demeaning that many Europeans would rather starve than go through the process.[30] Again, shame was mobilised by trade unionists. Shame was used to dispute unemployment statistics and was also held up as proof of lower-class respectability; that they would rather starve than compromise their dignity was heralded as a testament to white workers' moral strength. To feel shame in this context was to stake out the boundaries of white propriety.

It is clear that government statistics did not reflect the true extent of the unemployment problem. The figures provided by the Labour Bureau differed from those provided by the Unemployment Registry, and the Select Committee on Unemployment commissioned by the government in 1932 admitted that its own appraisal of 8 per cent combined male and female unemployment was probably an underestimation. However, while it is probable that some were ashamed of their unemployed status and therefore unlikely to register, the figure of 25 per cent unemployment in 1932 produced by the RLP's independent research appears inflated.[31] The Southern Rhodesian government were equally fearful of the growth of a poor white class and therefore unlikely to deliberately underestimate the number of white unemployed by such a large margin. The Rhodesian figures are striking precisely due to their relative insignificance: by 1933 the number of unemployed in the United States had almost reached a quarter of the civilian labour force over fourteen years of age, while in the United Kingdom the average unemployment rate from 1931–34 was around 20 per cent.[32] Whites in Rhodesia were in a sheltered position compared with the effects of the Depression on the working class internationally. Objectively, these figures should not have precipitated a crisis and yet the discourses surrounding unemployment and poor whiteism during these years were centred upon alarmist prophecies of racial decline. What was significant about the settler colonial context that precipitated such a panicked and fearful response to what were relatively quite low rates of unemployment?

Perceptions of white poverty and racial decline

Southern Rhodesian approaches to poverty and unemployment were largely influenced by international debates surrounding 'poor whiteism'. Certainly, the phenomenon was conceptualised, both by Rhodesian officials and white trade unions, mostly as a South African, and specifically Afrikaner, issue.[33] Other non-British nationalities were noted as harbouring predispositions to poor whiteism. Many non-British whites were deliberately hired by employers in the lesser-skilled occupations and therefore commanded lower wages. The 1914 Immigrants Regulation Ordinance had reference to particular undesirable ethnic groups: Levantines, Europeans from eastern Europe, Europeans from south-eastern Europe, low-class Greeks, low-class Italians and 'Jews of low type and mixed origin and other persons of mixed origin and continental birth'.[34] In these typologies descriptions of 'low-type' ethnicities were overlaid with a repetition of 'low class'. Low class inferred low racial status and the possession of one led to the development of the other.

While anti-Afrikaner sentiment eased after the vote on responsible government it did not entirely dissipate. Several Afrikaners trying to enter Southern Rhodesia complained to union authorities in the late 1920s that they had been discriminated against at the border. In 1929 Hendrik David Verheen was told by an immigration official at Beitbridge that he needed £80 to proceed across the border. Verheen had produced £80 but the official raised the required sum to £90. When Verheen said he could produce £90, the official replied that 'it is useless as your government is only sending in the Dutch people to out-vote us ... we do not want any Dutch families in Rhodesia'.[35] The Rhodesian Immigration authorities replied that it was not racial, but because they thought him and his family likely to become public charges, pointing out he was a farmer and bricklayer by trade.[36] Jan Rayvenstein, a Netherlands national who went under the name 'Jack Robinson' was deported in 1931 as an 'undesirable inhabitant' by Salisbury authorities who noted 'he had associate[d] continually with criminals, prostitutes and Coloured persons and was frequently under suspicion in connection with illicit gold dealing, the supply of liquor to natives and the commission of other crimes'.[37] That Jan Rayvenstein specifically chose the decidedly English-sounding Jack Robinson as an alias not only suggests that he potentially used this name to evade detection or the possibility of being recognised as a former convict, but implies a will to be seen to assimilate and shed stereotypes associated with Dutch origin.

The 1914 Immigrants Bill allowed for potential migrants to be refused entry to Southern Rhodesia on economic grounds, but this had primarily been directed at keeping unskilled whites out. Yet as the Depression intensified, and the position of skilled whites across southern Africa became increasingly precarious, the clause was now being used against the migration of skilled employees and keeping out those who might take jobs that could be performed by whites already in the country. The closure of mines in Northern Rhodesia compounded fears of white unemployed artisans – better educated and experienced – being offered jobs, which, the RLP argued, should go to home-grown Southern Rhodesians. In 1930 a law was passed to restrict migration from Northern Rhodesia. One engineer wrote to Keller lamenting that he was about to be replaced by a man from Krugersdorp despite 'willing and able' men residing in Southern Rhodesia.[38] The RLP, far from championing the rights of an international white working class, were struggling to keep white workers from Northern Rhodesia and South Africa out.

Poor whiteism was fundamentally an ideological construction; a set of beliefs embedded in the association of poverty with miscegenation, racial decline and the inability of whites to live and rule in Africa.[39] The concept of poor whiteism only emerged in the 1890s despite a much longer history of European material impoverishment across Southern Africa. During the late nineteenth century the new liberalism and social imperialism of Britain influenced South African approaches to poverty; no longer conceptualised as the result of individual failings, poverty was refashioned as the consequence of social structures and environments. This coincided with the rise of racial taxonomies, the growth of the working class and increased social unrest in 1880s Britain, all of which shook ideas regarding the inevitable progress of civilisation. In popular eugenic discourses poor whiteism was a symptom of societal decline; it was proof that racial purity was susceptible to being infected by environmental factors.[40]

Poor whiteism was also a transnational construction. In the 1930s eugenic societies found renewed impetus in Western Europe, the United States and a number of African settler societies, particularly South Africa and Kenya. Across these contexts poor whiteism meant much more than material impoverishment. It signified a range of behavioural and racial defects. The Southern Rhodesian *Report on Unemployment* defined poor whites as 'men accustomed to and content with a very low standard of living', who lacked any sense of ambition or responsibility and preferred to live with continual assistance from the state. They continued that the poor white should be treated differently to the 'impoverished European' as it was 'by the standard of living, and the psychological traits, more than actual financial position, that the class is defined'.[41] This discussion centred upon notions of the undeserving and deserving poor distinguishing between those who were unemployed because they found themselves in unfortunate circumstances and those who found themselves in poverty due to their own fecklessness. As one MP of the ruling Rhodesia Party argued, poor whites and those engaged in relief work were in that position 'through their own carelessness'.[42]

The *Report on Unemployment* identified that around one hundred of all registered unemployed in 1933 should be classified as 'poor whites'. Of the hundred identified as 'poor whites' seventy-nine were considered to be drunks and it was noted with fear that many of this number were registered voters.[43] There was particular concern over the evidence that some men had brought their wives and children to Nyson near the work camp at Mtao and had erected 'slums'. Many of these images rested on the trope of profligacy in the lower classes: that these people were poor and would reproduce undesirable behaviours in their children and that their untrammelled sexuality and uninhibited self-control would be replicated within the large families that they could not afford to sustain.[44] Notably, reproductive profligacy was also associated with a lack of control considered to be inherent to Africans.[45] The men at Mtao and Stapleford were specifically isolated to prevent a permanent 'poor white' settlement from developing.[46] In this regard, Southern Rhodesia was relatively successful. The figure of one hundred poor whites pales into insignificance when compared with South Africa, whose Carnegie Commission identified a total of three hundred thousand poor whites in 1930. Rhodesia's experience of poor whiteism was largely confined to the fear of a poor white class developing rather than its actual existence. Nevertheless, during the 1930s state authorities were becoming increasingly concerned that sections of the white poor, especially those in the relief camps, actually *enjoyed* doing unskilled work and living in degraded environments. The commissioner of labour, G. E. Wells, commented that those employed in relief camps 'had come to regard relief work as providing permanent employment of a character not uncongenial to them'. Some 25 per cent of the men at Mtao had resided there for somewhere between two and eight years and in some cases the men had turned down offers of employment outside the relief system. It was reasoned that conditions in the camps were not poor enough to encourage them to look for outside employment.[47]

The RLP and RRWU reflected popular eugenicist ideas and fears regarding the association of poverty with the erosion of racial boundaries. The *Review* noted with alarm how unemployment would lead Rhodesian whites to endure social debasement, writing that the unemployed men of South Africa 'must consort in slums with negroes and half castes to whose jeers and insolence he and his womenfolk especially are then subject'. This, they argued, led to white men selling liquor to Africans and white women being forced into prostitution.[48] Selling liquor to Africans proved to be a quick source of income to a layer of poor whites in South Africa, many of whom were incarcerated or deported if caught. The consumption of alcohol by lower-class whites stirred British colonial anxieties; across the empire more broadly the visibility of drunk whites was seen as endangering British identification as the ruling superior race.[49] These categories existed in dialectical tension: poor whiteism was both a cause *and* a consequence of a range of transgressive behaviours and attitudes. Criminality, alcoholism, miscegenation and familial breakdown were interrelated phenomena of moral decline.[50]

Daphne Anderson, a self-described 'poor white', gives some insight into these dynamics. She observed that during the 1930s the Southern Rhodesian state was particularly 'alarm[ed] at the number of white men who had joined the native loafers on street corners or who lay about on the grass of the municipal parks'.[51] Moreover, Anderson recalled how her own grandmother was sent back to England for crimes of alcoholism, which damaged family honour and undermined white prestige. Her aunt had initiated the deportation precisely because she 'was afraid for her reputation, knowing that her mother's drunken stories in the town had become well known'.[52] Britons who fell into irretrievable poverty could be repatriated to Britain as 'distressed British subjects'.[53] Such shameful figures had to be concealed. The *Review* suggested that those who failed to live up to the 'ideals of the race' should be repatriated to 'stagnate' in Britain 'where their shame would not be exposed and they could die off and leave the fair fields and industries of South and Central Africa to the tender mercies of the half-baked and coddled "child races" of fanciful Colonial Office officials'.[54] Deportation was preferable to the shame of unemployment, of failing to meet white standards of living, of poverty, all of which compromised the ability to maintain appropriate cultural and social distance from Africans. If whites could not maintain their racial superiority they should be sent 'home' to prevent such shame. When they returned to the home country they would 'die off'. These whites were not meant to survive it seemed, either in Africa or Europe.

Unemployment and poverty were also seen as inhibiting white workers from commanding deference from Africans. Lawrence Vambe, a prominent African journalist, noted that the Depression intensified the level of bile and hatred directed from white workers to Africans:

> Especially deep was their humiliation arising from the fact that they were seen doing pick-and-shovel tasks by the Africans, who walked or rode their bicycles past them. As it was, the Africans did not have to starve or go on the dole. If they lost their jobs, they simply returned to their villages, where they grew their own food. Probably for the first time, the European workers understood that black people had a freedom which they themselves did not possess. The indigenous people seemed unaffected by the white man's financial system that had gone so crazily wrong and brought poverty, insecurity and bitterness to men who had always behaved like demi-gods ... Their bitterness showed itself openly in the streets and on outlying roads. Those of them who knew our language swore at innocent black passers-by, using the most obscene terms in Chisezuru.[55]

In this scene whites work on pick and shovel, using their hands in the mud and dirt, while Africans appear carefree, riding bicycles, the imagery of urban, recreational modern life. Rawdon Hoare, although as a settler with a vested interest in representing Africans as content and well paid, observed that on the streets of Salisbury 'the majority of hotel and household servants can be seen riding expensive bicycles, dressed in attire of the latest fashion, while many white men ... plough their way on foot along the dusty roads'.[56]

The repetition of this particular image indicates that the Depression was widely perceived to subvert race and class hierarchies. Whites had continually preached the virtues of European culture and systems of governance, but this system had created unemployment and threatened the ability of white workers to lay claim to their presumed racial superiority. Vambe hints at white workers' envy of African landholdings and their position of semi-proletarianisation. White wage labourers had no such security; there was no plot of land waiting for them; they had to find work, emigrate or accept state relief. This must have been particularly galling; whites, whose self-identification as the productive driving force in the country, creating wealth and prosperity on what would otherwise be unprofitable, disused land, were now confronted with figures of Africans, whose links to rural villages were able to provide for them during the Depression.[57] Africans seeing whites working menial jobs and living in relative poverty brought the assumption of white racial superiority crashing down. Liberal MP Jacob Smit outlined why whites walking the streets – their unemployed and destitute status laid bare for all to see – was a particular problem as 'it might have to some extent a very bad effect on the minds of the natives when they see these white people doing the work which in the past was only done by natives'.[58] The debased white gave the black man confidence. This confidence was despised and feared. The confidence to challenge white authority, to refuse to follow instructions or display submissive behaviours, was the same confidence that led to revolt and rebellion against white rule.[59] As white workers suffered and felt their racial prestige under attack, they turned increasingly to violent intimidation and hostility in order to reassert their presumed superiority. Letters to the *Review* proliferated, complaining of Africans laughing, talking or walking in the street.[60] In part, the transgression lay in the incursion of African bodies into those urban and residential spaces imagined as white, but it was also the visible reminder of African contentment and individual agency. White workers desired Africans to perform their own humiliation; for them to accept that they were a lower race and to behave accordingly. When automatic deference was not forthcoming, frustration and bitterness resulted.[61] One letter from a white constituent to his RLP MP complained of 'insolence' from an African staff member as he 'asked the boy to open the gate, and the cheek I had from that little munt would make anyone's blood boil. After taking the law into my own hands I had to open the gate'.[62] Here anger was characterised as a natural reaction of white men to this transgression. African insolence damaged white prestige by defying whites' needs, not only to be served, but to be served

with appropriate obeisance.[63] Poorer whites, unable to command deference from Africans, were seen as a threat to the racial order itself.

Contesting white poverty

The reactions of the RLP and RRWU often appear inconsistent or
contradictory. They claimed that poor whites would 'die off' but might
simultaneously multiply at vicious speed; they recycled the idea that
poverty resulted from individual failing, but also painted the poor and
unemployed as innocent victims of an indifferent global system. These
contradictions surfaced as elite discourses were refracted by lower-
class whites; images of indolence and decline came into conflict with
workers' self-identification as the builders of empire and bearers of civilisation. While accepting many dominant ideas about poor whiteism,
in most cases the RLP and RRWU strove to mobilise sympathy for
these figures of white wretchedness. The *Review* commented upon
white children who walked around in the street barefoot, completely
unaware of the impropriety of their lacking aesthetic signifiers of class
and race. Nakedness signified savagery in colonial discourses and to
be barefoot was a sign of racial degeneracy.[64] RRWU described 'horrible dens … insanitary conditions, families of ten wandering about the
sanitary buckets, picking up crusts on account of inability to get sufficient rations from the Department'. RLP MP Major Walker pressed
this point arguing that there were

> families living in starvation. Government relief rations are not able to
> maintain these people. I can give an instance of a family of nine chil-
> dren and two parents receiving relief rations from the Government of a
> value of £1 a month. Is that sufficient to maintain life in any white or
> even black community? … When I went into some of these homes I was
> horrified; my heart bled.

This poverty and wretchedness did not necessarily refer to starvation
or homelessness, but rather an inability to afford domestic staff and
the iniquity of consuming mealie meal; namely, the failure to adhere
to 'white' standards of living.

Both the RLP and RRWU used white poverty to challenge the characterisation of white workers as lazy and insisted that those thrown
into poverty were at the behest of unscrupulous bosses and international capitalism as well as 'do-gooder' missionaries intent on
educating Africans. They were also keen to highlight the apparent
criminalisation of poverty as a stain on the Rhodesian government.[65]
RLP MP Jonathan Malcolm denounced Mtao and Stapleford as 'penal
settlements' and pointed to the despicable conditions white men were

forced to live in; some men in the camps were not provided beds or basic amenities.[66] These men, it was argued, had not lost consideration of white standards or white civilisation, but had been let down by a self-serving government and an exploitative global system. In 1934 a strike broke out at Stapleford over the conditions in the camp and the RLP called for the camps to be abolished. It was argued that the debased conditions meant that the men sent to the camps 'must inevitably become poor whites'. White men deserved proper work in the towns, not to be abandoned in outposts or to be made dependent on charity. The government had *created* poor whites.[67]

The figure of the wretched white abandoned and betrayed by the settler state was used to agitate around racialised labour practices. White workers feared that once they were replaced, they would never regain particular categories of work.[68] The *Review* argued that allowing Africans to compete with whites for jobs threatened 'our dominance as a race, our prestige, our usefulness in the vaunted trusteeship of the children races'.[69] White worker representatives utilised the language of trusteeship, and prevailing rhetoric regarding the idea that Africans should be civilised and uplifted by colonial powers, in order to argue against African education and social mobility.

Despite attempts to frustrate the growth of a skilled African workforce and an educated African middle class, the number of Africans earning a living through independent trading and businesses rose from 864 in 1930 to 3,545 in 1938, including in skilled and semi-skilled trades usually dominated by white wage earners such as building, plumbing and carpentry.[70] Domboshawa, the first state school for Africans, had opened in 1921 in Mashonaland followed by Tjolotjo in Matabeleland. Despite relatively small numbers, this social group was seen as a particular threat to the racialised order. Further concern emanated from the perceived impertinence of Africans in organising themselves into trade unions. Although African organisations were still in their infancy and relatively weak, the 1927 African mine strike at Shamva and efforts to extend the South African Industrial and Commercial Workers' Union into Rhodesia in the same year had unsettled white workers.[71]

Within the *Review* it was often suggested that elite whites and missionaries had formed a nefarious alliance with Africans against white labour. In reality most missionaries held paternalist assumptions about African development and were divided among themselves regarding to what extent African brothers and sisters in Christ should be transformed into social equals.[72] Nevertheless, missionaries received particular contempt from white labour organisations. The *Review* were particularly critical of Frank Hadfield who they accused of indulging African laziness:

Then up spake spurious Hadfield –
(A missioner he be) –
'I will protect the Native;
The Native shall be free;
His children shall not labour,
nor his able bodied toil;
this land is theirs, theirs only;
Theirs shall remain the soil.'[73]

One picture printed in the *Review* depicted Africans hand in hand with a missionary as MPs; whites appear asking Africans for jobs, serving Africans in restaurants and chauffeuring them around town. The Africans were drawn wearing top hats and smoking cigars – the aesthetic markers of the aristocracy. The white aristocracy were likewise castigated as lazy by white labour; if allowed to ascend Africans would simply become another parasitic class. But the African, the image implied, lacked the gentlemanly character despite his superficial appearance of civility. One figure forces a white woman to walk in the gutter and she appears helpless, her honour and physical safety compromised.[74] Africans, in other words, could never be truly civilised (Figure 8).

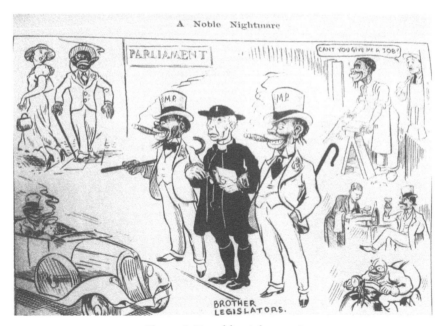

Figure 8 'A noble nightmare'

There was considerable contradiction within white labour's position. In one breath Africans were labelled as irredeemably uncompetitive in statements that proclaimed the natural and inherent higher productivity of white labour; at the same time employers and missionaries were repeatedly condemned in the strongest terms for enabling Africans to compete.[75] This competition, it was argued, would not 'elevate the native, but ... degrade the white man'.[76] One picture printed in the *Review* illustrated white workers' concerns over African progression into 'white' jobs (Figure 9). One white worker laments, 'What is to become of our children?' The African is presented as a gift, a child's toy: inanimate, innocuous and controllable. But the white workers see through Santa Claus's disingenuous offer for Africans 'to work your engines and your plough' and recognise the seemingly harmless figure was in fact a dangerous threat to white civilisation. The spectre of Cecil Rhodes stands with the workers; a tacit assertion that white workers were the true inheritors of the pioneering spirit embodied in Rhodes.

White labour felt increasingly threatened as the ranks of the white unemployed swelled. Africans seen to be performing 'white work'

Rhodesia's Santa Claus

Figure 9 'Rhodesia's Santa Claus'

were routinely harassed. White workers also complained to management, attempted to shame those firms that hired African staff in skilled positions and threatened industrial action in a bid to maintain their racialised monopoly over certain jobs.[77] White workers also drew upon Black Peril to limit African mobility. In 1932 one letter to the *Review* explicitly accused the media and state officials of minimising 'the facts' of Black Peril. The writer claimed that white women were frequently attacked in Bulawayo and called for African mobility to be restricted in the form of a curfew for Africans and 'prohibition of [their] use of side walks'.[78]

The boundaries of 'white male work' reworked

Despite assertions of natural superiority the reality was that many whites in the colony had few skills and had received little or substandard education. Compulsory education for whites up to fifteen years old was only initiated in 1930.[79] The inability of some whites to acquire skilled employment had to be dealt with by representatives of white labour who were keen to project an image of the respectable white wage earner. In particular the Depression encouraged the RRWU and RLP to reassess the racialisation of particular occupations. White workers had relied on possession of skilled work or redefining the work they performed as skilled, as a means of racial differentiation. But the Depression prompted the RLP and RRWU to demand that whites in Southern Rhodesia fill all levels of work, including that nominally performed by Africans. Central to this was a debate concerning the definition of 'white work'. The RRWU warned that it was precisely the attitude of whites in South Africa – that certain grades of work were beneath them – that had caused the poor white problem.

In the early 1930s the RLP and RRWU placed demands on the railway administration and tried to push through legislation in parliament that advocated the employment of whites in unskilled positions, including the most menial tasks in the colony such as cleaning, domestic service and delivering letters. In part this argument reflected a turn towards more segregationist discourse and the 'two-pyramid' policy of complete separation of the races in Southern Rhodesia, but this itself involved a reimagining of the place of the white worker in African settler colonies.[80] The Civilised Labour Policy, enacted by Herzog's Pact government in South Africa during the 1920s, which saw state initiatives to hire unskilled whites at 'civilised' rates of pay, no doubt also influenced the demands of white workers across Southern Rhodesia.[81]

In the eyes of many white labourers, so-called demeaning work was better than the shame of unemployment. Work was seen as

[91]

something that made a man; manual labour engendered character and status while worklessness eroded the key bases from which lower-class whites performed their racial identity. Thus, the respectability invested in skilled work was extended to unskilled categories of work. It was argued that reliance on Africans had made whites effete, soft and despotic.[82] White men, it was reasoned, should retain pride in all types of work; suffering in menial jobs on low pay was character building. White men performing these roles was used to proclaim European self-sufficiency on one hand and to demonstrate the uselessness and super-fluity of African labour on the other.

In 1933 the RRWU called upon the railways to ease the burden upon white families by replacing Africans with whites as engine cleaners, painters, office boys, call boys, learner cooks, pantry boys and bedding boys. This unskilled work was demanded for white youths rather than white men. Such menial work was a rite of passage for them; many older trade unionists were likely to have fulfilled low status jobs in the United Kingdom prior to migrating to Rhodesia and some would have performed such jobs within the colony. Trade unionists variously professed that they had been cleaners at some point, while others admitted to scrubbing railway floors and even working alongside Africans cleaning cutlery.[83] Yet while African 'boys' would be fulfilling these roles for the rest of their employment, reflective of dominant racial ideology that embedded Africans' perennial status as children, for white youths this was simply a transitory stage before they entered manly and respectable employment. Unskilled work was recognised as having a corrupting effect if undertaken over a long period of time.

While these organisations argued that white youths should be engaged in unskilled labour, they still maintained that those employed must keep up white standards. Keller argued, in response to offers of farm employment for young urban whites, that this would be inappro-priate as they would ultimately become farm labourers and 'work side by side with the natives on the farms'.[84] If whites were to take on menial jobs, proper racial protocol must be upheld, and some RRWU officials admitted that not all white youths were properly instructed in the correct behaviours. There was particular alarm from RLP members over white boys selling newspapers on the streets of Bulawayo; white boys on street corners were highly visible and also isolated from other white workers.[85] The RRWU were particularly concerned that some white youths had been duped by management into transgressing racialised labour protocols and that employers were refusing to hire those who displayed awareness or caution of established white labour practices in favour of more ignorant sections of the white population. In one account relayed at the 1933 RRWU annual conference, four 'young lads' passed tests to work alongside gangers on the railways and were told that they 'must do the same work as the natives do. Worryingly, three of the boys were perfectly willing. The fourth said, "I do not know I shall have to consult my father first!" Three were taken on and the other was left.'[86] White gangers usually had three or four Africans helping them, and while it was acceptable for white youths to work in menial jobs, it was argued that their impressionable minds should not be exposed to African labourers in such a manner. Doing the same work as Africans, it seemed, was only appropriate as long as sufficient distance was maintained between black and white.

Despite arguing for reserving unskilled occupations for whites, fears persisted regarding what this might engender in the European mind, particularly the malleable mind of the Rhodesian youth who could be tricked into some sort of shared experience with African workers if he was not continually guided and guarded. This reflected dominant ideas that young whites were particularly susceptible to the moral inflictions of poor whiteism. In 1933 Wells suggested that the sixty youths aged twenty-one and under who were employed on relief schemes be dismissed as it was damaging 'from a psychological point of view'.[87] Close proximity to poor whites would encourage youths to imbibe the work-shy character of their peers on the relief works just as proximity to Africans could lead to a blurring of racial identity.[88]

During the nineteenth century there was increased emphasis on childhood as formative stage of life; the experiences of childhood would determine the thoughts, feelings and behaviours of the adult self.[89] In the settler context it was accepted that children must be prepared and equipped to take on the burden of directing and controlling the indigenous population if the future of white civilisation was to be protected.[90] The continuation of white supremacy relied upon reproducing gendered and racialised behaviours; the socialisation of children into white mores, white pastimes, white preferences, white mannerisms and of course, white employment. As Ellen Boucher has argued, 'the act of setting explicit standards about how children should be raised – what values they should exhibit, what identities they should perform – provided a powerful means to demarcate the boundaries of the nation'.[91] In the wake of the instability wrought upon the family unit by the Depression the Rhodesian state developed increasingly aggressive interventionist policies with regards to child welfare, including removing children from parents deemed unable to maintain white standards and placing them in institutions designed to mould proper white citizens.[92]

Youth had evocative imaginary power in the machinations of politicians and empire builders. It is no wonder workers leapt on to this powerful symbol that could invoke allusions to racial improvement and the future of white civilisation.[93] Certainly, youth had instrumental value in agitation for improved conditions in the workplace. Arguments for workers' compensation laws were often made through allusions to the breakdown of the family unit. Jonathan Malcolm of the RLP detailed how accidents and fatalities had seen white women enter the labour market, which meant children were left at home unattended and unable to complete their education. White children were 'compelled to enter the labour market insufficiently equipped and probably on an unskilled basis, and the daughters may be compelled to marry into a lower social scale than they were accustomed to'.[94] In the pages of the *Review* pictures of white children were captioned 'White Hopes of Rhodesia' and in its political cartoons the RRWU was often represented by a small white boy. This focus on the youth also alluded to a sense of permanence; these were *Rhodesian-born* youths, the first generation of whites born on Rhodesian soil. Trade unions used white children to self-identify as defenders of the vulnerable and innocent. When Keller's suggestion for hiring white youths in government posts was rejected he argued that this amounted to 'ousting white youth from the country'.[95] Keller invoked the figure of white homelessness and destitution, the death of white civilisation and spoke of betraying the white youth of the country who 'are standing helpless, one could almost say in the streets of our towns, and the government will not help them'.[96]

White women in the workforce

Fears of African progression into white jobs and of families falling into poverty also encouraged a temporary modification in attitudes towards white female participation in wage labour. The RRWU and RLP had consistently argued that women should stick to their 'natural roles' in the home as mothers and wives. White women in the workplace were an affront to masculinity. As one trade unionist put it, female wage labour endangered 'a most sacred law of nature that a father must provide food and all necessities of life for his family'. While single white women in wage labour proved less threatening, it was argued that married women should only take on formal employment in exceptional circumstances 'to keep the wolf "POVERTY" at a distance'.[97] Blame was usually directed at employers for the destruction of the family and of 'natural' roles, rather than the women workers themselves. Female employment was seen as just another way in which employers would attempt to undercut white male wages. Providing for dependants was figured as a privilege that reaffirmed the pride male labourers were expected to have in their work. But achieving white standards of living was the paramount concern: female employment, despite the subversion of idealised gender roles it entailed, could be accepted if it prevented the greater sin of poverty.

By 1930 the *Review* was including historical pieces on brave women workers and the oppressive conditions they toiled under in eighteenth- and nineteenth-century Europe and argued that the settler government should be finding employment for women.[98] In the same year the RRWU issued a special invitation for women to join the union, although this appeal reinforced women's roles as aiding and supporting men (Figure 10). The RLP became more vocal in its support for white women workers and criticised the low wages of women working in tea shops and restaurants.[99] Increasing fears of replacement by African workers saw the RRWU rally around the idea that white women should be used instead of Africans as drivers while the RLP argued for white 'girls' to replace Africans in service in white hostels.[100] These demands for white women to be hired as drivers demonstrate the intensity of white male fears of being undercut or replaced by Africans: women were not only encouraged to take on clerical or various feminised occupations but work that was traditionally deemed the sole pre- serve of white men. White female employment was the lesser evil. Not only were extra female wages becoming more necessary in cer- tain households to keep poverty at bay, but white labour organisations recognised that it would be much easier to push white women back

The Branch Secretary

Figure 10 'The branch secretary'

into the home than it would be to push Africans back into unskilled positions.

Notably, the number of white women who registered themselves as unemployed in 1936 was over eleven times more than the nine identified in 1921. This is explicable in part by the increased white female population in the colony, which had risen by around 75 per cent over the same period. But this insufficiently explains such a rise in unemployment statistics. Rather it demonstrates that more white women were actively looking for employment and considering them-selves as 'out of work'. During the Depression the proportion of eco-nomically active European women increased. In 1926 20 per cent of European women over the age of fifteen were in economically active occupations. In 1931 this had risen to 24.8 per cent, which represented 17.6 per cent of all economically active European persons (see Table 2 in Chapter 1). The Depression had propelled more white women into wage labour. Despite changing roles for white women traditional notions of white femininity persisted and the impact of unemploy-ment on white women was largely framed in terms of the breakdown of established gendered norms.

Yet the use of census data in this way can obscure certain types of work performed by white men and women. Doris Lessing recalled that during the 1930s 'desperately thin anxious young white men kept turning up on the farms, walking, to ask for jobs', while 'letters arrived from women *begging* to be allowed to look after children or come for a week to do the sewing'. In Lessing's family home, Mrs Mitchell, a white woman from a 'frightful level of poverty' who 'always smelled of spirits' was employed to 'help' her mother with daily tasks.[101] Lessing knew that Mrs Mitchell 'must have been desperate' to be hired as a nursemaid and housekeeper, perhaps widowed, deserted or perhaps escaping a brutal husband. It is likely that such instances of casual work often went unrecorded by the state. We know very little about such methods of generating income for the poorest or most vulner-able white women in Rhodesia; hidden by shame and its short-term, casual nature. What is evident, however, is that the reality of hunger and poverty among a layer of whites eradicated any strong aversion to performing 'black work'.

State backlash

In 1933 Wells declared that the 'real remedy' to unemployment was the 'clear recognition of the fact that there is very little scope in Southern Rhodesia for the semi-skilled artisan, and still less for the unskilled man', so-called 'unemployables'. The solution would be one in which 'these classes ... be reduced'.[102] Stricter immigration policies and better education for the whites already in the colony were deemed essential. Calls for unskilled work coupled with demands that whites be paid wages that enabled a 'white standard of living' were unsurprisingly dismissed by employers and the government. The colonial secretary argued that the type of jobs the RLP were agitating for white youths was 'blind alley employment', continuing that jobs such as domestic service seemed out of the question as white girls, let alone boys, were reluctant to lower themselves.[103] Government officials argued that when white men did these jobs they were by no means more efficient than Africans. In fact, because of white workers' prejudices, they failed to complete basic tasks. Harry Bertin, MP for Salisbury South, recalled his visit to Umtali to attend a political meeting. When he arrived he expressed astonishment that nobody seemed to know that the meeting was taking place. It was explained to him that a white boy had been tasked with the job of publicising the event and that he had regarded it as 'beneath him. He said that it was a piccanin's job and not one that he ought to do'.[104] Such pronouncements flew in the face of white workers' claims to an inherently higher productivity and efficiency.

In the view of many employers and politicians the white worker was the cause of his own predicament; he had been too forward, too proud, too antagonistic and had failed to recognise his natural role and status in society. It was white workers who had refused to work because they had overvalued their own wages, had expected to get paid because of their skin colour rather than their skill and had viciously campaigned against the African worker, who, in the words of one Rhodesia Party MP, at least had the propriety to know his proper place and worth in society. White workers in Rhodesia were nothing more than a class of delusional arrivistes who had erroneously invested in fantasies of unlimited social status and economic success. While white, they were still fundamentally workers, and should learn their place. The unionism and radicalism during the early 1920s that sought to establish this elevated status of white workers was now being paid for in full. Certainly after the fall of white labour strength 'troublemakers' were targeted in retrenchment schemes and the RRWU complained of the favouritism of railway management shown towards those Europeans who had worked during the railway 1929 strike.[105] Management utilised the retrenchment caused by the Depression to discipline its workforce and remove undesirable elements. At Wankie Colliery the reasons given for individual retrenchment included being less 'useful' than other members of staff as well as marital condition; it was reasoned that married men with dependants had greater need for employment.[106] Yet this also reflects the notion that those who had failed to attract a wife were ultimately less-desirable men in the eyes of Rhodesian society.

Furthermore, white workers' erroneous classification of particular white jobs as 'skilled' increasingly came under fire.[107] By no means a neutral observer, Alexander Thomson, Rhodesia Party MP from 1924, was particularly vocal on this issue. In his role as the general manager of Wankie Colliery from 1908 to 1933 Thomson had presided over an authoritarian regime and engaged in several brutal industrial disputes with his white and black employees. As Ian Phimister's research has detailed, Thomson set out to ruthlessly suppress trade unionism, break strikes and generally proved indifferent to the suffering of those he employed.[108]

As an MP, Thomson attacked the basis of white workers' claims to higher pay and pretensions to status. In the Legislative Assembly he argued that a bricklayer was classed as such even if he had 'only built fowl houses in Vrededorp with clay bricks with dagga for mortar', just as those listed as blacksmiths may have only had experience as drill sharpeners or anchor smiths.[109] The reference to Vrededorp, one of the poorest *fietas* in Johannesburg, reinforced the association of poverty and a lack of education with Afrikaners.[110] But importantly it challenged the self-identified skill and racial purity of many white workers. Employers faced problems in hiring whites in lower-grade jobs as they demanded pay equal to that received by fully trained miners despite their lower skill. If employers made the mistake of taking on such men, Thomson warned of 'continual trouble in regard to pay' and unionisation. Employers, he argued, 'would rather employ kaffirs on what may be considered white jobs, even if the latter were not very expert, rather than put up with the trouble to which they are exposed if they employ Europeans in any numbers'.[111]

White labour continually hit back at these denunciations. In a 1932 Select Committee on Unemployment, Keller once again recommended policies that would employ whites in road building, prohibit Africans from being employed as drivers on mechanically propelled transport and allocate all government posts to Europeans (apart from 'completely unskilled labour'). He also called for a review of building works and subsidising employers to hire non-African labourers. These suggestions were rejected by parliament: for being too expensive, for bringing whites into disrepute by performing menial tasks and ultimately for being unnecessarily extreme for the situation. Keller responded in his characteristically hyperbolic style and declared that if government policy was not immediately altered 'the conspiracy of silence, the deliberate suppression of the facts, and the minimising of the most terrible problem we have facing us, will conceivably lead men to the threat of revolution'.[112] While Keller normally strove to cultivate an image of a respectable and reserved white workforce who shunned radical militant excesses and Bolshevism, when white workers faced 'the most terrible problem', namely, the twin prongs of African competition and white unemployment, the representatives of white labour did not hesitate in drawing upon the language of violent upheaval and revolution. These actions were posed as necessary to save white civilisation itself.

Keller and the RLP continued to make impassioned speeches about the seriousness of white unemployment well into the late 1930s.[113] However, unemployment dwindled and was eventually offset by the wartime economy; by March 1940 there were only 450 persons on the register of the Employment Bureau, most between the ages of twenty-two and forty.[114] Widespread labour shortages and a lack of skilled white manpower became the pressing issue for white labour in the Second World War and continued to characterise the labour market during the remainder of white minority rule.

The 1934 Industrial Conciliation Act

The experience of the Depression precipitated the ascendancy of segregationist ideology. Under the leadership of Godfrey Huggins, the Reform Party moved towards preventing competition between white and African workers. While the 1920 Industrial Disputes Ordinance had set up the principle of arbitration within industry in response to the white radicalism of 1919 and 1920, the 1934 Industrial Conciliation Act (ICA) strengthened the principle of arbitration and limited the autonomy of white trade unions. It was passed in part as a response to a strike of European workers within the building industry who felt threatened by being replaced by African workers.[115] The ICA served a double function of protecting white workers from competition from African workers by effectively erecting a colour bar but also as a means to curb trade union power.[116] The ICA stated that trade union officials who refused to pass over information regarding their internal affairs to the minister of labour faced a £500 fine and/or two years imprisonment. Furthermore, the Act effectively prohibited strike action throughout the colony.[117]

Some trade unions such as the AEU proved supportive of the Act, but it was not universally well received.[118] While appreciative of the idea of the colour bar, the Act itself was regarded by the RRWU as a superfluous measure designed to restrict trade union power. It was also denounced as an inefficient response to prevent white unemployment.[119] The RRWU decried having to give their membership details over to the Registrar of the Act and opposed what they deemed to be unnecessary influence and meddling in their own private affairs.

Moreover, the principles of arbitration laid down in the Act referred to 'employees', thus omitting African workers from the Act's purview; 'employees' only referred to European workers. African workers remained under the jurisdiction of the draconian 1901 Masters and Servants Ordinance.[120] Harry Davies argued that it was a bill that administered the law 'upon differences of nationality or colour'. Thus the RLP accused the government of imposing a law based upon racial discrimination. If, Davies argued, Africans were to enter European industries, they must be 'paid a wage as a citizen to enable him to maintain life on a European basis'.[121] The RLP moved to amend the bill so that it included Africans under the term 'employee', which was rejected. The motivations behind admitting Africans under the definition of 'employee' emanated from pervasive fears of undercutting rather than solidarity.

The ICA has been interpreted as the incorporation of white workers into the Rhodesian community. Yet, these assertions tend to smooth over how the nature of this alliance was internally contested. This incorporation was not made on the terms dictated by white labour and neither did it precipitate the erasure of class division and antagonism.[122] It also failed to prevent Africans from entering skilled work. The remaining chapters will demonstrate how this process of assimilation of white workers into the settler body politic remained incomplete.

Conclusion

The ways in which racial identity was performed was neither uniform across the settler community, nor static and unchanging across the colonial period; markers of difference shifted and racial identities were reconfigured in response to particular circumstances. During the Depression fears of poor whiteism and anxieties around racial decline became central to the lived experience of white workers and a formative element in the expression of race. Racial identity was made *through work*. Yet heightened unemployment threatened to compromise the ways in which European workers performed their whiteness through removing the ability to provide for dependants and undermining their self-identification as the productive force behind empire. In response, in contrast to dominant interpretations of European attitudes to manual labour, white workers did not only fulfil certain menial manual jobs, but actively argued for them and attempted to invest this work with new meanings of pride and respectability.

The Great Depression did not unfold uniformly across colonial Africa. The experiences of European workers and the responses of various colonial states were diverse. In Kenya immigration restrictions largely prevented the emergence of a white social class dependent on wage labour, but the administration was still compelled to intervene and provide subsidies and loans to its white farmers, many of whom were forced to temporarily leave their farms.[123] Fewer than three hundred farmers were forced to leave permanently, but 'undesirable' whites, such as criminals, alcoholics or the long-term unemployed, could be repatriated as 'distressed British subjects'.[124] While deport-ation proved to be a preferred method for the authorities in Kenya and, as previously detailed, in Katanga, Southern Rhodesia adopted a more mixed strategy; the presence of white bodies was fundamental to the desired character of its settler colonial project and it followed a South African model in establishing work colonies and legislating greater pro-tection for white workers. Yet unlike South Africa, Southern Rhodesia never had to contend with the poor white problem on a large scale and as an ideological project it never functioned with the same signifi-cance in nationalist projects and state building. Through its restrictive immigration policies, the absence of a large white rural population and the ability to deport undesirables if necessary, Southern Rhodesian authorities were able to shape and discipline its white population with methods unfitted to the South African context.

In many ways, poor whiteism in Southern Rhodesia existed more as a moral panic, sharing many characteristics with the periodic Black Peril scares of southern Africa in the first half of the twentieth cen-tury. Just as the low rate of incidences and accusations of black men attacking or raping white women were disconnected from the high level of fear and press it generated, settler fears of poor whiteism were detached from the reality of white poverty in Southern Rhodesia. Such phenomena deserve attention precisely because of the disproportionate reactions they provoked.[125] As a transnational ideological construction, poor whiteism manifested itself differently not only across national contexts, but also across social groups. This episode demonstrates the varied responses of white social groups to the Depression, but also illustrates how discourses of poor whiteism and eugenics were not merely projected on to white workers and the white poor but were internalised, reproduced and challenged by the objects of these ideo-logical narratives.

Notes

1 Of course, such ambitions were not always realised in practice. In Northern Rhodesia the colonial administration's plans for African labour were hamstrung by poor financial resources and opposition from powerful mining interests. See Elena Berger, *Labour, Race and Colonial Rule: The Copperbelt from 1924 to Independence* (Oxford: Clarendon Press, 1974), pp. 19–41. See also Moses Ochono, *Colonial*

Meltdown, Northern Nigeria in the Great Depression (Athens: Ohio University Press, 2009).

2 Susan Parnell, 'Slums, Segregation and Poor Whites in Johannesburg, 1920–1934', in *White But Poor: Essays on the History of Poor Whites in Southern Africa, 1880–1940*, ed. Robert Morrell (Pretoria: University of South Africa, 1992), p. 127; Vivian Bickford-Smith, 'South African Urban History, Racial Segregation and the Unique Case of Cape Town?', *JSAS*, 21:1 (1995), pp. 63–78.

3 Bogumil Jewsiewicki, 'The Great Depression and the Making of the Colonial Economic System in the Belgian Congo', *African Economic History*, 4 (1977), pp. 153–176.

4 Roos, 'Work Colonies'.

5 See, for example, Saul Dubow, *Scientific Racism in Modern South Africa* (Cambridge, UK: Cambridge University Press, 1995); Grace Davie, *Poverty Knowledge in South Africa: A Social History of Human Science, 1855–2005* (New York: Cambridge University Press, 2015). Specifically for the role of poor whiteism in the genesis of the modern South African state and apartheid, see Dan O'Meara, *Volkskapitalisme: Class, Capital and Ideology in the Development of Afrikaner Nationalism, 1934–1948* (Cambridge, UK: Cambridge University Press, 1983).

6 Coates, *Convicts and Orphans*; Errante, 'White Skin, Many Masks'; Yedes, 'Social Dynamics'.

7 Giovanni Arrighi, 'The Political Economy of Rhodesia', *New Left Review*, 39 (1966), p. 37 (original emphasis).

8 Phillip Stigger, 'Minute Substance versus Substantial Fear: White Destitution and the Shaping of Policy in Rhodesia in the 1890s', in *White But Poor*, pp. 130–150.

9 'The Unemployment Problem', *RRR*, April 1934, p. 10.

10 Thus Stanlake Samkange asserts that 'Keller objected to Europeans performing any kind of manual labour'. 'History of the Rhodesia Labour Party', p. 30; Carol Summers, 'Boys, Brats and Education: Reproducing White Maturity in Colonial Zimbabwe, 1915–1935', *Settler Colonial Studies*, 1:1 (2011), pp. 132–153.

11 Kennedy, *Islands of White*, p. 153.

12 For the process of restricting white workers' employment in unskilled work in South Africa, see Davies, 'Mining Capital'.

13 See chap. 4 in Phimister, *Economic and Social History*.

14 Nicoli Nattrass and Jeremy Seekings, *The Economy and Poverty in the Twentieth Century in South Africa* (Cape Town: Centre for Social Science Research, 2010), p. 8.

15 Stigger, 'Minute Substance', p. 137.

16 The average number of unemployed men from March to December 1922 was 281.8. From January to September 1923 this decreased to 268.1. Fred Eyles, *Southern Rhodesia Report Upon the Census Taken on 3rd May 1921* (Salisbury, Rhodesia: Government Printers, 1922), p. 17. In 1921 the census recorded 216 males and nine females as unemployed. On 31 October 1922 and 1923 records showed forty four and fifty five as employed on relief works respectively. NAZ: S480/95 C.H. Berger's Records of Unemployment; 'Editorial', *RRR*, December 1931, p. 15.

17 Lunn, *Rhodesian Railway*, p. 125.

18 *RRR*, December 1932, p. 14.

19 This figure has been reached through estimating the number of adult European males in 1933 at 21,000 by averaging the number of European males over the age of fifteen from the 1931 and 1936 censuses.

20 G. E. Wells, *Report on Unemployment and the Relief of Destitution in Southern Rhodesia* (Salisbury, Rhodesia: Government Printers, 1934), p. 8.

21 These figures represent only those who stated they were out of work in a particular industry. It has ignored the statistics on the economically active and inactive as well as the elderly and the independently self-sufficient. *Census of Population, 1936* (Salisbury, Rhodesia: Department of Statistics, 1943).

22 Lunn, *Rhodesian Railway*, p. 125.

23 Roos, 'Work Colonies'.

24 Wells, *Report on Unemployment*, p. 7.
25 Phimister, *Economic and Social History*, p. 93.
26 Samkange, 'Rhodesia Labour Party', pp. 4, 17.
27 See Passmore *et al.*, *Source Book of Parliamentary Elections*.
28 *Debates of the Legislative Assembly* (Southern Rhodesia: Government Printer, 1932), p. 412.
29 Edward Higgs, 'Fingerprints and Citizenship: The British State and the Identification of Pensioners in the Interwar Period', *History Workshop Journal*, 69:1 (2010), pp. 52–67.
30 'Plight of the Workless', *RRR*, December 1931, p. 19.
31 *Debates of the Legislative Assembly*, 1932, pp. 1815, 431.
32 Universities National Bureau, 'The Measurement and Behaviour of Unemployment', *National Bureau of Economic Research*, 1957, http://core.ac.uk/download/pdf/6871122.pdf, p. 215 (accessed 5 November 2019); James Denman and Paul McDonald, Labour Market Statistics Group Central Statistical Office, 'Unemployment Statistics from 1881 to the Present Day', *Labour Market Trends*, 104 (1996), p. 6.
33 Lowry, 'Rhodesia 1890–1980'.
34 NASA: 117/74 Southern and Northern Rhodesia Immigration Law, Volume 2, 'Letter from Office of the Chief Immigration Officer, Bulawayo, 15 May 1929, to the Commissioner for Immigration and Asiatic affairs, Pretoria'.
35 NASA: 117/74 Southern and Northern Rhodesia Immigration Law, Volume 2, 'Letter from Hendrik David Verheen', 30 November 1929.
36 *Ibid.*, 'Letter from Premier's Office, Southern Rhodesia', 20 March 1930.
37 NASA: P.M. 93/64.
38 *Debates of the Legislative Assembly* (Southern Rhodesia: Government Printer, 1933), pp. 336, 347.
39 Morrell, *White But Poor*.
40 Saul Dubow, 'Race, Civilisation and Culture: The Elaboration of Segregationist Discourse in the Inter-War Years', in *The Politics of Race, Class and Nationalism in Twentieth Century South Africa*, ed. Shula Marks and Stanley Trapido (New York: Longman, 1987), pp. 71–94; Ann Laura Stoler, *Carnal Knowledge and Imperial Power: Race and the Intimate in Colonial Rule* (Berkeley: University of California Press, 2010).
41 Wells, *Report on Unemployment*, pp. 24–25.
42 *Debates of the Legislative Assembly* (Southern Rhodesia: Government Printer, 1934), p. 1831.
43 Wells, *Report on Unemployment*, p. 26.
44 Lee, *Unreasonable Histories*.
45 Karen Jochelson, *The Colour of Disease: Syphilis and Racism in South Africa 1880–1950* (Oxford: Palgrave in Association with St Anthony's College, 2001), p. 57.
46 Wells, *Report on Unemployment*, p. 14.
47 *Ibid.*, p. 2.
48 'The Story of a Crime', *RRR*, January 1925, p. 19. See also *Debates of the Legislative Assembly*, 1932, p. 421.
49 Harald Fischer-Tiné '"The Drinking Habits of Our Countrymen": European Alcohol Consumption and Colonial Power in British India', *Journal of Imperial and Commonwealth History*, 40:3 (2012), pp. 383–408.
50 Jonathan Hyslop, 'Undesirable Inhabitant of the Union … Supplying Liquor to Natives: D. F. Malan and the Deportation of South Africa's British and Irish Lumpen Proletarians 1924–1933', *Kronos*, 40 (2014), pp. 178–197; Neil Roos, 'Alcohol Panic, Social Engineering, and Some Reflections on the Management of Whites in Early Apartheid Society, 1948–1960', *Historical Journal*, 58:4 (2015), pp. 1167–1189.
51 Anderson, *Toe-Rags*, p. 205.
52 *Ibid.*, p. 151.

53 On repatriation, see John Lonsdale, 'Kenya: Home County and African Frontier', in *Settlers and Expatriates: Britons Over the Seas*, ed. Robert Bickers (Oxford: Oxford University Press, 2010), p. 87; and Will Jackson, 'Poor Men and Loose Women: The Poor White Problem in Kenya Colony', *Journal of Colonialism and Colonial History*, 14:2 (2013).

54 'Editorial', *RRR*, June 1932, p. 9.

55 Lawrence Vambe, *From Rhodesia to Zimbabwe* (London: Heinemann, 1976), pp. 58–59.

56 Hoare, *Rhodesian Mosaic*, p. 66. See also Frank Clements, *Rhodesia: The Course to Collision* (London: Pall Mall Press, 1969), p. 52.

57 Despite the dominance of migrant labour systems the number of Africans permanently settling in towns and mining centres was increasing. Nevertheless, the image of an inherently rural African workforce remained potent. Not only did it fit into companies' interests to continue paying single men's wages, it enabled the government to ignore African unemployment. For some responses of Africans to the economic crisis, see Wolfgang Dopcke, '"Magomo's Maize": State and Peasants During the Depression in Colonial Zimbabwe', in *The Economies of Africa and Asia in the Inter-War Depression*, ed. Ian Brown (London: Routledge, 1989), pp. 29–58.

58 *Debates of the Legislative Assembly*, 1932, p. 419.

59 Brett Shadle, *The Souls of White Folk: White Settlers in Kenya, 1900s–1920s* (Manchester: Manchester University Press, 2015).

60 'A Sufferer', 'Letters to the Editor: A Complaint Against the Native', *RRR*, July 1933, p. 21.

61 On prestige, see Kennedy, *Islands of White*; Shadle, *Souls of White Folk*.

62 *Debates of the Legislative Assembly*, 1933, p. 873.

63 See Allison K. Shutt, '"The Natives Are Getting Out of Hand": Legislating Manners, Insolence and Contemptuous Behaviour in Southern Rhodesia, c.1910–1963', *JSAS*, 33:3 (2007), pp. 653–672.

64 Philippa Levine, 'States of Undress: Nakedness and the Colonial Imagination', *Victorian Studies*, 50:2 (2008), pp. 189–219.

65 'The Unemployment Problem: Full Reports of Labour Members Speeches', *RRR*, April 1934, pp. 9–16.

66 *Debates of the Legislative Assembly*, 1934, p. 1818.

67 'Men Without Hope', *RRR*, May 1932, p. 7.

68 Wells, *Report on Unemployment*, p. 1.

69 'Editorial', *RRR*, June 1932, p. 9.

70 Phimister, *Economic and Social History*, p. 190.

71 Sabelo J. Ndlovu-Gutsheni, 'Mapping Cultural and Colonial Encounters, 1880s–1930s', in *Becoming Zimbabwe*, p. 71; 'Inyazura Branch Notes', *RRR*, March 1928, p. 28.

72 See West, *African Middle Class*, pp. 39–40.

73 Van Short, 'A "Lay"ette for the Labour Triplets', *RRR*, December 1928, p. 21.

74 In Bulawayo a Vigilante's Association emerged in 1932 with stated aims to protect white women. Ranger, *Bulawayo Burning*, p. 67.

75 See *RRR*, March 1928, p. 28; *RRR*, December 1928, p. 21.

76 'Editorial', *RRR*, July 1932, p. 9

77 Vambe, *Rhodesia to Zimbabwe*, p. 165.

78 Llewellyn P. Raaf, 'Outrages on White Women', *RRR*, March 1932, pp. 36–37.

79 Bob Challiss, 'Education and Southern Rhodesia's Poor Whites, 1890–1930', in *White But Poor*, pp. 151–170; Summers, *Civilization to Segregation*, pp. 178–180.

80 'A Policy of Segregation', *RRR*, June 1934, p. 27.

81 See Jeremy Seekings, '"Not a Single White Person Should Be Allowed to go Under": Swartgevaar and South Africa's Welfare State, 1924–1929', *Journal of African History*, 48 (2007), pp. 375–394.

82 This point was made by educational legislators during the same period. See Summers, 'Boys, Brats'.

83 *Minutes of the 1930 RRWU Conference*, pp. 195–196.
84 *Debates of the Legislative Assembly*, 1933, p. 382. Summers notes that manual agricultural training for white youths was rejected by the settler population who demanded more academic schooling, but overlooks that while the RLP may have rejected agricultural manual work, manual labour in the towns was regarded in a different light. Summers, 'Boys, Brats', pp. 145–146.
85 *Debates of the Legislative Assembly*, 1933, p. 368.
86 *Minutes of the 1930 RRWU Conference*, p. 196.
87 Wells, *Report on Unemployment*, pp. 10–11.
88 *Ibid.*, p. 12.
89 Ellen Boucher, *Empire's Children: Child Emigration, Welfare and the Decline of the British World, 1869–1967* (Cambridge, UK: Cambridge University Press, 2014), p. 6.
90 Fiona Paisley, 'Childhood and Race: Growing up in the Empire', in *Gender and Empire* ed. Philippa Levine (Oxford: Oxford University Press, 2004), p. 251.
91 Boucher, *Empire's Children*, p. 13.
92 Ivo Mhike, 'Intersections of Sexual Delinquency and Sub-Normality: White Female Juvenile Delinquency in Southern Rhodesia, 1930s–c.1950', *Settler Colonial Studies*, 8:4 (2018), pp. 575–593.
93 Boucher, *Empire's Children*; Rebecca Swartz, *Education and Empire: Children, Race and Humanitarianism in the British Settler Colonies, 1833–1880* (Basingstoke: Palgrave, 2019).
94 'Workers and Compensation Laws', *RRR*, June 1929, p. 17.
95 *Debates of the Legislative Assembly*, 1933, p. 367.
96 *Ibid.*, p. 368.
97 Hugh Killeen, 'Female Unemployment', *RRR*, November 1921, p. 35.
98 'Women Workers of the Past', *RRR*, December 1930, p. 55.
99 'Tackling Unemployment Problems', *RRR*, November 1933, p. 11.
100 *Debates of the Legislative Assembly*, 1933, pp. 374–375.
101 Lessing, *Under My Skin*, pp. 129, 65–66.
102 Wells, *Report on Unemployment*, pp. 3–4.
103 *Debates of the Legislative Assembly*, 1933, pp. 865–868.
104 *Ibid.*, p. 871.
105 Headquarters of the Zimbabwe Amalgamated Railwaymen's Union Bulawayo, *Minutes of the 1933 RRWU Conference* (Bulawayo: RRWU, 1933), pp. 6–7.
106 NAZ: S480/1460 Copy of Letter to Mr Keller, 11 February 1929, p. 1.
107 See General F. D. Hammond, *Report on the Railway System of Southern Rhodesia, Under the 'Railways Enquiry Act, 1924'* (Salisbury, Rhodesia: Government Printer, 1925).
108 See Ian Phimister, *Wangi Kolia: Coal, Capital and Labour in Colonial Zimbabwe, 1894–1954* (Johannesburg: University of Witwatersand Press, 1994).
109 *Debates of the Legislative Assembly*, 1933, p. 353.
110 Oluwadamilola Okunlola, 'Memories of Fietas from the Late 50s to the 70s', in *Oral History: Representing the Hidden, the Untold and the Veiled*, ed. Christina Landman (Pretoria: University of South Africa, 2013), pp. 65–83.
111 *Debates of the Legislative Assembly*, 1934, p. 1825.
112 'Is Government Serious About Unemployment?', *RRR*, June 1932, pp. 18–19.
113 *Debates of the Legislative Assembly* (Southern Rhodesia: Government Printer, 1939), p. 829.
114 *Debates of the Legislative Assembly* (Southern Rhodesia: Government Printer, 1940), p. 1958.
115 See Max Jerry Mutyavaviri, 'Labour Legislation in Zimbabwe in Historical Perspective' (unpublished doctoral thesis, University of Zimbabwe, 1989), p. 190.
116 See Phimister, 'White Miners'.
117 'The Conciliation Bill', *RRR*, March 1934, p. 19.
118 Lunn, *Rhodesian Railway*, p. 102.

119 'Editorial', *RRR*, March 1934, p. 6.
120 See Phimister, *Economic and Social History* and van Onselen, *Chibaro* for details.
121 *Debates of the Legislative Assembly*, 1934, p. 96.
122 Lunn, *Rhodesian Railway*, pp. 10–11.
123 David Anderson and David Throup, 'The Agrarian Economy of Central Province, Kenya, 1918–1939', in *The Economies of Africa and Asia in the Inter-War Depression*, ed. Ian Brown (London: Routledge, 1989), p. 12.
124 Lowry, 'Rhodesia 1890–1980', p. 139.
125 Jock McCulloch. *Black Peril, White Virtue: Sexual Crime in Southern Rhodesia, 1902–1935* (Indiana: Bloomington, 2000).

CHAPTER THREE

The Second World War

The Second World War was not simply a European conflict, but a global, and specifically imperial, struggle.[1] Over half a million African troops from various dependencies fought for Britain during the war.[2] Yet in Southern Rhodesia the notion of training Africans how to use guns unnerved settlers who held on to perennial fears of rebellion against white rule. The total number of African males on full-time service was 15,153; but only 1,505 of them ever served outside Southern Rhodesia's borders. Despite settler attempts to shield Africans from potentially radicalising influences, the war created conditions that precipitated widespread African challenges to white authority. Certainly, the Second World War is usually noted as a watershed moment in the history of sub-Saharan Africa, a period of social, economic and political change that ushered in an era of mass nationalism and signalled moves towards the ending of European colonial empires across Africa.[3] In Southern Rhodesia settlers were able to prevent majority rule for another thirty-five years, but they proved less successful in their efforts to curtail African dissent, frustrate African trade unions, stem the rise of an African middle class or prevent African movement into towns and cities.[4]

Capitalism is a dynamic system. Class formations are continually reshaped by changes in capitalism as some industries decline in importance and newer ones take their place. This process brings new layers of workers into wage labour while discarding others.[5] The Rhodesian workforce was continually restructured by new demands created by emerging industries. These changes disrupted the ways in which particular occupations were understood as racialised and gendered categories, as well as broader class formations and identities. Across the period of minority rule, men and women of white British, white non-British, Coloured and African racial groups fought to variously challenge or uphold racialised and gendered patterns of recruitment, wages and working conditions. The ability of particular groups to challenge the status of particular occupations, skill grades and industries as white, black, male or female work relied on the interplay between settler ideologies, the demands of Rhodesian industry and the struggles of particular social groups within these processes.

While settler agriculture and mining had benefited from migrant labour systems, the Second World War stimulated the expansion of secondary industries that generally held a marked preference for stabilised African workforces as the import of foreign goods was disrupted.[6] In Southern Rhodesia manufacturing established itself as the second most important source of national income by the late 1940s. The number of factories increased from 294 in 1939 to 473 in 1948 and the gross output of these factories grew from £5.4 million to £25.8 million over the same period. By 1946 out of a total of 368,000 black wage labourers, 183,000 were employed as industrial workers.[7] In South Africa the proliferation of new semi-skilled positions in manufacturing threatened the racialised legal classification of 'skilled' and 'unskilled' work. Black, Coloured and white female workers – referred to as 'dilutees' – were increasingly used in semi-skilled work, particularly in factories, as employers proved reluctant to hire relatively expensive white men. As Nancy Clark has demonstrated, previous labour policies that sought to plot race to skill (and therefore wages and working conditions) were put under considerable strain.[8]

Part 1 of the chapter explores the Coloured and non-British white men and white women who entered the labour force during this period, as well as those white male workers of British descent who stayed behind during the war. White British workers' loyalty to empire and the war effort was tested as working conditions deteriorated and as they felt their dominance over urban spaces and semi-skilled work erode. When white British men reluctantly accepted they could no longer maintain their monopoly over certain occupational categories fierce debates erupted over the desirability of particular racialised and gendered groups. Britishness remained a central component of discriminatory hiring practices. Yet employers and white British male workers held conflicting ideas over the desirability of hiring particular racial others to ease skilled labour deficits. These debates reveal how hierarchies of race and nation sometimes uneasily overlapped as trade unionists discussed if a non-white Coloured, who was a British subject, was more or less desirable than a white, but non-British, European.[9]

The problem was partly one of classification. For Zygmunt Bauman, modernity is characterised by its drive to unambiguously classify, categorise, order and segregate. Yet the complexity of everyday life regularly evades such straightforward classification; ambivalence continually threatens modernity's zeal for orderliness. Ambivalence, according to Bauman, 'is the acute discomfort we feel when we are unable to read the situation properly and to choose between alternative actions. It is because of the anxiety that accompanies it and the indecision which follows that we experience ambivalence as a disorder ... as discomfort and a threat'.[10] In Rhodesia both Coloureds and non-British whites were sources of anxiety and discomfort among settlers because they repeatedly defied simple categorisation in colonial epistemologies. Imperial and colonial historians have stressed the incompleteness of colonial knowledge and argued that colonial structures repeatedly failed to fix static categorisation to complex and fluid political and social relationships.[11] This failure of colonial classification, I argue, resulted in the systematic production of *racial ambivalence*. For white workers this ambivalence expressed itself in confusion over how racial hierarchies worked in practice and pervasive fears that their ability to perform racial difference was under threat.

These debates over who should perform different types of work reveal the often arbitrary and imprecise character of race, but also point to a relative fluidity in how white women's femininity was conceptualised and instrumentalised by white worker organisations. Attitudes towards white female wage labour were shifting globally. In the United States and the United Kingdom the Second World War has received considerable attention as a period of transformation for women as they entered the workforce in record numbers and in more diverse occupations than ever before.[12] Southern Rhodesia provides an interesting point of comparison with these trends. While white women did enter the workforce in greater numbers, there was not a notable shift towards women performing 'male work' and women remained in traditional 'feminine' occupations. Alongside interrogating how the war impacted upon gendered patterns of employment, this chapter looks at white women's unequal treatment in the workplace, the resistance offered up by white women regarding their conditions of employment and the ways in which they were policed and encouraged to remain in the home.

Part 2 of the chapter shifts focus to white workers' attitudes towards perceived and actual threats posed by African urbanisation, class differentiation and trade union militancy. Notably, the chapter demonstrates that white workers were not universally hostile to African strikes. Duncan Money has shown that on the Copperbelt the attitudes and actions of white miners towards African strikes varied between indifference, aggression and encouragement.[13] In Southern Rhodesia, taken off guard, white workers' responses to African militancy were confused and inconsistent. Reactions to the 1945 railway strike and 1948 general strike reflect a tortured combination of support for workers' rights and racial supremacy.

There had been somewhat of a resurgence in effective white trade union organisation on the mines as the South African Mine Workers' Union had decided to extend its membership to Southern and Northern Rhodesia in 1937, which led to the formation of the Associated Mine Workers of Rhodesia (AMWR).[14] Both the AMWR and RRWU failed to reach a consensus over the best ways to pacify African challenges to their own status, in particular, emerging African trade unions. The RLP and newly formed Southern Rhodesia Labour Party (SRLP) were also bitterly divided between themselves over the question of African inclusion in their organisations. Responses to African urbanisation, in contrast, consisted of much more straightforward denunciations and acted to articulate broader fears regarding the precarious position of white workers and their perceptions of a fixed and ahistorical African 'nature'. Africans concentrated in towns and cities, particularly the unemployed and ascendant middle classes, increasingly became the locus for a number of fears regarding 'detribalisation' and the breakdown of traditional African social structures.

In *The Souls of Black Folk* W. E. B. Du Bois wrote that black Americans were

> born with a veil, and gifted with second sight in this American world – a world which yields him no true self-consciousness, but only lets him see himself through the revelation of the other world. It is a peculiar sensation, this double-consciousness, this sense of always looking at one's self through the eyes of others, of measuring one's soul by the tape of a world that looks on in amused contempt and pity.[15]

African Americans' experiences of racism shaped their identities, thoughts and perspectives of themselves; but this 'second sight' also involved a marginalised positionality that gave them a unique insight into American society writ large and white folk in particular. Historians of African settler colonialism have increasingly drawn upon Du Bois's writings in this regard. Following Brett Shadle's work on Kenyan settlers, Part 2 shifts focus to African perceptions of settlers, as well as the acute awareness of settlers to this gaze, in order to understand how racial ideologies were internalised, experienced and shaped daily interactions and relationships.[16] I argue that Africans observed status, rank and class differentiation among settlers and provided damning assessments of low-class whites. White workers' responses to this African gaze were characterised by a mixture of violence, venom and humiliation.

Part 1 Conditional nationalism, racial ambivalence and white womanhood

White workers' war nationalism

In *The Myth of the Blitz* Angus Calder argues that British wartime propaganda popularised the idea that Britain was captured by a uniform national spirit and shared experience of war that obscured the reality of widespread social antagonism, inequality and suffering across Britain in the 1940s.[17] Wartime propaganda and the public memorialisation of the war in Southern Rhodesia likewise masked existing social tensions by presenting an image of nationalist fervour and a burden willingly and equally shared. The war provided ample opportunity for settlers to proclaim their loyalty to Britain and empire. Southern Rhodesia proportionately volunteered more white men for the war than any other territory in the empire including Britain. European males on full-time service from 1939 to 1945 totalled 9,187; 6,520 of which served outside of the colony.[18] By late 1942, 52 per cent of the European male population between eighteen and forty were serving or had already done so.[19] It was a sacrifice that Rhodesians would draw upon in later years to emphasise the 'betrayal' of the British state.[20]

Those left behind to work in Rhodesia's industries and services saw themselves as central to the war effort. The symbolism of war and nationalist notions of sacrifice, duty and loyalty became a potent device in white worker agitation as well as curbing those demands.[21] While in 1940 Davies and Keller warned against docility and an acceptance of current conditions, arguing that capitalistic greed would not bow its head, Keller's opening speech to the 1942 RRWU conference spoke of 'non-cooperators and conscientious objectors in our own ranks', whom he accused of sabotaging the war effort.[22] This was in part due to the involvement of Keller and Davies in the national war government from 1940, but also because conscientious objectors defied the image of the patriotic white worker and proclamations of Keller and Davies that men would 'gladly' volunteer and submit themselves. Moreover, the Soviet Union had become a British ally in 1941, dampening left-wing opposition to the war in Britain. When a small number of men refused to comply with manpower investigations Keller threatened that if there was 'a worker who thinks he should be privileged any more than the soldier fighting for him' he should re-evaluate his position 'before they all have cause for regrets'.[23]

Nevertheless, white worker demands were not tempered by a sense of duty. The RRWU forced the railway administration into arbitration in 1942 and members felt as though the war was being used as an excuse by employers to refuse to meet their demands.[24] Both Northern and Southern Rhodesian governments had to intervene to prevent escalating action on behalf of RRWU when they reached an impasse with the railway administration and agreed to set up a body to look into railwaymen's demands.[25] Long hours remained a key point of contention. In May 1944 drivers, firemen and guards could work anywhere between 63 and 74.7 hours per week.[26] Occupational divisions resurfaced as many manual workers felt they carried an unequal share of the increased wartime workload. The RRWU complained that while clerks enjoyed time off, manual workers were 'likely to be kept "going to it" until the point of complete exhaustion is reached'.[27] The AMWR cheered successful strikes in South Africa and hinted at the possibility of repeats in Southern Rhodesia.[28] Mine workers were dismayed when Leslie Smith, who had won a by-election in 1943 for the RLP, was dismissed by Shabanie mine upon being elected to parliament. Uproar in the AMWR saw the *Granite Review* accuse mine management of being Nazis and warned that mine workers had not ruled out strike action.[29] The arrest of Northern Rhodesia Mine Workers' Union General Secretary Frank Maybank, incarcerated for 'subversive activities' and leading a strike of white miners, elicited widespread condemnation from white trade unionists in Southern Rhodesia.[30] Loyalty to the war effort, it seemed, did not supersede loyalty to other white British workers.

Moreover, support for the war itself was not always evident. The *Granite Review* repeatedly printed material from a female anti-war group. One article urged white women not to 'wait for the men' to act, and lamented the devastation wrought by war.[31] Perhaps such outright anti-war sentiment would have emasculated the union proper, who maintained a professed loyalty to the war cause and expressed the joy to be had in serving the empire. White women, however, could agitate on the basis of the death of children through bombing, and of husbands and sons in the fields. Associating anti-war sentiment with women safeguarded against accusations of cowardice and effeminacy. Yet proclamations of loyalty to the war effort in the *Granite Review* sat uneasily beside the inclusion of anti-war material and the threat of strike action.

The war also provoked wider concerns about the broader loyalties of white workers. Although the RRWU and AMWR liberally applied the word 'fascist' to anyone who disagreed with them, it was clear that they were having trouble within their own ranks with Nazi-sympathisers. Despite the *Review* regularly containing articles about the anti-working-class and anti-trade union dimension of fascism, up until the outbreak of war they repeatedly printed pro-Nazi material submitted by their union members. Only in 1938 did the *Review* state it would not print pro-Nazi letters.[32] Yet considering the pervasiveness of racial ideologies and notions of inherent difference and superiority, it is not entirely surprising that ideologies of the *Herrenvolk* appealed to a layer of white workers. Opposition to fascism seems to have come out of the recognition of the anti-working-class and anti-democratic basis of fascism as well as nationalist feeling towards Britain, rather than outright hostility to the racial element of Nazism.

Allies, enemies and refugees: non-British whites, Coloureds and racial hierarchies in the workplace

Britain's imperial and colonial ties were fundamental to her wartime economy and military strategy. From the outset Rhodesia threw herself behind the war effort, not least because settlers defined themselves through notions of sacrifice, duty and loyalty to empire. Over ten thousand men were stationed in Southern Rhodesia as part of the Empire Air Training Scheme (see Figures 11 and 12). While most RAF recruits were British, they also consisted of Rhodesians, South Africans, Australians, Greeks and Frenchmen.[33] British newcomers were initially excitedly welcomed by more established settlers, but new arrivals quickly became a source of panic. In particular those of working-class origin were singled out as failing to conform to Rhodesian standards of white behaviour. Hylda Richards remarked of the RAF men arriving that they failed to meet

> the obligations of the white man in a black country. They cat-called after our Rhodesian girls, and when repulsed, fraternised with Coloureds and natives. We old settlers had brought up our children to believe that England was a wonderful country, and the English a wonderful race ... When our sons saw these under-privileged, under-nourished, under-educated lads with their bad teeth and bad manners, they were aghast and when they saw them with the Coloureds and the natives they were horrified.[34]

One white woman interviewed in 2016 recalled that her mother had repeated that the men from the RAF who settled in Rhodesia were commonly known as 'the riff raff'.[35] Many white settlers' 'British values' were those of an idealised middle-class rural England. Deprived and unrefined, these working-class men failed to conform to their fantasies of Britishness. In her semi-autobiographical novel, *A Proper Marriage*, Lessing conveyed this sense of racial and national betrayal felt by white settlers as British soldiers arrived in the colony. For Rhodesians

Figure 11 Making Christmas pudding, RAF Hillside

'it was their own people they were expecting – and more: themselves, at one remove, and dignified by responsibility and danger'. Yet those who arrived were

> a race of beings in thick, clumsy greyish uniforms; and from these ill-fitting cases of cloth emerged pallid faces and hands which had – to people who above all always had enough to eat and plenty of sunshine – a look of incompleteness ... they could not own these ancestors; their cousins from Home were a race of dwarfs, several inches shorter than themselves. They were not burnt and brown, but unhealthy and pale.[36]

Notably, both Richards's and Lessing's observations on the disjuncture between established Rhodesians and working-class Britons utilised the language of racial degeneration and renewal. These descriptions categorised newly arrived Britons as unhealthy elements of the white race. Yet the stated problem was not only one of a defunct racial physicality, but also one of a defective white *mentality*. Certainly, it appeared that most new arrivals had failed to understand the appropriate forms of interaction:

> Several innocent men had brought Coloured women into the bars of an evening, and had violently resented being asked to leave. Others were observed offering black men cigarettes on street corners, while talking to

Figure 12 RAF men at Cecil Rhodes's grave

them, or even walking with them. It was rumoured that quite a number of them had actually gone into the homes of servants of the city, in the native location.[37]

Despite evidence of fraternisation and sexual relationships between British arrivals, Coloureds and Africans, liberal racial attitudes were by no means uniformly adopted by the soldiers and there were numerous reports of rape and sexual harassment of black women by British men.[38] Middle-class Rhodesians such as Richards felt compelled to note their outrage but it appears white labour generally turned a blind eye to the transgressions of their British counterparts. While in the *Herald*, concerned Rhodesian citizens complained about the visibility of drunken RAF recruits staggering in the streets of Salisbury, the RRWU defended their drinking and excesses. Furthermore, they denounced Prime Minister Huggins's intervention and perceived meddling in the affairs of the RAF.[39]

Of greater concern to the RRWU was the growing presence of non-British whites. The war led white workers into complex, and often inconclusive, discussions regarding the desirability of particular non-British workers. Historians have largely explained white worker hostility towards foreign Europeans through economic competition and the fear of being undercut.[40] While this is an important factor, it only partially explains white worker antipathy towards non-British whites. Manual workers, already aware of their own low status and the stereotypes associated with them, did not want their respectability further compromised through having to defend themselves against association with the dominant derogatory stereotypes of national 'others'. The myth of British superiority was willingly accepted by many white workers who believed that their own work was of a higher quality to that performed by other nationalities and ethnicities. Xenophobia, nationalism and the confusion created by the racial interdeterminancy posed by these social groups combined with material concerns of undercutting on a racially stratified labour market.

Hostility towards non-British groups generally intensified during the war period. There was suspicion of Afrikaners harbouring pro-German attitudes despite the absence of overtly pro-Nazi Afrikaner groups such as the Broederbond or Ossewabrandwag that existed in South Africa.[41] Some Afrikaners refused to fight for the Allied forces. Others were prepared to defend Rhodesia, but proved unwilling to declare allegiance to the British Empire. Those who refused to submit to Rhodesian authorities were coerced into forced labour and had their rights severely restricted: they lost their voting rights, all opportunities of government employment and government financial assistance

Figure 13 Women marching at RAF base at Hillside

and were sometimes forced to endure humiliating punishments.[42] Beyond the war anti-Afrikaner sentiment did not entirely dissipate; an immigration report in 1949 was alarmed that Afrikaner immigration had 'increased unduly' and that some of this number may have been South African Nationalist Party sympathisers. Immigration officials estimated that Afrikaners accounted for one-third of the white population.[43] As a largely rural population, Afrikaners were not looked upon as a particular threat within the labour market by other white workers. Yet, Afrikaners were seen as particularly uneducated and apathy to the RLP in at least one district was explained through noting the 'preponderant Afrikaner vote, a vote which is particularly difficult to educate'.[44]

While the presence of those involved in the RAF training scheme was contested among established settlers, the presence of refugees and enemy internees provoked more straightforward denunciations. A total of over 12,000 German, Austrian and Italians were interned in Southern Rhodesia as well as 1,624 Polish refugees who were put into camps across the colony at Gatooma (Kadoma), Fort Victoria, Salisbury, Tanganyika and Umvuma (Mvuma).[45] Doris Lessing had become an alien by her marriage to Gottfried Lessing, a German refugee, and as a result had to report to the Alien's Office once a week. Her fingerprints were taken and restrictions placed on her movement. Anything fifty miles beyond Salisbury was off limits without express permission of the Rhodesian state, although she admitted that this was not rigorously enforced.[46] Italians were treated with considerable suspicion and were accused of harbouring pro-fascist sympathies while the Polish were associated with the equally undesirable Jewishness and communism. When Communist Party recruitment propaganda surfaced in the colony it was blamed upon the increasing presence of 'newcomers'. Most disturbingly, as one letter to the *Herald* argued, this propaganda embodied 'the dangerous peculiarities of the communistic thinkers ... they are firm believers in equality of race and colour'.[47]

The Rhodesian Communist Party, with no official links to the Soviet Union, existed for around eighteen months. By Lessing's accounts, a few of the members were Rhodesian trade unionists; others were working-class RAF recruits, such as Frank Cooper, 'a cockney [whose] hatred of the middle and upper classes was expressed perfectly in communism'. There were also some non-British Europeans among their number. The group had attempted to get in touch with leading black trade unionists including Joshua Nkomo but failed to make any headway. Outside of this semi-formal party there was a group of communists in the RAF camp comprised mostly of the ground crew, but they were mostly working class and did not invite Lessing or the pilots recruited from Cambridge and Harrow who they saw as 'luxurious and privileged'.[48]

Fears around political subversion combined with xenophobia so that non-British whites were imagined both as racist fascists out to exterminate and enslave and sexually promiscuous communists hell-bent on equality and multiracial orgies. Anxieties concerning the lax sexual morals of new arrivals were confirmed when Polish women living in Tanganyika refugee camp were found to be having sex with the African servants that had been provided for them. Lawrence Vambe went as far as to describe the female camp as 'an unofficial brothel'.[49] White women's relationships with black men and their presence in African locations was seen as having deleterious effects upon African minds, with the potential to stir up a frenzy of Black Peril.[50] As detailed in Graph 4, Polish women were the only European national group with more women than men in the colony. This in itself may have caused concern over unattended women existing outside of male control. The women were relocated to a camp in Gatooma, their perceived indiscretions dealt with much more severely than those of the RAF men who went around openly with African women. This reflected the relative power of British RAF men in comparison to female Polish refugees, but also wider attitudes towards interracial sex: white men having sex with black women was regarded as a lesser sin than white women sleeping with African men.

Debates over whether to let internees and refugees remain in the country as settlers after 1945 centred upon their perceived ability to conform to the mores of Rhodesian society. There was particular concern that allowing undesirable nationalities into the country would result in a huge Coloured population.[51] Despite some pleas to stay from internees and refugees, most were forced to leave shortly after the war ended (Graphs 3, 4 and 5).

Non-British whites were perceived to blur already unstable racial boundaries. Doris Lessing's short story set during the war, 'The Black Madonna', follows Michele, an Italian internee and bricklayer by trade whose painting skills catches the attention of the local white women. Described as unkempt and drunk, 'there was a good deal of talk among the ladies about the dignity of labour, a subject in which they were well versed; and one felt they might almost go so far as to compare a white man with a Kaffir, who did not understand the dignity of labour either. He was felt to lack gratitude'.[52] That Michele seemed to hold no aversion to heavy manual labour cast further suspicion on his racial character. Nonetheless, Michele is hired by the local white women to build a model village for a war re-enactment. Captain Stocker, a British settler charged with monitoring Michele's progress, criticises Michele's slow pace, his failure to perform the requisite deference to those of British stock and Michele's repeated and open fraternisation with Africans. Yet the Captain quickly abandons his role overseeing Michele's work and instead spends days conversing and drinking with him. The longer the Captain spends

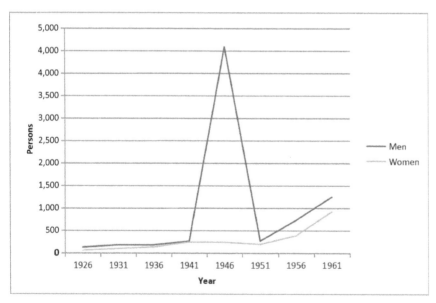

Graph 3 Numbers of Italian men and women in Rhodesia, 1926–61

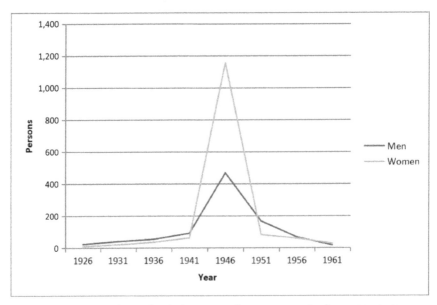

Graph 4 Numbers of Polish men and women in Rhodesia, 1926–61

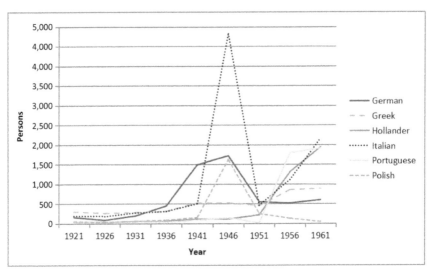

Graph 5 Total male and female minority European
populations in Rhodesia, 1921–61

with Michele, the more emotionally vulnerable he becomes; he cries aloud and speaks openly about his sexual relationships with African women. This failure to guard his own white behaviours is ultimately the Captain's downfall and he is given a period of time off by his superiors. Sent to recover in hospital, Michele visits the Captain with a gift of a painting of an African woman and, at his bedside, begins to mock the local white woman who laud his talent, claiming that 'they know nothing – savages. Barbarians'. Overwhelmed, the Captain tells him to get out. Michele's recognition of African woman's humanity coupled with his open denigration of white women produces intense anger in the Captain. Yet his frustration with Michele is in part born of jealousy. Michele does not understand – or refuses to follow – appropriate racial protocol expected of whites in Rhodesia. The Captain's own racial interactions remain a secret and produce inner turmoil and anguish. Michele does not feel this shame; neither does he judge the Captain for his transgressions. The Captain envies Michele's ability to live outside the prescribed racial behaviours. Yet he recognises that his proximity to Michele could result in another lapse and longs for distance from Michele to restore his own respectability. Here, Lessing conveyed prevalent stereotypes assigned to Italians at the time – indolence, sexual proclivity and constant inebriation; but also captured the deep hypocrisy that this white othering entailed. Vocal denunciations of interracial sex were often predicated on the disavowal of existing sexual desires towards racial others. For settlers, moreover, transgressive white behaviours were transmissible; physical distance from undesirable whites was a necessary preventative measure to ensure particular standards were maintained.

Prior to the war white trade unions repeatedly attempted to frustrate non-British Europeans entering into skilled trades.[53] With the declaration of war new national enemies were clearly defined. Italians were expelled from RRWU in July 1940 and white trade unionists regularly protested against their employment. However, a considerable number of the Italians in the camps were skilled artisans, some of whom possessed university degrees in engineering, and the government and private employers alike were keen to utilise their skills.[54] Italians 'of good health and character' were employed in the Rhodesia Air Training Group so as to release airmen for service, although they would work under supervision and not on 'secret work' or final assembly.[55] The agricultural sector employed 297 Italians in 1943, which rose to 600 by 1944.[56] Notably, the agricultural sector was devoid of an organised white trade union or large number of white employees to rally against their employment.

The exact position of particular groups within racial and national hierarchies was not always apparent. This presented a particular problem for white British workers attempting to enforce a strict racial division of labour. Significant confusion arose over how race should be structured into the workplace as it became increasingly evident that white skin was not necessarily preferable in every instance. In 1943 and 1944 the railway administration had approached RRWU regarding rehiring Italians who had been gangers before they had been interned. The RRWU repeatedly decried the measure. Yet the railway management insisted that this was a last resort; they protested that they had consistently attempted to hire white youths within the colony to work as gangers on the railways, but had failed to stir any interest. The RRWU lamented that the Rhodesian youth were spurning the role. Despite their attempts to characterise the ganger as a fulfilling, respectable career, RRWU had failed to prevent its racialisation.[57] In 1945 the shortage had reached 64 out of a total of 242 ganger positions and in the same year at the conference of the RRWU it was finally accepted that railwaymen could not maintain their position on British preference.[58] The matter was put to the conference bluntly: 'Which do we want: Coloured gangers or Italians?'

Some trade unionists came to the defence of Italian workers. Jimmy Lister, prominent member of the RRWU and MP for the SRLP, pointed out that most Italians were members of the union prior to the war and most had come out in the 1929 strike. He commented: 'I am concerned with a man as a worker and not as a national ... I would rather have a loyal foreigner than a Britisher who scabs in a strike.' In contrast, Roy Welensky argued that the shortage of Rhodesian and British recruits had been caused when the RRWU allowed Italians to fulfil the ganger role in the first place. No respectable Briton would want to take work that was associated with Italians, who had driven down the prestige of the ganger and accepted low wages. The problem was allowing non-British whites to take skilled and semi-skilled work in the first place. Nevertheless the motion passed that Italians should be employed as gangers with the important caveat that if men returned from war and wanted a job Italians had to be replaced.[59] However, even as men returned from the war, the railways struggled to attract gangers and by 1946 wastage of this position had rose to an average of twenty-five per year.[60] The conundrum over relaxing British preference for Coloureds or Italians did not recede. As pressures mounted further concessions were made in 1948 as the principle of hiring Polish and Italian artisans was accepted in order to deal with the increasing problem of the inadequate provision of houses for European staff.[61] Jimmy Lister had apparently changed his position and stated a marked preference for

Coloureds to be employed rather than Italians 'as, after all, the former were British subjects'.[62] In some ways this was articulated as a matter of *loyalty*: who would support, or at least be unable to challenge, the interests of white British men.

More generally the position taken towards Coloured workers was in a state of flux. The 1946 *Report into the Position of Coloureds* set out to identify skilled employment opportunities for the Coloured population. There were very few Coloured journeymen in skilled trades in contrast with South Africa where it was more common for Coloureds to fulfil semi-skilled and skilled positions. The railways employed around sixty Coloureds as gangers, porters and cooks. Only six Coloured persons were employed on the mines with membership of the Chamber of Mines, although others found some skilled work on small mines.[63] The building industry claimed it had no Coloured apprentices or journeymen. The 1941 census showed fourteen Coloured men working as bricklayers, although this was independently organised and the commission questioned whether they could be regarded as skilled journeymen without holding the requisite professional qualifications. Unorganised trades provided greater opportunities for Coloureds to progress into skilled positions.[64] The furniture industry employed twenty Coloured journeymen and forty-four apprentices and Coloured women were hired as upholsterers and machinists in the clothing industry. Employers in this industry stated a preference for Coloured labour and the report estimated this industry could provide work for fifty to sixty men and four to five hundred women.[65]

The commission identified two barriers to Coloured progression: the lower educational qualifications of Coloureds and the reluctance of employers to take them on out of fear of trouble from white labour. The first barrier lay in the racist provision of education in the country; the second, the commission concluded, derived from the fact that whites would resent working alongside Coloureds, both out of racial prejudice and fear of economic competition. The commission lacked any real solution and concluded that until prejudice was eroded, or until a boom period arrived with plenty of work for all, little could be done; Coloureds would have to patiently wait.[66]

White trade unionists justified their opposition to Coloureds in skilled positions through assertions that Coloured labourers were not substantially different enough from Africans that they could maintain distance and command appropriate authority. Rhodesia Railways and the agricultural sector had the highest number of Coloured workers in supervisory positions over African labour, but neither proved entirely comfortable with the situation. The Council of the Southern Rhodesia National Farmers' Union argued that the readiness with which Coloured labourers fraternised with Africans was cause for concern and prevented their promotion to higher positions. Coloured farm workers relapsed into inappropriate contact with Africans due to 'the absence of opportunity of social intercourse with their fellows [and] the absence of domestic comforts and standard of living and personal bearing which would make such conduct distasteful to them'.[67]

In 1947 a delegate to the RRWU conference attempted to define which mixed-race persons were appropriate for skilled and supervisory work. He complained of a ganger who 'was either a Coloured or a Euro-African: these men were not the same as the Cape Coloured because they actually associated with the natives, and the gangers did not want to work with them because it lowered the status of gangers. And the natives themselves would not work under these gangers'. The member stated that they did not have a problem with the administration hiring St Helenians or Coloureds, but strongly objected to 'half-castes'. Such differentiation relied upon subjective interpretation of behaviour rather than ancestral heritage. As previously stated, the classification of mixed-race persons as 'native' or 'Coloured' in part relied upon an individual's possession of 'white behaviours'.[68] The RRWU demanded that individuals were removed from the position of ganger if they were found to be 'living after the manner of an African'; Coloureds had a responsibility to maintain distance from their African workers if they wanted to retain semi-skilled and skilled positions.[69]

This self-identification and external categorisation as 'culturally European' was essential for Coloureds to be tolerated by white workers. Loyalty to white interests also informed these racial classifications. During the 1945 railway strike of African workers, Coloureds had remained at work with the European staff.[70] Coloureds who abandoned 'white' behaviour, which included self-imposed ostracism from fellow African workers, or were prepared to support African industrial action, lost their usefulness as a socio-economic barrier between white and black. Notions of loyalty played important functions across different imperial contexts in articulating the boundaries of racial identities. Certainly, Coloured categorisation and identity in many ways shared some common characteristics with that of Anglo-Indians. Concentrated in railway communities across India, Anglo-Indians were talked about – both by Europeans and by themselves – in terms of loyalty to empire and England.[71]

The threat of undercutting and the pervasiveness of racial and national hierarchies, while important in explaining the chauvinism of RRWU, does not adequately address why particular ethnic or national groups were preferred in specific instances. As well as matters of loyalty, white prestige was at stake. Encouraging non-British whites with their lax sexual mores, dubious political affiliations (whether fascist or communist) and presumed lower standard of living, to take up permanent residence in the colony could compromise white superiority writ large. White trade unionists, as shown in Chapter 1, struggled to reconcile the notion of respectability with the reality of white workers' experiences. The increased presence of these whites of 'lowly' racial status within the ranks of white labour threatened to tarnish this social group more broadly in Rhodesian society. Non-British whites could also be corrupting influences. The employment of Coloureds offered a safer option as their racial status was arguably more fluid; an individual's status as Coloured was under constant negotiation depending upon their perceived attributes and racialised behaviours. While Coloureds could be redefined as 'natives' if they failed to behave in the 'correct ways' it would be harder to deny Italians their European ancestry. The presence of Italians, moreover, could create a larger and therefore stronger Coloured population.

This spoke to the relative elasticity of nationalist rhetoric and racial classification. The importance of loyalty to Britain and empire proved conditional when used to curb the wages or working conditions of British whites; but was stressed as an insurmountable essence of the ideal worker in the face of competition from other non-British white workers. Nevertheless, by the end of the 1940s RRWU had to concede that it had lost the position of ganger to non-British whites and Coloureds; the ganger had been racialised and, as a lonely and low-paid job, was thoroughly inappropriate for socially aspirant white males. The infringement on what had previously been regarded as a white position was increasingly visible. Yet another group offered the opportunity to retain the association of some jobs with white respectability: white women.

White women and the nuclear family

Alongside immigration, biological and social reproduction was necessary to ensure the continued existence of the settler state. Family life was seen as central to strengthening and developing the colony, and this had important consequences for how white women's roles were envisioned. Marriage and family life were thought to have a tempering effect on men's excesses; white women were seen to engender stability and prevent the temptations of interracial sex. Cullen Gouldsbury, a keen observer of white Rhodesian society who wrote verse for the glory of empire, surmised that white women were important 'to lessen drink, to tame the bachelor colonial', but stressed that their role was one that was essentially subordinate and passive, indeed 'hardly more than ornamental':

To swish the skirt: to smile: to flirt,
to captivate the detrimental! –
To spend our cash, to cook our hash;
To sew for us the sportive button,
To reign within the house of tin,
and coax our goat to taste like mutton.
Yet still, we fear, the day draws near
When women will no longer heed us,
When beings in skirts will scorn our shirts,
And bid the heathen savage feed us.[72]

White women outside of the home and out of the control of their husbands were perceived to threaten the fabric of white society. As homemakers they were supposed to maintain white standards and provide a barrier between their children and corrupting racial influences, particularly African domestic staff.

In 1947 Southern Rhodesia's Department of Public Relations warned prospective settlers that while 'natives are very fond of children ... the entire charge of children – and especially little girls – should never be left either to a native boy or native girl. No white girl should ever be left alone in the house without white supervision'.[73] These relationships were not simply personal matters, but were informed and disciplined by official colonial practice and ideology.[74] As a result of her parents' poverty, Daphne Anderson's servant took what was deemed an inappropriate role in her upbringing: her relationship with her servant was so close Anderson's first language was not English, but Shona. As a child she was unaware of the perceived incongruous nature of this contact, but as she aged she increasingly recognised the impropriety of this relationship, which incited shame and a fear that it could compromise her social standing. Imagining of a wealthy woman, Anderson wrote, 'What would she say if I told her that I had been brought up by native servants and had been treated as one?'[75] Her estranged father and aunt were forced to intervene to separate Anderson and her sister from the servant, reintegrate them into white respectability and instruct them in the appropriate relationships and performances regarding Africans.

White reliance upon domestic staff was noted in the *Labour Front*, which described 'the utter dependence of the European on the African' and continued that

we see the results of this evil of dependence all around us. We all know the woman who has given up the struggle and with the resigned attitude of 'leave it to the boy' has sunk herself and her family to a level far below that of any civilisation, to a level, in fact, dangerously near to that of the African she despises ... we are retrogressing, our children are becoming dependants on the race they despise ... as the culture of other white cultures are moving forward, we are moving backward.[76]

Over-dependence upon African servants produced lazy whites who had no recognition of the moral value of work. Moreover, mothers who abandoned their assigned roles in the home were accused of bringing not only their families but the entire race into disrepute.

The nuclear family was the site of biological reproduction and of racial thinking. Yet the white family also reproduced the *skilled workforce*. White workers who wished to maintain the skilled monopoly on jobs thus had an interest in maintaining a high reproduction rate. The *Review* contended that low wages had prevented the ability of the white race to reproduce and expand and claimed that

the number of children, with too few exceptions, is limited to one or two per family ... all considerations of family are governed by financial expediency. If state assistance were granted and parents made allowances for over three children, then a nightmare of future financial worry would be removed, and there would be every chance of having healthy, instead of undernourished, children.[77]

For government employees the marriage allowance, introduced in 1909, meant that white civil servants were entitled to a supplementary sum in line with their wages; the higher paid the civil servant, the more money he would receive as a marriage allowance. This incremental rate alludes to the fact that the allowance was not about staving off poverty, but rather endeavoured to enable men of different classes to achieve particular idealisations of domesticity and familial life. Men under the age of twenty-six proved ineligible, perhaps reflecting the extended bachelorhood of many men in Southern Rhodesia as they competed for the attention of a limited number of white women. The allowance was finally abolished in the early 1950s and incorporated into a flat wage rate.[78] Significantly, extra wages paid to male employees centred upon concerns about the ability of white men to provide for their dependants and was used to argue against white women's entrance into the formal economy.

The insignificance attached to white women's work has often been underscored by misogynistic assumptions. Notions that women did not care about their careers because they could not break from natural attachment to the nuclear family, only took on jobs so that they could spend money on frivolous luxuries (which more often than not were pointed out to highlight narcissistic or shallow tendencies) or essentially saw their employment as a temporary measure before marriage has had the effect of erasing the importance of women's wage labour. Kate Law and Ushehwedu Kufakurinani have restored agency to white women and challenged the one-dimensional view of 'gossipy' house-wives by looking at the ways in which white women contested the ideology of domesticity. White women's involvement in civic and public life, voluntary organisations and paid employment spoke to diverse experiences of women in the country, but also their evolving roles both 'as agents of change and as cultural intermediaries' and as staunch defenders of white rule.[79]

Of course, many white women were not passionate about their careers; neither did their wages form the bulk of family incomes. Some white women were unable to conceive of subversive woman-hood under the strength of conservative gender ideologies. Yet white women's aversion to wage labour had just as much to do with poor wages and working conditions and the type of boring, repetitive jobs they were offered. Marriage restrictions, unequal wages and working conditions for men and women, as well as ideological stress upon the family and traditional gender roles, combined to create conditions in which women were encouraged to remain in the home upon marriage. Yet women were motivated by a complex range of financial, social and emotional needs and desires. The types of work they performed must take this complexity into account. White women were variously encouraged to take up wage labour due to boredom and isolation in the domestic sphere, attempts to carve out their own independence, financial need, as well as a sense of patriotism and duty to the country and empire. Their entrance into wage labour, moreover, was a highly contested process in which meanings attached to gender and race were both reaffirmed and subverted.

Jonathan Hyslop has argued that campaigns against mixed marriages by white men in South Africa during the 1930s were inflamed by the increasing entrance of Afrikaner women into industrial labour. By arguing for certain protections for white women, men sought to re-establish gender hierarchies, but this also helped men and women to coalesce around a white racial identity.[80] The next section explores broad trends of white female wage labour and, together with Part 2, demonstrates that white women's labour and sexuality were equally potent devices in articulating the boundaries of white racial identity and controlling the movement both of white women and African men.

Patterns of white female employment

While the number of white women working on farms, including those owning, managing or assisting as wives or daughters, amounts to a small fraction of economically active white women, discussions around female agricultural labour nonetheless reveal the particular roles envisioned for both white men and women in the colony. At its height farming accounted for 11.7 per cent of female activity in 1926, which steadily declined to around 1 per cent by 1969. White wives were likely to have been involved in some elements of farm operations, acting as medics for farm labourers, running farm shops and assisting with necessary administrative duties.[81] White women were discouraged from pursuing agricultural work, both as wage earners and as independent land owners. They were warned that they would not be able to handle the climatic conditions nor the loneliness characteristic of farming. But the primary concern of colonial authorities lay in the potential of lone white women overseeing African labour. This raised images of potential inappropriate contact with Africans, but also white women's frailty and vulnerability. White female employment was generally undesirable, but in many cases it was deemed unacceptable. Jobs that involved duties with the potential to deepen interracial familiarity between white women and black men or lower the prestige of white women – such as barmaids – were widely condemned.[82] In 1922 the *Report for Agricultural Openings for Women* issued by the Society for the Oversea Settlement of British Women had warned that 'the African' 'respects a man, whereas he does not respect a woman'. The Society instead suggested poultry farming on the condition that 'they will have the protection of a married man and his family ... the object of such an arrangement is that the native labourers may know that there is a white man other than an ordinary European employee who may be called upon to take command of affairs if necessary'.[83] The 'ordinary European employee' was not regarded as possessing sufficient authority to control African workers. Implicit here is the suggestion that those European men who were unable to find a wife were lacking; in controlling Africans they were as worthless as white women and children.

Over the period of minority rule women generally remained in traditional welfare and caring professions, administrative work and unpaid work that supported their husband's profession.[84] White women listed in the census as domestic servants and maids doubled from 145 in 1926 to 310 in 1936, but by the 1960s this figure was below 100. Very occasionally, one or two women appeared on the census in other unexpected categories – as industrial foremen, motor mechanics, vulcanisers, well sinkers, water drillers and painters and decorators. Clerical work was the largest single occupation for women in Rhodesia from 1926 until 1969. This sector accounted for around a quarter of white female employment during the 1930s and had increased to 59.3 per cent by 1969 (see

Table 4 European women's occupations as a percentage of total economically active European women, 1926–69

Year	Clerical (%)	Teachers (%)	Nurses (%)	Shop assistants (%)	Hairdressers and beauty (%)	Farmers (%)
1926	39.2	–	8.3	16.9	0.3	11.7
1936	26.3	10.2	10	9.9	2.1	4.8
1941	39.3	4.6	10.4	11.6	1.9	4.3
1946	39.4	7.6	9.4	10.3	1.7	3.6
1951	44.9	6.7	5.9	13.4	1.1	2.5
1956	44.6	5.8	5.6	11.9	1.1	1.9
1961	56.1	7.5	4.7	12.1	1.6	1.3
1969	59.3	8.4	5.3	8.6	2.2	1.4

Table 5 Percentage of women performing clerical work across Rhodesia, the United States and Canada[a]

Year	Southern Rhodesia (%)	United States (%)	Canada (%)
1920	–	48.4	41.8
1926	28.9	–	–
1930	–	52	45.1
1936	44.4	–	–
1940–41	51.4	52.6	50.1
1946	50.9	–	–
1950–51	67.9	60.2	56.7
1956	71.9	–	–
1960–61	66.9	67.8	61.5
1969	57.4	–	–
1970–71	–	74.6	68.9

[a] Data for the United States and Canada was taken from Kim England and Kate Boyer, 'Women's Work: The Feminisation and Shifting Meanings of Clerical Work', *Journal of Social History*, 43:2 (2009), pp. 307–340. The data for Southern Rhodesia refers only to European women.

Table 4 and Graph 7). The feminisation of clerical work in the twentieth century was a general trend across Western societies although this process occurred at a slightly slower pace in Rhodesia, as indicated by Table 5.[85] This can be explained in part by the ratio of women to men, but also reflected the relative strength of conservative gender ideologies and employment policies that favoured white men.

Employment opportunities for white women were largely determined by marital status. Formal employment was expected to cease upon marriage.[86] Many married women earned less than their single counterparts, regardless of their experience or qualifications. For example, a woman who had been earning between £380 and £570 per annum as a teacher in 1951 would be reduced to earning a maximum of £270 upon marriage.[87] Despite labour shortages very little was done to improve working conditions to encourage women to enlist or remain in their chosen careers. Nursing suffered from perpetual shortages across the period of minority rule and intensified during the Second World War. By 1939 there was a shortage of thirty-five registered nurses in government hospitals, which steadily rose to 121 in 1946.[88] In line with the 1930 Civil Service Regulations, women gave up nursing upon marriage and could only be rehired on a temporary basis. In 1948 out of sixty-two resignations, marriage was responsible for forty-five. In order to become a registered nurse, women had to be at least eighteen years old and training took four years to complete.[89] As most women were married by their early twenties this produced a poor return on the investment in nurse training for the Rhodesian state. One white nurse who started work in Gatooma in 1930 claimed that medical author-ities intervened in nurses' lives in attempts to prolong their careers as single women. She recalled that if nurses were making friends and enjoying their social lives they might be transferred to work under an 'unpopular matron'. Likewise, if a nurse had accepted a marriage pro-posal from a local man she could face being transferred to 'the other end of the country'.[90] These point to coercive, rather than incentive-based, methods of retention.

As part of the civilian workforce during the Second World War women comprised 33 per cent of total employed in the United States and 39 per cent in the United Kingdom.[91] In Southern Rhodesia the European figures were slightly lower at 27.9 per cent but this neverthe-less marked a substantial shift in employment patterns (see Graph 6). As the Second World War continued the employment of young white men was increasingly seen as a waste of training resources by the civil service as it was anticipated that they would soon be called up for mili-tary service. By 1940 civil service recruitment had a white female prefer-ence where possible as it was presumed that women would be available for a longer period of time. Experienced female civil servants were for-bidden to leave their posts if no other women could fill the vacancy.[92] The Women's Auxiliary Territorial Service was formed in June 1940 to ease labour shortages that were already apparent. White women were employed as clerks, drivers, postwomen and mess assistants in training camps.[93] By the end of the war a total of 1,510 white women would have served in full-time capacity, 137 of whom served abroad (see Figure 13).[94] More generally, attitudes towards acceptable work for white women only slightly modified. White women worked in the new munitions factories, Rofac and Sofac, located in Bulawayo and Salisbury respectively. In both factories white women dominated the labour force, albeit under white artisan male supervision.[95] It was also thought that women might be introduced into various manual trades including within the electrical industry as armature winders and in various roles within the printing industry.[96]

However, the replacement of white men by women was slow and by no means enacted on a wide scale.[97] Factory work was still a generally undesirable job for white women. Daphne Anderson noted that the white women who worked as tobacco packers were usually 'from the poorer parts of the town, Afrikaans girls from Ardbennie or Hatfield … daughters of railway men or engine drivers from the Railway Married Quarters, sad faced older women reputed to be widowed but suspected of being divorced or deserted'.[98] The training of women to replace men in skilled clerical positions was seen as a less contentious move that would not compromise women's femininity. Nevertheless those directing the training process held reservations about women with poor education from lower-class backgrounds progressing through

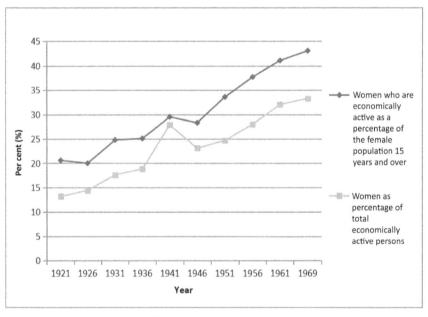

Graph 6 Economically active European women as a percentage of adult European women and of totally economically active European persons, 1926–69

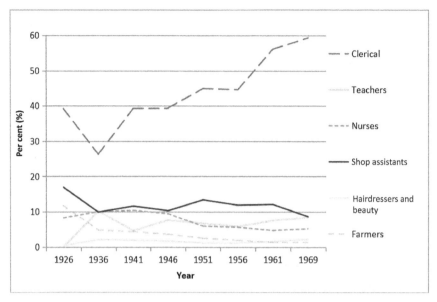

Graph 7 European women's occupations as a percentage of
total economically active European women

training programmes. Rivell's Commercial Classes noted that ever
growing numbers of young women with little to no training were
being absorbed into commercial work, and would be 'kept on at a low
standard of wages and ... add to the government's "difficulties" in the
inevitable depression period which will follow the war'. Rather than
advocate training for these inexperienced women, they suggested that
'beginners' should not be given the option to attend training events as
'schools would be inundated with all kinds of girls where general education is poor and who would only make indifferent workers at the end
of their training'.[99]

White women generally had little chance for promotion, suffered
poor conditions and working rights and could be hired at lower wages
with fewer benefits than their male counterparts. While many accepted
their terms of employment, some white women offered limited resistance to their conditions. Law and Kufakurinani have argued that in the
face of criticism that suggested their entrance into formal employment
spelt the end of the family, white female workers argued conversely
that their employment enabled them to provide a greater home life and
opportunities for their children.[100] Moreover, in some cases women
were successfully incorporated into existing trade unions. However,
white women's pressure upon their trade union representatives failed

to result in significant gains. Certainly, immediately before the outbreak of the Second World War, RRWU maintained its hostility
towards hiring women. One letter blamed railwaymen and their wives
for taking employment away from the white youth of the country.[101]
Particular disdain was reserved for married women and in 1940 RRWU
pressed for all married women to be fired and replaced with single
women.[102]

In 1941 the railways employed 2,414 white men and 206 white
women, yet this gender imbalance eased as over 40 per cent of white
male clerical staff were released for war duty. In 1943 around 15 per
cent of the total European railway staff were on active service, which
saw numbers of white women employed rise to 413.[103] Female clerks
employed as a wartime measure on the railways began on a starting
wage of £180 to £202 per annum. White women were also entitled to
annual increments of £15 and by 1943 experienced clerks could receive
up to £262.[104] Such incentives suggest employers were keen to retain
their female staff. In 1945 RRWU accepted the principle that the union
should fight for white male and female clerks to share the same grading
and therefore receive the same wages, but in 1947 white women were
still earning over 30 per cent less than their male counterparts.[105] Wage
disparities persisted even in occupations dominated by white women.
In 1940, out of 500 white teachers only 166 were men. In the same
year, in the highest grade men earned £860 to £1,100 per annum, while
women earned £700 to £900. Perhaps unsurprisingly due to the gendered ratio of the profession and organisation, the Rhodesia Teaching
Association pushed for equal wages from the Second World War.[106]

There is also some evidence of independent white women's organisation in the workplace. In 1939 over one hundred white women
attempted to establish an organisation that placed wages 'on a civilised
standard'. They asked for a minimum wage of £10 a month, but were
summarily dismissed by the Chambers of Commerce who also rejected
their attempt to form a union. There was also agitation over sixty-
six white women employed on piecework at the United Cigarette
Company who received £7 a month. While the Industrial Inspector was
keen to stress the contentment of the women, the RLP pointed out
that in the absence of a trade union they were less likely to speak out
about their wages and conditions in fear of reprisals and victimisation.
An attempt to unionise these low-paid women by better-paid women
proved unsuccessful. While initial meetings attracted at least twenty-
five, management threatened to dismiss them if they attempted to
form a union.[107] Other white women were able to utilise the skills
shortage to their advantage when negotiating their contracts; when
applying for a clerical job Daphne Anderson highlighted the shortage

of white men during her interview to successfully demand that her prospective employer pay her what a white man would receive.[108]

While white labour organisations had unsuccessfully argued for minimum wages to be officially instated across the colony for years, the entrance of white women into low-paid work in larger numbers during the war equipped white labour organisations with compelling images of virtuous and vulnerable women at the mercy of greedy employers. They argued that white women in factories worked in deplorable conditions that amounted to 'sweated labour' and were forced to inhabit charitable subsidised hostels, in which they slept on wire stretchers with no mattresses, because they could not afford decent accommodation. This was not entirely uncommon. Immediately before the outbreak of the war Doris Lessing had been offered a job as a window dresser by the owner of a large retail shop for women and local town councillor, Mr Barbour. He offered the job on such a poor rate that Lessing would have to live in a 'hostel for poor girls' that was subsidised by the government. Lessing summarily rejected the job and admonished Mr Barbour for using his political weight 'to get cheap labour for his shop'.[109] Likewise, the RLP accused commercial houses of paying white women between £2 and £5 a month while knowing that a 'reputable' lodging would demand at least £6 or £7 a month. Jimmy Lister claimed that white women were working as shop assistants in Umtali on £2 a month and without sufficient wages, it was feared that white women would lower themselves in order to generate extra income.[110] The RLP claimed that in paying poor wages 'sometimes immorality is the result'. Some of the white women who worked in the factories had to supplement their wages by working in the bioscopes after their shifts had finished. This meant that women had to walk the streets alone at night and the RLP asserted that this had led to one or two women being attacked.[111]

Despite shifting gendered labour patterns the Rhodesian state continued to stress the role of housewife and mother and retain discriminatory employment practices. In the 1950s the *Chigwidden Report* argued that there was no popular feeling from women to remove marriage restrictions. Women supposedly preferred the freedom and flexibility that came with part-time work, which allowed them 'to take their holidays when their husbands are on leave, to transfer from one centre to another with their husbands and to relinquish their employment at short time notice for domestic reasons'.[112] Maternity pay was discussed in the social security report of 1944, but it concluded that the 'peculiar conditions' of Rhodesia meant that 'the personal care and protection of mothers for their children [was] highly desirable'. Maternity pay would encourage women away from their important roles as mothers.[113]

There was a slight decrease in the percentage of adult European women noted as economically active in 1946 as men returned from war. But white female employment continued to grow and there was a growing tendency for women to stay in employment after marriage. At its 1946 Annual Congress, the Federation of Women's Institutes in Southern Rhodesia called for an end to the marriage bar.[114] Some 24 per cent of married white women in 1951 were in employment and they accounted for 49 per cent of all economically active women.[115] For employers, white women were attractive as they could be paid less than their male counterparts and, importantly, their employment did not create the intensity of backlash from white male workers that hiring Africans would have done. White male workers saw the need to keep women in the home to protect their own self-image as providers, but white female employment had its advantages. It kept Africans, Coloureds and non-British white men from permanently usurping these roles and it increased white workers' family incomes. By couching recruitment in terms of a war effort, white women could be reminded that this was a temporary patriotic measure, not a fundamental change in their 'natural' roles in society.

Hostilities towards white female employment re-emerged when white women failed to return to the home in the post-war period. Therefore while AMWR applauded women's effort and aptitude in 'performing functions which are not usually associated with their sex such as oxy-acetylene welding and soldering', they also vehemently argued that women had become too bold and that they had to make the choice between chivalry and equality. If women wanted to be treated as equals on the labour market, then 'women who were competitors must be treated as men'.[116] The image of purity and helplessness was conditional on white women acting in ways that supported existing gendered power relations. White women who went to work in defiance of white men were seen as threats to the white nuclear family and reconceptualised as self-interested perversions of femininity.

Part 2: African urbanisation, militancy and class formations

Concerns regarding white female autonomy outside of the home took place in the context of the unprecedented movement of Africans into schools, cities and towns, semi-skilled work, trade unions and on to picket lines. In struggling against these incursions into 'white spaces' white workers clung on to the policy of 'parallel development'. Yet many European workers were outraged that skilled work was performed by Africans even within their allocated spheres of 'development'. The Bulawayo branch of the RRWU successfully passed a motion to agitate

[136]

for the replacement of African typists with Europeans in the Native Affairs Department, and in Salisbury and Gwelo European artisans had successfully fought for a monopoly over building accommodation in the African reserves.[117] While white unions pressed to extend their monopoly of skill into emerging industries, employers and state authorities recognised that the growth of secondary industry could not 'be secured on an exclusive "white labour" policy'. Inflated rates of European pay were not sustainable and many employers had introduced Africans into semi-skilled work. Percy Ibbotson, author of a report into African urban conditions, neatly captured the emerging orthodoxy when he stated that 'racial prejudice and discriminating legislation cannot battle successfully against economic facts'.[118]

The policy of segregation enabled Europeans to imagine Africans as fundamentally rural beings; incontrovertibly swaddled by tradition and custom, bound in primordial stasis.[119] Yet it had become increasingly clear to state authorities that the changing labour demands required the permanent settlement of Africans in urban areas not only be tolerated but encouraged. More broadly, increasing pressure upon rural landholdings as a result of land apportionment had accelerated urbanisation across sub-Saharan Africa. Urban areas offered employment in domestic services, unskilled government work, the railways and retail. They also offered avenues to escape conscription into compulsory labour schemes, such as those initiated as part of the Compulsory Native Labour Act, which provided labour on European farms and in extractive industries over the course of 1942–46.[120] Many African women saw urban areas as less restrictive than rural areas and as providing opportunities to evade the authority of overbearing in-laws, parents and husbands.[121] The city was the site of multiple struggles over established gendered and racial boundaries. Just as white women's autonomy caused unease for settler patriarchs, African women's independence in urban areas provoked paranoia from African churches, rural elders and those elite urban Africans who felt that maintaining control over African women's activities was central to their own respectability.[122]

Cities had been cultivated as white spaces in which the demographic weakness of whites across the colony could be temporarily disavowed. It was here that Rhodesia could be imagined and visualised as a white man's country. Race and space were co-constructed; making settler colonial space relied not only on physically laying claim to territory but also involved reimagining spaces as white.[123] As African urbanisation intensified settlers correspondingly reconceptualised Africans as parodies of modernity; threats to white women and white civilisation and plagues on Rhodesian racial and national health. Settlers were also increasingly perturbed about the visibility of Coloureds and Indians in 'white' areas. When financial barriers failed to prevent Indians from buying residences in European areas, the future mayor of Bulawayo, J. M. Macdonald, claimed with conspiratorial flair that 'the insidious infiltration and encirclement by the Indians in Bulawayo was part of a deliberate and calculated policy'. Despite the fact the 1946 census showed only 2,911 'Asiatics' in the country, Macdonald argued that Indians were franticly buying up land as India was being overrun with her 'teeming millions'.[124] He claimed multiracial spaces encouraged 'the intermingling and intermarriage of the races – the bastardisation of the nation' and implored that segregation was the only way to 'hand our children a country clean, healthy and virile as we found it'.[125]

Africans and other non-white groups were seen to carry infectious diseases over to the white population and this provided a powerful justification and motivation for urban segregation.[126] The preoccupation with African health was felt acutely among whites who had to labour beside them. The *Granite Review* printed the numbers of Africans with silicosis and infectious diseases on the mines while the Trades and Labour Council in Bulawayo passed resolutions in 1942 to press for compulsory medical examinations for all Africans seeking employment 'to minimise and eliminate venereal and other diseases'.[127] Africans were deemed unable to control their base erotic desires, afflicted by hypersexual disorders and regarded to disproportionately carry sexually transmitted diseases (STDs). While this sexual desire of Africans was controlled in the rural areas by traditional customs, many settlers believed that in the absence of these constraints, the sexual desires of urban Africans were unchecked.[128]

White trade unions aggressively complained about Africans performing skilled work, but they also complained viciously about Africans *not* doing work. Urbanisation had increased the visibility of so-called 'loafers'. As argued by Jocelyn Alexander, the right to the city was underpinned by employment status and settler authorities believed unemployment created rootless individuals while work was seen as a corrective and preventative to nationalism, radicalism and discontent.[129] The RLP argued that Africans developed an immoral character in the city and explicitly identified urbanisation as the main cause of crime in South Africa.[130] The *Review* printed complaints that police camps had been turned into breweries and drunken Africans wandered the streets at night without a policeman in sight.[131]

The relative absence of white men intensified concerns over isolated white women. In 1947 the Department of Public Relations advised 'women new to the country must remember that there may be prying eyes. Make sure that your curtains are adequate and are drawn at night

... precautions should be taken, especially when the women are on farms or are forced to live alone'. Farming districts were singled out as places where women would be at particular risk in the event of husbands and sons being engaged in military service abroad or as part of the war effort in the towns. As a protective measure these women 'very often [had] iron bars fixed across their bedroom windows and a loaded shotgun stood against the wall at the bedside'. Yet even in the towns white women were warned not to assume that their safety was assured, especially if they were 'sleeping alone'. The Department of Public Relations advised that bars should be fixed to downstairs bedroom windows especially in accommodation for single white women.[132]

In 1940 the *Review* printed a spate of reports of African attacks upon Europeans, most involving axes or 'kaffir picks' and one case resulting in the murder of a railwayman's wife.[133] This murderous spree was explained in numerous ways. One letter sent into the *Review* by 'Sentinel' criticised the journal's coverage, making the simple point that not all Africans were murderers and thieves but argued that those Africans who had resorted to crime had been taught to behave badly by Europeans. In particular, 'European indolence' had disastrous effects on African mentalities. 'Sentinel' recalled that when one railway painter was sent to paint a station the white painter stretched out the work by two extra weeks and that 'to my knowledge most of the work was done by his native assistants'. He had observed European workers

> walking to a job, their hands in their pockets and natives following carrying tools, timber, etc. I have seen railway natives putting concrete into position. I have also seen natives on engines breaking coal. Now if the white man wants to protect his trades, he must be prepared to treat them as jealous possessions, not push work off on to the native, and then whine about 'undercutting' and 'missionaries' ... The truth of the whole matter is that we cannot do without natives, and for some incomprehensible reason we hate them for it.[134]

The response was furious and asserted that the average African was a thief and a murderer.[135] But the common theme among the many letters that were sent to denounce 'Sentinel' and his apparent misunderstanding of Africans, was the contention that Africans' attitude towards women was proof of insidious murderous character. One response contended 'that the age-old custom of natives, in their natural environment, is a general tendency to make the women do all the work, even the tilling of the lands, whilst the male members of the tribe spend their time hunting and drinking beer'.[136] This all went back to central principles of labour: work made a man and, according to white labour organisations, African men neither worked in their reserves, where they were emasculated through their reliance on female manual labour, nor in the towns, where they sat on street corners and spurned opportunities for work.

Yet despite such protests, trying to stem the tide of African urbanisation, was, in the words of General Smuts, like trying 'to sweep the ocean back with a broom'.[137] White workers could do little but complain and increase their harassment of Africans who they deemed to have crossed into 'white' areas. When four white artisans employed on the railways were forced to move from their homes in order for Africans to take up their cottages they smashed the sinks and cut the electricity and wiring as they left in protest.[138] Africans living in white quarters represented an incursion into white spaces, a loss of white territory and the implicit suggestion that what was acceptable for white workers was also appropriate for African artisans. This recourse to violence represented the frustration felt by these white artisans at the mere association with their black counterparts and also their desperation to aggressively remind Africans that they were indeed different and subordinate.

The rise of elite Africans

Despite repeated attempts by the state to align skin colour to the contours of class, from the earliest days of white occupation African class differentiation existed and was exacerbated by the uneven development of capitalism in the region. Very few educated or professional Africans were able to amass substantial amounts of personal wealth. Yet, as Michael West has argued, this African social group offended and threatened settlers purely by their ambitions and achievements.[139] Due to discriminatory educational provision Africans educated up to standard six or seven were generally regarded with high social status and until 1945 only two Africans had received university education in Southern Rhodesia. Most had to go abroad to Europe or the University of Fort Hare in South Africa.[140] Yet the growing manufacturing sector demanded not only a stabilised workforce, but one that was increasingly skilled. In response, from 1940 to 1950 government expenditure on African mission schools rose from £72,655 to £527,088 and over the same period the number of students doubled.[141]

As African workers took on increasingly skilled roles, white workers variously denied that the work Africans performed was actually skilled, or denigrated it as producing inadequate sub-European standards of craftsmanship. Clements Kadalie's autobiography gives some indication of the treatment white workers meted out to Africans taking on semi-skilled and skilled positions. Kadalie was born in Nyasaland and became a qualified teacher at sixteen before moving to South Africa and founding the Industrial and Commercial Workers' Union. He faced considerable resentment from the whites he laboured beside, including one white female typist who 'could not tolerate seeing me in the same office at my desk doing the same clerical work as herself ... She definitely hated me'.[142]

During early years of white rule educated, professional and wealthy Africans looked to settlers for acceptance and equality and made evolutionary political demands rather than desiring the radical overthrow of Rhodesian society. They used the language of 'civilisation' to fight for the political and economic rights they felt they were entitled to by proving they were above the 'average' African.[143] While the African middle class during these earlier years clung on to the idea of racial partnership under the axiom of 'equal rights for all civilised men', not all Africans saw every white as civilised. The white manual worker had little education compared with the African elite. Many white workers were considered to be conceited, deluded and inexplicably angry at those Africans who failed to laud white mediocrity as excellence.

Joshua Nkomo was one of these few highly educated Africans who would later go on to found and lead the Zimbabwe African People's Union (ZAPU) and eventually serve as vice president in independent Zimbabwe. Before his entrance into nationalist politics he was employed on Rhodesia Railways in the Department of African Affairs and was elected to lead the African trade union. He described how his superior, a welfare officer who had no training and only 'education up to school leaving level' was paid £100 a month, while he himself was paid £12 a month despite holding a university degree. Nkomo refused to attend the daily morning line-ups in which African employees were searched by the compound police, who, Nkomo stated, 'decided I was some new sort of animal, and left me alone'. Generally he described those whites who worked directly with him as 'well meaning' but nevertheless admitted that his promotions, personal office and access to a telephone and typewriter, meant that he was often the recipient of anger and insults from white staff who complained about his presence and sought to exclude him. Nkomo observed that he was not invited to the white employees' 'tea club' but maintained that these passive aggressive behaviours did not unsettle him.[144]

Herbert Chitepo, the first African barrister in Rhodesia and subsequent leader of the Zimbabwe African National Union (ZANU), recalled how he was forced to use fire escapes, rather than stairs or lifts, across the office buildings of Salisbury. His wife Victoria was a highly educated teacher with degrees from the University of Natal and the University of Birmingham and also an impressive political activist in her own right. While on a shopping trip to one of the stores in Salisbury she had witnessed a sales assistant fired on the spot by her manager – outraged that the assistant had allowed Victoria to try on a pair of shoes. Chitepo later remarked that the continued discrimination, not only in industry and parliament, 'but [also] in the shops, on the staircases, and at office counters ... denied to the African his essential dignity as a person, and violated his sense of dignity and self-respect'.[145]

Many more Africans failed to secure suitable employment that matched the qualifications they held. Alexander Kanengoni, a trained teacher who left his position to join the liberation forces in 1974, captured this deflation of unrealised potential in the fictional character of Noel, a young black man who worked at the Rhodesia paper factory:

> At the guillotine, virtually no thinking and absolutely no creativity was required. He would stand there, rechannelling back on to the conveyor belt stray chunks of sliced paper with his mind completely closed ... Every day the first thing to catch his eye would be his GCE 'O' level certificate hanging in a battered frame on the wall ... a dusty, bleached piece of greenish paper ... the symbol of his dashed dreams and frustrations. He had now got used to looking at it without feeling anything. The certificate had failed to get him anywhere. The best it had done was to squeeze him in at the end of the guillotine.[146]

Likewise in Charles Mungoshi's, *Coming of the Dry Season*, the central character Paul Masaga, goes to the city to find work armed with educational certificates but finds nothing but poverty and frustration. After two years of searching for work, he is offered an unskilled job. Yet Paul is immediately fired by the illiterate white foreman, who reasons, 'I don't want any bloody thinkers here. I want somebody to listen and obey orders and do what he's told.'[147] Uneducated whites did not want to work alongside educated Africans who threatened to lay their own inadequacies bare.

In 1947 T. S. Hlabangana wrote to the *Labour Front* to complain that Europeans were hired as teachers in African schools, which restricted the already limited employment avenues for educated Africans. As well as warning of a 'fanatic nationalism' that would emerge as a result of closing off avenues of progression, Hlabangana questioned the ability of whites to fulfil all skilled positions. His evaluation of the 'level' of whites was damning; whites had allowed themselves to become unskilled, uneducated and complacent:

> The lack of balance in the economic structure of the country has lowered the general level of European skill. It is not very necessary for Rhodesian Europeans to acquire higher education since their skins give them

sufficient physical and financial protection. This has given Europeans a false and certainly temporary security and will ultimately lead to the emergence of a 'poor white' class.[148]

The figure of the poor white, often used by white labour in order to argue for greater protection, was now being used by Africans to indict racialised economic structures and condemn white workers as lazy. In doing so they inverted racial stereotypes of slothfulness and productivity. Such assertions of humanity were feared and hated by the majority of white labour. It was not just that educated Africans posed a threat in taking jobs from Europeans; education appeared to imbue Africans with a propensity to challenge their position of inferiority. The government warned new settlers against hiring the 'half-educated unreliable type' as domestic servants. Those with some education were 'impertinent and inclined to talk back'.[149]

Ezekiel Makunike was one such highly educated African who graduated from an American Methodist Mission School in the 1940s and went on to obtain a bachelor's degree in India. He was a trained teacher and headmaster at several schools before becoming a journalist. In one instance Makunike had forgotten to display his learner sign in his car while driving and was reprimanded by a white policeman. The policeman repeatedly demanded that Makunike call him 'Sir'. Makunike refused, reasoning that 'the honour to be called "Sir" must be deserved'. The white police officer responded by threatening to 'smash' Makunike who was summarily asked to report to the police station. At the station it transpired that the white officer had been convinced to back down as he had been warned of Makunike's status and knowledge of the law by some of the African sergeants.[150] Makunike, in this refusal, publicly accused the white policeman as being unworthy of respect. The policeman threatened violence when Makunike's actions subverted the settler hierarchy, but was ultimately cowed into silence. This small triumph over white authority was atypical to be sure, but it was precisely this type of challenge to settler power that whites feared.

The RRWU claimed that while educated Africans may have declared that they were different from the average African, they could not escape their tribal loyalties and immorality. Many white workers were at pains to emphasise that educated Africans could simply not be trusted. The supposed deviousness of educated Africans was fictionalised in several short stories published in the *Review*. In one of these stories, 'Panjandria', a headman's ten wives are arrested for stealing from a local white farmer and the headman offers his messenger some goats to fix the situation. The messenger convinces an African clerk employed at the native administration office to deceive his employer into believing the African wives were innocent in return for a female goat. This African clerk looks down upon the uneducated African messenger, referring to him as 'scum', but knows he can deceive his white employer who duly releases the women. Despite the weight given to white testimony in Rhodesian society it is the white farmer who is disbelieved. These narratives castigated educated Africans as having an inflated sense of self-importance as well as the overly familiar and naïve employer.[151]

There were other reasons for white workers to fear Africans from this social stratum. The *Review* noted that due to an educated African fighting a municipal court case in Bulawayo a precedent had been set for all Africans to use the pavement, and as a result the towns were 'infested with arrogant, impudent, and filthy products of the compound'.[152] The law had only been repealed in 1934 after Masotsha Ndlovu had arranged for Sithupha Tshuma to openly defy the law and fight the cause on appeal.[153] In 1940 the scribe for RRWU's Umtali branch declared that he had witnessed three Africans 'with their typical insolence and disregard of women's feelings, swagger along the pavement ... and deliberately, three abreast, force a white woman to step into the street and on to the pavement to avoid them'. He described his 'black rage' at this incident, and more so that he felt hopeless to stop what was going on: 'I had to sit tight in my car without a murmur, for the simple reason that the law of this country has established the right of a filthy, cheeky and ignorant native to consider the pavements as much as his right as a dainty, clean and sensitive white girl would!'[154] The response of visceral anger and violence was not uncommon. In 1949 the general manager of Rhodesia Railways was forced to appeal to RRWU to instil discipline in white workers whose violent behaviour towards African staff meant the latter were becoming increasingly unruly. Europeans had taken 'discipline into their own hands and just hammer[ed] the African', which had resulted in a loss of 'confidence ... in his European supervisors'. Educated Africans were specifically mentioned as being particularly liable to respond negatively to violence. The general manager had some sympathy for white workers in this regard and admitted he knew of 'the irritation [Africans] can cause', but ultimately demanded that Europeans kept their 'hands off the African'.[155]

African labour militancy: the 1945 and 1948 strikes

Education was likewise blamed for increasing industrial militancy; many educated Africans had taken leading roles in emerging trade unions and entered into cross-class alliances. Such alliances had been fostered by the experience of oppression under minority rule in general, but more measures such as the 1946 Urban Areas Act that had severely limited the mobility of the black bourgeoisie, prohibiting them from trading in white areas and forcing them to live with poorer black workers, undoubtedly strengthened the basis for collective action.[156] Charles Mzingeli, a mission-educated activist and owner of a Salisbury-based grocery store, led the reconstituted Reformed Industrial and Commercial Workers' Union (RICU) in 1946. The Bulawayo African Workers' Trade Union (known as the Federation) emerged in late 1945 led by Jasper Savanhu, editor of the *Bantu Mirror*. A rival group called the African Workers' Voice Association was established in 1947 by Benjamin Burombo, a successful businessman based in Bulawayo.

African men and women had resisted capitalist exploitation and colonisation from the earliest stages of white rule, during which dance societies, mutual aid societies, burial societies and religious groups such as Watch Tower whose millenarian prophesising had an idiosyncratic proto-socialist bent, flourished. While the political articulacy of such groups can tend to be overstated, they nevertheless evidence African resistance to and navigation of capitalist exploitation and alienation.[157] Charles van Onselen has demonstrated how workers used various strategies to evade, challenge and subvert the work demanded of them. Acts of defiance included loafing, sabotage of work processes, intentional slowness, attacking and damaging mine property, as well as the property of managers and white miners.[158] Although there had been sporadic instances of collective action in these early years, under conditions of harassment, surveillance and repression, the growth of political organisations was stifled and there was no systematic attempt to organise workers until 1927 when the Southern Rhodesian branch of the Industrial and Commercial Workers' Union (ICU) was founded.[159]

Across sub-Saharan Africa, labour unrest intensified during the Second World War and employers faced pressing needs to devise new methods of controlling labour.[160] In Southern Rhodesia the 1940s saw an increase in independent African trade unions and the 1945 and 1948 strikes are widely recognised as important instances of collective resistance in Zimbabwe's history.[161] Teresa Barnes has argued that this resistance was underpinned by the issue of social reproduction, as migrant labour ideology that provided accommodation, rations and wages for single men proved increasingly outdated. The demands that emerged in these struggles were directly influenced by the growing numbers of women and children living in urban areas.[162] Urban conditions for Africans were characterised by overcrowding, disease, malnutrition, lacking or non-existent sanitation systems and an acute poverty that was exacerbated by wartime inflation. The *Report on Urban Conditions* in 1945 noted that when taking into account wages and rations many Africans must had been approaching starvation point.[163] Various commissions argued that an increase in wages, proper accommodation, hostels for women, recreational facilities and other social welfare should be instigated.[164] But successive warnings on the gravity of the situation went unheeded by authorities. The railways were particularly slow at building housing for African employees despite serious overcrowding. From 1936 to 1944 the number of African men, women and children in the Bulawayo municipal location had risen by 81 per cent.[165] The number of Africans living in the Bulawayo railway compounds rose from 1,469 men and 309 women in 1933, to 2,436 men and 1,147 women in 1945, an increase of 66 per cent and 271 per cent respectively.[166]

Alongside management dragging its feet to meet new requirements, the shortage of skilled artisans and the intransigence of the RRWU who refused to allow Africans to complete skilled tasks in building work further slowed progress.[167] Such obstructions did not occur when Europeans faced housing shortages. During the 1940s the RRWU reluctantly supported motions to employ African artisans to build houses for white railwaymen in Northern Rhodesia owing to a lack of European artisans; African artisans were deemed temporarily acceptable to prevent white homelessness. The overcrowding in African areas, however, was an insignificant concern to RRWU.[168]

The Rhodesian Railways African Employees' Association (RRAEA) was formed in March 1944 in Bulawayo following a strike two years previously over mealie-meal rations and its membership quickly grew to two hundred African workers.[169] The RRAEA aimed to improve the conditions of all African employees and stressed moral, mental and physical improvement of its members. They also sought affiliation to the RRWU, which the latter obstinately refused.[170] After its inception, the RRAEA had written to the general manager about a range of issues, including union recognition, all of which were flatly ignored. On 27 September 1945 the administration informed the African workers of a new flat rate of three pence per hour, which would indicate a reduction in wages for some staff. Just under a month later around 80 per cent of the ten-thousand strong African workforce took part in the strike. In less than a fortnight strikers had returned to work on the agreement that an inquiry be made into their working and living conditions.[171]

There was confusion over the attitude RRWU members should have towards the strike. The multiracial SRLP gave approval to the railway strikers, arguing that it was conducted in an 'admirable' manner, with strong organisation and discipline. They remarked impressively that strikers in Salisbury had destroyed beer stocks to prevent drunkenness on the picket.[172] The *Granite Review* also noted these characteristics and praised the strikers' unanimity and refusal to back down from principles, which was something to be desired within the ranks of white labour.[173] However, the RRWU were keen to argue that the cause of the strike resulted from the insistence of the government and missionaries to provide African education. It was pointed out that the railways were almost 'crippled' by the African strike. They argued that by putting the railways in the hands of cheap African labour, Africans could hold the administration to ransom.

The *Review's* branch notes in the immediate aftermath of the strike reveal divergent opinions over the use of white labour to break the African strike. Many railwaymen were unhappy about taking on black roles in the production process and there was evidence that whites restricted their work to the transport of essentials. The RRWU executive directed the branches 'not to damage the cause of the African in his desire to improve his conditions' but maintained that essential services must be continued.[174] Kenneth Vickery has shown that while Roy Welensky, leader of the northern section of the RRWU, would go on to claim he had argued that white men should not take on black jobs as 'it's not our job to break another union', at the time he admonished the RRWU leadership for failing to print in the *Review* 'a full record of the native strike and the efforts of the union to keep things going'.[175] Vickery has also indicated that the refusal to perform tasks usually performed by Africans may have actually been more of a reflection of white workers' distaste of menial work rather than a sense of solidarity. The taboo of being a 'scab' and confusion over the novelty of the situation would have also played a role. A simple aversion to performing 'black work' certainly does not explain the report in the *Labour Front* that one white union branch was on the verge of coming out on strike alongside the African workers.[176]

As Vickery has noted, perhaps the most unexpected reaction to the strike was that of the railway administration, who held pervasive fears of industrial activity flaring up in European quarters.[177] Management feared Africans galvanising Europeans into action. The general manager, Mr Skillicorn, declined to meet with the strikers, reasoning that 'if the natives were allowed to do this there would be no reason why the Europeans should not do so too'.[178] In the past, public opinion had often been mobilised against white industrial action through allusions to African rebellion. Rawdon Hoare recalled that on the eve of the 1929 railway strike elite settlers feared that 'riotous "whites"' would 'cause grave discontent amongst the native tribes'. Those with memories of the 1896–97 rebellions cautioned how quickly Africans could be goaded into action.[179] Employers, the government and the Argus press variously argued that white workers were being irresponsible by threatening white unity and giving Africans ideas about rebelling against their bosses.[180] Certainly on multiple occasions strikes and demands of black workers were influenced by white action and trade union organisation.[181]

Yet Europeans were unlikely to offer meaningful support to African grievances. Both Africans and Europeans repeatedly crossed the other's picket lines. During 1919 between three and four hundred white miners went on strike across the Rezende, Falcon, Shamva and Gaika mines.[182] There was particular concern from management and the government that Africans should be kept busy, not only to minimise the loss to productivity but because 'trouble' would undoubtedly arise from a thousand Africans being left idle. Mr Southwell, the manager at Rezende, argued that they could keep the mine running at full capacity with only twelve white men and 'a considerable number of highly intelligent natives'. The threat was explicitly laid down by management writing in the *Rhodesia Herald* that 'the board have for long realised that too many white men have been employed' and that they would continue to use African labour 'until such a time as they can obtain a supply of non-union men'.[183] Herbert Walsh, president of the miners' union, denied the possibility that Rezende mine could function without its fifty European miners. That twelve Europeans could uphold production was denounced as 'so palpable an inaccuracy as to require no contradiction whatever'.[184] This was an affront to white declarations that only they had the requisite skill to perform such labour. Similarly, during African strikes strike-breaking may have emanated from the desire to cover white weakness: what the 1945 railway strike demonstrated above all was white dependency on African labour and the productivity of Africans that white workers were so eager to dismiss.

In the wake of the railway strike the fear of independent African organisation was rife. Word of the strike had spread and in the immediate aftermath there were instances of strike action in the Umtali area, of brickworkers in Bulawayo and sanitation workers in Salisbury.[185] With one humiliating defeat and signs of spreading unrest, authorities were quick to act at any whiff of organisation and harsh punishment was meted out. In November, several Africans employed in the building industry were reported in the *Rhodesia Herald* as being charged under the Masters and Servants Act for refusing to work. The African employees claimed they had not refused work, but had merely complained about their sleeping quarters and asked what their employer was going to do about it. The magistrate fined each African 10s and fourteen days of hard labour, which could be suspended on the condition that they immediately returned to work. The magistrate had informed the defence that the Africans 'had gone the wrong way to better their conditions'. They should rely on their master and the native commissioner in the future.[186] Likewise mine management at Rezende blamed the railway strike for encouraging dissatisfaction in the ranks of their African labour explaining that 'as the railway boys had got more they wanted more'. Demands of a £15 rise were quickly squashed. The white AMWR cheered management actions as a necessary show of strength and declared that all African demands should be crushed with similar fervour.[187]

Repression and surveillance did not quash African militancy for long. Although African railway workers had won modest pay rises and slightly improved working conditions as a result of the 1945 strike action, the sluggish pace of improvement failed to ease discontent. In January of 1948 the report of the National Native Labour Board recommended some increases in wages and improvements in conditions of service for railway workers just as more strike action seemed imminent. While the Native Labour Board postured that reforms were underpinned by a humanist ideology in which 'natives must be regarded as human beings with human needs and not merely units in a labour force', the president of the Salisbury Chamber of Commerce summarised the motivations behind the reforms more succinctly: 'We must get more work out of the native.'[188] It was stressed that for the expansion of secondary industry to take place 'an improvement in the efficiency and purchasing power of the native is not merely desirable but essential'.[189]

The improvements awarded to railway workers did not go unnoticed and became a basic universal demand for Africans to agitate around. While many black trade union leaders advised restraint, workers bypassed their representative's advice and prepared for collective action. On 14 April widespread strike action began and by the end over one hundred thousand Africans had taken part. Lasting over a two-week period, by the end of April employers' organisations had agreed to a basic wage of 30s a month in urban areas and 25s in rural, that extra rations should be given to men with wives and all Africans should be entitled to ten days leave a year with full pay and overtime pay – although these were suggestions and not binding on employers.[190]

During the strike Vambe described fear and panic engulfing white Salisbury, as 'for the first time since the 1896 rebellion, white people were compelled to swallow their pride and wash their own dishes, cook for themselves, empty their own dustbins, do their own shopping and collect their own letters. Meanwhile their black employees paced up and down the streets and loudly jeered at them.'[191]

Lessing provided a different picture of white Bulawayo residents: 'roaming the streets armed to the teeth, looking for Africans to beat up and punish'.[192] The RRWU appear to have refrained from making public pronouncements about the strike in the *Review*. Perhaps the RRWU recognised the fragility of the political situation and feared that their commentary would provoke black railway workers who had not taken part in the action. For years white labour had noted with fear the wide-scale industrial activity both to the south and north of the colony, notably the Copperbelt disturbances of 1935 and 1940 in Northern Rhodesia and the 1946 strike of African mine workers on the Rand, but white trade unions repeatedly postponed taking a definitive stance on African trade unions in their own territory. The AMWR had been asked in 1942 by African workers to form an African workers' union, but took no immediate action, recommending discussion of the matter in branches.[193] It was only after the 1945 strike that RRWU gave full consideration to the issue of African trade unions. Some white trade unionists pointed out that independent African unions would be too radical for public opinion, while others argued that it marked the beginning of the end for white domination of artisan trades. One RRWU executive committee member posited that their white daughters 'would be unable to obtain employment because the native would not wish to be served in shops by Europeans. He would wish to be served by his own people'.[194] As white male unemployment was becoming less convincing as an argument to prevent Africans from taking jobs in conditions of white labour shortages, white female unemployment was instrumentalised to undermine African progression. Nevertheless, in 1946 the RRWU passed a motion to 'guide and assist' African trade unions, although the *Review* indicated some rank-and-file dissatisfaction with the decision and had to persuade its members that recognition was the best form of control.[195]

The African branch and the RLP

The question of African organisation also surfaced in the ranks of the RLP. The RLP's popularity peaked in 1939 as they gained 33.18 per cent of total votes cast and seven out of a total of thirty seats. In 1940 Harry Davies and Jack Keller resigned from the RLP to form their own Labour Party as Davies's appointment in the Southern Rhodesian national government cabinet as minister of internal affairs had been accepted in defiance of the RLP Congress. While this original split was ostensibly about personality disputes and attitudes to participation in the national war government, the central issue that kept the two wings of labour from reconciling was the attitude taken to African involvement in politics and trade unionism.[196] In 1938 Colonel Walker, an MP for the RLP, had been approached by a small number of Africans who stated that 'the Labour Party was the party of the workers and therefore the proper party for them to join'.[197] With no racial prohibitions in the constitution, they were accepted. After the split in 1940 the Davies/Keller faction altered their constitution so it stipulated that 'no member of the aboriginal tribes or races of Africa, nor any person having the blood of any of the aboriginal tribes or races of Africa, and living among and after the manner thereof shall be admitted to membership'.[198] The RRWU were initially split over whether to support the Keller/Davies (RLP) or the multiracial Lister/Maasdorp (SRLP) faction, but the RRWU leadership eventually gave their support to Davies and Keller while the AMWR resolved to neither give nor receive assistance from the multiracial party.[199] The *Granite Review* repeatedly denounced the SRLP and summarised: 'We wonder if the engagement of some of the sons and daughters of those who are members of [the SRLP] will be announced to be Mr or Miss Jim Fish ... we do agree that justness and fairness should be given to the African but EQUALITY never.'[200] The AMWR openly accused the multiracial SRLP of accepting Africans purely out of financial expediency and low membership. In accepting African members the SRLP had brought 'trade union members to the level of the African'.[201]

Over the course of the early 1940s several attempts were made to reunite the two labour parties, but the issue of African inclusion remained contentious. Keller disparagingly commented upon the presence of Africans at SRLP's 1942 conference, pointing out the hypocrisy of certain members of the SRLP and the irreconcilability of the African's nature with genuine political unity and solidarity. The African delegates were merely loafers in comrades clothing: 'I can visualise those five native gentlemen being distinguished by the kindly reference to them as comrades, but when they go outside and walk on the pavements they become loafers ... how can you call them loafers in one direction and comrade in another?'[202] The progress of the 1945 conference, which was initiated to reconcile the two labour parties, was severely hampered, according to the *Labour Front*, by 'a political blunder of the first magnitude on the part of the SRLP' who had dared to sit their African members next to white women. They argued that white labour was the proper guardian of African interests. They certainly did not want Africans speaking or fighting for themselves. Instead, they argued, an all-white committee of men (and explicitly no women), should be appointed to deal with all matters concerning Africans.[203] The SRLP were further portrayed as capitalists and enemies of the empire and therefore, enemies of the white race itself. One letter printed in the *Herald* from an 'old trade unionist', applauded the labour split, glad to be rid of the SRLP, whose party line he said was dictated by the Soviet Union and whose members had brought about 'a strange state of affairs [in] that white men in this country should associate politically with the native in preference to cooperation with people of their own colour'.[204] The issue of white women's chastity and relationship to black men was repeatedly invoked in trade union and Labour Party print material.[205] The dehumanising language used to describe black men coupled with the image of white female vulnerability invited the white readership to share in a collective feeling of disgust and outrage, but also questioned what brand of 'Rhodesian socialism' white workers should invest in.

The SRLP failed to achieve ideological uniformity or consensus on African participation among its members. Some members of the SRLP were more committed to African equality than others. Doris Lessing and other communist sympathisers had been recruited by Gladys Maasdorp specifically so that they could support the existence of the African branch, but their ideas had little sway with the wider party.[206] Moreover, in the SRLP there was a division between left-wing socialist elements based in Salisbury and those such as Donald Macintyre, who loathed the African branch and did all he could to ensure another did not spring up in Bulawayo.[207] Macintyre had been elected as a Labour member for central Bulawayo in 1933 and afterwards served as the mayor for Bulawayo, becoming the chairman of the finance committee during the 1940s, which made him responsible for the African location.[208] When accused of inviting Africans to rule, Macintyre had to confirm that 'there was no intention on the part of the executive to organise the native within the political structure of the colony'.[209] He refused to spend money on improving the Bulawayo location and actively obstructed repeated attempts to improve conditions.[210] His membership of the SRLP probably had more to do with his fractious relationship with Keller and Davies rather than political alignment with its more radical or liberal leanings. The AMWR repeatedly labelled Macintyre as a bourgeois enemy of white workers.[211] Keller likewise denounced Macintyre in parliament and argued his loyalties lay with his own businesses rather than white workers.[212] Macintyre aside, several branches in the SRLP attempted to remove the African branch even after the RLP split.[213]

More broadly, the organisation was still essentially a paternalist organisation with populist policies. Any radicalism was hamstrung by the belief that they could get the majority of white workers to align themselves with African political organisation. One SRLP member strenuously denied that the party had agitated for African enfranchisement and argued that 'the only natives who belong to the SRLP are those who have qualified for and obtained the vote. They did this themselves without the assistance from the SRLP'.[214] Thus the SRLP differentiated between 'civilised' Africans and the uneducated mass. African members were required to be literate, which limited potential for membership growth. Certainly, there were only thirty-one African members by 1944.[215] The SRLP could not escape the logic of race and African membership was justified through appealing to a set of mythic liberal 'traditions of our [white British] race'.[216]

Nevertheless, the *Labour Front*, newspaper of the multiracial SRLP, printed commentary from leading African trade unionists, including RICU leader Charles Mzingeli. It also contained excerpts from John Strachey's *Why You Should Be a Socialist* and not infrequently references to Marx, Engels and Lenin. The *Labour Front* acknowledged that European standards were only achieved through the exploitation and oppression of Africans.[217] The SRLP attempted to defend its position by pointing out that the franchise had been open to Africans since 1922 and denounced Keller and Davies, noting that 'racial discrimination was responsible for Hitler and if Rhodesia adopts an anti-native, anti-Jew, anti-foreigner complex it will eventually lead her into terrible trouble'.[218] At the 1946 RRWU conference Jimmy Lister had argued that

> no one could now say that African workers were something quite apart from European workers ... it would ill become a European trade unionist to deny to others what he demanded himself ... they hated the natives because they feared him, and they feared him because they knew in their own minds that their standard of intelligence was not much above that of the native.

If, Lister continued, statistics were correct, three hundred thousand Africans in employment would soon become four hundred thousand in the next few years and holding back African advancement in such numbers would prove futile. Rather than make an enemy of Africans, they should be incorporated into existing trade union structures. The issue, Lister argued, was that increasingly less skill was needed to fulfil tasks on the railways but 'this bought the European worker closer to the native than most would admit'.[219] The skill gap between black and white, despite white trade unions' best efforts, appeared to be closing. Yet white trade unions would not accept this, preferring to deny any hint of similarity in the skill or work performed. Jimmy Lister's views were far from universal. He was castigated by the RLP for 'denigrating [his] own country'. Speaking on India at a public meeting in Umtali he was lambasted for saying that imperialist governments 'represented the financial interests. They are concerned with the profits to be made'. Lister questioned the ideological basis of empire, which, he argued, had not uplifted but destroyed civilisations. The *Granite Review* denounced Lister's apostasy to the imperial mission and argued that India was characterised by internal strife and famine before British rule.[220] Yet Lister appeared to have some limited influence on the white workers he organised alongside. Doris Lessing recalled that Lister had managed to get his branch (comprised of white workers) to vote in favour of the RLP African branch:

> When asked by us how he had done it, for we needed to know how it was done, 'I just let them have it, that's all it is. I said I was ashamed of them as working men, they needn't expect me to run things for them if they turned their backs on basic socialist principles.' And he recited:

> For a'that and a' that
> It's coming yet for a' that,
> That Man to Man the world o'er,
> Should be brothers for a' that.

> To show us how he had shamed his fellow white workers with Burns.[221]

Lessing was clearly surprised that anyone could get white workers to vote in this way. Certainly, these unexpected votes cannot just be explained through Lister's power as an orator or the respect he commanded among his fellow white workers. Rather it illustrates the continuing power of shame and pride in disciplining white worker behaviour, the potency of appeals to working-class and socialist principles, as well as the familiarity of at least some of these workers with Robert Burns's appeals to dignity and self-respect among working men. In this instance at least, Lister's admonishments that their behaviour amounted to a failure to act as working-class men fighting for socialist principles seems to have worked against the pull of racial ideologies and their interests to protect themselves against lower-paid workers. This was of course, the exception rather than the rule, but indicates that racial and socialist ideals were understood and acted upon in complex and diverse ways.

This complexity is reflected in the experiences of Bob Wharton, a white bricklayer and trade unionist who had moved from Britain with his wife, Alison, and their four children during the 1930s. While his position as a trade unionist gave him pride, the contradiction between socialist ideals and his racist actions elicited deep shame. Lessing, his neighbour, observed that while Bob, like many other white workers, hated capitalists and feared black competition, 'he was always uneasy, always guilty about it ... he was standing shoulder to shoulder with his white mates, keeping the black men out of skilled work. He knew it, and he was tormented by it'.[222] When Alison Wharton became pregnant, fearing the added emotional and

[154]

financial burden, she gave herself an abortion. Alison had to be rushed to hospital, yet Bob 'was too proud to ask for the relief hospitals give to poor people. They sold what furniture they had', downsized to a smaller house that consisted of two rooms and sold their motor car. As the family slipped further into poverty Bob increasingly turned to alcohol and after one heavy night of drinking was found dead at the bottom of a flight of stairs.[223]

Notions of the deserving and undeserving poor and the dynamics of shame, anger and pride that were rooted in poverty and class never entirely receded. During the 1940s Lessing worked as a junior secretary in a legal firm, which brought her face to face with a steady stream of 'poor whites', most of whom had failed to escape from debts accrued during the Depression:

> Some were men who drank and their wives had left them. They stood glaring at me with furious reddened eyes, or were ashamed and would not look at me ... Some men had been brought low by the illness. The women had babies in their arms or children pulling them by the hand, the tired, just-coping women of real poverty. Often the names on the cards were Coetzee, or van der Hout, or van Huizen, or Pretorius or van Heerden ... this wasn't slump time, it was war time, there was work. Mary [Lessing's superior] disapproved of these smelly shabby people cluttering up her nice clean office. She thought they should all be punished.[224]

The problems of 'poor whiteism' had not been entirely eradicated. Settler authorities noted that some Europeans were housed in sub-white 'slums' across the cities. Jimmy Lister and Colonel Walker visited a 'slum' in Salisbury South and described

> what at one time had been a large house but which was now divided into ten separate rooms and in these ten rooms there were about 40 people living in a disgraceful state of overcrowding. In one room there was a man, his wife, and six children. I ask him how he managed to put up the children and he said that the room was occupied by his wife and himself and the six children slept on the verandah.[225]

Overcrowding and disease were seen as phenomena that had to be restricted to African areas in order to achieve differentiation. Labour representatives used increased economic prosperity to argue for social welfare programmes similar to those being implemented in post-war Britain. The social security plan advocated by the RLP included a medical service, old-age pensions, widows' and orphans' allowance, disability allowance and unemployment benefits.[226] Unemployment benefit was only to be made available for Europeans, Coloureds and Asiatics.[227]

White poverty was still commented upon with zealous fervour, but RRWU emerged from the war stronger than it had been in the 1930s. White railway workers won pay rises in 1946 and 1947 and white miners revitalised their trade union organisation.[228] Economic depression after the war was regarded as inevitable. Yet the anticipated unemployment crisis never appeared. The 1946 census identified only 568 Europeans 'out of work', representing less than 1 per cent of the European population over fifteen years of age.[229] Shortages continued to intensify. In 1948 the number of notified vacancies reached 836 and the *Herald* noted that building artisans were in great demand. Rhodesia Railways had 111 noted vacancies while the mines had twenty one. In the same year it was noted that the number of unemployed was kept well below four hundred persons.[230]

Both the RLP and SRLP were about to enter terminal decline. Bitter divisions had plagued the parliamentary labour's existence. As Stanlake Samkange has argued, the RLP often intensified the divisions within the labour movement rather than overcoming them.[231] In the 1939 election the RLP were gaining a respectable 33.18 per cent of the total vote. In 1946 this had fallen to 16.69 per cent for the RLP and just 5.61 per cent for the SRLP, winning three and two seats respectively. Keller was returned to parliament in the 1954 general election by the railway enclave Raylton, who remained loyal until his death in 1959.[232] The last ditch attempt by Colonel Walker to initiate a third 'united' Labour Party in 1945 failed as the question of the colour bar could not be overcome.[233] The SRLP increasingly rejected control by the trade union bureaucracy, recognising their fundamentally reactionary interests. By 1945, the RLP claimed a racially exclusive membership of just over five hundred.[234] In the same year the president of the SRLP declared 'in a country where there are roughly twenty Africans for every European, a white labour party, or even one which is mainly concerned with white interests, is an anachronism'.[235] In 1948 the SRLP conducted discussions regarding the future of their party. Under conditions of falling popularity, funds and activity, the SRLP was resigned to admit that no progressive party could produce effective change 'under the aegis of Labour because it was associated with trade union reaction'.[236] Despite the members voting to carry on under the SRLP, the days of the party were numbered. Certainly, the period had incontrovertibly damaged both wings of labour and political representation of labour failed to recover. Centre-right parties were willing to concede to white workers' demands in return for their loyalty in the suppression of the African majority.[237]

Conclusion

The relationships between white male British workers and the black, white non-British, white female and Coloured 'dilutees' who were hired in increasing numbers in an expanding range of roles point to the complex way gender and racial hierarchies were understood.[238] The ability to control African labour was a recurring theme in the discussions over the suitability of particular social groups for different types of employment; white women, non-British whites, Coloureds and low-class whites were all seen as unable to command sufficient authority or deal with African staff in an adequate manner. White trade unions' attitudes towards hiring white women, Coloureds and non-British whites were dictated by pragmatism; all of these incursions could be tolerated if it meant that Africans could be kept out of skilled trades. However, this failed to prevent African progression into what were deemed white jobs.

The rhetoric of black criminality and loafing acted to articulate anxieties concerning a number of interrelated phenomena that contributed to a sense of emasculation for white men. White women could humiliate white husbands by becoming a source of income, or they could put themselves in danger by taking on unsuitable jobs; yet black men in employment could impoverish the daughters of white trade unionists by obstructing them from pursuing respectable careers. White British men attempted to re-establish their position by arguing against the autonomy, progression or physical mobility of particular social groups deemed to be a threat. They demonised Africans as they encroached on spaces, jobs, behaviours and attributes that had been imagined as white; they accused non-British whites of damaging white prestige and adding to the Coloured population; and they argued that the SRLP and employers had endangered white women and encouraged Black Peril. They also sought to control white women; to reposition them as weak and frail at a time when their increased autonomy outside of the home threatened the gendered division of labour and some of the ways in which white workers' masculinity was performed. By portraying women as helpless from the advances of African men and unscrupulous employers, trade unions dominated by white male workers laid claim to a virtuous masculinity. Yet white women were not seen as entirely helpless, especially if they took on work in defiance of white men. White women were still dissuaded from taking on jobs that were perceived to damage white prestige, compromise a woman's femininity or that brought them into inappropriate contact with black men. Their experiences of work were conditioned by the ideological importance of the white family and the reproduction of the race, which located women in the home.

Initial reactions to the 1945 strike and debates over African trade unionism demonstrate a level of confusion from white workers. The RLP preached a racially exclusive socialism but it is clear many individuals were unsure about how this idiosyncratic ideology should be translated into practice. Inconsistent or muted reactions to black working-class action sprung from the tension between loudly proclaimed socialist ideals and the reality of powerful racial interests. In many instances white workers responded to these phenomena with anger and violence. This reflected frustration over their inability to control the labour process, the racialisation of work and the physical and social mobility of Africans more generally. White workers' racial attitudes had not necessarily hardened from previous decades; rather, the growth of secondary industry had opened the door for a class of semi-skilled African workers who were essential to the Rhodesian economy. Thus, the power of white workers to punish and discipline as they saw fit was increasingly scrutinised and curtailed by employers. Many employers relied upon white workers to play a coercive role in the workplace, but this coercion had to be measured and controlled. Changing labour demands produced new tensions and power dynamics in the workplace; balances had to be struck.

Notes

1 See Ashley Jackson, *The British Empire and the Second World War* (London: Hambledon Continuum, 2006).
2 David Killingray, *Fighting for Britain: African Soldiers in the Second World War* (Woodbridge: James Currey, 2010).
3 Alois Mlambo, 'From the Second World War to UDI, 1940–1965, in *Becoming Zimbabwe*, pp. 75–114.
4 Kenneth P. Vickery, 'The Rhodesia Railway Strike of 1945, Part One: A Narrative Account', *JSAS*, 24:3 (1998), pp. 545–560; Kenneth P. Vickery, 'The Rhodesia Railways African Strike of 1945, Part Two: Cause, Consequence, Significance', *JSAS*, 25:1 (1999), pp. 49–71; Raftopoulos, 'Nationalism and Labour'; West, *African Middle Class*; Ian Phimister and Brian Raftopoulos, ' "*Kana sora ratswa ngaritswe*": African Nationalists and Black Workers – The 1948 General Strike in Colonial Zimbabwe', *Journal of Historical Sociology*, 13:3 (2000), pp. 289–324; David Johnson, 'The Impact of the Second World War on Southern Rhodesia, with Special Reference to African Labour, 1939–1948' (PhD Dissertation, SOAS, 1989).
5 Karl Marx, 'Wage Labour and Capital' (1847), www.marxists.org/archive/marx/works/1847/wage-labour/ch09.htm (accessed 5 November 2019).
6 Jackson, *Second World War*, p. 231.
7 Phimister, *Economic and Social History*, pp. 253–259.
8 Nancy Clark, *Manufacturing Apartheid: State Corporations in South Africa* (New Haven, CT: Yale University Press, 1994).
9 For an overview of hostilities towards Afrikaners, Italians and other non-British whites during this period see George Bishi, 'Kith and Kin? Rhodesia's White Settlers and Britain, 1939–1980' (unpublished doctoral thesis, University of the Free State, 2018).

10 Zygmunt Bauman, *Modernity and Ambivalence* (Cambridge, UK: Polity, 1991), pp. 1–2.
11 Ann Laura Stoler and Frederick Cooper, 'Between Metropole and Colony: Rethinking a Research Agenda', in *Tensions of Empire: Colonial Cultures in a Bourgeois World*, ed. Ann Laura Stoler and Frederick Cooper (Berkeley: University of California Press, 1997), pp. 1–56.
12 Penny Summerfield, *Women Workers in the Second World War: Production and Patriarchy in Conflict* (London: Routledge, 1989), chap. 7.
13 Duncan Money, '"No Matter How Much or How Little They've Got, They Can't Settle Down": A Social History of Europeans on the Zambian Copperbelt, 1926–1974' (unpublished doctoral thesis, University of Oxford, 2016).
14 Ian Phimister, 'White Miners', p. 196. Also known as AMWU.
15 W. E. B. Du Bois, *The Souls of Black Folk* (Oxford: Oxford University Press, 2007), p. 9.
16 Shadle, *The Souls of White Folk*; Roos, 'Ideas for a Radical History of White Folk'.
17 Angus Calder, *The Myth of the Blitz* (London: Pimlico, 1992).
18 MacDonald, *War History*, appendix, p. i.
19 Jackson, *Second World War*, p. 230.
20 Smith, *Great Betrayal*.
21 Jeremy Krikler, 'The Commandos: The Army of White Labour in South Africa', *Past and Present*, 163:1 (1999), pp. 202–244.
22 Commune, 'Letter to Editor, Cost of War and Cost of Living', *RRR*, May 1940, p. 25.
23 'Keller's Opening Address to Conference', *RRR*, August 1942, p. 6.
24 'Railway Dispute', *Granite Review*, September 1942, p. 3.
25 'The Railway Dispute', *RRR*, November 1942, p. 1.
26 Vickery, 'Rhodesia Railway Strike Part One', p. 547.
27 *RRR*, March 1940, p. 8. B.N.99; 'An Unwise Policy', *RRR*, November 1940, p. 14.
28 'Workers' Great Victory in Sweet Strike', *Granite Review*, November 1942, p. 9.
29 'Dismissal of L. T. Smith M. P., Insiza', *Granite Review*, July 1943, p. 1.
30 'Arrest of Frank Maybank', *RRR*, November 1942, p. 11. See also Money, 'The World of European Labour'.
31 Ferrugina, 'For Women Only', *Granite Review*, September 1943 (repeated 1944), p. 6.
32 'Editorial', *RRR*, April 1938, p. 3. 'Letters', *RRR*, January 1934 were written by 'Swastika'. See also 'Letters', *RRR*, February 1934, p. 18; March 1934, p. 17; April 1934, p. 17.
33 Johnson, 'Second World War', p. 40.
34 Hylda M. Richards, *Next Year Will Be Better and the Verse of T. Hylda Richards* (London: Hodder & Stoughton, 1952), p. 200.
35 Interview with Sharon Smith, Chris May and Jackie Wright, white women aged between sixty and ninety, Essex, November 2016.
36 Lessing, *A Proper Marriage*, p. 216.
37 *Ibid.*, p. 217.
38 Vambe, *Rhodesia to Zimbabwe*, p. 136; Robert Blake, *A History of Rhodesia* (New York: Alfred. A Knopf, 1978), p. 234.
39 B.N.99, 'Here We Go Round', *RRR*, November 1940, p. 5.
40 Phimister, 'White Miners in Historical Perspective', p. 190.
41 For fears over Nazi sympathisers among white South African troops, see Neil Roos, 'Education/Sex/Leisure: Ideology, Discipline and the Construction of Race Among South African Servicemen During the Second World War', *Journal of Social History*, 44:3 (2011), pp. 811–835.
42 Gustav Hendrich, 'Allegiance to the Crown: Afrikaner Loyalty, Conscientious Objection, and the Enkeldoorn Incident in Southern Rhodesia During the Second World War', *War & Society*, 31:3 (2012), pp. 227–243.
43 *Ibid.*, p. 1.
44 'The Eastern Districts Result', *RRR*, September 1938, p. 11.
45 See Baxter Tavuyanago, Tasara Muguti and James Hlongwana, 'Victims of the Rhodesian Immigration Policy: Polish Refugees from the Second World War', *JSAS*,

38:4 (2012), pp. 951–965; Martin R. Rupiah, 'The History of the Establishment of Internment Camps and Refugee Settlements in Southern Rhodesia, 1938–1952', *Zambezia*, 22 (1995), pp. 137–152.
46 Lessing, *Going Home*, p. 132.
47 'Communists and the Natives: Party Not Wanted in Colony', *Rhodesia Herald*, 26 March 1948, p. 11.
48 Lessing, *Under My Skin*, pp. 247–249, 304, 314.
49 Vambe, *Rhodesia to Zimbabwe*, p. 138.
50 Carina Ray, 'The White Wife Problem: Sex, Race and the Contested Politics of Repatriation to Interwar British West Africa', *Gender & History*, 21:3 (2009), pp. 628–646. See also McCulloch, *Black Peril*.
51 Vambe, *Rhodesia to Zimbabwe*, p. 159.
52 Lessing, 'The Black Madonna', in *African Stories*, p. 13.
53 See Phimister, 'White Miners', p. 190.
54 Johnson, 'Second World War', p. 25.
55 NAZ: S801/2 Italian Labour Service (1944–1945), General Policy and Administration.
56 *Ibid.*, p. 27.
57 'Salisbury Branch Notes', *RRR*, October 1945, p. 21.
58 'Shortage of Gangers on Railways', *Rhodesia Herald*, 2 November 1945, p. 6.
59 Headquarters of the Zimbabwe Amalgamated Railwaymen's Union Bulawayo, *Minutes of the 1945 RRWU Conference* (Bulawayo: RRWU, 1945), pp. 50–52.
60 *Report of the Commission of Inquiry Regarding the Social Welfare of the Coloured Community of Southern Rhodesia, 1946* (Salisbury, Rhodesia: Government Printer, 1946), pp. 69–70.
61 Headquarters of the Zimbabwe Amalgamated Railwaymen's Union Bulawayo, *Minutes of the 1948 RRWU Conference* (Bulawayo: RRWU, 1948), p. 77.
62 *Ibid.*, p. 79.
63 *Report of the Coloured Community*, pp. 58–60.
64 *Ibid.*, pp. 34–35.
65 *Ibid.*, p. 49.
66 *Ibid.*, pp. 21, 33.
67 *Ibid.*, pp. 61–62.
68 Lee, *Unreasonable Histories*.
69 Headquarters of the Zimbabwe Amalgamated Railwaymen's Union Bulawayo, *Minutes of the 1947 RRWU Conference* (Bulawayo: RRWU, 1947), p. 118.
70 Vickery, 'Rhodesia Railway Strike Part One', p. 553.
71 Alison Blunt, ' "Land of Our Mothers": Home, Identity, and Nationality for Anglo-Indians in British India, 1919–1947', *History Workshop Journal*, 54:1 (2002), pp. 49–72.
72 Cullen Gouldsbury, 'For Women Only: Land Settlement in Rhodesia, Rider Haggard's Report Condemned', in *Songs Out of Exile: Being Verses of African Sunshine, Shadow, and Black Man's Twilight* (London: T. Fisher Unwin, 1912), pp. 23–24.
73 Rhodes House Oxford, *Southern Rhodesia's Welcome to Women: Facts and Figures for the New Settler* (Salisbury, Rhodesia: Department of Public Relations, 1947), p. 11.
74 Boucher, *Empire's Children*, p. 145. For the contests, ambivalences and intimacies that domestic service involves, see Stoler, *Carnal Knowledge*; Karen Tranberg Hansen, *Distant Companions: Servants and Employers in Zambia, 1900–1985* (Ithaca, NY: Cornell University Press, 1989).
75 Anderson, *Toe-Rags*, p. 197.
76 'Retrogressive Rhodesia', *Labour Front*, January 1946, p. 26.
77 Assegai, 'Matters of Moment: Racial Suicide', *RRR*, May 1942, p. 8.
78 Brenda Manjiche, 'Implementation and Impact of the Marriage Allowance in Southern Rhodesia, 1914–1953' (BA Dissertation, University of Zimbabwe, 2012).
79 Law, *Gendering the Settler State*; Kufakurinani, *Elasticity in Domesticity*.
80 Jonathan Hyslop, 'White Working-Class Women and the Invention of Apartheld: "Purified" Afrikaner Nationalist Agitation for Legislation Against "Mixed" Marriages, 1934–9', *Journal of African History*, 36:1 (1995), p. 60.

81 Kirkwood, 'Settler Wives'.
82 McCulloch, *Black Peril*, pp. 95, 105.
83 *Report for Agricultural Openings For Women* (London: Society for the Oversea Settlement of British Women, 1922), p. 5.
84 See Shirley Ardener and Hilary Callan, *The Incorporated Wife* (London: Croom Helm, 1984).
85 Clerical work includes those described in the census as clerks, typists, stenographers, bookkeepers and, in the 1969 census, computing machine operators.
86 Kufakurinani, *Elasticity in Domesticity*, chaps 3 and 4.
87 T. S. Chigwidden, *Report on the Public Services of Southern Rhodesia, 1951–1952*, quoted in Magaya Tinashe Aldrin, 'A History of the Rhodesia Teachers Association' (BA Dissertation, University of Zimbabwe, 2007), p. 32.
88 Ivo Mhike, '"A Case of Perennial Shortage": State Registered Nurse Training and Recruitment in Southern Rhodesia Government Hospitals, 1939–1963' (BA Dissertation, University of Zimbabwe, 2007), p. 39; 54.
89 *Ibid.*, pp. 12, 59–60.
90 E. R. Cole, 'Gatooma Hospital', *RNN*, 5:2, June 1972, pp. 1–2.
91 Margaret Walsh, 'WomanPower: The Transformation of the Labour Force in the UK and the USA Since 1945', *Recent Findings of Research in Economic & Social History*, 30 (2001), www.ehs.org.uk/dotAsset/4e68f7d2-4ddb-4d34-889d-30c831beb6b1.pdf (accessed 19 August 2017), p. 1.
92 Monica King, 'Serving in Uniform: Women in Rhodesia Defence Forces and the Police, 1939–1980' (BA Dissertation, University of Zimbabwe, 2000), p. 32.
93 *Ibid.*, pp. 17–20.
94 J. F. MacDonald, *The War History of Southern Rhodesia, 1939–1945, Vol. 2* (Bulawayo: Books of Rhodesia, 1976), appendix, p. i.
95 Johnson, 'Second World War', p. 154.
96 NAZ: S482/198/40 Letter to Prime Minister from the Controller of Industrial Manpower, 9 March 1942, p. 1.
97 King, 'Serving in Uniform', p. 14.
98 Anderson, *Toe-Rags*, p. 228.
99 NAZ: S482 198/40 Letter to Mr Sutherns from Rivell's Commercial Classes
100 Kufakurinani, *Elasticity in Domesticity*, p. 95; Law, *Gendering the Settler State*.
101 Fairplay Always, 'Letters: Live and Let Live', *RRR*, September 1939, p. 26.
102 *RRR*, February 1940, p. 6.
103 Headquarters of the Zimbabwe Amalgamated Railwaymen's Union Bulawayo, *Minutes of the 1943 RRWU Conference* (Bulawayo: RRWU, 1943), p. 35.
104 W. Skillicorn, 'Women Clerks Employed as a Wartime Measure: Conditions of Employment', *RRR*, June 1944, p. 5.
105 *Minutes of the 1945 RRWU Conference* , p. 75; 'Salaried Staff Enquiry', *RRR*, January 1947, p. 5. Figures worked out from a female maximum of £347 4s per annum and a male maximum of £508 10s.
106 Aldrin, 'Rhodesia Teachers Association', pp. 30–38.
107 *Debates of the Legislative Assembly* (Southern Rhodesia: Government Printer, 1938), p. 1023.
108 Anderson, *Toe-Rags*, p. 338.
109 Lessing, *Under My Skin*, p. 198.
110 *Debates of the Legislative Assembly*, 1938, pp. 1004–1009.
111 *Debates of the Legislative Assembly* (Southern Rhodesia: Government Printer, 1939–40), p. 1972, pp. 831, 995.
112 Chigwidden, *Report*, quoted in Aldrin, 'Rhodesia Teachers Association', p. 85.
113 *Report of the Social Security Officer* (Salisbury, Rhodesia: Government Printer, 1944), p. 77.
114 Kufakurinani, *Domesticity*, p. 102.
115 *Census of Population, 1951* (Salisbury, Rhodesia: Government Printer, 1954), p. 18.
116 'Munitions Manufacture in Rhodesia', *Granite Review*, June 1942, p. 5; 'The Idea of Chivalry', *Granite Review*, August 1946, p. 1.

117 Headquarters of the Zimbabwe Amalgamated Railwaymen's Union Bulawayo, *Minutes of the 1946 RRWU Conference* (Bulawayo: RRWU, 1946), p. 158; Ibbotson, *Urban African Conditions*, p. 18.
118 Ibbotson, *Urban African Conditions*, p. 82.
119 Bill Freund, *The African City* (Cambridge, UK: Cambridge University Press, 2007).
120 Johnson, 'Second World War', pp. 335, 214.
121 Barnes, '*We Women*', p. 110.
122 Raftopoulos, 'Gender, Nationalist Politics'.
123 Tracey Banivanua Mar and Penelope Edmonds (eds), *Making Settler Colonial Space: Perspectives on Race, Place and Identity* (Basingstoke: Palgrave Macmillan, 2010).
124 *Report on the Census of Population Held on 7th May 1946* (Salisbury, Rhodesia: Central African Statistics Office, 1949), p. 3.
125 'Move to Prevent Indians Buying Property in European Areas', *Rhodesia Herald*, 23 January 1948, p. 10.
126 Gwyn Prins, 'But What Was the Disease? The Present State of Health and Healing in African Studies', *Past & Present*, 124 (1989), pp. 159–179; Maynard Swanson, 'The Sanitation Syndrome: Bubonic Plague and Urban Native Policy in the Cape Colony, 1900–1909', *Journal of African History*, 18:3 (1977), pp. 387–410.
127 'Need for Trade Union Unity and Planning', *Granite Review*, August 1942, pp. 1–2.
128 The association of Africa and Africans with STDs has proved particularly durable. See Jochelson, *Colour of Disease*.
129 Jocelyn Alexander, ' "Hooligans, Spivs and Loafers"?: The Politics of Vagrancy in 1960s Southern Rhodesia', *Journal of African History*, 53 (2012), pp. 347, 354.
130 'European or Native? At the Crossroads', *Labour Era*, April 1946, p. 5.
131 BN.99, 'Murder Most Foul', *RRR*, March 1940, p. 29.
132 Rhodes House Oxford, *Southern Rhodesia's Welcome to Women*, p. 34.
133 'Umtali No. 1 Branch Notes', *RRR*, March 1940, p. 41.
134 Sentinel, 'Letter to the Editor', *RRR*, April 1940, pp. 25–26.
135 G. H. Browne, 'Letter to the Editor', *RRR*, May 1940, p. 26.
136 Klipspringer, 'Letter to the Editor', *RRR*, May 1940, p. 28. See also J. A. P. Evans, 'Letter to the Editor', *RRR*, May 1940, p. 29.
137 Percy Ibbotson, *Report on a Survey of Urban African Conditions in Southern Rhodesia* (Bulawayo: Federation of Native Welfare Societies, 1943), p. 75.
138 Vambe, *Rhodesia to Zimbabwe*, pp. 159–160.
139 West, *African Middle Class*, p. 13.
140 Vambe, *Rhodesia to Zimbabwe*, p. 165.
141 West, *African Middle Class*, pp. 48–49.
142 Quoted in Ian Phimister, 'An Emerging African Proletariat: The Shamva Mine Strike of 1927', in *Studies in the History of African Mine Labour in Colonial Zimbabwe*, p. 61.
143 West, *African Middle Class*, pp. 21–23, 109.
144 Joshua Nkomo, *The Story of My Life* (London: Methuen, 1984), pp. 40–46.
145 Quoted in Kealty, *Politics of Partnership*, p. 380.
146 Alexander Kanengoni, *Vicious Circle* (Basingstoke: Macmillan, 1983), p. 7.
147 Charles Mungoshi's, *Coming of the Dry Season* (Nairobi: Oxford University Press, 1972), pp. 39–41.
148 T. S. Hlabangana, 'The Colour Bar Again', *Labour Front*, July 1947, p. 17.
149 Rhodes House Oxford, *Southern Rhodesia's Welcome to Women*, p. 13.
150 Ezekiel Makunike, *I Won't Call You Sir: Black Journalist's Encounters in White-Ruled Rhodesia* (Harare: SAPES, 1998), pp. 25–27.
151 'Panjandria', *RRR*, December 1940, p. 95.
152 BN.99, 'Here We Go Round', *RRR*, February 1940, p. 11.
153 Ranger, *Bulawayo Burning*, pp. 81–82.
154 'Umtali Branch Notes', *RRR*, March 1940, p. 41.
155 Headquarters of the Zimbabwe Amalgamated Railwaymen's Union Bulawayo, *Minutes of the 1949 RRWU Conference* (Bulawayo: RRWU, 1949), p. 99.

156 Phimister, *Economic and Social History*, p. 266; West, *African Middle Class*, pp. 23, 109, 136.
157 Phimister, 'An Emerging African Proletariat', p. 69.
158 Van Onselen, *Chibaro*.
159 Phimister, *Economic and Social History*, p. 264.
160 Clark, *Manufacturing Apartheid*, p. 118.
161 Vickery, 'Rhodesia Railway Strike Part One'.
162 Barnes, '*We Women*'; van Onselen, *Chibaro*.
163 'Report on Urban Conditions in Southern Rhodesia', *African Studies*, 4:1 (1945), pp. 10–12. For first-hand descriptions of the terrible conditions Africans were forced to live in, see Ranger, *Bulawayo Burning*, pp. 149–150.
164 Ibbotson, *Urban African Conditions*, p. 80.
165 Calculated from statistics given in Ibbotson report as number of total Africans increases from 6,077 in 1936 to 11,006 in 1944.
166 Vickery, 'Rhodesia Railway Strike Part Two', p. 54.
167 Johnson, 'Second World War', pp. 342–345.
168 *Minutes of the 1946 RRWU Conference*, p. 158.
169 Vickery, 'Rhodesia Railway Strike Part One', p. 550.
170 David Johnson, 'Urban Labour, World War II, and the Revolt of the Working People in Colonial Zimbabwe', *South Asia Bulletin: Comparative Studies, Africa and Middle Class*, 15:2 (1995), p. 75.
171 Vickery, 'Rhodesia Railway Strike Part One', pp. 550–548.
172 'Thinking Aloud', *Labour Front*, November 1945, p. 14.
173 'Broken Record', *Granite Review*, November 1945, p. 2.
174 'Broken Hill Branch Notes', *RRR*, December 1945, p. 91.
175 Vickery, 'Rhodesia Railway Strike Part One', pp. 559–560.
176 'Thinking Aloud', *Labour Front*, November 1945, p. 14.
177 *Ibid.*, p. 547.
178 'Mr Skillicorn Gives Evidence on the African Workers' Strike', *Rhodesia Herald*, 9 November 1945, p. 12
179 Hoare, *Rhodesian Mosaic*, p. 190.
180 Kennedy, *Islands of White*, p. 139.
181 See Lunn, *Rhodesian Railway*, p. 130. On the 1929 strike, see Ranger, *Bulawayo Burning*, pp. 51–52; Dacil Jeuf and Ewout Frankema, 'From Coercion to Compensation: Institutional Responses to Labour Scarcity in the Central African Copperbelt', *African Economic History Working Paper Series*, no. 24 (2016), p. 32.
182 'Correspondence', *Rhodesia Herald*, 23 December 1919, p. 20.
183 'Mine Workers Strike', *Rhodesia Herald*, 16 December 1919, p. 5.
184 Herbert Walsh, 'Letter', *Rhodesia Herald*, 23 December 1919, p. 7.
185 Vickery, 'Rhodesia Railway Strike Part Two', p. 67.
186 '34 Natives Who Refused to Work', *Rhodesia Herald*, 30 November 1945, p. 3.
187 'Native Strike', *Granite Review*, December 1945, p. 8.
188 'Natives' Right to Higher Wages', *Rhodesia Herald*, 9 January 1948, p. 9.
189 'Higher Wages for African Rail Workers', *Rhodesia Herald*, 1 January 1948, p. 1.
190 'Suggestion to Improve Native Labour Conditions', *Rhodesia Herald*, 9 April 1948, p. 11.
191 Vambe, *Rhodesia to Zimbabwe*, p. 245.
192 Lessing, *Going Home*, p. 252.
193 *Granite Review*, December 1942, p. 12.
194 *Minutes of the 1946 RRWU Conference*, p. 149.
195 'African Trade Unions', *RRR*, November 1946, p. 3.
196 Samkange, 'Rhodesia Labour Party', pp. 53–90.
197 ICOMM: pp.zw.srlp. 1, Memo Re. Split SRLP from RLP, p. 1.
198 ICOMM: pp.zw.rlp.RLP.1938, Constitution, p. 2.
199 *Ibid.*
200 'The Labour Party vs the Rhodesia Labour Party', *Granite Review*, December 1941, p. 6.

201 'We Have Been Sold', *Granite Review*, October 1941, p. 6.
202 Hopeful, 'Correspondence', *Granite Review*, April 1942, p. 9.
203 'Resolutions on Labour Unity: New Appeal to Parties', *Rhodesia Herald*, 21 December 1945, p. 1.
204 'Letters to the Editor', *Rhodesia Herald*, 21 December 1945, p. 2.
205 'Are You a Socialist?', *Granite Review*, November 1945, p. 8.
206 Lowry, 'Impact of Anti-Communism', p. 172.
207 Ranger, *Bulawayo Burning*, p. 120.
208 *Ibid.*, p. 119.
209 'Unsatisfying', *Granite Review*, November 1941, p. 1.
210 See Ranger, *Bulawayo Burning*, chap. 3.
211 'The Labour Party vs the Rhodesian Labour Party', *Granite Review*, December 1941, p. 6.
212 Ranger, *Bulawayo Burning*, p. 120.
213 M. C. Steele, 'White Working-Class Disunity: The Southern Rhodesian Labour Party', *Rhodesian History*, 1 (1972), p. 69.
214 'Letters to Editor: SR Labour Party and Native Policy: Liberal Statement Denied', *Rhodesia Herald*, 26 October 1945, p. 2.
215 Steele, 'White Working-Class Disunity', p. 66.
216 ICOMM: pp.zw Memo re: Split SRLP from RLP.1946.
217 P. M. Loveridge, 'Readers Forum', *Labour Front*, July 1944.
218 'Labour Discord Not Due to Personalities', *Rhodesia Herald*, 4 October 1945, p. 6.
219 *Minutes of the 1946 RRWU Conference*, pp. 150–152.
220 'Britain, India and Mr. Lister', *Granite Review*, February 1944, p. 7.
221 Lessing, *Under My Skin*, pp. 307–310.
222 Lessing, *Going Home*, pp. 241–242.
223 *Ibid.*, p. 239.
224 Lessing, *Under My Skin*, pp. 315–316.
225 *Debates of the Legislative Assembly*, 1939–40, p. 1972.
226 'Social Security Plan of Labour Party', *Granite Review*, March 1944, p. 9.
227 *Report of the Social Security Officer*, 1944, p. 84.
228 Lunn, *Rhodesian Railway*, p. 105.
229 *Report on the Census 1946*, p. 79.
230 'Fewer Unemployed in Colony', *Rhodesia Herald*, 7 May 1948, p. 12.
231 Samkange, 'Rhodesia Labour Party', p. 4.
232 Passmore *et al.*, *Source Book of Parliamentary Elections*, p. 156.
233 'Letters to the Editor, Move for Labour Unity', *Rhodesia Herald*, 7 September 1945, p. 2.
234 *Labour Era*, 1 December 1945, p. 5.
235 'Presidential Address of SRLP', *Labour Front*, p. 1.
236 ICOMM: pp.zw.srlp. 5 Minutes of Informal Congress of SRLP.1948, p. 4.
237 Samkange, 'Rhodesia Labour Party', pp. 104–105.
238 Clark, *Manufacturing Apartheid*.

CHAPTER FOUR

The 'multiracial' Central African Federation, 1953–63

Discussions of a white labouring class in the period beyond the 1950s have generally been limited to fleeting references to their support for the Rhodesian Front and other right-wing groups. Waning interest in white workers has reflected radical historians' understandable preoccupation with nationalist movements and African trade unions in the period from the early 1950s, but has also been influenced by the tendency of some radical historiography to fixate upon the ebb and flow of struggles at the point of production, at the expense of struggles fought out at the cultural level in people's daily lives and experiences. Thus as white industrial action declined from the 1920s, historians correspondingly paid less attention to white workers. This shift could also be partly explained through trends popular since the 1970s in which class is conceptualised as a set of particular shibboleths, traditions and aesthetics attributed to coherent class identities. As particular signifiers of class have changed or disappeared across the twentieth century, many historians and cultural theorists have clamoured to announce the end of the working class *tout court*, rather than being attentive to the specific ways in which class formations reconfigured.[1]

Alongside white workers' dampened radicalism and lack of industrial action in comparison with other industrialised nations, the RLP dissolved as the century progressed. White workers increasingly failed to possess particular signifiers associated with traditional working-class identities. In 1957 Doris Lessing concluded that among settlers 'there is no class feeling, only money feeling'.[2] Ian Phimister and Alfred Tembo have summarised that 'by the 1950s and 1960s almost all settlers saw themselves as whites rather than workers, as a privileged aristocracy of labour'.[3] Yet white workers continued to occupy distinct class positions that offer unique perspectives from which to interrogate broader settler colonial processes. Moreover, their self-identification *as workers*, was never eradicated.

This chapter covers the period in which Southern and Northern Rhodesia joined with Nyasaland in the Central African Federation from 1953 to 1963. The Federation's main architects, Godfrey Huggins and Roy Welensky, were keen to stress the federal government as a barrier against majority rule and as a route to independence and dominion status. Garfield Todd served as prime minister from 1953 to 1958 as part of the United Federal Party (UFP) and initiated a series of modest reforms in Southern Rhodesia under the new mantra of 'multi-racialism'. For white workers in Southern Rhodesia, the Federation and its rhetoric of multiracialism provoked concern over the dilution of the colour bar. The 'black North', with a much smaller class of white labourers, had historically seen greater progression of Africans into semi-skilled and skilled trades. Welensky attempted to mobilise white workers' support for the Federation by pointing out that white artisans on the Copperbelt were the best paid manual workers in all of Africa despite all of the 'Colonial Office interference'.[4]

But even with these assurances, pressures for African advancement intensified during the Federation period and threatened to erode the edges of the colour bar and white workers' monopoly of skilled employment. Labour shortages and the threat of African advancement sparked renewed interest in ideas of a white labour policy, the removal of Africans from the ranks of labour and reinvigorated efforts towards producing a tiered educational system that would ensure every settler could achieve a white standard of living. The process of imagining a completely white labour force also required that the figure of the poor white be invested with new meaning. 'Undesirable' work and wages had to be reconceptualised as outward expressions of pioneering spirit and respectability. Despite the broader context of decolonisation, these debates demonstrate settlers' optimism over the future of Southern Rhodesia and the tenability of a continued European presence and power.[5]

The Federation period witnessed intensifying pressures to allow jobs that historically had been performed by whites to be released to Africans. White workers continued to justify racist wage structures and their monopoly of skilled jobs in the face of growing domestic and international opposition and this was done through appealing to ideas that particular gendered and racialised bodies had definite limits of productivity. White worker identity was in part informed through maintaining a monopoly over the most senior grades and skilled positions in the colony. African advancement and African industrial organisation and upheaval threatened these dynamics. How white workers reacted to

these phenomena offer insights into how white workers saw themselves; as skilled, as educated, as creators and producers, as bearers
of modernity. Africans were imagined through an inverted mirror
image of these traits against which white labour could contrast itself.
White labour identity, as well as being informed by the structural position of white workers within the capitalist settler colonial state, was
also an evolving relational social category shaped by its positionality
to classed, racialised and gendered others. When Africans challenged
their own positions within the settler hierarchy through their demands
for entry into skilled jobs and equal wages they threatened not only
to proletarianise sections of this contradictory class and dismantle its
privileges within the labour market, but to remove the ways in which
white labour imagined itself as a distinct layer of Rhodesian society. If
white labourers performed and articulated their racial identity through
work, African progression into jobs that had historically been fulfilled
by whites jeopardised the ways in which white workers conceived
themselves as racially superior. This was not simply an attack on pay
and living conditions, it denied white workers a crucial means of racial
differentiation.

In the 1940s one friend of Doris Lessing, an 'old revolutionary' from
Europe who had spent his early years in Southern Rhodesia in isolation,
had desperately implored her to leave: 'This is a damned corrupting
country. We should get out quick. We should all get out. No one with
a white skin can survive it. People like us are too few to change anything. Now *get out* ... I'm getting out by the first train.' He ignored his
own advice and within a few years had become engaged to the daughter
of a large Rhodesian manufacturer, boasted of his new found wealth
and had embraced the mores of the white society that he had previously held in such contempt. Lessing observed numerous such transformations. She had left Southern Rhodesia for the United Kingdom
in 1949 to return in 1956 as a journalist and found that many of her
old socialist friends and settlers once considered 'wild revolutionaries'
and 'dangerous citizens' now loudly trumpeted the Federation as a
benevolent, civilising force.[6] Here, white racial thinking was unavoid-
able. Certainly, in some accounts Rhodesian settler society appears to
have similar power to the malevolent forces in *The Stepford Wives* or
Invasion of the Body Snatchers in its ability to eliminate difference
and enforce conformity.

Alison Shutt and Tony King have argued that the transient nature
of the settler population meant that re-education was a constant task.
Cecil Rhodes, early frontier myths, hostility to apartheid and promotion of the multiracial franchise as a central part of settler identity became important in the socialisation of new immigrants under

[167]

Federation.[7] However, the success of settler socialisation tends to be overstated. Moreover, while some historians have acknowledged that divisions were created during the Federation, there is little consensus regarding the nature of these fractures. For example, Donal Lowry has noted migrants with a more conservative outlook who desired to escape the British post-war Attlee Labour government as well as the 'Bengal Chancers' and 'Poonafontein Rifles' who arrived in Rhodesia from newly independent India.[8] In contrast, Alois Mlambo has noted that post-war immigration of middle-class professionals created differences between 'Old Rhodesians' and new arrivals with the latter holding relatively liberal racial ideas, preferring paternalist multi-racialism than outright segregation and opposition to majority rule.[9] White liberals mingled with elite blacks at garden parties and political meetings held by societies such as the Capricorn Africa Society and the Interracial Association of Southern Rhodesia, who invested in a vision of progressive franchise. Such liberal reformers, as Canadian journalist Patrick Kealty wrote in 1963, 'consist[ed] of people who are almost always highly educated and above the intellectual average – doctors, lawyers, students, professors, clergymen – people who feel the prick of conscience'.[10]

The emigration of lower-class whites has generally been overlooked in historical analysis. Contemporary commentators, in contrast, were deeply animated by the growing numbers of working-class settlers. Lessing herself was particularly critical of these arrivals, who she saw as being motivated purely by greed. Racial conflict, moreover, became increasingly explained through the presence of racist working-class migrants.[11] Cyril Dunn, African correspondent for the *Observer*, explained that

> Rhodesia has been described as the Working Man's Colony and it seems to be the case that many newcomers still come from the lower ranks of British society. After years of subservience, a newcomer finds himself suddenly promoted into a kind of aristocracy. A sense of racial superiority is of all feelings the most easily acquired and (let it be confessed) is by no means a disagreeable sensation. When it appears that the status and security of his job, his place in society and his many privileges all depend upon the rigid maintenance of an aloof dignity in white men, he can rarely feel impelled to interfere with this arrangement in the interests of an abstract social justice.[12]

Migration, the expansion of secondary industries, labour shortages and high labour turnover rates also destabilised established labour organisations. The white workforce was internally fragmented between established settlers and newcomers and between the trade union bureaucracy and the rank-and-file membership. This chapter uses the 1954 firemen's strike on Rhodesia Railways to show how white trade union bureaucrats cooperated with the state to remove undesirable elements from their ranks. White trade union complaints over the incongruent attitudes of newcomers and the behaviour of unruly Rhodesian-born youths expressed wider concerns over the failure of racialised socialisation and integration into the wider settler ideals.[13] Of particular concern was the fear that some newer white workers harboured socialist and non-racial ideas. Moreover, sections of white settlers had failed to achieve the elevated social status they expected through their racial identification. Records from the railway administration that white workers were approaching the railways for financial assistance highlight the subjective notion of poverty; workers saw themselves as unable to live a 'white lifestyle' on the wages they received. The reaction to white workers' protests against African advancement and the heavy-handed reaction to the firemen's strike are used here to emphasise the conditionality of white workers' privileges.

These upheavals created by European immigration often expressed themselves through competing definitions of Britishness. The Federation period was marked by growing conflict between Britain and the settler government as the issue of majority rule loomed. Bill Schwarz has argued that during this conflict, the perception that two types of Briton existed deepened. The first were the colonial settlers, who saw themselves as combining a hardy realism with an a posteriori knowledge of African affairs. The second type of Briton laid claim to metropolitan and urbane sophistry.[14] However, this tends to overlook that within Rhodesia established settlers and newcomers also offered competing definitions of who was, and who was not, *authentically* British. These contests over British identity demonstrate competing claims to a superior character, politics and way of life. Accusing others of not being British was a way of positioning one's views and beliefs as a legitimate expression of 'Britishness' while marking others out as fraudulent or degenerate.

Labour shortages and threats to white male monopoly

From the 1930s settler governments had pushed for closer union between Northern and Southern Rhodesia and Nyasaland, but successive British governments had frustrated its implementation on the grounds that it was detrimental to African interests. Partly in response to the election of the National Party and establishment of apartheid in South Africa in 1948, British attitudes relaxed.[15] Africans in Nyasaland and Northern Rhodesia, however, feared the extension of segregationist practice and indefinite delays to majority rule. Dr Hastings Banda, prominent in the Nyasaland African Congress, and Harry Nkumbula, president of the African National Congress (ANC) in Northern Rhodesia, both mounted vigorous campaigns against Federation. African opinion in Southern Rhodesia, on the other hand, was mixed and organised opposition to Federation generally muted. While Europeans in Northern Rhodesia and Nyasaland were wary of Southern Rhodesia exerting undue control, they generally supported Federation. In Southern Rhodesia 63 per cent of the overwhelmingly white electorate voted in favour of Federation. Despite vocal African opposition in Northern Rhodesia and Nyasaland, an agreement was eventually reached in which each territory would keep their own constitutions, relationship with Britain and control over African affairs, but a federal legislature would assume control over defence, economic policy, European education, taxation, external trade, transport and services such as electricity.[16]

The Federation was a period of huge growth. The European population had more than doubled between 1946 and 1956 from 82,386 to 177,124.[17] The number of manufacturing establishments had risen from 435 in 1946 to 724 in 1952 and by the following year the manufacturing sector employed over seventy thousand persons. African urbanisation increased, as did African participation in wage labour.[18] In 1946 Africans in the formal wage economy totalled 376,868; a decade later this had risen to 609,953.[19] Over the same period the number of African and Coloured staff employed by Rhodesia Railways increased by 77 per cent from 13,113 to 23,210, while the number of Europeans had increased by 110 per cent to 9,903.[20] The railways were becoming proportionately whiter; in 1939 there were 330 Africans employed per 100 Europeans, but by 1958 this had decreased to 212 Africans employed per 100 Europeans.[21] The Copperbelt experienced a similar shift as the number of white miners increased both in relative and absolute terms, accounting for 11.3 per cent of the total workforce in 1947, which grew to 18.4 per cent in 1961.[22] In contrast, in 1954 one white miner employed at Wankie would oversee one hundred black miners.[23] This in part demonstrates the heterogeneity in the dynamics of labour within particular occupations – not all white workers were inevitably working with a gang of African labourers beneath them. Although a racialised hierarchy would have undoubtedly existed, different sectors and occupations experienced different racialised working practices. Moreover, this meant that whites who envisioned themselves purely as overseers of African labour were sorely disappointed. Lunn has argued that on the railways 'there are strong indications that the racial demarcation line after 1947 increasingly became one of supervision as much as skill', yet this data reveals countervailing tendencies in the racialised organisation of labour (see Table 6).[24]

Despite the growth in the settler population and increasing numbers of Africans entering the workforce, labour deficits continued. Rhodesia Railways had suffered labour shortages from 1945 and the administration complained of a shortage of enginemen, guards and shunters 'despite intensive recruiting campaigns'.[25] In 1956, while 2,370 European staff were hired there was wastage of 1753. By 1957–58 wastage remained high at 1,584 and 1,697 respectively.[26] More generally across the colony it was suggested that over three thousand European builders were estimated to have been forced to leave Southern Rhodesia as a result of being overworked due to shortages.[27]

Despite shortages the Department of Labour professed it struggled to place unskilled whites and white women were noted as exceptionally difficult to place.[28] There were some avenues for permanent unskilled positions for women, such as the 130 women employed by Woolworths store in Salisbury, and temporary work was often found for women in retail over the busier Christmas period.[29] But it was argued that women on the unemployment registers were most likely 'pin money queens' and therefore not 'genuine unemployed'.[30] Nevertheless, white women continued to enter the labour force in ever greater numbers and married women were increasingly likely to remain in employment. Additional white female income became increasingly important in sustaining the conspicuous consumption of luxury goods.[31] The 1956 census pointed out that the proportion of economically active European women was 'among the highest in the world'. It recorded that 25.2 per cent of

Table 6 Railway employees north and east of Bulawayo[a]

Year	European	African and Coloured
1946	3,843	11,420
1947	4,251	12,972
1948	4,556	13,485
1953	7,792	19,516
1954	7,846	19,978
1955	8,505	20,885
1956	9,122	21,930
1957	9,789	23,273
1958	9,895	20,805

[a] Collated from *Rhodesia Railways Report of the General Manager for the Years Ended 31 March 1957–59* (Bulawayo: General Manager's Office, 1957–1959).

European women in the Federation were economically active compared with figures of 27.6 per cent in England and Wales in 1951; 21.7 per cent in the United States in 1950, 19 per cent in Australia in 1954 and 16.3 per cent in South Africa in 1951. In Southern Rhodesia 58.3 per cent of economically active European women were married while 28.2 per cent of the total married European women were in employment.[32]

Although more white women appear to have been recruited by RRWU, including one woman on the branch committee in Salisbury, married women found little protection from the union.[33] In 1954 a motion for white female clerks to be paid the same rates as white males was unanimously adopted at the RRWU conference. This was not a move towards gender egalitarianism; the motion further suggested that hiring women should be made as expensive as possible to encourage their return to the home.[34] When the railway administration began to replace married white women with single white women in 1957, the RRWU failed to protect its married female members.[35] Some union members argued that women should not be kept in the home, reasoning that women worked for reasons beyond money to spend upon frivolous items and had 'the interest of the railway at heart'.[36] It was pointed out that many married women had a lot of skill and dedication to the job that younger women did not possess.[37] Yet married women's unemployment was less unseemly than their single counterparts': 'Should [the young] be forced to "walk the streets" seeking employment because of the presence of an artificial "no vacancy" barrier which at this stage in our development can only be justified for sentimental reasons?'[38] It was agreed that while the wives of lower-grade men should be able to enter wage labour, the wives of station masters, grade clerks or senior grade clerks were frivolously taking up employment. Letters from railwaymen suggested that married women should be employed on a monthly basis and got rid of immediately if any single man applied.[39]

Despite obvious desire on behalf of some white women and non-British Europeans to enter the workforce, employers and white trade unions preferred to follow restrictive recruitment patterns in the face of continuing labour shortages. Plans to bring out railwaymen from Italy were decried by white unions and were eventually abandoned despite chronic shortages. This was further frustrated by restrictive immigration policies, which stipulated that the number of 'foreign' Europeans allowed to enter the colony was limited to 8 per cent of total white immigration.[40] There was particular concern over the fact that during the first six months of 1950 immigration from the Union of South Africa vastly outnumbered that from Britain. While 22 per cent of arrivals came from Britain, 69 per cent of immigrants were from the Union.[41]

The Rhodesian state increasingly believed that many men had no intention of remaining in their stated employment after being brought into the colony. In 1951 immigration policies were updated to prevent new immigrants from changing their stated occupations or industries without approval from the Immigration Selection Board or until they had acquired domicile. Although it was noted as a 'regrettable interference with the economic freedom of the subject', it was deemed necessary as recruits were leaving in order to find employment in 'more attractive' industries 'almost immediately' upon arrival.[42] By 1954 Rhodesia Railways were owed £17,280 in expenses by 213 recruits who had resigned or absconded. Reports from railway recruiting officers in Britain indicated that they had been 'fleeced' by some of the applicants, who after receiving the expenses at the interview did nothing further to come to Rhodesia.[43] Further to this, a 'post-war restlessness' was thought to be affecting the men, which meant they did not want to stay in a particular country or profession and employers had observed a 'wandering' tendency of white labourers. Wankie and Shabanie were failing to attract local recruits and complained of a large turnover of European daily-paid men. Miners and artisans stayed in employment for a few weeks before moving on. In most cases they moved to the Copperbelt, although mine owners explained this movement through the 'natural "roaming" tendency on the part of the worker who knows there is a job "over the hill"' rather than the higher wages offered in Northern Rhodesia.[44] Those brought out from Britain to work in the outposts of the railway system often quickly left to take up employment in Salisbury and Bulawayo as these positions proved lonely and lacked the community and facilities of the larger centres. Manufacturing offered work in towns with better hours. Other recruits were noted as simply failing to accustom themselves to Rhodesian life.[45] Attracting immigrants was one thing, making them stay put or act in ways that seamlessly slotted them into the settler community was quite another.

A white labour scheme

While white labour was deemed to be suffering from 'restlessness', the African affliction was diagnosed as inadequacy and indolence. Perceived problems of African labour were summed up by the pronouncement of one Liberal MP that 'they are inefficient. They are deteriorating. There are not enough'.[46] African farm labour was believed to be particularly disloyal and incompetent, although low wages and poor conditions were never used to explain this malaise. As labour shortages showed no sign of abating, arguments that only a white labouring class was capable of meeting the needs of an expanding industrial Rhodesia appeared with renewed vigour. The same Liberal MP posited that while Africans may have some use as domestic servants or farm hands, new industries required *white* workforces: 'When we talk about these large schemes – Kariba Gorge, Sabi Valley, oil from coal, secondary industries – I cannot see our doing anything very much on indigenous labour.'[47] Restrictive immigration policies had historically sought to control the number of white workers in the colony, but labour shortages reinvigorated the question over the future character of Southern Rhodesia. The *Review*, perturbed about African incursion into semi-skilled jobs, particularly the increasing visibility of African bus drivers and conductors on public transport, demanded immigration of whites who would fall into 'lower-income groups'.[48] Lower-class whites who would be contented with lower-paid jobs were seen as vital to upholding the colour bar and keeping particular semi-skilled jobs white.

The United Party were the most vocal in their support for a white labour policy in which Europeans were to be brought into the colony on fixed contracts in unskilled and semi-skilled employment. In the words of one United Party MP, in the absence of a white working class 'from which to draw physical energy ... the European races in this Colony will degenerate'.[49] The growth of an established white working class and peasantry was perceived as engendering permanence and stability; whites would not have to fear being numerically overwhelmed by Africans while a larger white population would improve settlers' chances of claiming dominion status.[50] Uneducated, unskilled whites might find a future in Rhodesia. It was argued that South Africa had been built up by a 'poor white' peasantry, who were very different from the scourge of poor whites of the 'mentally or physically defective' type. Southern Rhodesia could benefit from encouraging the growth of a poor white peasantry, who themselves would give birth to the next generation of miners and railway workers.[51]

The specific demands for a 'white peasantry' at first seem out of place; this social class no longer existed in Britain, nor indeed most of the industrialised West. This image that harked back to a preindustrial class who were envisioned as working the land and reproducing the settler population, in some respects mirrored aspects of African rural social reproduction and urban migrant labour. In the context of high labour turnovers and 'wandering' white labourers, this appeal to a stabilised white peasantry was not simply an appeal to an anachronistic idealised rural pioneer; it represented a longing for ties to the land that invoked a sense of permanence. It was a desire to make urban whites rooted to the land through familial ties. But in order to bring out unskilled whites, the discourses surrounding poor whiteism had to be restructured. Poor whiteism had to be extricated from discourses of degeneracy and invested with new meanings. The *good* poor white had to be popularised as enhancing settler rule; as an essential buttress of white domination.[52]

These new white workers would be prohibited from having African domestic staff as those pressing for the scheme did 'not want every immigrant who comes in here to have a native to polish his shoes. He had to do some work himself'. African labour was envisioned as being entirely replaced by Europeans.[53] The tobacco industry initiated a pilot scheme in 1949 using half a dozen farms to evaluate the potential of using white manual labour on a large scale. While the pilot scheme was hailed as a success, moves towards engaging white labour on a widespread scale did not progress. Antipathy towards poor whites remained and the scheme was rejected in the Legislative Assembly by twelve to eight votes and was criticised for trying to implement a policy of indentured labour for Europeans. Moreover, it was thought that the scheme would encourage the settlement of 'a second-class European population'.[54] Such a population would require huge subsidies from the government in order to educate its children and to attain a respectable white standard of living. Opposition to white labour policies primarily came from a desire to utilise cheaper African labour. Whatever a lower-class white could be paid, employers were well aware Africans could always be paid less. Despite increasing interest in white labour policies, the economic importance of African labour to Rhodesian industry, agriculture and domestic service could not be denied. Rhodesia was already struggling to accommodate its unskilled and uneducated white population and if employers refused to employ whites in place of Africans, Rhodesia would be left with an insurmountable unemployment problem.

Many of the unskilled whites resident in the colony were seen as being a product of inadequate educational provision. White boys were emerging from primary education who were only suited for manual, repetitive work. While these whites could perform 'a number of mechanical jobs' it was admitted they could not compete for these jobs with Africans. The Education Department was implored 'to pay particular attention to these children *to enable them to take their place in the white community of Southern Rhodesia'*.[55] Integration and assimilation required acquiring an appropriate level of education, displaying the ability to command a distinguishing income – and therefore to live a white lifestyle. In 1951 it was estimated that 25 per cent of Europeans aged sixteen would fail to pass Standard Seven examinations at the end of their secondary education.[56] Members of the Legislative Assembly suggested that employers should give afternoons off to white employees who were undertaking technical education. If Africans must advance, then Europeans must advance ahead of them.

Plans were drawn up to make sure that poor white boys were saved the indignity of menial work or unemployment. It was suggested that children aged between fourteen and fifteen who showed little academic aptitude should be streamed into an education with a 'vocational bias' in specialist technical high schools. Here it was hoped that low achievers could still be uplifted and prepared for a life in a respectable trade. Although poor educational performance for white girls was less of a concern, they were encouraged to enrol at Queen Elizabeth and Eveline in vocational courses that included 'commerce, shorthand and typing, book-keeping and commercial geography, domestic science and nursing and, in due course, dress-making, millinery, catering, hairdressing, commercial art and even armature winding'.[57]

Labour shortages did not lead to an easing of restrictive gendered or British-preference employment practices, but led to renewed discussions over education and the place of unskilled whites in the colony. Yet the white poor remained contested figures; what for some signalled a hardy authenticity to others held untold damage to white prestige, over-reliance upon the state and the entrenchment of uneconomic labour practices. The fears of degeneration and miscegenation bound up with poor whitesim persisted.[58] While Rhodesian-born youths had to be uplifted there was less support for bringing in unskilled whites into the colony.

African advancement

As the 1950s wore on, pressures to stabilise the African workforce and increase its spending power intensified alongside growing domestic and international pressure for decolonisation. Anxious not to become an international pariah, African advancement was seen as a means to protect against international criticism, to dampen nationalist fervour and militate against violent overthrow from below. White Rhodesian trade unions were also facing growing hostility internationally. At the International Labour Organisation (ILO) conference in 1959 Pat Lennon, the delegate elected by the all-white federal Trades Union Congress (TUC) and described by the *Central African Examiner* as a 'white supremacist', reported that he faced hostility from African members of the ILO, particularly Ghanaian and Guinean delegates who 'promised liberation and extermination'. Yet Lennon received the support of other white commonwealth trade unionists. In defence of Rhodesian trade unionism, a Canadian delegate pointed out his own trade union did not accept black members. While the British delegates seemed concerned with the treatment of Africans in the Federation, Lennon was assured that this was simply an issue of misinformation.[59] However the relationship with British trade unions was tense. The RRWU painted British trade unions as sanctimonious; they themselves were unwilling to work with undesirable Europeans, but 'if you come from Africa and have a black skin you are automatically right, but ... if your skin is white you are some kind of pariah'.[60] This feeling no doubt intensified with the British Labour Party's pronouncement in 1956 that they would demand a multi-racial franchise in the Federation when they came to power.

Progress for African workers was painfully slow. In 1956 African staff on Rhodesia Railways had won the right to be paid in cash rather than in rations and a new African senior staff grade was introduced to, in management's words, create 'a responsible middle-class group in the African community'. Only 185 Africans were affected by the new grade, representing a meagre 0.8 per cent of all Africans employed by the railways.[61] In 1957 Robert Kawanga became the first African to hold the position of assistant stationmaster on the railways at Luchenza in Nyasaland.[62] It is not coincidental that this limited African progression first took place where settlers were demographically weakest. Similarly, the first African nurse to be promoted from state registered nurse (SRN) to nursing sister in 1962 was based at a hospital in Lusaka, Northern Rhodesia.[63]

Common tropes re-emerged to reject African advancement: unrest among African workers; the supposed inherent backwardness of Africans, which framed them as the antithesis to industry (Figure 14); the 'annihilation of the European', poor whiteism and the greater exploitation of all workers.[64] White trade union support for African advancement was generally limited to support for gradual pay increases: a well-paid African workforce was less of a threat to white workers. White trade unions justified inequalities in pay and work conditions through the seemingly liberal mantra of 'equal pay for equal work'. Yet this demand concealed a reactionary core. 'Equal pay for equal work' gave a veneer of impartiality to the differential values attached to particular types of work and the values assigned to the racialised and gendered bodies performing the work. Therefore, while the RRWU acknowledged that Coloureds carried out the same work as Europeans, differential pay was justified through the important caveat that 'their *potential* value is not as great as that of the Europeans'.[65] In 1959 Coloureds could expect to receive approximately 90 per cent of European pay for performing exactly the same job.[66] The potential value of African labour was pegged at an even lower rate. The federal TUC claimed that Africans could only produce a fifth of a European's output in the same time period and therefore should be paid a fifth of the European's wage.[67]

Distinct racialised groups of workers were seen as having definite limits of what they could conceivably produce: each race commanded

Figure 14 'Beware of trains'

its own internal logic of productivity just as every race was separated by a static hierarchy of 'living standards'. As Rhodesian settler Peter Gibb argued in 1961, protections for white wages were necessary precisely because 'if a European youth leaving school were to take on a menial job on the present African wage standard he might as well commit suicide because he will starve anyway'.[68]

White workers used this language in order to lay claim to equality and liberalism while supporting and demanding racist structural inequalities in the labour market. Thus RRWU's general secretary argued that denying employment to anyone based upon colour was 'fundamentally wrong', accused management of exploiting African workers and portrayed RRWU as the champion of all workers of all races.[69] Europeans arguing for the 'rate for the job' knew that employers, if they had to pay Africans and Europeans the same wage, would always hire the latter over the former. In 1956 when the government enforced a law that required white workers and black workers in the building industry to be paid

[178]

the same wages, building employers immediately began sacking their African workers, causing the opposition to this law to perversely come from African workers; desperate to have a low-wage job than none at all.[70]

Yet white labour's demands for the rate for the job invited a back-lash against white workers who were castigated as greedy, overpaid and underworked. While high rates of pay were initially justified to attract skilled labour, times had changed and now 'a vast amount of money will be frittered away paying Africans far more than is justi-fied either by their standard of living or by the intrinsic value of the more advanced jobs they will get ... So the lower grade of European was and is overpaid. Now the African is to be overpaid too!'[71] The *Central African Examiner* likewise argued that white workers' demands for the rate for the job would ruin the Rhodesian economy and that European pay rates were unreasonable.[72] Even the RRWU admitted at its 1959 conference that the 'rate for the job' was a farce intended only to keep the African out of European jobs and that 'sooner or later someone would call their bluff, because it was not a realistic policy to adopt'.[73]

Despite the existence of African trade unions since the 1920s not one was recognised by official conciliation machinery. The Industrial Conciliation Acts of 1934, 1937 and 1945 excluded Africans from the definition of 'employee'. This exclusion was in part justified through the rhetoric of responsibilities and rights and contrasting the perman-ence of white employees with the supposed transitory and seasonal nature of African labour. In the Legislative Assembly it was argued that because Europeans had a long tradition of organised labour, whites had a natural understanding of the principles of bargaining. Trade unionism was pitched as something 'traditional' to white workers, a product of industry and modernity, infused with notions of respect-ability and responsibility and, importantly, something that Africans neither required nor were ready for.[74]

Nevertheless, the fact that Africans were independently organising themselves into trade unions could not be denied and in 1947 the Native Labour Boards Act had set up two regional boards for arbitration matters. The first provision for registration of an African trade union did not take place until the Rhodesia Railways Act of 1949. African trade unions were weak during the Federation period, wracked by internal factionalism, personality disputes and harbouring a complicated and often tense relationship to the growing nationalist organisations.[75] But their existence presented a threat that was not underestimated by the Rhodesian state. In 1952 the minister of native affairs admitted that moves towards facilitating African organisation must be limited as the 'premature organisation of unskilled primitive labour is fraught with grave dangers to the worker himself'.[76] The question of African unionisation for the government, employers and white workers alike was first and foremost one of control. Enacting repressive measures to squash industrial organisation had failed; incorporation and facilitation was the new agenda under Federation.

The 1954 Native Industrial Workers' Union Bill finally made collective bargaining machinery available to Africans. Between December 1954 and March 1955 there were twenty-five African industrial unions registered although the *Review* evaluated them as 'badly organised and inefficiently run'.[77] The AMWR and the AEU agreed to incorporate African branches in 1954. The AMWR general secretary had explained the benefits of incorporating an African branch as a 'sub-section' of the European union; all African grievances would be taken to the white leadership and 'the European union would then be in a position to know the aims of the African workers. Then, if the African claims were just, the European would be the first to recognise them and put them forward'.[78] Multiracial unionism offered a strategy to strangle radical African trade unionism as African demands could be mediated through the conservatism of skilled white members. Some white workers also saw incorporation as a means to prevent Africans being used to break European strikes and counter communist infiltration.

In 1959 the ICA allowed Africans to join trade unions but unskilled union members had less voting power, which effectively devalued African votes within multiracial unions. The Act encouraged industry-based unions, rather than cross-industrial occupational-based unions and unions were prohibited from making political alliances in a bid to prevent them allying with nationalist groups. Agricultural and domestic workers remained under the Masters and Servants Act.[79] In 1960 the RRWU agreed to open up the union to all non-Europeans employed in grades covered by the National Industrial Council (NIC) for the railway industry.[80] Despite predictions that 40 per cent of RRWU membership would immediately leave if their union was allowed to become 'an almost black one', by August 1961 there were 176 Africans in NIC grades, the majority of whom became members of RRWU.[81] After repeatedly lamenting poor attendance at branch meetings, Umtali admitted that it was 'nice to have twenty-two new members whatever their colour'.[82]

There was considerable division over the extent to which some jobs should be given over to African workers. One member of the RRWU union executive argued that the position of steward on the trains was inappropriate for whites as the pay was low and could not sustain a white family. The white stewards, he argued, were causing their children shame as a result of failing to afford blazers or shoes and 'he or she goes to school feeling shabby and ill at ease. This could be the

[180]

start of an inferiority complex – a bad thing for a European in Africa'. Whites had to *feel* and project their superiority.[83] Although previously a steward himself, it was a job he believed whites should release to black workers.[84] These suggestions were met with incredulous hostility. While it was agreed that the position of steward was undesirable, the rank and file appeared to defend the job as one performed by 'fully trained' men who were 'justly proud of the position they hold in spite of its attendant discomforts'. White men could take pride in this work. The image of Africans providing corridor service on night trains provided further justification for stewarding to remain white.[85] Demands for low-skilled and undesirable jobs to be staffed by Europeans may have had better support from the more uneducated and unskilled sections of the white workforce, but also reflected a resolve not to compromise over any aspect of African progression.

With regards to the public service, Kufakurinani has shown that white women often occupied semi-skilled jobs, which would be the first to be offered to African men, and as such they vociferously denounced plans for African advancement as well as moves towards equal wages between black and white men.[86] On the other hand, nursing shortages had proved so intense that, in contrast to the general tendency of white workers to fiercely defend white monopoly of skill, some white nursing and medical staff had urged the government to train African nurses from the 1940s.[87] Four-year training courses for Africans to become registered nurses commenced in September 1958 but African nurses were restricted to the treatment of African patients.[88]

The fears behind the prohibition of African nurses treating whites were summed up by a letter sent to an RLP MP in 1933. The writer asserted that Africans working in European hospitals defiled unwitting patients and expressed 'shock' at witnessing 'the natives bring my wife from the operating theatre and lift her into bed ... It is a well-known fact that natives carry all kinds of diseases and yet our doctors allow these natives to handle our wives when they are in a state of unconsciousness'.[89] Africans who worked in white hospitals had the chance to observe whites at their most fragile, their most vulnerable. While shortages in the medical profession encouraged greater tolerance towards African advancement, the notion that unsanitary Africans must be kept separate from hospitalised whites meant that this progression was only encouraged in forms that supported existing segregationist practice.[90]

In 1959 the federal government drew up proposals for the railways that broke down jobs such as ticket issuers, lorry drivers and dining car stewards into three or four pay grades, which both Africans and Europeans would progress through.[91] The AEU and RRWU decried the scheme as back-door fragmentation and deskilling. The Railway African Workers' Union (RAWU) were also suspicious of the scheme, which was seen to offer little real advancement. Over two hundred RRWU members from Gwelo, Salisbury and Umtali met and passed a vote of no confidence in their president. The AEU protested by calling a twenty-four-hour strike on 21 January. European unions protested that Africans would work for a proposed four-year 'testing period' during which Africans would be placed on a basic wage £10 below the minimum European rate for the job.[92] Others were more adamant that not even at double rate for the job would they allow Africans to impinge on European work.[93] The railway administration assured workers that no one currently working on the railways would face a pay cut. The testing period, they argued, was purely a safeguard to ensure European standards were being maintained. Yet the white unions' bluff was finally called as the railways offered every job on the rate for the job. RRWU and AEU were able to reduce the proposed four-year training period to one year. This was accompanied by an assurance that Africans could be removed from their posts if they failed to produce 'European standards' of work. White workers were fundamentally too weak and the needs and desires for cheaper labour too great to completely prevent such changes.

The firemen's strike

Struggles over African progression were reflected within industrial action taken by both African and white workers over the period.[94] After the 1948 general strike the Subversive Activities Act was passed in 1950 in order to quash political dissent and punish worker militancy. Nevertheless, the 1950s saw an unprecedented number of wildcat strikes of European workers across Northern and Southern Rhodesia. European railway workers had not taken strike action since 1929 and the last large European strike had taken place in 1932 in the building trade. Significantly, both of these occurred prior to the introduction of arbitration machinery under the 1934 ICA, which had effectively prohibited strikes in the colony.

The short-lived strike of Rhodesia Railways' firemen in 1954 is an under examined flashpoint in white trade union history, which offers insight into the general problems of labour retention that characterise the Federation period and the failure to rapidly inculcate newer immigrants with appropriate settler mentalities. For white railway workers, the railways represented more than the mobility of goods and persons, but held the promise of upward social mobility in the settler community. However, many of the immigrants who moved from the

United Kingdom failed to transcend the boundaries of class and status they were trying to escape. While the strike ostensibly emanated over pay and conditions, it was also fuelled by an assertion of certain rights and privileges that framed white workers' identity, including the right to organise. In particular it shone light upon the growing hostility between the conservative trade union bureaucracy and the rank and file of the RRWU, which represented around three-quarters of all European staff on the railways at the time of the strike. The strike and subsequent fallout demonstrated the extent to which the elite feared that white labour had a latent radicalism that could be stirred into frenzied industrial action.

Tensions had been building among low-paid workers for a considerable period. The RRWU had entered arbitration in February 1953 and while a basic pay increase was won for all grades the arbitration received a mixed response from RRWU members. In particular married men claimed they were unable to support their families on basic rates of pay.[95] Lower-skilled and lower-paid positions were often understood to be appropriate only for younger, single men from which they would gradually progress after gaining relevant experience. However, staff shortages had forced the administration to hire older experienced men in 'shunting' grade, which was considered a 'learner' grade. As a result the firemen's wage of £39 per month did not match what many older Europeans expected as a basic rate.[96] Moreover, the high number of resignations on the railways fuelled the belief that the administration were bringing out experienced workers with families from the United Kingdom under false pretences. For white railwaymen, an appropriate wage was determined just as much by age and marital status as it was by race and gender. The RRWU argued that men with years of experience and skill were being hired in low-skilled work.[97] It was considered unsightly for older white men with dependants to be employed on such low wages. The existence of this layer of whites failing to attain white standards of living within the railway community threatened to bring down the prestige of railway workers more generally. White workers were keen to present an image of social mobility and respectability, which demanded ensuring every white employed by the railways was able to project an air of prosperity and achievement.

The railway administration and RRWU had to repeatedly state that the firemen could not take action outside of the arbitration machinery and threatened that any man taking illegal strike action would be prosecuted.[98] Nevertheless firemen continued to call for strike action and there were calls from some quarters to form a new independent railway union.[99] As agitation over pay from the firemen's section increased, Charles Taylor, a British trade unionist and fireman who had been resident in the colony for thirteen months, was singled out as a ringleader of the continuing dissent and was expelled from the union on 31 May. Particularly unnerving to the administration and the government was the aptitude Taylor had shown in organising and rallying the men. On the first day of the planned strike the Criminal Investigation Department (CID) searched Taylor's house and found what they claimed to be a 'draft manifesto of standard communist type', which provided grounds for his arrest on 4 June. On hearing this news, firemen voted to carry on with the strike at midday on the same day and Taylor was deported to the United Kingdom.

The rapidity with which Taylor was deported without trial emanated from deep-seated fears of the administration and government that white workers could hold the country hostage through paralysing the railways. The government belatedly justified the deportation on the basis that Taylor had lied to enter the colony; Taylor's wife had confirmed he had been a member of the British Communist Party from 1943 to 1953 and a propaganda secretary for a local branch in Derbyshire, all of which was used to discredit Taylor and the firemen's demands.[100]

The strike went ahead in spite of interventions by the railway administration, the RRWU's executive and the government. While initially consisting solely of firemen, the strike gradually extended to include some sympathetic engine drivers and shunters who were angered by the heavy-handed response.[101] The firemen refused to negotiate with the president of the RRWU when he met with them to convince them to return to work and demanded separate representation as they distrusted the leadership who had seemingly aided the state to deport Taylor.[102] Garfield Todd, on the other hand, refused to negotiate with the strikers and would only deal with official RRWU representatives. The strikers eventually agreed to return to work on conditions of no victimisation, a fair trial for Taylor and a special commission into their claims. While strikers at Salisbury agreed to end the strike on 7 June, men at Bulawayo refused to trust reports of men returning to work from the RRWU leadership and management, and as a result did not end their strike until 10 June, only after Salisbury strikers had been flown out to Bulawayo to confirm the reports (see Figure 18).

The administration, RRWU executive and the rank and file provided competing explanations as to the strike's causes. Management maintained that the ringleaders of the strike had no concerns over firemen's pay.[103] They were accused of taking advantage of ill feeling in order to have a holiday, and it was noted that it was not entirely 'irrelevant that [the] strike came a day or two after payment of wages for May and coincided largely with Whitsun holidays'.[104] The RRWU executive committee asserted that the initial 1953 arbitration had been successful. The men, it was argued, had no real grievance but had been riled up by Taylor and his communist propaganda. Taylor was portrayed as a demagogue who did not care about the firemen's concerns but who was obsessed with striking and had deviously tricked the men into his own agenda that included ousting the general secretary and appointing himself as leader. One delegate at the 1954 RRWU annual conference recalled that he had met Taylor in the Zawi mess room where Taylor was talking about the recent strike of Africans at Wankie and had denounced the government's actions to break the strike. Taylor had continued to defend the rights of Africans to strike and even declared: 'My views about the African are these. When my daughter grows up, if the African is fit to have my daughter, he can have my daughter.'[105] Protecting white women was an axiomatic element of white masculinity within Rhodesia. By symbolically offering up his own daughter to an African man, Taylor had transgressed a constitutive element of white masculinity. The executive committee used anecdotes of Taylor's communism and liberal racial attitudes to justify their actions towards the strikers and attempt to erode the fireman's loyalty to him. Taylor's guilt was reaffirmed through these tales of his inability to meet the characteristics and behaviours expected of white workers.

However the publicity that Taylor had garnered in his defence was seen as having the potential to jeopardise essential recruitment of skilled workers from the United Kingdom. Taylor had received support from trade unionists in Britain and declared in the British press that he would not let the matter lie. Moreover, Taylor had returned to Britain and openly challenged the myth of social mobility in Rhodesia. He publicised that men were in debt; new arrivals were disgruntled at their low pay and often 'did not know where their next meal would come from'. Taylor further described his own experiences in damning terms: 'One day I did the unmentionable thing in Rhodesia: I borrowed money from my "houseboy" to buy milk for the kiddies.' Taylor understood that he was contravening white standards of behaviour. He offered a view of reliance and dependence upon African domestic staff; an image Rhodesian white labour had put considerable effort into emphatically denying. He hit back at the RRWU leadership as 'smug and lazy', accusing them of ignoring the rank and file and effectively acting as part of management rather than as the representatives of labour. According to Taylor, part of the reason why firemen took action was due to the administration's offer for improved conditions being restricted to the 'UK men', while Afrikaans-speaking men who made up half of the front-plate staff were offered no improvements.

Taylor described the offer as a 'disgraceful' suggestion that 'would have worsened racial feeling and destroyed all hopes of unity for a generation' and he cheered that when the strike eventually came UK and Afrikaans men walked out together. Taylor also vocally criticised the conditions of Coloured prisoners in the Cape, where he was stationed before deportation to Britain.[106]

How did the firemen allow themselves to be led by a man whom Rhodesian authorities considered to be such a deviant? The RRWU leadership argued that new arrivals had not fully adjusted to the Rhodesian trade union modus operandi or settler culture more generally.[107] Management likewise reasoned that the cause of the strike was down to mass recruitment of new European staff. In 1954 of the 8,000 Europeans employed by the railways 5,200 had less than eight years of service. Although recruits were screened, management admitted that with their huge recruitment drive, it was inevitable 'that some of the less desirable found their way into the country'. They further noted that: 'It was apparent for some time that many overseas recruits were fairly strongly influenced by socialist ideas and felt that labour should negotiate on more militant lines. This feeling among certain grades of recruits goes back some years.'[108] Sam Wright was employed by Rhodesia Railways from 1950 to 1976 and recalled that employees recruited from Britain were 'the most vociferous, in union matters ... it was a constant ding-dong between them and management' and dismissed some of their demands and rationale as 'completely absurd'.[109]

To militate against continuing dissent, as well as initiating more stringent screening processes, it was suggested that railwaymen be forbidden from marrying until they had reached a certain wage, something that was already in place for army personnel, policemen and bank employees.[110] This, it was thought, would prevent the growth of impoverished families and dissatisfaction from married employees. The Department of Labour likewise expressed a preference for men to come out individually and establish themselves before bringing out their families, as the infrastructure could not bear added population.[111] Without the requisite housing and services, white recruits were living in conditions below what they had anticipated and as a result were seen as being more susceptible to communist influences and industrial action. The settler state, railway administration and RRWU itself desired the settlement of white families; families were seen to engender stability and permanence. During the 1950s the *Review* printed a series of illustrations that stressed the role of the railwayman as essentially familial: a suburban man able to keep his family in comfort, a nation builder and source of pride for wives and children

(Figures 15 and 16). Yet economic conditions meant the immigration of families had a potentially radicalising effect.

European immigration was intended to maintain racialised employment practices and ease skilled labour deficits, but this was conditional on new arrivals being socially mobile and being able to perform a particular imagined white identity. The social mobility that Rhodesia promised its white workers was embodied in figures such as Roy Welensky who had risen from a position as a railwayman to the premiership. His mother had died when he was eleven and he stayed with his father in a poor part of Salisbury with Indians and Coloureds as neighbours. He was sent to a charitable school and in later years recalled that other children would jeer at him and his classmates and call them 'free school loafers'. Yet, Welensky maintained that he had improved himself through hard work, and even set about reading 'the classics' while on the footplate. Notably, Welensky did not attempt to obscure this upbringing or his former poverty, he wore it as a badge of honour.[112]

Yet this social mobility was neither universal nor automatic. In the year of the strike the Women's Guild had dispensed government rations of 1s 6d per person to sixteen European families and twenty-nine Coloured families every month for the preceding year. They gave a further ninety-six European families and seventy-four Coloured families second-hand clothes and shoes.[113] In a bid to prevent radicalisation the railway administration set up a welfare fund for its European staff in 1956 whose purpose was 'to give assistance for the relief of distress amongst railway employees by means of loans or grants in cash or kind', and in its first year dealt with 1,532 cases of white distress.[114] By 1957, 28 per cent of all European employees were approaching the administration for financial assistance.[115] From these statistics it is unclear what qualified as 'distress' for European workers: whether this was an inability to provide for dependants, to pay African domestic staff or to attain a social standing befitting of white skin. What is clear, however, is that many white workers felt that they impecuniously existed at the edges of white propriety.

The RRWU executive's assertions of confidence and moves towards providing financial assistance to Europeans at the bottom of the wage scale failed to quell dissent. The close relationship between employer and trade union bureaucracy fostered by the ICA was coming under greater scrutiny from rank-and-file members. There were reports of raucous meetings full of insults and jeering towards officials and the *Review* was forced to repeatedly extol the virtues of the current leadership and list their accomplishments in fighting for improved conditions.[116] Branch scribes continued to submit notes that defended

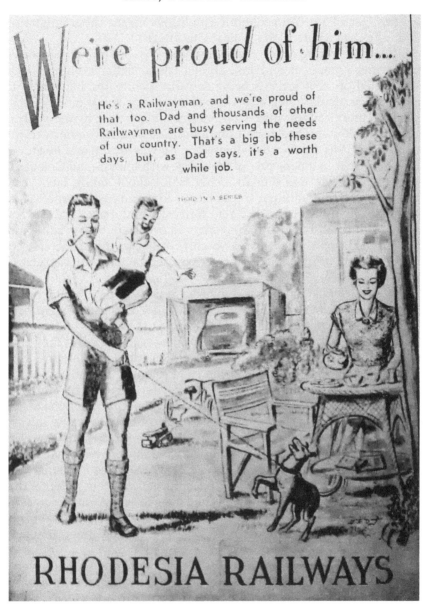

Figure 15 'We're proud of him'

Figure 16 'We're proud of him'

Taylor and denounced the leadership. The strike, in their opinion, was not a result of Taylor's interference but of 'bureaucratic administration ... allied with clueless but abundant supervision on the part of many junior officials'.[117] Despite the RRWU's annual conference passing several motions of confidence in the union leadership, branch scribes complained that delegates had voted against the prevalent feelings of their branch members. Branches also accused the incumbent leadership of causing a wave of resignations from the union.[118] The union bureaucracy in turn accused branch scribes of disruption and of 'flouting of authority', but the dissatisfaction failed to subside.[119] A year on, Que Que branch continued to call for a special conference and a motion of no confidence in the executive committee.[120] Figure 17, printed in 1959, suggests in-fighting continued long after the initial fallout.

During the 1954 conference there were several failed attempts to remove this conservative layer from the union leadership. Lower grades in the union were keen to prohibit railway officials – including inspectors and instructors – from serving on the executive committee, under the contention that these higher grades were effectively working as part of management. This motion was lost by nine to fourteen.[121] A motion to reduce the number of years a man had to be part of the union to be elected to the NIC from five to three years was likewise summarily rejected by the conference.[122] In this way, the union sought to control the potentially radical elements of its membership. They

Figure 17 'A typical Bulawayo branch meeting'

WANT

Railwaymen Back On The Job

Figure 18 'Railwaymen back on the job'

recognised that this meant that many delegates to the NIC were
disliked and not the first choice of its members but the RRWU leadership saw this as a necessary measure to prevent newcomers with
dangerous ideas from holding positions of power in the union. In
particular, it sought to control communist infiltration. At the same
time, while white labour's structural position engendered animosity

[191]

towards black workers and inhibited the likelihood of solidarity, such racial attitudes could not be taken for granted. The newcomer who had not yet been adequately drilled in the racial protocols expected of Rhodesian labour had to be prevented from diluting the union's attitude to African workers.

This in part reflected dominant ideas that established settlers had intricate ways of knowing the African population that were unobtainable to the newly arrived settler. As Sam Wright acknowledged, while recent settlers could achieve amicable relations with Africans they 'never quite had the same association as those African born' who possessed an 'insight into the ways and nature of the Africans'. Wright commented that the more recent immigrants displayed an 'unfortunate variety of attitudes' with complete disregard for the 'boundaries of personal contact that was acceptable'. Unlike the established settler, newcomers did not understand the full implications and 'dangers of too much familiarity which was not to the comfort of either party'.[123]

As discussed in Chapter 1, the contention that newer settlers and lower-class whites were the most violently racist section of society and the most likely to blur or transgress established racial boundaries was common and persisted over the period of minority rule. Lawrence Vambe observed that post-war British working-class immigrants gloated in their sudden elevated status and argued that they 'wanted to experience how it felt to have someone beneath them ... the lower they came down the social scale, the coarser they proved to be'. Vambe singled out the white lift attendants in the skyscrapers across the city as being 'particularly abominable'.[124] British journalist Richard West asserted similar sentiments and claimed that 'working-class immigrants ... understood nothing of Africa'.[125] When African sex workers appeared in greater numbers in the white lower-class suburb of Waterfalls during the 1950s this was explained through the presence of newly migrated white artisans. On one occasion a white policeman stationed in Waterfalls caught two white men having sex with two African women. This would be noted on the men's immigration records and a second offence would likely have resulted in deportation. The white policeman arrested the men and ordered them to get in the back of his vehicle with the African constables on duty. This provoked indignation from the white men who replied, 'We're not getting in the back with these bloody kaffirs.' The policeman noted the apparent contradiction, 'They didn't mind shagging kaffirs, but they didn't want to travel in a truck with them.'[126]

Fears of liberal racial attitudes seeping into RRWU from the rank and file were somewhat misplaced. When an executive committee directive ordered that white drivers should work with unqualified firemen to break the strike it was vociferously condemned as an attack on the colour bar. Initial reports sent between railway management suggest that railway authorities were keen not to use Africans to perform work usually done by Europeans as they feared it would strengthen the strikers' resolve and garner support for their action from other sections of the European workforce. However, rank-and-file members accused the executive committee of giving 'the right to the administration to place any human being of any colour on an engine and call him a fireman'. One delegate argued in defence of the union that their role was to break up illegal strikes: 'It even warranted the use of European convicts on the footplate. Everybody would have been done out of a job. There was also the example to the African. They were putting it in their heads how to get rid of all Europeans in the country; if the illegal strike had been successful they would have "had it".'[127] The trade union bureaucracy who dominated the conference generally agreed that strikes were not considered a useful tool any longer due to their potential influence upon African workers.[128] They accepted principles of arbitration and came down heavily on any action outside of its direct control. Yet what this episode demonstrates is precisely a lack of control over white labour on the railways.

Young apprentices were singled out as being particularly unruly and insubordinate by the railway administration. As well as receiving a substandard education, the absence of fathers during the Second World War was blamed for creating a disjuncture in the white nuclear family, which had resulted in widespread recalcitrance among young recruits.[129] The family was envisioned as an important unit for the socialisation of children in imparting particular racial and gendered behaviours. Yet in the absence or aberration of the nuclear family unit, perceived dysfunctional traits could take root. More generally the *Review* condemned railway employees' behaviour in the canteens, noting that 'the managers and European staffs of some canteens have been insulted; African servants have been assaulted; furniture and equipment have been broken, and utensils have disappeared at an appalling rate'.[130] Concerns over the sobriety and respectability of the rank and file also persisted (Figure 17).

Letters to the *Herald* bemoaned the high expectations of new arrivals and pointed to the fact the firemen's wage reflected its low skill. While these newcomers would have had a lowly status in Britain 'governed simply by the type of trade in which they were employed, not by the colour of their skin. After a spell in the colony it beats into their brains that they are Europeans and must therefore enjoy this so-called European standard of life'.[131] Dissatisfaction was seen as a consequence of new arrivals' unrealistic expectations. Another letter expressed shock at the behaviour of new immigrants and asked, 'If they are not satisfied then why do they stay, and upset others?'[132] The accused 'lawlessness and irresponsibility' of Taylor, argued one letter, amounted to 'the negation of those qualities which we term British'.[133] Established settlers used particular ideals of 'Britishness' against new British arrivals to present themselves as the true inheritors of this national identity. These Rhodesian claims to uphold and embody authentic British ideals and characteristics would only be made with increasing frequency and fervour into the 1960s and 1970s.[134]

Some strikers admitted that their primary concerns were not about pay. At Dett, railwaymen listed demands about street lighting, water and electrical shortages and general home conditions. They specifically complained about their nursing sister, who had caused a 'certain amount of friction' due to the fact she was 'of a type above the average driver, fireman and guard and does not socially mix too well'.[135] In a similar vein, Sam Wright, while usually at pains to emphasise uniformity among Europeans on the railways 'in skills [and] social sophistication' was forced to admit that 'dotted in this rather homogenous crowd, were a few exceptions who stood out a bit like sore thumbs'. Those he noted as standing out were not the poor, but those from the 'higher class of society', one a 'pompous' superintendent and another a doctor, scarred from 'duelling' who walked around 'with such an air of conceit and self-importance as to become a figure of ridicule and mockery'.[136]

Railway workers attempted to influence railway spaces by controlling the movement and presence of particular racial and classed groups. Numerous complaints over an unwanted African presence littered the *Review* and the management-owned *Rhodesia Railways Magazine*, which described 'hordes of Africans, their beds, furniture and possessions that are daily to be found scattered all over the station' and 'the hordes of "loafers" who sprawl all over the station premises at all hours of the day and night'.[137] Demands for separate African and white railway stations abounded. Coloured identity was also in part mediated through demands to be separated from the African areas. A Coloured platelayer's wife described her anger at being forced to travel in fourth class with African travellers.[138] Physical distance and separation reinforced claims to particular racial identities. But this animosity extended to upper-class whites. Railwaymen attempted to cultivate the railways as a white space; but it was also fundamentally a classed space. The white families of the Dett railway community were angered by a middle- and upper-class incursion into their delineated communities. The presence of such figures was a reminder of their social inferiority and the class divisions many were trying to transcend, but also pointed to the limitations of white social integration and an inclusive Rhodesian identity. Workers at Dett attempted to utilise the strike action to set forward their own demands regarding the white railway community and who was and was not a part of it.

As well as demanding particular rates of pay according to marital status and experience, the strike itself was a reaction to the treatment of Taylor. White men took strike action as an assertion of the right to organise and as a flagrant challenge to the RRWU leadership. There was particular anger over the heavy handedness of the state in squashing the strike. Within hours of the firemen announcing their strike, a state of emergency was declared across the colony. The CID searched the homes of strike leaders and several were arrested, dismissed from the railways or subsequently demoted. Keller, who had retired from the railways and become a full-time MP, openly criticised the RRWU leadership and complained of 'gangster' tactics, claiming that Garfield Todd and Roy Welensky had descended on his home to interrogate him and his links to the strikers.[139] In the wake of the strike Keller moved a motion to repeal section 8 of the Peace Preservation Act, which allowed the governor to make regulations in the event of strikes. The Act allowed the government to pass laws without parliament; to use forced labour, to hold people without trial and to arrest without warrant 'anyone whom they suspect ... merely suspect – of having said or done something which might in their opinion adversely affect the efficiency of an essential industry'.[140] Keller denounced the Act as a fascist decree and claimed Rhodesia was a police state, reminding the assembly that he had been assured that under no circumstances would the Act be used against white workers. Presumably he believed such measures were necessary to deal with industrial action involving African workers, but impinged on the civil liberties of Europeans.

The Legislative Assembly upheld that the Act should be used against both black and white workers in the interests of 'freedom'. Europeans could not be seen to openly flouting the law and punishment had to be meted out. The government also argued that they could not let a European strike continue when they had acted with brutal force against recent African strikers at Wankie.[141] All union power had to be curbed and wildcat strikes could not be tolerated. Europeans had a price to pay for their privileged position in the labour market. One MP reminded white labourers that 'the European artisan is not only in a specially favoured position under the law but he also in consequence has special duties to the community in which he lives ... in the presence of an almost overwhelming mass of uncivilised and unskilled labour [his duty] is to act moderately and temperately in industrial disputes'.[142] The firemen's short-lived strike failed to unsettle established union structures despite widespread anguish within the rank and file. The state had reacted brusquely to the actions of the firemen and reminded white workers that their privileged place within the settler community was conditional. In turn, many white workers saw their relationship to the state as one characterised primarily by suspicion and antagonism rather than co-option or partnership. The presence of policeman armed with aggressive weapons spying on a trade union meeting in Figure 17 underscores white workers' recognition that the state would employ coercive methods to ensure white discipline.

African industrial action

Instances of African industrial action during the Federation period were met with harsh brutality and repression. During the 1954 Wankie Colliery strike Todd deployed considerable military force to police 16,000 strikers. White miners, railwaymen and even clerks went down into the pits to keep production going.[143] After an inadequate basic wage increase in 1956 the RAWU, which had amalgamated the separate Northern and Southern Rhodesian African unions in 1955, called a strike that saw 7,500 Africans lay down tools for three days.[144] Police were armed with truncheons and used tear gas on striking Africans who had gathered in Bulawayo.[145] Unlike in 1945 where RRWU had acted with confusion and indecision over the 'correct' attitude towards African industrial action, in 1956 the Bulawayo branch admitted candidly that 'it has been our duty to do everything in our power to keep the job going which is nothing less than breaking the strike'.[146] The strike was used by the RRWU to demonstrate the irresponsibility of Africans, their immorality and unfitness for advancement and unionisation.[147] As well as strike-breaking, white employees sometimes rallied themselves into unofficial patrols or paramilitary units.[148] On hearing rumours of strike action in 1961, a volunteer police force of railway employees gathered to guard the workshops.[149]

Management were keen to publicise the loyalty of their European staff; it not only created a sense of camaraderie between white employees and management, but acted to discipline and dishearten African strikers. During a strike of African workers in 1952 the *Rhodesia Railways Magazine* claimed that a small number of Europeans actually outperformed the usual African workforce. It was noted that Europeans had eagerly fulfilled 'any odd job that was required of them'. Again in 1961 it was claimed that full production was maintained in the mechanical shops despite a thousand Africans leaving the shop floor.[150] Across white railway communities men and women rallied to support strike-breakers. Wives and daughters of railwaymen provided encouragement and support, but also took on cleaning roles, acted as messengers and served tea to the remaining workers.[151] Gendered and racialised hierarchies translated into the types of jobs people took on in strike-breaking. Those likely to take on the most menial of tasks and therefore the jobs most associated with Africans were women and non-British whites. During a 1956 strike the *Rhodesia Railways Magazine* specifically mentioned the Greek and Italian employees fulfilling roles of cleaning and handling coal.[152]

The image of Europeans performing menial 'African jobs' was used to emphasise the autonomy and self-reliance of white workers. The ability of whites to fulfil these tasks were celebrated as ' "palefaced" tea and "wash-up" boys, office cleaners, messengers, appeared miraculously from nowhere to aid the hardy labourers and to disprove the frequent observation that Rhodesians would be "lost" without the Africans to wait on them'.[153] Denying the centrality of African labour was at the core of how white workers envisioned themselves as the motor force behind Rhodesian industry and progress; African strike action allowed white workers to profess their loyalty to the wider settler project, prove their claims of innate white productivity and refute allegations of dependence on African labour.

The end of Federation

Under the leadership of Garfield Todd, the UFP's 'multiracialism' amounted to a limited number of reforms. Alongside removing prohibitions on Africans buying alcohol, Todd oversaw increased spending on education and supported extending the franchise to 'educated' Africans, most of whom were nurses and teachers. Yet Michael West has persuasively argued that the Federation's liberal reforms cannot be explained through the influence of particular individuals but must be located within broader 'economic and political transformations'.[154] Increased spending on education is best understood as a response to the growth of new industries that demanded educated and stabilised workforces, rather than of the influence of a small band of liberals.[155] Certainly, Todd regarded himself as firmly within the mainstream of Rhodesian politics. He had defended land apportionment and was quick to act against independent African organisation, ruthlessly suppressing African coal strikers in 1954 as well as the railway strikers of 1956. His ideal of partnership was fundamentally paternalist and generally circumscribed to black intellectuals and the respectable middle classes.[156]

Todd was nonetheless seen as a liability within the UFP. In 1958, after the announcement of a basic rise in wages for some African workers, a coup against Todd by members of his own cabinet saw his replacement by Sir Edgar Whitehead.[157] For many African elites, this extinguished any remaining hope in racial partnership.[158] In urban areas, anger mounted over low pay, poor living conditions, inadequate housing provision and extortionate travel expenses. The implementation of the Native Land Husbandry Act, which sought to individualise landholdings and control settlement in the reserves, had further fermented discontent.[159] These wide-felt grievances coupled with a growing pessimism in Federation propelled the rise of mass nationalism from the mid-1950s and forged stronger links between rural and urban struggles.[160] As the Federation years drew to a close, the brutality of the Rhodesian state intensified in response to challenges to settler power.[161] Jocelyn Alexander described these last years of Federation as 'the worst political violence since conquest'.[162] As the Southern Rhodesian ANC gained supporters, a state of emergency sought to suppress nationalist organisation. The National Democratic Party replaced the banned ANC in 1960 and in the same year African discontent erupted in the *Zhii* riots spread throughout urban areas.[163] The government used public order acts to restrict trade union activity and intimidate leaders. Over thirty high-ranking African trade unionists were held in prison and the state defended sending police members to trade union meetings.[164] The National Democratic Party denounced the 'Federation of inequalities' and paid particular attention to discriminatory practices in which 'people of the same qualifications receive different salaries because of their skin colour'.[165] Nationalists questioned why 'those whose annual income is £16 per annum should shout sky-high in praise of Federation and its economic advantages together with those with white skins whose semi-skilled white workers receive an average of £1,134 an annum'.[166] Africans also struggled for basic human dignity. One white nurse recalled a successful strike of African student nurses in 1962 who demanded to be called by their names, rather than by number. Yet she recalled that this simple demand was denied by the matron, which inevitably prolonged the strike.[167]

Meanwhile, settler politics were set to lunge rightward. From the Second World War, the same political and economic transformations that had offered some opportunities for skilled and middle-class Africans had simultaneously sidelined the interests of white workers, farmers and the white middle classes who stood to benefit from the elimination of African competition.[168] These various settler factions found their political salvation in the RF. When the UFP declared its intention to repeal the Land Apportionment Acts and continue to implement a series of liberal reforms, the RF promised settlers it would uphold the voting qualifications that ensured white dominance and maintain unequal land patterns. In 1962 the RF won thirty-five seats and ushered Winston Field into power, swept to victory on the back of votes of rural areas and lower-class whites.

The RF received on average 55 per cent of the vote in each district and received the highest support in farming districts of Gwelo Rural and Rusape. Seventeen out of nineteen rural constituencies voted in RF candidates.[169] The RF also polled well in older districts populated by lower-class whites including Waterfalls, Queen's Park and Hatfield and the mining centres Shabani and Gatooma. Certainly, in the run up to the 1962 election the RF specifically targeted white workers. Its publicised principles included a defence of the racialised welfare state and the introduction of unemployment benefits, an assurance the RF would support the rate for the job, prevent fragmentation and ensure 'that the skilled worker is protected from discriminatory wage practices and from unfair competition arising from a lowering of standards and the exploitation of cheap labour'.[170] Although the RF generally found electoral success across the country, they received less support in the more middle-class urban districts including Borrowdale, Greendale and Arundel.[171]

Reluctant to commit himself to UDI, Winston Field's leadership of the RF proved short-lived and Ian Smith was set to rise to the premiership in 1964.[172] A farmer and former RAF fighter pilot in the Second World War, Smith became the face of white settler minority government. Smith was by no means a natural ally of white labour. He was critical of trade union power and the demands of white workers, 'especially when these powers were in the hands of people who are socialistically inclined'.[173] Under Smith's leadership, the RF would maintain a strained yet interdependent relationship with white workers. In the same year Smith rose to power, a government report estimated that if wastage trends prevailed, industries would suffer a deficit of skilled and professional workers totalling between 23,000 and 35,000, or 13 per cent to 18 per cent by 1970.[174] The problem of labour shortages refused to abate. While white workers became an important ally to the RF as the settler community rallied around the banner of white supremacy to forestall majority rule, the country's labour needs meant that the RF's professed commitment to white workers and the colour bar was compromised from the outset.

Conclusion

Bill Schwarz has argued that the history of the Federation is a history of the struggle over the future of racial whiteness.[175] Despite the wider context of decolonisation across the British Empire and neighbouring British African colonies, white workers' focus on the future pointed to an unbridled optimism for sustained white rule. Rhodesians saw themselves as different, unique and able to ride the tide of independence sweeping the continent. The Federation also witnessed a shift from white workers' demands for a colour bar that excluded Africans from particular roles to discriminatory pay on the basis of engrained inefficiency. 'Rate for the job' allowed European workers to utilise the dominant rhetoric of multiracialism to perversely prevent any meaningful steps towards racial equality. Despite some limited reforms, progress for Africans was fundamentally lacking. High labour turnovers and widespread shortages accentuated white labour's transient and fluid character, which complicated efforts at a united resistance to African advancement.

Widespread labour shortages reinvigorated debates over potential alternatives to African progression, but economic necessity won out over white supremacist idealism. Fantasies of eliminating Africans from the labour process altogether remained pipe dreams as long as white reliance upon African labour remained.[176] Discriminatory gender recruitment patterns also continued in the face of continuing labour shortages and turnovers. Yet despite poor conditions and low pay, from 1946 to 1956 economically active European adult women as a percentage of all economically active European persons rose from 23.1 to 28 per cent (see Table 2 in Chapter 1).

The mobility afforded to particular Europeans to traverse imperial locations destabilised established settler practices and frustrated labour organisations attempts to cultivate a coherent white worker identity. White labour upheavals revealed the general weakness of a divided labour movement, but also the struggles to determine the boundaries of a white standard of living. It is clear that despite the existence of the colour bar and a series of racialised welfare measures, not to mention the huge wage disparities between African and European workers, substantial numbers of white workers continued to see themselves as hard done by and living either in or on the edge of poverty. Moreover, white workers were not successfully co-opted by the settler state. While European workers had a privileged position in the labour market this was in exchange for a regulated apathy and hamstrung trade union power. For employers and state authorities the use of repressive force was not out of the question; policing settler boundaries was a constant process.

Under the limited 'multiracialism' of the Federation, European trade unions were forced to remove their racial exclusivity in order to curb African social mobility. At the breakdown of Federation the RRWU pressed for a scheme that reallocated Europeans working on the Northern Rhodesian and Nyasaland lines to Southern Rhodesia. The railway administration assured its white employees that none would lose their jobs through displacement in the drive to Africanise skilled positions in newly independent states. In 1965 there were still over 1,600 'non-Zambian' railway employees in Zambia.[177] On 1 July 1967 the unitary railway system that crossed international borders ceased to exist. In Zambia RRWU members feared their racial boundaries, which were in part articulated and delineated through the monopoly of higher-paid skilled positions, would be eroded. By February 1968 all RRWU branches in Zambia had closed and by 30 June in the same year 1,006 railwaymen had been repatriated to Southern Rhodesia.[178] Moving south in the event of the territorial breakdown allowed for these workers to maintain internal borders, which enforced racial inequality just as decolonisation threatened to remove them.

Multiracialism under Federation was in many ways an attempt to make surface-level changes while leaving the structures of racial inequality intact; an abortive attempt to reconcile the contradictions between the continued proliferation of semi-skilled positions, ongoing labour shortages and pre-existing racialised labour structures. Fearful of being replaced and undercut by African workers, white workers played a key role in the conservative reactionary backlash to Federation policies. As Nyasaland and Northern Rhodesia moved towards independence and majority rule, the RF's populism offered a means for white workers to protect their status and privilege. For the most part, white workers were eager to uphold the colour bar and stifle African progression and were willingly incorporated under the RF's banner of white supremacy.

Notes

1 See Hobsbawm, 'Forward March'; Andre Gorz, *Farewell to the Working Class: An Essay on Post–Industrial Socialism* (London: Pluto, 1982). For criticism, see Willie Thompson, *Postmodernism and History* (Basingstoke: Palgrave Macmillan, 2004).
2 Lessing, *Going Home*, p. 64.
3 Ian Phimister and Alfred Tembo, 'A Zambian Town in Colonial Zimbabwe: The 1964 "Wangi Kolia" Strike', *International Review of Social History*, 60 (2015), p. 53.
4 Roy Welensky, 'Federation and Railwaymen', *RRR*, April 1953, p. 5.
5 See also Julia Tischler, *Light and Power for a Multiracial Nation: The Kariba Dam Scheme in the Central African Federation* (Basingstoke: Palgrave Macmillan, 2013).
6 Lessing, *Going Home*, pp. 60, 86, 149–150.
7 Shutt and King, 'Imperial Rhodesians'.
8 Lowry, 'Anti-Communism', pp. 172–173. See also Blake, *History of Rhodesia*, p. 274.
9 Mlambo, 'From the Second World War to UDI', in *Becoming Zimbabwe*, p. 77.
10 Kealty, *Politics of Partnership*, p. 243.
11 David Caute, *Under the Skin: The Death of White Rhodesia* (London: Penguin, 1983), p. 115; Peter Gibbs, *Avalanche in Central Africa* (London: Arthur Barker, 1961), p. 50; Richard West, *The White Tribes: Revisited* (London: Private Eye/Andre

Deutsch, 1978); Blake, *History of Rhodesia*, p. 282; Cyril Dunn, *Central African Witness* (London: Victor Gollancz, 1959), p. 204.

12 Dunn, *Central African Witness*, p. 207.
13 Such concerns about unruly youths were prevalent across Africa at this time. See Andrew Ivaska, 'Of Students, "Nizers", and a Struggle Over Youth: Tanzania's 1966 National Service Crisis', *Africa Today*, 51:3 (2005), pp. 83–107; Andrew Ivaska, *Cultured States: Youth, Gender and Modern Style in 1960s Dar es Salaam* (Durham, NC: Duke University Press, 2011).
14 Schwarz, *White Man's World*, p. 347.
15 *Ibid.*, p. 343.
16 Blake, *History of Rhodesia*, pp. 261–268.
17 Southern Rhodesian Census 1946 and 1956.
18 Raftopoulos, 'Nationalism and Labour', pp. 81–85.
19 C. M. Brand, 'Politics and African Trade Unionism in Rhodesia since Federation', *Rhodesian History*, 2 (1971), p. 89.
20 *Rhodesia Railways Report of the General Manager for the Year Ended 31 March 1956* (Bulawayo: General Manager's Office, 1956), p. 6 (this includes those employed on the Southern Section operated by South African Railways).
21 'African Advancement in Industry', *RRR*, November/December 1959, p. 5.
22 Ian Phimister, 'Workers in Wonderland? White Miners and the Northern Rhodesian Copperbelt, 1946–1962', *South African Historical Journal*, 63:2 (2011), p. 215.
23 Ian Phimister, 'Lashers and Leviathan: The 1954 Coalminers' Strike in Colonial Zimbabwe', *International Review of Social History*, 39 (1994), p. 172.
24 Lunn, *Rhodesian Railway*, p. 142.
25 *Rhodesia Railways Report of the General Manager 1956*, p. 11; BRMA: SD16: Strike, Firemen, 1954, Rhodesia Railways Letters, Press Cuttings (hereafter SD16: Strike, Firemen), Report, p. 2.
26 *Rhodesia Railways Report of the General Manager 1956*, p. 11.
27 'Bulawayo No. 1 Branch Notes', *RRR*, July 1954.
28 NAZ: Department of Labour Reports for 1959 and 1960.
29 NAZ: S2239 Southern Rhodesia Department of Labour, *Report for the Month of June*, 1958, p. 3.
30 NAZ: S2239 Southern Rhodesia Department of Labour, *Report for the Month of October*, 1958, p. 1.
31 'More Married Women Are Now Working', *RRR*, July 1956, p. 6.
32 Census, 1956, p. 9.
33 'Salisbury Branch Notes', *RRR*, June 1950, p. 27.
34 Headquarters of the Zimbabwe Amalgamated Railwaymen's Union Bulawayo, *Minutes of the 1954 RRWU Conference* (Bulawayo: RRWU, 1954), p. 154.
35 'Replacement of Married Women Employees', *RRR*, December 1957, p. 1
36 'Married Woman', Lusaka, Letters to Editor, *RRR*, April 1955, p. 11.
37 'Broken Hill No. 2 Branch Notes', *RRR*, February 1959, p. 17.
38 'Bulawayo Salaried Supervisors Branch Notes', *RRR*, February 1959, pp. 15–16.
39 Francois, 'Pin Money Queens', *RRR*, May 1955, p. 11.
40 *Debates of the Legislative Assembly* (Southern Rhodesia: Government Printer, 1951), p. 3584.
41 TNA: LAB 13/204 Memorandum: Immigration, 8 September 1950
42 'A Revision of Policy', *Rhodesia Herald*, 5 April 1951, p. 5.
43 BRMA: SD16: Strike, Firemen. Report, p. 4.
44 NAZ: S2239 Southern Rhodesia Department of Labour, *Report for the Month of July*, 1960, p. 1; Phimister, 'Workers in Wonderland?', p. 197.
45 BRMA: SD16: Strike, Firemen. Report, p. 3.
46 *Debates of the Legislative Assembly*, 1951, p. 3576.
47 *Ibid.*; Tischler, *Light and Power*.
48 'Editorial', *RRR*, April 1951, p. 1.
49 *Debates of the Legislative Assembly*, 1951, p. 3584.
50 *Debates of the Legislative Assembly*, 1950, pp. 2815, 2828.

51 *Debates of the Legislative Assembly*, 1951, p. 2880.
52 For debates over white immigration during the RF period, see Josiah Brownell, *The Collapse of Rhodesia: Population Demographics and the Politics of Race* (London: I. B. Taurus, 2011).
53 *Debates of the Legislative Assembly*, 1951, pp. 3608–3610.
54 *Ibid.*, pp. 3588–3610.
55 *Ibid.*, p. 2861 (emphasis added).
56 *Ibid.*, p. 2936.
57 *Ibid.*, pp. 2857–2867.
58 Timothy Parsons, *The Second British Empire: In the Crucible of the Twentieth Century* (Lanham, MD: Rowman & Littlefield, 2014), p. 154.
59 'ILO Conference and Meeting with British TUC', *RRR*, August 1959, pp. 10–11.
60 'Whither Trade Unionism?', *RRR*, August 1957, p. 6.
61 *Rhodesia Railways Report of the General Manager 1956*, p. 16.
62 *Federal Newsletter*, 30 November 1957.
63 Masakure, 'On the Frontline of Caring', p. 109.
64 *Federal Newsletter*, 2 October 1959; 'Fear that Railway Plan Will Make Poor Whites', *Rhodesia Herald*, 31 July 1959.
65 'The Unions Case Summed Up', *RRR*, November 1954, p. 7 (emphasis added).
66 *RRM*, December 1959, p. 50.
67 '"Trade Unionists Throughout the Federation Meet in Bulawayo": Conference Opened by Mr T. C. Rutherford President of South African Trade Union Council', *RRR*, July 1955, p. 5.
68 Gibbs, *Avalanche in Central Africa*, p. 97.
69 'African Advancement in Industry', *RRR*, November/December 1959, p. 4.
70 Lessing, *Going Home*, p. 106.
71 TNA: DO 35/7460: *Northern News*, 17 December 1959
72 *The Central African Examiner*, 19 December 1959, p. 6.
73 *Minutes of the 1954 RRWU Conference*, p. 276.
74 *Debates of the Legislative Assembly* (Southern Rhodesia: Government Printer, 1956), p. 2585.
75 See Raftopoulos, 'Nationalism and Labour'.
76 *The African in Southern Rhodesia Industry* (Bulawayo: Rhodesian Institute of African Affairs), pp. 22–23.
77 'Future of Trade Unions and Industrial Conciliation Machinery', *RRR*, June 1956, p. 10.
78 *Minutes of the 1954 RRWU Conference*, p. 264.
79 Brand, 'Federation', p. 90; Mlambo, 'Second World War to UDI', p. 103.
80 *Fortnightly Summary*, 9 April 1959.
81 'Que Que Branch Notes', *RRR*, July 1956, p. 25; 'Constitutional Proposals', *RRR*, August 1961, p. 4.
82 'Umtali, No. 5 Branch Notes', *RRR*, October 1960, p. 20.
83 See Will Jackson, 'Bad Blood: Poverty, Psychopathy and the Politics of Transgression in Kenya Colony, 1939–59', *Journal of Imperial and Commonwealth History*, 39:1 (2011), pp. 73–94; Ann Stoler, *Race and the Education of Desire: Foucault's History of Sexuality and the Colonial Order of Things* (Durham, NC: Duke University Press, 1995).
84 'Mr Matthews Says Goodbye as an Executive Member', *RRR*, January 1955, p. 16.
85 W. A. Chapman, 'Letters to Editor', *RRR*, February 1955, p. 12.
86 Ushehwedu Kufakurinani, 'Negotiating Respectability: White Women in the Public Service of Southern Rhodesia', *Online Journal of Social Sciences Research*, 1:4 (2012), pp. 115–124.
87 Masakure, 'On the Frontline of Caring', p. 43.
88 'Miss O. R. Norton's Farewell', *RNN*, 8:2, June 1975, p. 17.
89 *Debates of the Legislative Assembly*, 1933, p. 873.
90 See Lynette Jackson, *Surfacing Up: Psychiatry and Social Order in Colonial Zimbabwe, 1908–1968* (Ithaca, NY: Cornell University Press, 2005), chap. 2.

91 TNA: DO 35/7460 African Advancement on Rhodesia Railways (Note for the Secretary of State for the Colonies), p. 1.
92 TNA: DO 35/7460 *Federal Newsletter*, 29 January 1960, p. 8.
93 *Minutes of the 1954 RRWU Conference*, p. 276.
94 Money, 'The World of European Labour'; Phimister, 'Lashers and Leviathan', pp. 165–196.
95 'Arbitration Award', *RRR*, April 1954, p. 1.
96 TNA: DO 35/4831 Deportation of Charles Taylor: Secret: Inward Telegram from High Commissioner of Federation to Commonwealth Relations Office.
97 *Minutes of the 1954 RRWU Conference*, p. 25.
98 'Firemen Told: Illegal to Strike at this Stage', *Rhodesia Herald*, 21 May 1954, p. 13.
99 'Railwaymen Give Notice to Union, Que Que', *Rhodesia Herald*, 4 June 1954, p. 1; 'Mr Went's Resignation Demanded', *Rhodesia Herald*, 3 June 1954, p. 1.
100 TNA: DO 35/4831 Deportation of Charles Taylor: Inward Telegram to Commonwealth Relations Office: From UK High Commissioner.
101 'Salisbury Engine Drivers Out', *Rhodesia Herald*, 7 June 1954, p. 1.
102 BRMA: SD16: Strike, Firemen. Letter to Chief Mechanical Engineer, 16 June 1954, no. 368/33, p. 2.
103 BRMA: SD16: Strike, Firemen. Report, p. 2.
104 TNA: DO 35/4831 Deportation of Charles Taylor: SECRET: Inward Telegram from High Commissioner of Federation to Commonwealth Relations Office.
105 *Minutes of the 1954 RRWU Conference*, pp. 222–224.
106 Charles Taylor, 'Why I was Deported from Rhodesia', *Daily Worker*, 6 July 1954.
107 *Minutes of the 1954 RRWU Conference*, p. 210.
108 BRMA: SD16: Strike, Firemen. Report, p. 2.
109 Sam Wright, *Tracks Across the Veldt: Memoirs of a Rhodesia Railwayman, 1950–1976* (Bognor Regis: Woodfield, 2005), p. 47.
110 *Minutes of the 1954 RRWU Conference*, p. 25.
111 TNA: LAB 13/204 1820 Memorial Settlers Association, Requisitions: Southern Rhodesia.
112 Dunn, *Central African Witness*, pp. 175–177.
113 'Work of Guild of Loyal Women for Salisbury's Needy Families', *Rhodesia Herald*, 1 May 1954, p. 3.
114 *Rhodesia Railways Report of the General Manager for the Year Ended 31 March 1957* (Bulawayo: General Manager's Office, 1957), pp. 11–12.
115 *Ibid.* Some 2,781 employees had approached the railways in 1957.
116 'Salisbury No. 1 Branch Notes', *RRR*, June 1954, p. 6; 'The Union's Case Summed up', *RRR*, September 1954, p. 12.
117 'Bulawayo No. 1 Branch Notes', *RRR*, September 1954, p. 15. For more criticisms of leadership and support of firemen's strike, see, 'Choma Branch Notes', *RRR*, October 1954, p. 20; 'Salisbury Branch Notes', *RRR*, June 1954, p. 23; 'Bulawayo No. 4 Branch Notes', *RRR*, June 1954, p. 24.
118 'Que Que Branch Notes', *RRR*, October 1954, p. 22.
119 'The Unions Case Summed Up', *RRR*, October 1954, p. 7.
120 'Que Que Branch Notes', *RRR*, July 1955, p. 22.
121 *Minutes of the 1954 RRWU Conference*, pp. 251–255.
122 *Ibid.*, p. 244.
123 Wright, *Tracks Across the Veldt*, pp. 45–46.
124 Vambe, *Rhodesia to Zimbabwe*, p. 159; Gibbs, *Avalanche in Central Africa*, p. 49.
125 West, *White Tribes*, p. 45.
126 Brian Taylor, interviewed as part of the Rhodesian Forces Oral History Project, http://researchdata.uwe.ac.uk/104/138/roh-oh-tay-br-appr.pdf, p. 16. (accessed 5 November 2019).
127 *Minutes of the 1954 RRWU Conference*, p. 230.
128 *Ibid.*, p. 211.
129 *RRR*, October 1951, p. 3.
130 'Editorial: Our Canteens', *RRR*, March 1952, p. 2.

131 Toothpick, 'Payment on Results', *Rhodesia Herald*, 7 June 1954, p. 5.
132 Contented Citizen, 'Wages on the Railways', *Rhodesia Herald*, 2 June 1954, p. 7.
133 'Mr Todd's Warning on Communism and Federation', *Rhodesia Herald*, 7 June 1954, p. 1.
134 Schwarz, *White Man's World*, p. 398.
135 BRMA: SD16: Strike, Firemen. Letter to Chief Mechanical Engineer, 16 June 1954, no. 368/33, p. 3.
136 Wright, *Tracks Across the Veldt*, pp. 34, p. 87.
137 Mrs E. M. Black, Bulawayo, 'Over to You', *RRM*, March 1954, p. 40. See 'Over to You', February 1954, p. 38; March 1955; October 1955, p. 48, for more examples of complaining of African presence at railway stations. Or from December 1955, p. 62, demands from 'Bulawayo' for apartheid to be implemented across all stations. *Rhodesia Railways Magazine* was launched by the administration in 1952 and replaced the *Railways Bulletin*, which had been in press since 1921 to challenge the monopoly of the *Review*.
138 'Over to You', *RRM*, February 1954, p. 50.
139 TNA: DO 35/4831 Deportation of Charles Taylor: Letter from Keller and Stoney, p. 1; *Debates of the Legislative Assembly* (Southern Rhodesia: Government Printer, 1954), pp. 968–972.
140 *Ibid.*, p. 919.
141 TNA: DO 35/4831 Deportation of Charles Taylor: SECRET: Inward Telegram from High Commissioner of Federation to Commonwealth Relations Office.
142 *Debates of the Legislative Assembly*, 1954, pp. 940–946, 956.
143 Phimister, 'Lashers and Leviathan', pp. 189–191.
144 *Rhodesia Railways Report of the General Manager 1957*, p. 14.
145 Ranger, *Bulawayo Burning*, p. 202.
146 'Bulawayo No. 1 Branch Notes', *RRR*, October 1956, p. 13.
147 'Illegal and Morally Wrong', *RRR*, October 1956, p. 1.
148 Phimister, 'White Miners'.
149 'Strike Scare', *RRM*, September 1961, p. 5.
150 'African Strike', *RRM*, July 1952, p. 28.
151 *RRM*, November 1961, p. 7.
152 'Railways Maintained Full Service During Recent Strike of Africans', *RRM*, November 1956, pp. 23, 52.
153 'Broken Hill: African Workers Strike', *RRM*, July 1952, p. 26.
154 West, *African Middle Class*, pp. 50–51.
155 *Ibid.*
156 *Ibid.*; Dunn, *Central African Witness*, pp. 80, 160–164.
157 Raftopoulos, 'Nationalism and Labour'.
158 West, *African Middle Class*, p. 213.
159 Ian Phimister, 'Rethinking the Reserves: Southern Rhodesia's Land Husbandry Act Reviewed', *JSAS*, 19:2 (1993), 225–239; Stoneman and Cliffe, *Politics, Economics and Society*, p. 21.
160 Raftopoulos, 'Nationalism and Labour', p. 92.
161 See the Law and Order (Maintenance) Act and Emergency Powers Act, both enacted to strengthen the coercive functions of the state.
162 Alexander, 'Hooligans, Spivs and Loafers', p. 349.
163 Ranger, *Bulawayo Burning*, chap. 7.
164 TNA: LAB 13/1533 Committee on Freedom of Association: Case No. 251 Complaint Presented by the World Federation of Trade Unions Against the Government of the United Kingdom in Respect of Southern Rhodesia, p. 38. LAB 13/1533 Department of Labour 1962.
165 *RADAR*, 9:24 December 1960, p. 2.
166 *RADAR*, 10:14 January 1961, p. 2.
167 Interview with Shirley Webb, retired nurse, aged seventy, Harare, May 2015.
168 See Arrighi, 'Political Economy of Rhodesia'; Stoneman and Cliffe, Politics, Economics and Society, p. 18.

169 Anthony Lemon, 'Machinery and Voting Patterns in Rhodesia, 1962–1977', *African Affairs*, 77:309 (1978), p. 520.
170 ICOMM: Rhodesian Front Principles, 1962.
171 See Passmore *et al.*, *Source Book of Parliamentary Elections*.
172 Blake, *History of Rhodesia*, p. 360.
173 'Industrial Conciliation in the Melting Pot, *RRR*, 'July 1951, p. 6. For RRWU hostility to Smith, see 'Editorial', *RRR*, 'July 1951, p. 1.
174 *The Requirements and Supplies of High Level Manpower in Southern Rhodesia, 1961–1970* (Salisbury, Rhodesia: University College of Rhodesia and Nyasaland, 1964), p. 1.
175 Passmore *et al.*, *Source Book of Parliamentary Elections*, p. 170.
176 See debates in South Africa between Apartheid purists and realists, centring on the question of the removal of black labour from the white economy. Deborah Posel, 'The Apartheid Project, 1948–1970', *The Cambridge History of South Africa, Vol II*, ed. Carolyn Hamilton, Bernard K. Mbenga and Robert Ross (Cambridge, UK: Cambridge University Press, 2011), pp. 319–368.
177 'Editorial', *RRR*, September 1965, p. 1.
178 'Zambia as We See It', *RRR*, March 1968, pp. 9, 17.

CHAPTER FIVE

White fights, white flight and the Rhodesian Front, 1962–79

It has long been apparent that those who hold our destinies in their hands do not regard the white manual worker as important. This attitude is not confined to our own industry. It is to be seen in the building trade, in the mines and in various industrial plants. You, who wield a shovel, you, who fashion wood, you, who lay bricks – your daily bread is assured for a little longer, but such modes of occupation are being made untenable for your sons.[1]

Cheap black labour has spoilt them ... Outside southern Africa the majority would be unemployable.[2]

In 1947 Indian independence marked the beginning of the end for the British Empire. Its disintegration was rapid; by the 1960s the United Kingdom had lost formal control over most of its African possessions. Yet as Britain retreated from her former colonies, settler commitment to white supremacist rule strengthened across southern Africa.[3] The RF swept to power in 1962 on the back of promises to uphold segregation, land apportionment, the colour bar and maintain white rule. As Rhodesia made its bid for independence Britain insisted upon constitutional changes that would allow for majority rule. This was obstinately refused and in the face of international pressure and nationalist agitation the RF declared Rhodesian independence in 1965.

International sanctions took effect from 1966 that entrenched Rhodesian illusions of a besieged righteous minority standing against a morally corrupt world. The RF turned to increasingly repressive measures to hold on to power. In response, the two dominant nationalist organisations, ZANU and ZAPU, formed armed wings; initial insurgency tactics comprised largely of guerrilla vanguardism waged from the rural areas in the north of the country.[4] The Federation's language of partnership was jettisoned. Yet the RF did not return to an emphasis on race despite its obvious centrality to the settler state;

[207]

UDI and minority rule was instead couched in language of maintaining 'standards', Christian civilisation and anti-communism.[5]

These platitudes were repeated and internalised; they variously motivated and justified many settlers to take up arms in defence of white rule and to withstand the uncertainty and remain in the country. Rhodesians themselves were not necessarily motivated by an ideological commitment to strict segregation. What bound Rhodesians together, according to Godwin and Hancock, was a desire for a 'pleasant life' and a collective, 'almost infinite capacity for self-deception'.[6] Certainly, Rhodesia's racial and national identity could never rely on white skin to overcome latent ethnic and social divisions. These cracks could only ever be temporarily plastered over by proselytising about an amorphous civilisation that sought to bind a heterogeneous white population against an equally nebulous backward and barbaric other.[7] It was precisely the ambiguity of Rhodesian identity that allowed different social groups to remake it in their own image.[8]

The RF era can broadly be split into two periods. The first is marked by economic buoyancy, increased white immigration and a guerrilla insurgency that failed to fundamentally impede the day-to-day functioning of white society. Yet from 1972 Rhodesia experienced economic downturn, intensification of the war, military conscription, mass emigration and growing pessimism regarding the future of white rule. Simmering under confident assertions of white power and the inevitable ascendency of Western civilisation, a growing doubt took hold regarding the ability of whites to 'stick it out'. White workers and trade unions were aware that their protected positions were under threat. In South Africa the National Party moved away from their white worker support base from the 1960s and embarked on a series of reforms that eroded the socio-economic position of white workers. This shift has generally been used to explain white working-class support for far-right groups, including the Afrikaner Weerstandsbeweging (AWB), who it was believed would restore white class privileges.[9] Yet as Danelle van Zyl-Hermann has shown, both of the major right-wing groups to split from the National Party – the Herstigte Nasionale Party and the Conservative Party – proved unsuccessful in their attempts to court white workers. White workers in South Africa were not automatically incorporated into the hard right and neither did they share a uniform or cogent strategy for combating or accommodating the dismantling of their privileges in the labour arena.[10]

The limited references to white workers in Rhodesia during the 1970s have tended to overstate harmonious relations with the RF and has been dominated by a narrative of white embourgeoisification. Otherwise it has mentioned trade union support for the right-wing

Republican Alliance.[11] While the interests of white workers were for a time secured within the cross-class alliance under the RF, as independence approached in the late 1970s they increasingly felt that it was their privileges that were being used as bargaining chips to protect elite white interests. Certainly the RF years saw increasing class resentment and antagonism among whites. Yet this volatility did not translate to automatic support for political parties to the right of the RF. Instead, these fears contributed to a reworking of white worker identity, which was increasingly articulated in reference to a double-edged notion of poverty; that there was both something transformative and crippling in manual labour and financial struggle. The notion that white workers had built the country and contributed most to the counterinsurgency effort intensified feelings that they had suffered the most to build and protect Rhodesia, only to be abandoned by the white elite.

Certainly, class shaped men's experience of the war as well as their (in)ability to evade conscription. White male workers went to war in order to protect their racial and gender privileges, but their absence from industry while they fought in the bush further destabilised established labour practices and eroded the very colour bar they were attempting to uphold. The white nuclear family, held up as a barometer of progress, civilisation and stability by settler colonial nationalists, disintegrated under the pressures of war. Anxieties of white victimisation flared as majority rule approached; rumours circulated among settlers that white families would suffer gratuitous violence at the hands of African nationalists and that whites were to be ousted from their jobs, homes and social clubs while the country plunged into economic ruin.

The settler state had entrenched a particular type of white masculinity; for many white men the demise of the white state became synonymous with the loss of the racialised and gendered power it had come to embody. This chapter ends with the argument that the complex material and psychological threats presented by majority rule and the increasing disruption to established social hierarchies were experienced as castration anxiety among white male workers.

Job fragmentation and class fissures

The image of a classless society in which every European lounged beside swimming pools waited upon by servants was manufactured by Rhodesian authorities to attract whites to the colony. Yet, even the most ardent defenders of a myth of white homogeneity occasionally slipped into descriptions of the 'undesirable' white areas, the respectable clubs and bars and their less salubrious counterparts. In Salisbury, while middle-class professionals would live in northern suburbs such as Borrowdale and Mount Pleasant with swimming pools and country clubs, the suburbs south of the railway line housed lower-skilled and manual working Europeans. Whites in Cranborne, Hillside and Braeside lived in noticeably smaller houses in close proximity to the Coloured area, Arcadia. Just west of Arcadia along the railway line lay Harare, the African township, followed by the city's major industrial sites, Workington and Southerton, and Lochinvar, a suburb for white railway employees (Figure 19).[12] Even in smaller districts, the spatial dimensions of race and class were readily observable. Peter Godwin remarked of the small company-owned mining town, Mangula, that 'you could determine people's status by altitude alone'. Above the African section at the bottom of the hill came larger houses for white miners and artisans, while the highest altitudes were reserved for professional and managerial whites. This affluent peak was disparagingly known by those who lived below them as 'Snobs' Hill'.[13]

These divisions deepened in the last years of minority rule. Settler rhetoric emphasised loyalty to kith and kin and declarations of being 'more British than the British'. Yet affluent British arrivals were keen to stress their difference from self-proclaimed 'Rhodies'. Amanda Parkyn arrived in 1959 and quickly made friends with well-educated Britons with professional careers in line with her own background. When her brother, Simon, came to visit he 'distinguished between our friends and people he called "Rhodesian", people with the strong accent very like South African, with its echoes of Afrikaans'. Additionally Parkyn highlighted that this dislike emanated from a perception that they were 'less well educated'. Simon described a rugby match between the British Lions and the 'coarse' Rhodesians, 'a very rough lot', who caused six injuries to Lions players. Simon continued: 'I'm afraid I don't like these Rhodesians; they have horrible short haircuts and are very hearty and simple. They all look exactly the same and can be recognised a mile off.'[14]

From the 1960s the Rhodesian state endeavoured to stabilise its power base by encouraging white immigration in what Josiah Brownell has termed a 'war of numbers'.[15] The RF loosened stringent immigration controls and previously 'undesirable' inhabitants entered in larger numbers, which further destabilised the already shaky pretences to cultural uniformity.[16] Snobberies were certainly not erased under a sense of inclusive 'Rhodesianness'. One white woman who lived in Mabelreign described: 'We all thought the railway ... if you worked on the railway. Ach no. They were low class. And especially if you lived "that side" of town. They called it the wrong side of the railway track.' Waterfalls, Cranborne and Hatfield were described as being populated by 'the dregs of society' as well as poor whites who worked on the

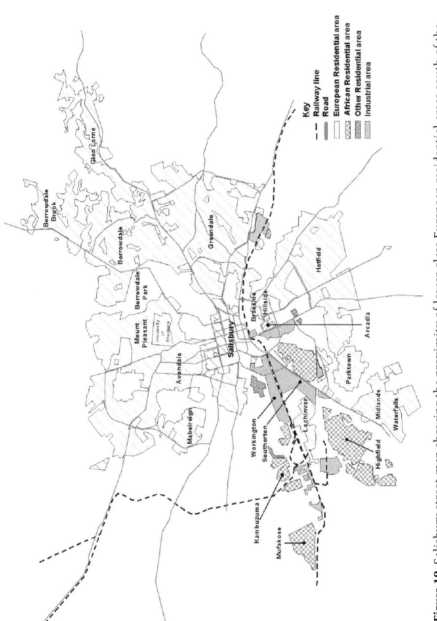

Figure 19 Salisbury street map showing the proximity of lower-class European residential areas south of the railway line to industrial areas and Coloured and African residential areas, c.1974

Key
- – – Railway line
- —— Road
- European Residential area
- African Residential area
- Other Residential area
- Industrial area

Glen Lorne

Borrowdale Brook

Borrowdale

Borrowdale Park

Mount Pleasant

University of Rhodesia

Avondale

Mabelreign

Greendale

Salisbury

Braeside

Hillside

Hatfield

Arcadia

Parktown

Workington

Southerton

Lochinvar

Midlands

Waterfalls

Highfield

Kambuzuma

Mufakose

railways, swept streets or collected rubbish. This woman remarked that many of these types were new immigrants and 'all they could get were those lowly jobs. And they all ended up on the other side of the railway line'.[17]

Divisions of status and skill continued to undermine any white class identity that existed. Increasing pressures upon white workers did not forge unity. The RRWU failed to contain sectional interests and in 1971 a rival organisation of engine drivers, the Railway Association of Locomotive Employees (RALE), emerged.[18] By August 1972 RALE had around eight hundred members and claimed it had come to represent 90 per cent of senior enginemen. The exchanges between RRWU and RALE were particularly bitter, with the latter accusing the former of being dominated by clerical grades who only fought for improvements in their own quarters. The RRWU had incensed RALE by agreeing to railway administration plans for the single manning of diesel locomotives, which also allowed guards to train to become diesel engine drivers.[19] The *Locomotive Express*, a small typed newsletter, sought to uplift the status of enginemen as a central part of the railway workforce and represented a desire to be separated from certain white workers on the railways, particularly the less-skilled clerical grades represented by RRWU. They claimed moral superiority and trumpeted their possession of skilled qualifications. When other sections of the railway staff were taking industrial action and militant activity RALE claimed that ' "working to rule" like strikes, was a system of blackmail resorted to when negotiators representing the employees fail[ed] to make out a case to prove the worth of their demands'.[20] In turn RRWU became increasingly critical of the enginemen, accusing them of being 'well off' and grossly exaggerating their perceived hardships.[21] On the railways at least, increasing pressures appeared to intensify rather than ameliorate existing fissures.

Despite increasing numbers of Africans in skilled trades, in 1969 whites officially made up 80 per cent of skilled manpower. The following year there were an estimated 25,000 skilled black workers employed comprised of 14,000 teachers, 10,000 skilled and semi-skilled industrial workers as well as some health care and public service workers. The Apprenticeship Training and Skilled Manpower Development Act of 1968 stipulated that only those who had completed an apprenticeship or equivalent trade test could be employed in skilled occupations. As apprenticeships were mainly given to whites African progression into skilled trades was frustrated.[22] Progression was highly uneven. In 1965, whereas mining had 76 European apprentices and no Africans, manufacturing industries had 120 European apprentices and six African apprentices.[23] Yet increasing numbers of Africans were receiving the requisite education to enter skilled trades. From 1970 to 1977 a maximum of 32,298 Africans were eligible to be recruited to skilled trades.[24] The percentage of apprenticeships completed by Africans rose dramatically from 2.3 per cent in 1962 to 18.1 per cent in 1975. In 1972 the engineering and motoring industry had reached agreements that allowed parts of the jobs to be performed by less-skilled persons, thus breaking the monopoly of white journeymen.[25] By 1975 the number of black apprentices in building and mechanical engineering outnumbered Europeans.[26]

The low calibre of white employees and growing numbers of skilled, educated Africans became increasingly visible. A number of young white Rhodesians interviewed about the future of the country in 1971 noted with unease the numbers of educated Africans who could not find suitable jobs. One remarked, 'I know someone who hasn't even got O levels and she is supervising an African with his A levels, and this African can't get any other job'.[27] Stanley Nyamfukudza, thrown out of the University of Rhodesia for participating in demonstrations against racism in the 1970s, noted that 'the streets of every town were crawling with young black people, burdened with armfuls of certificates', yet 'no white man, illiterate or otherwise, had any problem finding a supervisory job. It was a wonder that young people still went to school at all'.[28] Neither had multiracial trade unionism led to meaningful improvements. In the late 1970s about a fifth of RRWU members were black. Yet when black engine drivers complained that whites with lower qualifications and less experience were constantly promoted above them, Rhodesia Railways management 'merely reported that no solution had been found – the white drivers had dug in their north British heels'.[29] In 1972, when three junior Europeans had been promoted over more qualified non-European drivers, dissatisfaction came to a head. The RRWU summarily received resignations from ninety-six Coloured, Asian and African workers.[30]

The numbers of African women in wage labour had also dramatically increased by 56 per cent from 1969 to 1975 as employers attempted to reduce their wage bills. By 1975 there were 129,370 African women in primarily low-skilled and low-wage jobs.[31] One 1976 investigation into the potential of utilising African women's labour on a wider scale found that when employers were challenged for not hiring African women in secretarial and clerical work, they variously responded that African women were incompetent, uneducated and lacked initiative. However, many employers maintained that even if educated African women existed they would not 'fit in' with European female staff. Other firms claimed they would not hire African women as they could not provide the correct toilet facilities.[32]

While African women's progression into semi-skilled and skilled work remained severely limited, nursing offered one avenue for educated African women to gain respectable employment. Clement Masakure has shown that in African hospitals, white medical professionals were reliant on African staff to translate Western medicine to African patients and African nursing orderlies and SRNs reported that white nurses encouraged them to perform work outside of their established remit.[33] It appears that a layer of white nurses acknowledged the skill and quality of work performed by their African counterparts and African nurses were sometimes invited to speak at events organised by the white-dominated Rhodesia Nurses Association (RNA). Yet while the RNA may have seen their African counterparts as respectable women and applauded African nurses who had 'made sister grades and higher and of a calibre we can be proud of', they presented themselves as an apolitical force. When Mexico refused to grant visas to Rhodesian nurses to attend the International Congress of Nurses in 1973 the RNA replied that this was an outrage on their profession and claimed that all nurses had no choice but to 'nurse within the social, economic and political structures by which they are circumscribed by time and fate'.[34] The RNA generally embraced the idea that Rhodesia was a benevolent force for good that had dutifully responded to Kipling's call in the 'White Man's Burden' to 'bid the sickness cease'.[35] Moreover, most white nurses failed to extricate themselves from racial thinking endemic in Rhodesian society. In 1977 when an African nurse, Sister Chizarura, was appointed to the position of sister in charge at Dangamvura Polyclinic above her less-qualified white competitor, Sister Geddes, the latter immediately resigned as 'she was not prepared to work under an African'.[36] Formal workplace racial hierarchies remained intact and there is little evidence that respect within medical spaces translated into social mixing outside of them.

The *Report of the Commission into Racial Discrimination* noted that Europeans across the public service but 'particularly in the lower-income groups' were 'reluctant to accept the African either as a colleague on an equal footing or, even more so, as his superior'. Europeans had resigned 'rather than be forced to take orders from a senior African official'.[37] The *Public Service Report* further noted that Europeans would resent interacting with Africans if they were allowed to work in government offices. It was considered that allowing Africans to have access to information on 'personal matters' such as income, tax, customs and immigration, would prove insufferable. Notably, all of these categories allowed Africans greater insight into the social status of white individuals. These files held financial and social shame. Individual prestige would be subject to scrutiny through

[214]

access to bureaucratic files, and Africans would be granted the power to process a European's claim.[38] These positions in the civil service would enable Africans to *know* Europeans; specifically, where individual Europeans stood in the wider social system.

While it is widely appreciated that whites in postcolonial states across Africa have articulated any erosion of privilege as 'reverse racism', much less attention has been paid to how this rhetoric functioned within the settler state. By the 1970s the language of 'reverse racism' was common among white workers who repositioned themselves as victims. Job fragmentation was the medium of this 'discriminatory' agenda in which employers attempted to ease shortages by dividing up one skilled job into several semi-skilled parts, which would allow them to hire Africans on lower wages. The *Granite Review* spoke of the unfair 'job reservation in reverse'.[39] Yet the RRWU argued that they had been unfairly targeted by industrial leaders, and while they had secured 'rate for the job',

> job fragmentation is the evil advocated in Rhodesia today ... the manner in which fragmentation is advocated ... is racial discrimination in reverse ... It causes a further division between black and white in that to make it work, the upper grades must be redesignated into supervisory roles, but with greatly reduced complements, thereby denying promotion and promised advancement, but with greater hate motive.[40]

Job fragmentation was redefined as being *responsible* for racial tensions. The AMWR argued that job fragmentation was a threat to white and black artisans alike and criticised the African TUC of Southern Rhodesia as an 'organisation which encourages the separation of the races in the affairs of trade unions'. In 1972–73 the AMWR had around six thousand European members and one thousand African members. Its white leadership claimed it was 'second to none in this part of the world for looking after mine workers of all races'.[41] In response to such claims Phineas Sithole, president of the African TUC, argued that European artisans, their trade unions and the government policies that appeased them, in resisting what was 'emotionally called "job fragmentation"', had prevented the development of adequate training programmes. Sithole gave an assurance that Africans were not challenging Europeans' place in industry; they would not be replaced by Africans, 'but rather ... should find their place in the redefined technical hierarchy of modern industry'.[42] Such arguments appear remarkably moderate. However, African trade unionists were challenging white workers' self-identification as bearers of modernity. This appeal to modernisation inverted dominant tropes of backward, primordial Africans existing as an inflected mirror image of advanced, technical Europeans. The European worker had now become a barrier to development and relied on emotional appeals rather than economic fact. Sithole pressed for 'modern productive methods' including local training and the division of jobs into semi-skilled components. Craft unionism was an anachronism; the importation of skills may have been suited to the early twentieth century, but now retarded development.[43] This was particularly true of European engine drivers on the railways in their vocal concerns over dieselisation. Despite efforts to modernise the railway system, RALE argued that the ways in which dieselisation was being pushed through in Rhodesia was not about productivity but merely a prelude to undercutting and retrenchment.[44]

White trade unionists hit back at accusations of obstinacy and backwardness. They argued that the problem of shortages was not about Europeans' high expectations, or war and political instability; it was low wages and poor conditions.[45] For RALE, acute shortages were 'deliberately created' by employers. RALE publicised that South African national Sakie Du Beer was refused employment as a fireman on Rhodesia Railways despite having eight years' experience on South African Railways, having passed his drivers exam and being married to a 'Rhodesian girl'. RALE scoffed at the Salisbury recruiting office who had turned down his application because 'he was too tall'. Instead, RALE reasoned, the administration appeared to prefer hiring Africans as stokers and, after a short period, would promote them to enginemen.[46]

Sakie Du Beer was defended as a white man against African incursion. His wife's nationality gave his claim further legitimacy; she was not described as Afrikaner or British, but as a 'Rhodesian'. Luise White has argued that in the late 1960s, 'the workings around Rhodesian citizenship seemed to have become flexible, if not hollow'. By 1967 new immigrants could become Rhodesian citizens within two years.[47] In 1969 the census categories changed and no longer required participants' 'nationality' but their 'citizenship' status, reflecting the RF's desire to turn 'migrants' into 'settlers'.[48] This shift in the way the state defined its population points towards efforts to engineer a more amorphous white Rhodesian identity that could absorb other non-British nationalities. Yet this did not erase inter-European prejudices. In railway communities ethnic enclaves were encouraged through sectional housing patterns that placed different grades and job categories into separate railway housing. Men brought out from Greece or Italy to be shunters would be housed together.[49]

As settler rule came to an end in Angola and Mozambique, Rhodesia experienced an influx of Portuguese migrants, but the RRWU retained its British preference and argued that 'the "non-comprehendo" type … is a hazard in many ways – lowering of job standards, safety factors ignored or oblivious to'.[50] The Portuguese were identified as more likely to take 'lowly jobs' and were derogatorily referred to as 'sea kaffirs' or 'porks' – the latter derived from the cockney rhyming slang 'pork and cheese'.[51] Afrikaners also had a range of derogatory nicknames: *'japies'*, 'hairy-backs' and 'rock spiders'.[52] Some interviewees explicitly identified 'the poor' as Afrikaners as 'they weren't educated and they were really just railway workers or shopkeepers'. Yet many struggled to articulate what it was precisely that made these settlers different from those of British or Rhodesian stock: 'They were definitely not like us. They were white, but I dunno. They were a different culture. They were definitely not like us.'[53]

Nevertheless, non-British whites were always preferred to Africans. Individual Africans who the RRWU thought were undeserving of their positions were named within the *Review* and used as examples of 'discrimination' against the white worker. One Mr Bulle was singled out as he had been hired as a job analysis technician on a contract basis. The RRWU claimed that when they had enquired into why Mr Bulle was given the job, the administration responded that he was hired 'because he was an African', rather than his possession of any suitable qualification. While claiming that 'this in itself is contrary to this organisation's policy, which is non-racial', such actions amounted to harassment of African workers, some of whom were RRWU members.[54] Kafue branch tried to pass a motion removing Africans from the fireman grade due to 'incompatibility'.[55] Even in the face of huge pressure as shortages increased, white workers repeatedly complained that Africans were performing 'white' work.[56]

Despite a growing pool of suitable African candidates, skill shortages intensified. Economic sanctions placed on Rhodesia fostered the expansion of import replacement secondary industry, which experienced a growth rate of 212 per cent from 1966 to 1974 and required ever growing numbers of semi-skilled and skilled staff.[57] Finding eligible whites for the positions proved difficult. Economic expansion in Europe and Rhodesia's status as a pariah state with an ongoing civil war severely impacted upon attempts to attract skilled white recruits.[58] In a drive to attract skilled immigrants, taxes on incomes over £2,000 were reduced in the 1969 budget.[59] The maximum rate of tax was lowered to 40 per cent for single persons at R24,000 and married persons R28,000 to be in effect from the 1970 tax year.[60] While such measures may have been appealing to white men, such tax thresholds on family incomes dissuaded women from taking formal employment. In 1969 34,206 European women were economically active; 33,333 of these listed occupations in either full- or part-time work. This represented 42 per cent of European woman over fifteen years old. In comparison, in the

United Kingdom in 1971 about 55 per cent of women above the age of sixteen were in employment.[61] Despite assurances from the minister of finance that the 1969 tax reforms meant that women should be able to remain in employment after marriage without being penalised through tax rules, women continued to suffer.[62] This was despite warnings in 1969 that some essential services, particularly nursing and teaching, could face a total breakdown if women were continually discouraged from staying in employment upon marriage.[63]

The RNA argued that the tax law was 'one of the greatest deterrents to nurses considering returning to work'.[64] Many nurses continued to fail to enter formal employment after qualifying.[65] In 1970 questionnaires were distributed to nurses with SRN qualifications or equivalent in order to establish the causes of low retention rates across the profession. Most respondents quoted long hours and poor pay and conditions as fundamental problems with staff retention. Some 34 per cent of returned questionnaires were completed by women who had left nursing to take up work in clerical posts, shops, nursery schools and crèches.[66] Some 74 per cent of respondents expressed that, despite rises in wages, nursing pay did not compare favourably with other types of employment, but 94 per cent would consider returning to nursing in a hospital on a forty-hour, five-day week. There was also a significant desire to see married nurses acquire the same rights as their single counterparts. Married women were branded as part-time and felt as though they were forced to accept 'second-class status in respect of leave and promotion conditions'. The RNA pointed to further ways in which the nursing shortage could be overcome: overtime pay, extra allowances for night duty, more pay for more qualified staff as well as crèche centres for night staff with children.[67] However, these failed to materialise.

For the most part, skills shortages in the 1960s did not dramatically change women's role in the economy. Racial labour policies were modified by an elitist, gendered conservatism. Professions that demanded training such as teaching and nursing struggled to project the air of middle-class respectability that many white women coveted.[68] In certain sectors the number of women employed actually decreased. From 1961 to 1969 the number of women employed as shop assistants and in sales decreased from 3,735 to 2,854. The proportion of women to men employed in clerical work was also reduced. Whereas white women accounted for 66.9 per cent of all whites employed in clerical posts in 1961, this dropped to 57.4 per cent in 1969 (Table 4 in Chapter 3). The percentage of women over fifteen who were economically active rose by 2 per cent in eight years. This represents a slowing down of the entrance of women into formal employment. It certainly does not suggest a remarkable change from previous employment patterns (Table 2 in Chapter 1).

Intensification

The resolve of employers to Africanise certain positions hardened as shortages intensified.[69] The rigid five-year apprenticeship was castigated as outdated and there were moves to reduce the number of years an individual had to train before achieving journeyman status. In 1974, Roy Welensky, in contrast to the opinion espoused by his own old union, pointed out that white women had learned skills very quickly during the Second World War and there was no reason why Africans could not take up skills with similar speed. Attempting to fix particular occupations as white was useless, he declared, 'I can remember when every lorry driver had to be white … tell me where do you see white lorry drivers in this country today?'[70] In the same year the president of Bulawayo Chamber of Industries demanded that employers pursue an 'independent economic policy … geared to destroying the established and traditional pressure of the colour bar in commerce and industry'.[71] The *Survey of Engineering Manpower* estimated that Rhodesia had no more than a quarter of the total technicians it needed. Engineers had been fulfilling technicians' duties to keep production moving.[72] Mining companies in Wankie complained that shortages meant essential maintenance work was not being completed.[73] The president of the Chamber of Mines estimated that by 1978 Rhodesia would face a shortfall of 8,500 skilled artisans.[74] The former vice president of the Confederation of Rhodesian Employers noted a 'small but disconcerting commentary' regarding the average age of journeymen; in 1972 almost 22 per cent of artisans were aged fifty years old or above.[75] By 1974 the median age of engineers was 47.5. Older artisans were not being replaced by younger whites.[76]

While white skin could be a source of pride in Rhodesia it also engendered humiliation among those who had failed to secure elevated status. The RRWU lamented that a layer of railwaymen 'are ashamed of their condition as a worker. They all dream of a status in which they would not be called a worker or an employee, but something else. They abhor this status'.[77] Many white workers sought to ascend into the ranks of the middle class, which after all, was promised by the popularised image of a classless Rhodesia. The European youth were noted as disinterested in manual labour, even skilled artisan work. In 1974 a commission into technical education admitted that 'the image of the artisan [needed] to be enhanced in some fashion'.[78] Shortages in the building industry were explained as 'English [is] scarcely spoken on a building site [thus] European apprentices are not attracted to the industry'.[79] The skilled monopoly that white workers had fought so hard to protect was slipping out from underneath them. While white trade unionists posed this as the result of the actions of double-crossing governments, unscrupulous employers and African deception, the reality was that they had failed to create a popular representation of the working white that could attract the requisite number of white men to fulfil these occupations.

By the mid-1970s, as the initial benefits of import substitution waned due to a racially limited market, the Rhodesian economy had entered a crisis of overproduction/accumulation and from 1975 to 1978 Rhodesia experienced an average decline in GDP of 2.3 per cent.[80] South Africa's policy of détente with independent African states and the loss of Mozambique as an ally in 1975 compounded Rhodesia's isolation and reduced the country's ability to evade international sanctions. From 1974 to 1978 manufacturing production fell by 27 per cent and fifty thousand urban private sector jobs were lost.[81] In 1975 the percentage of black apprentices dramatically fell to 14.8 per cent from the 18.1 per cent of the previous year. The minister for labour warned of imminent job losses in unskilled and some semi-skilled trades, but shortages persisted in skilled employment and the apprentice intake rose by 28 per cent from 1974 to 1975.[82] As in previous economic crises, retrenchment affected Africans most severely. On the railways deficits grew while traffic decreased with the closure of the Rhodesian/Mozambique border in 1976. Total staff decreased from 21,248 to 20,708 in 1975–76, and would fall by a further 104 by 1977.[83]

As early as 1975 the *Railways Annual Report* expressed considerable concern over low morale, high turnover and the effect of military commitments upon staff shortages. White workers refused to allow Africans to perform skilled work but also refused to perform increased workloads themselves. The *Chronicle* reported that European workers at the Rhodesian Alloys firm in Gwelo rejected an offer for a shorter working week because reduced hours were offered with the caveat that Africans could be employed as artisans. This was denied by the management who argued that harmonious relationships existed between skilled staff. However they admitted that Europeans without artisan status had been particularly riled by the move.[84] The mining union AMWR likewise struggled over job demarcation and they attempted to prevent moves in which a skilled fitter would be made to perform another artisan's work, such as welding.[85]

Moreover by 1972 the war had entered a new phase. Military call-ups gradually intensified.[86] By 1978 men under the age of thirty-eight could be called for a maximum of 190 days a year, while those aged thirty-eight to forty-nine had a maximum service of ten weeks. The increasing age of those recruited saw sections of the military derogatorily referred to as 'Dad's Army', even though older recruits were kept from the front line.[87] Certainly, the burden fell disproportionately on the young.[88] The shared experience of military service was seen to flatten social distinctions among recruits; military camaraderie forged a reinvigorated sense of Rhodesian manhood. Rhodesian Army recruitment posters cast military service as the apotheosis of masculinity (Figure 20). For the first time some men from rural areas came into contact with 'rough guys, motor bikers and guys who took a lot of drugs'.[89] Yet just as military service offered paths to create a cross-class hypermasculine white identity, the processes of conscription, internal

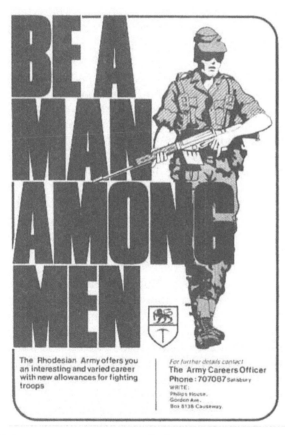

Figure 20 'Be a man among men', Rhodesian Army recruitment poster

hierarchies of rank and evasion of military service simultaneously brought class distinctions into sharp relief.

Attending university offered a route for wealthier middle-class Rhodesians to evade military service.[90] Many lower-class whites who went straight into the forces regarded students as 'draft dodgers'. Simon Krige, who spent his national service in the Rhodesian Army from 1974, remarked that there was a 'good chance' students who returned to Rhodesia during the university vacations would 'get beaten up'.[91] As the manpower shortage intensified deferments for university students were abolished in the late 1970s and whites were recruited directly as they left school. Yet even when university exemptions were removed class hierarchies structured military service. The police had higher entry qualifications and received higher pay. At least six O levels, which was later raised to three A levels, were required and the British South Africa Police (BSAP) had a higher proportion of university graduates than the army. In contrast, white recruits to the Guard Force that patrolled 'protected villages' were referred to as the 'dregs of society' and included those who had been deemed medically unfit for regular service. One white officer rank in this force, the keep commander (KD), 'was considered the lowest of the low and generally referred to in Guard Force jargon as the "Kaffir Dog" after his initials'.[92] It appears that the racial character of the white poor and 'unfit', even those ostensibly fighting for a 'white Rhodesia', was still under question. Money also bought military influence. At least one BSAP recruit secured their place not because of any academic achievement, but because his father was 'the general manager of one of the biggest building societies in the country'.[93] Another former BSAP recruit described the 'huge friction' caused by the ability of businessmen to evade military service as 'those who went to the war zones would be upset about their next-door neighbour who's making a lot of money and never goes into the sharp end'.[94]

Support for the Rhodesian troops also had a class character; one white woman who tried to raise money for the troops observed that the response was generally good, but 'the better dressed they were, the meaner they were [while] the more hard up a person was, the more she or he seemed to want to give'.[95] In turn, lower-class whites were repeatedly blamed for delaying a settlement and extending the conflict. David Caute noted that the Women for Peace, were mostly 'well-off and live[d] in tastefully inconspicuous luxury, quietly despising the poor white artisans in their bungalows who back Ian Smith'.[96]

White workers became increasingly embittered. It was clear to many soldiers that Africans were getting promoted above them in their absence. Employers were reminded that 'our men' were fighting to uphold standards in Rhodesia and that they were doing this in order to secure employment for themselves and their children.[97] One letter to the *Herald* claimed that big businesses were using European military commitments to push through Africanisation:

> A visit to the banks and business houses in the major towns and cities will show that the majority of employees are now young Africans, whose job opportunities are increasing rapidly while the career prospects of the young Europeans are decreasing fast due to continued military commitments ... these facts ... amount to racial discrimination against the white Rhodesians.[98]

Firms who advertised employment for men 'with no or very little call up' were lambasted as 'virtually abandoning [men] committed to their safety'.[99] One RF MP criticised the attitude of many employers towards men with military commitments as a 'national disgrace'.[100] Yet ironically, military service provided employment for those who had lost their jobs due to military commitments. One call-up noted that 'several people including one civil engineer who lost his job and because there's no unemployment pay or anything ... volunteer[ed] to be on permanent call-up so he could live fairly cheaply while he was on service. Although he was not paid very much, it was probably just about enough to meet his mortgage and a few basics'.[101] For some at least, the war that was fought to protect 'white standards' of living brought impoverishment and insecurity. The Apprenticeship authority admitted that 3,000 out of 3,800 apprentices were affected by the continuous call up.[102]

White workers themselves were finding it increasingly difficult to deny the role of Africans in industry. An investigation in 1975 revealed that many white mechanics recognised that without their assistants they would not be able to complete their workloads. One white foreman admitted that electricians got their 'untrained' African assistants to fulfil all of their duties while they were on military leave. Yet the mechanics and foremen interviewed in 1975 stated that under no circumstances would they accept Africans as apprentices.[103] In October 1978 Africans aged eighteen to thirty-five who had completed three years of secondary education or had signed up to complete an apprenticeship were made to register for call-up. Firms were instructed to withhold pay from Africans who failed to register. This was later expanded and any African under sixty who had ever registered for an apprenticeship was liable to be called up for service. Most absconded this 'duty'. As journalist David Caute observed, this measure was aimed at the Africans *'from whom the whites feared competition'*.[104] It was a belated and ultimately ineffective attempt to reassure white workers.

Brutalisation among lower-class recruits was also arguably more common as a result of this class differentiation in military service. As one ex-serviceman noted, the 'apprentices, guys who just lived, working in shops and that. They did six weeks in, six weeks out, six weeks in, six weeks out and they were hardened'.[105] White soldiers interviewed by David Caute candidly explained the violence they inflicted on Africans both in and out of uniform. Paraphrasing the language used by these whites, Caute noted Rod Maddox, a young member of the Rhodesian Light Infantry (RLI), admitted he and his friends 'got pissed, drove to a friend's house in Highlands, had some more beers, then attacked a car driven by a middle-class coon'.[106] Likewise, confrontations between white soldiers and Africans in Nyamfukudza's novel *The Non-Believer's Journey* centre upon lower-class whites and Africans with relative status. In the novel Sam – a teacher in Highfields – catches the attention of a white soldier at a roadblock when he presents his 'slick identity card – a concession made to the more successful or educated Africans'. Incensed, the white soldier attempts to humiliate Sam: 'Good job? Nice pay? ... Come on don't be coy ... I'm sure you make a lot more than I do on this fucking job! How much do you earn? ... This is a really smart one! This is a really clever, smart one and, my foot, is he cheeky! He even speaks good English, agh, it's too much!' The soldier's ire only intensifies as Sam is found to be carrying a relatively large amount of money (for an African). The soldier proceeds to physically assault Sam while yelling, 'Bloody hell man I am going to pull your fucking balls out!'[107] As explored below, the focus on his genitals was not incidental. Struggles to impose a hegemonic masculinity and restore manhood were inflected by class experience and central to the violence and experiences of white and black men in 1970s Rhodesia.

The erosion of the nuclear family

In her research on women and the guerrilla war, Tanya Lyons has demonstrated that both African and white women were prevented from fighting on the front lines, idealised as mothers and instrumentalised as innocent victims of the conflict. While African women had a much greater involvement in the military aspect of war, the RF insisted white women's most important work was providing emotional support to white men.[108] Some white women took on supportive volunteer roles, such as running canteens for Rhodesian troops.[109] Others complained that their efforts were not taken seriously enough and warned that 'enforced inactivity' would erode morale. They argued that it was 'psychologically disastrous for women not to be involved actively' and claimed that white women could benefit the war effort as they were of hardy 'pioneer stock'.[110]

From 1975 the army began to advertise for white women to enrol and the Rhodesian Women's Service was initiated so that women could take over from men stationed at bases to release them into the field.[111] Alison Ruffell, who had left nursing to take up administrative work in the Rhodesian Army in the 1970s, noted that senior-ranking men would open doors for them, although this technically went against protocol, 'and they'd wink at you and things, which is really not very appropriate'. In the context of widespread marital breakdown, the wives of men stationed in the army also 'weren't keen' that female recruits be stationed alongside men.[112] Certainly, Figures 21 and 22 illustrate how

F.A.C. : Forward Air Controller

Figure 21 'Airy up here/FAC'

In the Joint Operation Centre, Miss Junket
– we do EVERYTHING together!

Figure 22 'Joint operation centre'

white women were perceived in the army – as distractions or sexual objects to be harassed. White women's formal participation in the war remained low and by 1977 there were only forty-two white women police officers.[113] The following year seventy white women went on the first police reservists two day training camp for women. They were mainly from farming districts, over thirty years of age and married.[114] In the relative safety of the towns, some white women volunteered for the special police and patrolled suburban areas, although this was done for reasons of morale rather than the effectiveness of their actions.[115]

Despite white women's limited formal involvement in the conflict, the war profoundly disrupted established gender roles. Conscription interrupted interpersonal relationships and put increasing strains on the white nuclear family unit. As the 1970s progressed one out of every four marriages would dissolve; by 1979 this had risen to one in three and Rhodesia attained one of the highest divorce rates in the world. One consultant psychiatrist argued that women were increasingly pressured into 'premature sexual relationship[s]' before men left for duty.[116] At the same time the RF lauded the white family as the heart of Rhodesian society. The Termination of Pregnancy Act of 1976 saw practically no improvement on previous abortion laws and women's primary role was reaffirmed as one of bearing and raising children, although the numbers of abortions performed for white women continued to rise.[117] Many white wives felt acute isolation. Some complained they were excluded from social events and that while they were left at home to look after the children, their husbands carried on partying past midnight at hotels and nightclubs with junior female staff.[118]

Marriage and its breakdown could be a source of pain, enforced dependence and impoverishment. When Peter Godwin arrived in Filibusi, a small, isolated mining town, Ma Whitlock was highlighted to him as having a reputation for attempting to arrange extra-marital liaisons, much to the anger of her husband Jack, an unsuccessful miner. When Godwin asked her, 'Why don't you leave if you hate it so much?' Ma Whitlock replied, 'Leave? Where would I go? And with what? I'm the wrong side of forty and I've got no money of my own. No, Jack's got me trapped here in the bush.'[119] In the *Grass Is Singing* Mary Turner's hopelessness is precipitated by her marriage to the unsuccessful farmer, Dick. Mary marries because of the intense social expectations placed on her as she ages, rather than a desire for love or romantic companionship. Her marriage brings impoverishment, depression and eventually death. Such women appear regularly in the historical record.[120] Trish Pennington, the wife of Bob, a tobacco farmer interviewed by David Caute in the late 1970s, existed in a 'drugged lethargy'. David and Bob found her 'lying unconscious on the living room floor. Matthew, the cookboy bending over her ... gesturing helplessly towards an empty gin bottle'.[121]

For many white women, the marital experiences of Mary Turner, Ma Whitlock or Trish Pennington must have deeply resonated. Many deserted or divorced women complained that their (ex-)husbands had fled and refused to pay maintenance, leaving them destitute or unable to meet the costs of raising children.[122] The Rhodesian state removed children from single white women and placed them into care homes or boarding schools if it was believed that the single parent would be unable to meet the financial costs of supporting a white child.[123]

Single life presented its own problems, particularly for older white women. Many felt they required a male escort when going out to prevent harassment and shame. Finding appropriate white male escorts proved especially difficult for those over forty. One dating service – the Marriage Bureau of Rhodesia – reported that white men in their fifties refused to date women of the same age and preferred women in their thirties. The white men left over, one white women reported, were 'impotent – or nearly so ... it's alarming to see how many alcoholics are in this age group'.[124]

Yet many white women also used this disruption to established gender relationships to carve out their own independence. There were growing appeals for single mothers to come together to help each other with the demands of parenting and to mix socially. At least forty white women met monthly in Salisbury. There was a roster service for babysitting and transport services and the group promoted self-help and education.[125] Conscription had also reshaped the notion of white women's work. One interviewee recalled: 'When we had the Bush War the women in town worked. Because the men had gone and joined the army ... It saw the growth of where they were going and the jobs they got. Even though men weren't gone forever and ever, there were still lots of jobs that women could get that men used to do ... That's when women really worked.'[126]

Articles on women *as workers* and respectable business people also became more prevalent in the Rhodesian press.[127] In interviews, whereas women quoted nursing, teaching, retail, hairdressing and clerical work as acceptable jobs for white women, waitressing, bar work, hotel work and manual labour were still regarded as unthinkable.[128] Yet some younger women transgressed the norms laid out by older generations. Val Sherwall recalled working in an OK Bazaar as a retail assistant during her summer holidays as a young student, until her mother found out, 'horrified' that her daughter would be 'seen working in a place like the OK Bazaars' and forbade further employment.[129] Newcomers, or those who had spent a longer period of time abroad, were also much less likely to hold prejudices against particular types of 'low' work:

> There were quite a few [white women] in the nightclubs and the bars ... but I think people looked down on them. Like they were lowlifes. But there were a few. My cousin was a barmaid, which took us all by surprise ... but because she had been to England for a few years, and that's what she had been doing over there ... she came back and just marched into a bar ... they always expected us to get, not necessarily a degree, to get something when we left school, whether it was secretarial, nursing. They didn't want you to go and work in a bar![130]

Other white women arriving from Britain worked briefly as nannies or housekeepers for relatives without the attendant shame.[131] While established Rhodesian women were more cautious about the types of work appropriate for white women, some newer arrivals disparagingly noted the laziness fostered by Rhodesian society, an over-reliance on servants and a general unwillingness to work.[132]

This was shared by some employers who alleged a lack of commitment and work ethic among their white female staff. An investigation during 1972–73 found that European women in Posts and Telecommunications had twice as many sick days as European men and almost ten times as many as African men, undermining European trade union assertions that white males were inherently more productive than Africans.[133] Jeanne Shoesmith, committee member of the International Council of Women, wrote to the *Herald* pleading for an end to discrimination against married women in employment, but nevertheless asserted that some women work 'simply to keep themselves and their families in luxury'.[134] In reply to Shoesmith, one woman argued that women who worked did so because they were single or their husbands had died. Most white women were unskilled and had little to no qualifications, which, she argued, enabled employers to 'take advantage while claim[ing] all women work for "pin money"'. She demanded courses that would enable white women to acquire qualifications to 'maintain their present lowly status' against the 'claims of male employees' that gender discrimination in wages and conditions were essential as they had large families to provide for.[135] Many white women wrote to the *Herald* to emphasise that they could no longer expect to rely men.[136]

Increasingly panicked by Africanisation and the intermittent absence of white men, some trade unions displayed greater support for white women. The RRWU argued that the position of women on the railways 'sounds like a story of exploitation of cheap labour' and asked, 'Would any of the officers in our administration allow this to happen to any of their wives?' Support for equal pay was articulated as a component part of 'gentlemanly' behaviour. The men of the administration were accused of brutishness through allowing women to work in such degraded conditions. This agitation relied on constructing women workers as possessions of working men. The *Review* reminded its members of its motto 'united we stand', with the addition that '*they belong to us* and they are entitled to our support'.[137]

In 1973 the Committee of Lady Members was formed to deal specifically with the issues faced by women on the railways.[138] White women within the RRWU argued that as they had been 'expected to do the same work as a man' they must be paid the same wage. They added that they had often trained male recruits and corrected the work completed by their male superiors.[139] In a bid to stabilise railway staff, in 1975 white women below the age of sixty were offered the opportunity to be made permanent employees. A married woman, it was noted, 'should no longer be looked upon as occupying a chair awaiting single employees becoming available'. In industry and commerce women were already treated as permanent staff and the railways belatedly acknowledged that they were behind the times by continuing to treat women as transient and part-time additions. Yet most skilled women preferred to work in commerce and industry, which offered higher wages than those on the railways.[140] By 1978 RRWU were arguing for a united pay structure of thirteen pay grades, in effect assuring 'rate for the job', while acknowledging there was a need for a reduction in the wage gap between skilled and unskilled grades.[141] The unified pay structure was agreed upon and came into effect in November 1978, prohibiting discrimination between sexes.[142] However, white and black women across the country would have to wait for independence for the principle of equal pay to be established in law.

White male trade union support for white women was ultimately mediated through conservative gender ideologies and the RRWU reminded their members that they were 'not advocating for the women's lib'.[143] Perhaps as a consequence of the belated support to white women on the railways their participation in the RRWU had remained low. In 1976 150 white women were members of the RRWU, despite the railways employing in excess of seven hundred.[144] Moreover, resistance to women's employment persisted and wives of railwaymen were blamed for taking unnecessary work.[145] That wives of railwaymen, rather than married women more generally, were mentioned indicates that this resistance, at least in part, came from a desire of railwaymen to keep their own wives in the home.

There was also considerable pressure to conform to a particular pristine appearance.[146] White women were accused of not playing their part in relieving demoralisation on the railways by failing in their duties of beautification: 'Any modern suburban scene in the morning can testify to the bleary eyed wives, in rollers and nondescript costume, seeing husbands off to work. No wonder the man has little to boost him on his way.'[147] Women working on the railways were subject to similar scrutiny. The dress of 'our lady members' was noted as causing discontent, although at least one branch scribe took some sympathy with the women: 'Surely if the ladies are neat in appearance and conform to the requirements of modesty and cleanliness, taking into account what they can afford for clothing and cosmetics, what must they do to please some of the gentlemen?'[148] White women were expected to be beautiful for white men. Despite the professed conservatism of Rhodesian society, the Rhodesian press, trade union journals and magazines regularly printed pictures of hypersexualised women for the (white) male gaze. Often accompanied by a crass nationalist message, such images point to how, for white men at least, Rhodesianness was just as much about power over white women's bodies as it was over Africans (Figure 23).

The Rhodesian Front and the 'betrayal' of white workers

In the early 1960s disillusionment with the RF surfaced. Working men had supported the RF in order to maintain 'rate for the job', but in

Figure 23 'Too many weapons are in irresponsible hands'

[231]

the words of one white trade unionist, 'this confidence was misplaced, to say the very least'.[149] John Newington, the RF's MP for Hillcrest, repeatedly asserted the importance of protection of white workers and found support from other MPs including John Glieg and Edward Sutton Pryce, who were all elected in wards populated by lower-class Europeans. They shared the viewpoint of many white workers that the skilled labour shortage was a consequence of the failure of employers to appreciate their skilled workforce.[150] Newington noted an 'alarming' number of 'sub-standard youngsters coming out of European, Coloured and Asian schools'. He estimated at least 25 per cent of whites were 'below average in capacity and ability' and found it increasingly diffi-cult to find employment. Despite assurances from other RF MPs that job opportunities were sufficient, he asked:

> If there is no deterioration in job opportunity, one wonders where all the European women have gone who used to operate the cash desks in the supermarkets, where have all the European barmen gone, the receptionists, many of the telephone operators? Where have all the long-distance European road motor service drivers gone, except on the railways; where have all the building artisans gone?[151]

This image harked back to previous idealisations of a white man's country populated by hardy Europeans fulfilling all levels of employ-ment in society. It was an imagined past that erased the reality of the centrality of African labour, but one that nonetheless engendered the image of a mythical pantheon of pioneering white workers.

While removed from the heyday of the white radicalism, the RRWU nonetheless continued to propagate an image of itself through the lan-guage of class struggle. When retrenchment plans were announced in 1963 the RRWU responded, 'Let the economies and cuts start at the top'.[152] They retained ideas of difference between the 'productive staff', i.e. the grades represented by their union, in contrast to the supervisory and managerial staff who were dismissed as unnecessary addendum to the actual running of the railways.[153] The *Review* continued to print 'songs of the working man'. 'The happy paysheet clerk', written by a clerk in Bulawayo appeared alongside several songs from *Songs of Work and Freedom*, a collection of folk songs from the United States that glorified trade union struggle, class warfare and denounced the inequalities engendered by capitalism.[154] It also continued to carry biographies of leading figures including Herbert Walsh and Davy Payne and their struggles to establish trade unionism in Rhodesia.[155]

This was a sense of class division and an identity rooted in the con-cept of a working man. The fact that the sweeping tide of decolonisa-tion had failed to breach the white minority of Rhodesia was explained with allusions to this identity. Whereas other white settlements had failed, it was the presence of a particular type of white worker, which, in the eyes of one trade unionist, set Rhodesia apart; white workers were foundational to sustained white rule. One letter to the *Review* heralded this proletarian character of the remaining white bastions in Africa:

> My first impression of Rhodesia, after Kenya, was the throbbing vitality of the place. I saw grime-streaked Europeans shovelling coal and building houses, building a nation. I saw men sitting in a bar after a hard day's work with calloused hands and sweat-matted hair. I saw a people confident of the future who were prepared to perform all the tasks that had built a civilisation in the lands of their origin. I saw men who recognised that they could not create by sitting and looking. These people were proud and eager. I soon learned that this was the secret that stamped Rhodesia as different to the other African countries I had known. The white collar and the desk did not constitute the pinnacle of ambition for these Europeans.[156]

The manual labour white men had performed had *built the nation itself*. It was not high statesmen, colonial officials or industrial leaders who were responsible for the emergence of Rhodesia; it was the working man. They saw a country that they had built up in sweat and grime. Their calloused hands were proof of their struggle and sacrifice as well as a physical expression of their difference from the high statesmen and aristocrats of other colonies who had failed to create and maintain spheres of civilisation in Africa. It also fed into growing dissatisfaction and alienation from the 'colonial office' types. Guy van Eeden wrote in *The Crime of Being White* that despite the progress and civilisation bestowed upon Africans by settlers, the 'uppity types' of the colonial office who were described as a pompous mass of inward-looking toffs, frustrated this progress through working against the settlers and 'encouraging the nationalists'.[157] As well as drawing on images of white Rhodesians as an oppressed minority, this also reflected growing pride in relative poverty, a pride in enduring hardship and resourcefulness. It was precisely the idea that they had struggled and built civilisation 'with their hands', as the famous song by Rhodesian folk singer Clem Tholet proclaimed, which imbued a sense of rights and entitlement.[158]

One woman wrote into the *Herald* to stress the hardship whites had faced and recalled how her father, an engineer, had to do the work of 'an unqualified man' while the family lived in 'a small one-bedroomed flat'.[159] White trade unions were keen to stress how this struggle was one that they continued to endure. White poverty was reprehensible and bemoaned but simultaneously valorised. Suffering could be romantic *and* demeaning. RALE complained of being overworked, single men's accommodation was described as 'stone boxes which often do not favourably compare even with the stables provided for horses and it would appear that in some areas these single men are expected to live on grass'.[160] There was particular concern over the impact of rising prices and the effect this was having on the lower grades. In 1974 the RRWU complained that while the media covered recent investigations into the African urban poverty datum line, much less was said about white pensioners, many of whom were 'required to subsist, or barely survive, on pensions lower than those figures shown in the survey'. As Europeans had higher 'basic needs' the RRWU pressed that 'it leaves much to the imagination when one tries to visualise the type of meals these senior citizens are compelled to concoct, brought from the residue of the pension after the other compulsory needs have been met'.[161] Newington reported that in his constituency three male European pensioners had to come out of retirement to take on work to supplement their income. They were trained technical storemen who had been hired at two-thirds what they have been paid previously, which was gradually reduced to one-third before they were ultimately replaced by Africans.[162] What is interesting here is that these were *skilled* men; while it had been accepted that less educated and unskilled Europeans had a certain degree of instability, this signalled an attack on what was thought to be safeguarded employment. These accounts were not only used to highlight how certain individuals had been treated; they functioned as prophetic warnings. Individual tales were allegorical for *all* white workers. These elderly men were figures of vulnerability, first undercut then completely ousted.

In the early 1970s lower-class Europeans in the country were described as being in a state of unrest over wages. Gleig, Sutton-Pryce and Newington made several remarkably anachronistic and uneconomical demands in parliament. Employers were encouraged to pay inflated wages to their white semi-skilled staff.[163] Sutton-Pryce advocated that employers should take it upon themselves to find out whether particular jobs were desired by Europeans and if they were, that they should see to it that a reasonable salary was offered – in essence suggesting employers voluntarily increase their own wage bill.[164] These MPs who argued for protective measures were glibly dismissed by the rest of the party. When Newington denounced incursions into 'European jobs' in parliament he was shut down by the minister of labour who questioned what was meant by 'European jobs', pointing out that this category had shifted over time.[165] Whereas the demarcating lines of 'white work' had always been contested, many in the RF had begun to reject the very concept of a 'white job'.

This was begrudgingly recognised by some trade unionists. In one letter from a regular contributor to the *Review* it was claimed that the 'rate for the job' had failed to hold up the colour bar. He continued that the immigration policy was fundamentally flawed if 'rate for the job' was the only protection for white workers:

> I appreciate that those who possess certain skills are in demand, but what of their future? What of the future of their children? If anything is beyond doubt it is the fact that all our children are potential geniuses, fitted only for higher education and white-collar work. If the opportunity ceases to exist for your son to build a wall and for my son to plaster a ceiling and for Nobby Clark's boy to fire an engine then we may as well pack our bags and take ourselves to some part of the world where this type of work is still considered to be honest and honourable employment.[166]

When occupations became 'black', their respectability and transformative potential was sapped from them. Work could become infected by African hands. There was a tacit recognition that not all whites could secure skilled employment; whites did not have an inherent intelligence or skill that would protect them. The answer, this trade unionist argued, was explicit job reservation for whites. He warned against 'buying that house and building that swimming pool' as they would not be enjoyed by white children. The reference to 'Nobby Clark' – English slang for clerks associated with the richer middle class – warned that even the children of the wealthy would not be spared the humiliation of poverty and unemployment.

The minister of labour pointed out that there were already safeguards put in place for substandard Europeans; those who failed to meet entry requirements for apprenticeships on academic grounds could still be admitted if they were recommended by apprenticeship authority.[167] Yet protection could not be guaranteed under the RF. The unskilled European could not be uplifted.[168] In theory the RF was dedicated to upholding the colour bar.[169] Yet while deploring job fragmentation as 'lowering standards', the minister of labour highlighted the need for flexibility with regards to technological advance and therefore, 'motivations [when applied in] good sense, goodwill and a real concern for the interests of the country as a whole, and not merely their own self-interest' were to be encouraged, while 'motivations inspired by a desire to exploit cheap labour are to be deplored'.[170] The minister stated that if employers and employees 'freely – and I emphasise the word freely – decide on measures which appear to constitute fragmentation, they obviously have argued the matter out without duress or under any pressures and have had domestic reasons for including in their agreements'.[171] White trade unionists protested that they had been coerced into accepting such agreements.

Frustration over the failure of the RF government to secure white workers' standard of living encouraged bouts of militant activity. On 3 August 1964 AEU members in Northern Rhodesia went on strike lasting eleven days, while its two thousand members in Southern Rhodesia worked to rule in support. The AEU demonstrated their importance as the government despaired that 'a comparatively small number of people [could] break the railway system'.[172] The strike cost the railway administration an estimated £700,000.[173] While the South African railway union leant its support by refusing to accept goods consigned to Northern Rhodesia and the African RAWU declared its 'moral support', the RRWU refused to support the AEU.[174] The RRWU belatedly issued a directive for its Northern members to strike from 14 August to prevent the organisation looking ineffective. However, the strike was not unanimously supported among RRWU members. Gwelo defied the executive committee orders to work to rule, which was in any case declared ineffectual by management. This must have been disappointing for the RRWU as the AEU's action a week earlier had caused a severe backlog of goods.[175] While Livingstone branch members felt 'that to have to gone back to work when they did was capitulation in the face of government threats and management non-cooperation', other members resigned from the union because they disagreed with strike action.[176] This reflected the differing pressures upon white workers staffed north of the border, but also an uneven willingness for confrontation.

The RF's traditional power base came from professional, managerial and agricultural groups. Despite polling well among white workers and the fact that the MP for Bellevue, Wally Stuttaford, had been a railwayman before entering politics, only two RF MPs could be considered to be from 'artisan' stock.[177] White workers felt increasingly alienated from the RF. White trade unionists resented interference in their internal workings and increasing powers given to the minister of labour. In 1967 the Railway Industry Act of 1949 was replaced by the Industrial Conciliation Act, which applied to other industries across Rhodesia. The Railways Act allowed for eight representatives from the railways, six from RRWU and two from AEU. However the ICA sought to equalise representation to include the African RAWU, much to the dismay of the white unions.[178] The AEU increasingly protested the national labour policy and argued that successive ICAs had restricted freedom of association and the rights of trade unions. While the government sought to control the funding of unions under the guise of preventing communist infiltration into African unions the AEU claimed that 'in reality the restrictions introduced were equally restrictive to organised European labour and possibly more so'. The policy of the RF, it was claimed, was leading to a future 'with unions as puppets of the State performing according to a predetermined and regimented pattern of behaviour'.[179]

In 1969 railway staff were offered an 8.5 per cent pay rise, which was rejected by all three unions.[180] From 4 November the RRWU worked to rule and placed a ban on overtime from 5 November. When the AEU announced it would take strike action on 14 November the government promulgated the Emergency Powers (Maintenance of Railway Services) Regulations, which prohibited railwaymen from taking strike action. The regulations were only repealed in February 1970.[181] Amendments to the ICA in 1971 attempted to extend the ban on strikes into other industries. The minister of labour was pressured by the white TUC to forego an outright prohibition of strikes, but strikes could still be illegal if the president decided it 'would prejudice the public interest'.[182] In 1973 further proposed changes would give the minister of labour unprecedented control over arbitration, including the power to amend the terms of arbitration awards. In explaining these actions, the minister of labour asserted that while

> the strike weapon was an admirable tool when used to bring unscrupulous employers to their senses ... when used, as it is being used almost daily in many countries of the Western world, to blackmail whole communities into acceptance of the demands of small, perhaps insignificant, sectors of the community, I suggest the right to strike becomes less than a right.[183]

This was a pointed reminder of white workers' subordinate status within the RF and Rhodesian society more broadly.

Nevertheless draconian measures received criticisms from African and white trade unionists alike. Branch scribes of the RRWU decried 'the millstone hung round our necks by legislation ... which restricts our liberty as railwaymen and working men ... [I would] rather talk than strike ... but I object to my right to do so being taken away from me arbitrarily'.[184] In June 1973 the secretary of AEU called 'for a shelving of differences between all trade unions so that a united front could be formed, while the RRWU commented that trade unions were 'virtually in a position where they could not operate'.[185] In the same year the president of RRWU resigned, quoting that government interference in trade unions was 'destroying the instrument which differentiates us from totalitarianism *in whatever form it may take*'.[186] There is an implicit assertion here that Rhodesia, with its staunch anti-communism, was becoming just as authoritarian as communist regimes with state-controlled unions.

Rhodesia was a front-line state surrounded by an ever-growing number of independent African states dominated by political leadership that, at least in rhetoric, subscribed to Marxism–Leninism. It also had to defend itself from ZAPU and ZANU, variously funded by the Soviet Union and China, as well as the more explicitly Marxist ZIPA.[187] Anti-communism had an urgency for Rhodesia within the Cold War context that was far removed from the experiences of, for example, the United Kingdom. Anti-communism thus formed a large part of dominant political rhetoric and justifications for military action. While white trade unions had been consistently anti-communist, they did not shy aware from the language of class and attempted to use the RF's denunciation of communist totalitarianism against the party's own policies.

In 1969 disillusioned trade unionists had broken away from the RF in order to set up the Republican Alliance, which promised to uphold segregation and prevent majority rule. Its principles stated a commitment to pass laws, the rate for the job, 'to protect from cheap labour' and unemployment, to review multiracial trade unions, to oppose job fragmentation and to create white jobs, white social security and separate education for whites and Africans. It was also staunchly anti-communist and opposed to 'political' and wildcat strikes.[188] Despite policies that were aimed to garner lower-class white support the popularity of the Republican Alliance among workers was generally low. In the 1970 general election the Republican Alliance were overwhelmed.[189] While two executive members of AEU were members of the alliance, they received considerable backlash as over eighty lay members of the AEU petitioned that the two men resign from the party.[190]

White labour was never a homogeneous block, and did not respond in a uniform way to the impending changes. Moreover, the RF were not only worried about being outflanked from the right. Newington argued that government policy could have the unintended effect of pushing European workers into multiracial alliances, in which they would be 'forced to side with dissident and anti-government elements'.[191] White workers continued to be treated with suspicion as potentially subversive elements of society in need of conciliation and policing.

Demise of the white male worker

As majority rule swept across the last remaining African states, stories of imminent disaster, railway collisions and destruction of industry in black hands circulated among settlers. Following Mozambican independence, Denis Hills met numerous Portuguese families who 'looked like artisans and farmers' at Jan Smuts airport:

'Mozambique has collapsed and the Europeans are finished', one man told me, drawing a finger across his throat. 'You can't even get salt because when the blacks were told to treat stagnant water with oil to kill the mosquitoes, they poured oil over the salt pans too; and sugar is scarce because labourers don't like bending down to cut the cane at the bottom.' He had a repertoire of such stories.[192]

Reg Penrose, general secretary of RALE, reminded his readers that 'there was at least one accident a day' in Zambia following Africanisation.[193] Railwaymen often used the experiences of their white counterparts in Zambia in assessing their future fortunes. European railwaymen wrote to the *Review* complaining that the ascendancy of Ian Smith had worsened racial tensions between employees north of the Zambezi. At Victoria Falls a white engine driver had been arrested on the accusation of tampering with locomotives on the Zambian side. He was imprisoned for eight days but the European railway men at Wankie protested by refusing to handle traffic to or from Zambia until he was released.[194]

Particularly unnerving to European employees was the new-found confidence of Africans under an independent state. One European railwayman professed that the white workers were entirely apolitical and simply wanted to work but

> two Africans, representing themselves to be officials of UNIP, trespassed on to Club premises and began arguments about racial prejudice in the Club. One member objected to being called 'comrade', and with a mild Anglo-Saxon adjective, told them so. The outcome was an accusation that the European threatened to kill them. Whilst this is entirely false, it could lead on to more trouble and reprisals.[195]

What proved unsettling was the apparent nerve Africans had to enter European social spaces and challenge European behaviour. The United National Independence Party (UNIP) came under heavy criticism, in particular for apparently threatening the African Mine Workers' Union in order to prevent them from taking strike action on the Copperbelt. RRWU accused UNIP politicians of intimidating African trade union leaders and using 'gangs of loafers who threatened to kill anyone who obeyed the decision to strike'.[196]

In these narratives African independence signalled the end of trade unionism and democratic organisations. Accusations of nationalist infiltration were not purely instrumental in order to delegitimise real demands and discontent of African workers. The AMWR was particularly perturbed that over half of the Wankie workforce was comprised of Africans from Northern Rhodesia. At the Wankie Colliery strike in 1964 the AMWR noted women were wearing UNIP badges and that the crowds shouted UNIP slogans. They reported intimidation and violence towards 'ordinary' Africans who wanted to return to work.[197]

Settler anxieties had a mutative quality. Will Jackson and Harry Firth-Jones have explored their shifting bases and multiple expressions in Kenya; during decolonisation anxieties that had previously centred upon the African environment and tropical neurasthenia were transformed into fears of Africans as people.[198] Likewise, Sandra Swart, Danielle Dunbar and Nicky Falkof have variously demonstrated that in South Africa growing fears and panics around demonic activity, satanic worship and white family murder in the late apartheid years reflected deeper anxieties over white hegemony, the loss of political power and pessimism with leading political figures.[199] In Rhodesia, as the numbers of white civilian deaths increased in the late 1970s, horror stories of torture and mutilation at the hands of African nationalists increasingly circulated among settlers. Rhodesian state propaganda publicised the deaths of black and white civilians in gory detail, often with accompanying pictures, with particular emphasis on the mutilation of babies, children, missionaries and women. This focus on innocents, dependants and vulnerable civilians was used to indict African nationalists as inhuman savages and support the contention that the war was being fought to protect Rhodesia from sadistic communists and decidedly *not* about protecting racial privilege.[200]

White men also increasingly saw themselves as targets of African violence. The experiences of Hennie Buitendag, a white miner at Kitwe, who was detained without trial and tortured by Zambian policemen who thought he was a spy, were reported by the *Illustrated Life Rhodesia*. The article detailed how 'his body and private parts were burnt with lighted cigarette ends and matches'. He was then hung him from a tree and swung by his testicles and 'made [to] lie spreadeagled on the floor'.[201] Buitendag's experiences, which involved subordinate sexual positions and genitals, were not an isolated phenomenon. Tales of sexual humiliation and castration at the hands of Africans in newly independent states circulated among Rhodesian men.[202] The actual occurrence of white castration may not have been common, neither did it dominate official Rhodesian propaganda, but its power in rumours, gossip and the settler imagination should not be understated. Settler anxieties over race, gender, sexuality and power that in previous years had been expressed through Black Peril increasingly took the form of a generalised castration anxiety. Black Peril panics had revolved around attempts by white men to enforce racial and gender hierarchies; at their core were appeals to settler authorities to discipline and punish those who threatened white male power. Castration anxiety, on the other hand, was neither a call to action nor an attempt to wield power over black men and white women; its inner workings reflected pessimism over white rule, fears of impotence and the permanent removal of white masculinity.

This anxiety was arguably rooted in fears of revenge from the adult men whom settlers had called 'boys' for decades. From its outset,

Rhodesian settler colonialism unevenly eroded the multiple and shifting bases from which African men exercised authority and defined their manhood, whether rural landholdings, urban cash-earnings, marriage or control over women.[203] In the 1970s guerrilla warfare offered African men one way to reclaim an idealised 'tough' masculinity that Rhodesian settler colonialism had denied.[204] Masculinist language sought to delegitimise and suppress rival nationalist organisations, women, civilians and 'sell-outs', as well as justify the violence directed towards them.[205] Nationalist rhetoric also increasingly disrupted white workers' self-understandings. The ZANU Chimurenga song, 'Hapana Chavo' proclaimed:

Bhizinisi imba yamakavaka
Nezvidhina zveZimbabwe
Zvinobvaka muvhu reZimbabwe
Zvakanywa nemvura reZimbabwe
Munyika inoka yeZimbabwe
Zvichikanywa nemi vatema
Hapana chavo apa.
(Are structures built from Zimbabwean raw materials?
These come from the soil of Zimbabwe
Bricks made using Zimbabwean water
Bricks burnt using Zimbabwean fire
On this very Zimbabwean soil
They are made by you black people
They have no claim to anything.)[206]

This was a loud assertion that it was black labour that made Zimbabwe. Whites had 'no claim to anything'. The foundations of white workers' masculinity, itself constructed through work, claims to productivity and provision for dependants, became increasingly unstable. In one Greek cafe, white railway workers agonised over their futures: 'Our jobs will be given to blacks, the service will collapse like in Zambia, and no one will pay our pensions. Oh, and did you know? – the young white fellow who was kidnapped not long ago on the Beitbridge road was found with his penis stuffed into his mouth.'[207] White workers expressed their fear of losing work in the same breath as vivid depictions of castration. Certainly, majority rule and the loss of 'white work' reflected deeper anxieties around the removal of white male workers' gendered and racial power.

Dick Gledhill's novel *One Commando* is replete with descriptions of white castration. Gledhill had fought in the RLI from the mid-1970s and claims that his novel 'is very much based on fact ... the scenes I have tried to describe ... were not isolated cases. They happened with sickening regularity, on thousands of occasions'. Lieutenant

Colonel Ron Reid-Daly, a former captain of the RLI and founder of the Selous Scouts, lends his authority to the claims of authenticity in the foreword, confirming that the novel 'portrays a very real picture'. *One Commando* repeatedly describes Africans attacking white civilian families in gratuitous detail. In one particularly brutal scene a mother and daughter were raped and the father and son forced to watch before being castrated.[208] Encouraged by 'visions and nightmares' of the murder of his family in Kenya, Ray Hunter travels from Australia to Rhodesia to join the RLI. After successfully completing several missions, Ray becomes part of an operation to kill a particular African commander 'Tarzan'. Tarzan takes sexual gratification in killing and regularly orgasms as he inflicts violence. When Ray finally captures Tarzan, the white soldiers threaten to castrate Tarzan and pull down his pants, revealing his 'surprisingly small balls and penis'.[209] Evil guerrilla fighters in the novel are indicated by this deviant masculinity, acts of homosexuality and paedophilia. There are some 'good' Africans in this novel; but pointedly, multiracial alliances are formed through a shared masculine identity and reinforce colonial stereotyping regarding the warrior manly qualities of the Matabele in contrast to the supposed effeminacy of the Shona. Yet for all its harmful stereotypes and fanciful exaggerations *One Commando* provides insight into the self-perception of many white soldiers as manly womanisers and skilled combatants in contrast to their effeminate enemies, but also plays on underlying fears of emasculation and impotence. Notably, the protagonist Ray is able to retain his hypermasculinity by leaving Rhodesia on the eve of independence.

Despite claims that Rhodesians had the best fighting force in the world, there were considerable concerns over standards. Military service did not necessarily provide an uncomplicated sense of masculinity for all. Sometimes the denial or loss of masculinity generated sympathetic portrayals; Gledhill described 'Piet Grobler [who] had lost a leg and his testicles. He would never make love again. He was nineteen'.[210] Other white recruits were subject to bullying and harassment from more experienced soldiers who saw them as inadequately manly.[211] Figure 24 is taken from a comic book that aimed to raise morale among the troops. Although some of the humour was self-effacing, most was based on dehumanising caricatures of 'terrs' and white women. Here, the focus of this anxiety is an under-trained 'idiot' white youth. Military service was meant to re-enforce masculinity but many failed to meet the particular brand of machismo required for entry into this homosocial camaraderie. As Marc Epprecht has argued, with the militarisation of Rhodesian society, those who failed to meet the standards of hegemonic rough, womanising masculinity, could themselves be targets of violence.[212]

Figure 24 'No, you idiot – I said prick his boil'

Considering the broader context of European marriage breakdown, extra-marital affairs and loss of control over white women and a highly violent and brutal war, it is perhaps unsurprising that these fears were articulated in this way. White masculinity had in part been constructed through asserting control within the white nuclear family. Men who served in the Bush War feared what their wives and girlfriends got up to in their regular absences. One military history notes that from 1976 'a wave of poison pen letters reached the troops, suggesting their wives back home were indulging in orgies'.[213] In (male-authored) novels and memoirs white women's days appeared to consist of frivolous leisure activities and sexual infidelities. David Caute described the typical Rhodesian woman's day: 'Physical exercise ... afterwards, a bath, drinks, a cigarette, an afternoon with the kids, then, maybe, whatever man is not away in the Bush. "How do you expect me to survive on my own for six months?" Exercise is not enough.'[214] White women's independent sexuality was feared and abhorred. Keith Nell's memoirs detail how on a period of leave from the Rhodesian Special Air Service, Nell returned home to find a note left on the table, written by his girl-friend – and intended only for her friend – which described her affair and the man in question's 'pathetically small ... erect winkie'.[215] Later, Nell was angered by another white woman who refused his sexual advances in a bar and thought to himself: 'I wondered who she thought she was to treat me like scum while I spent months at war, risking my life and sleeping on the hard ground to keep her butt safe.'[216]

White women were never universally presented as uncomplicated vulnerable figures, as the literature on Black Peril attests,[217] but during the 1970s a layer of white women came under increasing scrutiny; many were seen as duplicitous, ungrateful for the sacrifices white men had made and were perceived as setting out to explicitly demean and belittle white manhood (Figure 25). Again anger and violence became the recourse of many white men struggling to retain their status and power. Domestic violence rose while brawls and fights between white men became increasingly frequent scenes in bars and social clubs.[218] Drawing on Hannah Arendt's theorisation of the antithetical relation-ship between violence and power – in which one intensifies as the other wanes – Jacqueline Rose has asserted that it is 'masculinity out of control, – masculinity in a panic – that is most likely to turn ugly'.[219] Rather than a demonstration of power, this heightened violence against women and other men is better understood in the context of generalised pessimism over the future of Rhodesia and the white mas-culinity it had embodied; as a desperate grasp of white men attempting to cling on to their diminishing racial and gendered power.

Towards majority rule

In 1976 the RF finally accepted proposals for majority rule within two years. Pressures had reached tipping point. Enthusiasm for the war dwindled as casualty rates rose. White immigration had fallen rap-idly from 1971 and ultimately sounded the death knell for the white skilled monopoly.[220] In 1977 the general manager of Trojan Nickel Mine admitted that the company now preferred to hire African artisans 'because the quality of the whites ... has fallen disastrously'.[221] The following year the chairman of Rio Tinto Rhodesia, a multinational mining corporation, announced that grades that had previously been entirely white were now at least 13 per cent African, but that still more needed to be done.[222]

By 1977 the RF had reneged on all of its founding principles.[223] Majority rule was inevitable. In the same year twelve RF MPs, including Edward Sutton-Pryce, a long-standing critic of RF's treatment of white

F.O.P. : Forfeiture of Pay

Figure 25 'Forfeiture of pay'

workers, split to form the Rhodesian Action Party (RAP). The RAP were grossly dissatisfied with Smith's negotiations towards a settlement with African nationalist organisations, but like the Republican Alliance, failed to command widespread support.

Wage freezes were announced in February 1977 to curb inflation.[224] The RRWU initially accepted the freezes, acknowledging that 'a war is being waged and that it has to be paid for' but emphasised that 'we were given an assurance from Mr. Smith *that the burden would be* shared'.[225] However, the RRWU argued that the civil service, railways and municipal workers were being forced to 'bear the brunt of the burden of deficit'.[226] White class resentment only intensified during the last years of white rule. The rich and the upper echelons of the RF were increasingly accused of buying property abroad and finding illegal ways to smuggle out their own wealth while ordinary whites suffered and were only allowed to leave with $1,000 if they chose to emigrate.[227]

RF ministers promised that there would be 'no Africanisation for the sake of Africanisation'. The minister of commerce and industry proclaimed there would be a place for skilled whites in the country as trainers of Africans.[228] Yet assurances did little to thwart white emigration, which only compounded skilled labour shortages. Africans could be increasingly observed in 'white' jobs and 'white' houses. Richard West observed that by mid-1977 mortgages and credits were available to middle-class blacks but often refused to whites 'whose future was looking increasingly unsure'. Social segregation was becoming less rigid and 'even in Meikles, that former bastion of the ace settlers, [there were] black guests and even a black hotelier rebuking a white barman'.[229] In urban hospitals, overcrowding meant white and black patients were often treated in desegregated wards.[230] Middle-class Africans increasingly purchased property in lower-class white areas. In October 1977 it was announced that Lochinvar, a residential area for white railway employees, was to become multiracial. By January 1978 Sixty-nine families had moved out of the area, most relocating to Waterfalls. Those who moved claimed that they left Lochinvar because of a lack of schools rather than fears of African neighbours.[231] Yet one white women was less candid and remarked that if Africans were allowed to move into white areas they would bring extended families 'who would indulge in such practices as defecating on the lawn'.[232] Not all white families reacted with such distaste. Godwin and Hancock noted that railwaymen in Lochinvar interviewed by a British journalist 'sounded like committed multiracialists'.[233] Exhaustion with the war had seemingly mellowed sections of white Rhodesia. By January 1979 laws outlawing residential segregation were repealed.[234]

One letter printed in the *Herald* argued that while most white workers would put up 'with the hardships of war' they would not suffer the indemnities inflicted by employers who continued to increase workloads but not salaries. The writer claimed that he had applied for fifty jobs in a three-month period and attended six interviews but had got no further in finding a job despite having considerable experience in sales and administration. He argued that he had no choice but emigration: 'I hate to leave this country which I consider home, but there is an old saying that "you get what you pay for".'[235] Another letter demanded compensation for whites who lost their jobs under Africanisation, suggesting eighteen months' salary, or three years' salary for those over forty-five, reflecting a pervasive fear about the future of white pensioners. He further demanded that Europeans should be able to sell their houses to the state at 'reasonable valuation' paid in cash while unemployed Europeans wanting to leave should have their fares paid.[236] Fears surfaced over lower-class whites without capital who might be stranded under an African government without financial assistance. The RF attempted to prevent the Old Age Pensions Repeal Bill that would get rid of the means-tested pensions of Coloureds, Asians and Europeans, which they argued meant that 'impoverished old people will in the future have to go cap in hand to government bureaucrats to ask for what was once theirs by right'.[237] This is an image of deference; it portrayed old pioneers who would have to beg to Africans for their 'rights'. While civil servants and MPs had their pensions guaranteed railwaymen were concerned that they would lose their pensions if they left the country.[238]

Emigrating or 'taking the gap' was motivated by a number of financial, social and psychological reasons. Lower-class whites feared that without protection from colour bars and industrial agreements their standard of living would deteriorate. Many more feared outright replacement in indigenisation policies, a rapid descent into poverty and an inability to secure 'respectable' employment. In Rhodesia unskilled white workers had always benefited from the bargaining strength of their skilled counterparts.[239] Many low-paid Europeans were supported by familial networks that included skilled members, who were now leaving in their droves.[240] White workers also resented that they could no longer act with impunity; one woman lamented the 'poor Afrikaner foreman at Karoi who got the sack just for doing what he'd always done – calling an idle kaffir an idle kaffir'.[241] Others could not stand the idea of living under a black government. Some were determined to stay in Zimbabwe, although this was not necessarily out of a sense of racial equality, despite protestations to the contrary. As one white apprentice based at Shabani Absestos Mine proclaimed, 'I'm not a racialist I'm prepared to work beside a munt or sit in a bar with one or some wog which I can tell you I was prepared to do a few years ago no way', reasoning that if he stayed, 'I can have a car and go fishing ... and have a drink four times a week and still have money in my pocket you try doing that in a pub in the UK'.[242] Yet as optimism over the potential of a continued 'pleasant life' dissipated, whites left in their droves.

Conclusion

A ceasefire was finally called in 1979, by which time 30,000 had died, 275,000 were wounded and 1.5 million refugees had been created by the conflict.[243] The narrative that white workers had built the nation only added to the acridity of white workers' responses to impending independence. As pressure upon white workers mounted, pretensions to multiracialism and a matter of maintaining 'standards' were abandoned in favour of more openly racist and segregationist discourse. Many white workers conflated their own fate with that of 'white civilisation' in its entirety; 'maintaining standards' was synonymous with upholding the colour bar and the gendered division of labour. Yet despite promises to protect these white standards, under the RF the colour bar had become untenable and Africans entered skilled work in ever greater numbers. The state's ideological commitment to the settler family saw continued discrimination against white women's employment. Nevertheless, as the 1970s wore on white women's roles as mothers and housewives were put under increasing stress as shortages intensified and military conscription disrupted daily life. While boundaries over black and white and male and female work shifted over the century, during the 1970s the very concept of 'white work' came under scrutiny.

The relationship of white workers to the RF is best characterised as a volatile cross-class alliance in which workers felt increasingly alienated and 'sold out'. The Lancaster House Agreement afforded protection to white landholders, but white wage labourers felt they had got a raw deal. Despite the twenty safeguarded white seats in the majority rule government and reconciliatory statements made by Mugabe asking whites to stay, fifty to sixty thousand whites left in the first four years of independence.[244] By 1987 the European population had reduced to 110,000 from its peak of 278,000 in 1975.[245] Clutching on to fantasies of white rule some relocated to apartheid South Africa. Others emigrated in the wake of increasing calls for indigenisation. By 2001 64,261 Zimbabwean-born whites were living in South Africa and 28,732 Europeans were counted in the 2012 Zimbabwean census – around a tenth of the population in the 1970s.[246]

Notes

1 'Livingstone No. 1 Branch Notes', *RRR*, October 1964, p. 12.
2 Denis Hills, *Rebel People* (London: George Allen & Unwin, 1978), p. 199.
3 John Darwin, *Britain and Decolonisation: The Retreat from Empire in the Post War World* (Basingstoke: Macmillan, 1988).
4 Michael Evans, 'The Wretched of the Empire: Politics, Ideology and Counterinsurgency in Rhodesia, 1965–80', *Small Wars and Insurgencies*, 18:2 (2007) p. 176.

5 Luise White, *Unpopular Sovereignty: Rhodesian Independence and African Decolonization* (Chicago: Chicago University Press, 2015), p. 29.

6 Godwin and Ian Hancock, *Rhodesians Never Die*, pp. 11, 50.

7 *Ibid.*, pp. 3–8; Joseph Mtisi, Munyaradzi Nyakudya and Teresa Barnes, 'Social and Economic Developments During the UDI Period', in *Becoming Zimbabwe*, pp. 115–140.

8 White, *Unpopular Sovereignty*, p. 29.

9 Johann van Rooyen, *Hard Right: The New White Power in South Africa* (London: I. B. Taurus, 1994), p. 34; David Welsh, 'Right-Wing Terrorism in South Africa', *Terrorism and Political Violence*, 7:1 (1995), p. 251.

10 Danelle van Zyl-Hermann, 'White Workers and South Africa's Democratic Transition, 1977–2011' (unpublished doctoral thesis, University of Cambridge, 2014), pp. 14–15, 78.

11 Mtisi *et al.*, 'UDI Period', p. 137; Godwin and Hancock, *Rhodesians Never Die*, p. 25.

12 P. A. Hardwick, 'Journey-to-Work Patterns in Salisbury, Rhodesia: The Contrast between Africans and Europeans', *Journal of Transport Economics and Policy*, 8:2 (1974), pp. 180–191. Figure 19 has been constructed from synthesising Hardwick's map on p. 181 with a street map of Greater Salisbury, and was completed with considerable assistance from my sister, Lesley.

13 Peter Godwin, *Mukiwa: A White Boy in Africa* (London: Picador, 2007), pp. 185–186.

14 Amanda Parkyn, *Roses Under the Miombo Trees: An English Girl in Rhodesia* (Beauchamp: Matador, 2012), p. 69.

15 Brownell, *Collapse of Rhodesia*.

16 Karin Alexander, 'An Analysis of Elements of White Identity and Ideology Construction in Zimbabwe', in *Zimbabwe: Injustice and Political Reconciliation*, ed. Brian Raftopoulos and T. Savage (Cape Town: Institute for Justice and Reconciliation, 2004), pp. 193–212.

17 Interview with Maureen Moss, retired white woman, Harare, June 2015; Godwin and Hancock, *Rhodesians Never Die*, pp. 29–30.

18 'Plan New Approach: Recognition Sought', *Locomotive Express*, 1, June 1972.

19 Dorothy Davies, *Race Relations in Rhodesia: A Survey for 1972–3* (London: Rex Collings 1975), p. 433.

20 'Plan New Approach: Recognition Sought', *Locomotive Express*, 1, June 1972, p. 2.

21 G. M. de Salis, 'Reply to RALE', *RRR*, July 1974, p. 10.

22 *Survey of Engineering Manpower 1974/5* (Salisbury, Rhodesia: Government Printers, 1976), pp. 16, 24–26.

23 H. W. Roberts, *Education and Training in Rhodesia*, Faculty of Education Occasional Paper No. 5 (Salisbury, Rhodesia: University College of Rhodesia and Nyasaland), p. 19.

24 Colin Stoneman, *Skilled Labour and Future Needs* (Catholic Institute for International Relations, 1978), pp. 11, 21–25.

25 W. F. Duncan, 'Labour Problems in Rhodesia: A Trade Union Viewpoint', *Rhodesian Journal of Economics*, 6:4 (1972), p. 16.

26 Stoneman, *Skilled Labour and Future Needs*, p. 14.

27 'The Voice of Young Rhodesia', *Illustrated Life Rhodesia*, 5 April 1971, pp. 16–17.

28 Stanley Nyamfukudza, *The Non-Believer's Journey* (London: Heinemann, 1980), p. 86.

29 Caute, *Death of White Rhodesia*, pp. 162–163.

30 Davies, *Race Relations in Rhodesia*, p. 430.

31 Duncan Clarke, *Unemployment and Economic Structure in Rhodesia* (Gwelo: Mambo Press, 1977), p. 24.

32 Joan May, *African Women in Urban Employment: Factors influencing their Employment in Zimbabwe* (Gwelo: Mambo Press, 1979), p. 66.

33 Masakure, 'On the Frontline of Caring', pp. 19, 32, 128.

34 'Miss Norton's Farewell', *RNN*, 8:2 (June 1975), p. 17; 'No Visas for Nurses', *RNN*, 6:2 (June 1973), p. 1.

35 Rudyard Kipling, 'The White Man's Burden: The United States and the Philippine Islands', first published in *McClure's Magazine*, 12:4 (1899), pp. 290–291.
36 Interview in Matthew Mataruka, 'History of Mutare African Municipal Workers 1945–1994' (BA Dissertation, University of Zimbabwe, 1995), p. 23.
37 *Report of the Commission of Enquiry into Racial Discrimination* (Salisbury, Rhodesia: Government Printers, 1974), p. 44.
38 *Ibid.*, pp. 35–39.
39 'Fragmentation of the Skilled Trades', *Granite Review*, October 1971, p. 12.
40 'Presidential Address to 1976 Convention', *RRR*, October 1976, pp. 1–4.
41 'Fragmentation', *Granite Review*, October 1971, pp. 4–5, 12; Davies, *Race Relations in Rhodesia*, p. 439.
42 Phineas Sithole, 'Labour Problems in Rhodesia', *Rhodesian Journal of Economics*, 6:4 (1972), pp. 11–12.
43 *Ibid.*, p. 13.
44 See 'Plan New Approach: Recognition Sought', *Locomotive Express*, 1 June 1972.
45 W. F. Duncan, 'Labour Problems in Rhodesia: A Trade Union Viewpoint', *Rhodesian Journal of Economics*, 6:4 (1972), p. 16.
46 *Locomotive Express*, August 1972, pp. 6–8.
47 White, *Unpopular Sovereignty*, p. 118.
48 See Constantine, 'Migrants'.
49 Interview with Barry Bright, white ex-railwayman, Bulawayo, June 2015.
50 'Foreign Labour', *RRR*, October 1975, p. 12.
51 Godwin, *Mukiwa*, p. 152.
52 Paul Moorcroft and Peter McLaughlin, *The Rhodesian War: A Military History* (Barnsley: Pen & Sword Military, 2008).
53 Interview with Moss.
54 'Rate for the Job', *RRR*, July 1965, p. 1.
55 'Editorial', *RRR*, May 1962, p. 1.
56 'Umtali No. 4 Branch Notes', *RRR*, January 1971, p. 16.
57 Mtisi *et al.*, 'UDI Period', p. 132.
58 *Report of the Commission of Enquiry into Racial Discrimination* (Salisbury, Rhodesia: Government Printers, 1974), p. 66.
59 Alec Schattil, 'The Report of the Franzen Commission and the Rhodesian Budget', *Rhodesian Journal of Economics*, 3:4 (1969), pp. 8–14.
60 Duncan, 'Labour Problems', p. 15.
61 Economically active figure includes unemployed, part-time workers and unpaid family workers. Housewives were considered economically inactive. For UK data, see Craig Lindsay and Paul Doyle, 'Experimental Consistent Time Series of Historical Labour Force Survey Data', *Labour Market Trends* (2003), pp. 467–475.
62 'Letter from Mr. Wrathall', *RNN*, 4:2 (June 1971), p. 6.
63 Schattil, 'Franzen Commission', p. 12.
64 'Nursing Staff Shortage Questionnaire', *RNN*, 4:1 (July 1971), pp. 13–14; Law, *Gendering the Settler State*, p. 105.
65 'Editorial', *RNN*, 4:1 (July 1971), p. 1.
66 'Nursing post' included work in doctors and dentists surgeries, private nursing and as health visitors.
67 'Comments and Suggestions', *RNN*, 4:1 (July 1971), p. 17.
68 *Ibid.*, p. 20.
69 'Employers Back Principle of Rate for the Job', *Rhodesia Herald*, 15 May 1974, p. 10; Ken B. Crookes, 'Labour Problems in Rhodesia: An Employer's Viewpoint', *Rhodesian Journal of Economics*, 6:4 (1972), pp. 2–3.
70 'Sir Roy Urges: Train Africans', *Rhodesia Herald*, 29 March 1974, p. 9.
71 'Train More Africans for Top Jobs – Plea', *Rhodesia Herald*, 10 May 1974, p. 3.
72 *Survey of Engineering Manpower*, pp. 16, 24–26.
73 'Colliery Gets Its Artisans', *Rhodesia Herald*, 20 June 1975, p. 15.
74 'Employers Back Principle of Rate for the Job', *Rhodesia Herald*, 15 May 1974, p. 10.

75 Crookes, 'Labour Problems', pp. 1–8.
76 *Survey of Engineering Manpower*, p. 26.
77 *RRR*, December 1978, p. 14.
78 *Report of the Commission of Inquiry into Further Education in the Technical and Commercial Fields* (Salisbury, Rhodesia: Government Printers, 1974), pp. 6–7.
79 Crookes, 'Labour Problems', p. 4.
80 Mlambo, *History of Zimbabwe*, p. 160.
81 Patrick Bond, 'The Rise and Fall of the Rhodesian Economy, 1965–1979: A Marxist Account of Space, Time and the Capital Accumulation Process', African Studies Seminar Paper given at the University of Witwatersrand African Studies Institute, 1993.
82 'Minister Tells Rhodesia to "Face the Fact of Job Losses"', *Rhodesia Herald*, 19 June 1975, p. 7.
83 *Rhodesia Railways Report of the General Manager, 1974–79* (Harare: NRZ, 1979), p. 1.
84 'Moves to Make More Jobs "Resisted"', *Bulawayo Chronicle*, 10 December 1975; 'Report of Statements "Incorrect"', *Bulawayo Chronicle*, 12 December 1975.
85 'Mineworkers Claim Denied by Employers', *Rhodesia Herald*, 15 October 1975, p. 3.
86 *Rhodesia Railways Report of the General Manager 1975*, p. 6; 'Railways Had Deficit of $36m', *Rhodesia Herald*, 7 January 1978, p. 3.
87 Mike Boardman, interviewed as part of the Rhodesian Forces Oral History Project, http://researchdata.uwe.ac.uk/104/178/roh-oh-boa-mi-appr.pdf, p. 27 (accessed 5 November 2019).
88 Hills, Rebel People, p. 201.
89 Simon Krige, interviewed as part of the Rhodesian Forces Oral History Project, http://researchdata.uwe.ac.uk/104/179/roh-oh-kri-si-edit.pdf, p. 5 (accessed 5 November 2019).
90 Godwin and Hancock, *Rhodesians Never Die*, pp. 113–14.
91 Simon Krige, interviewed as part of the Rhodesian Forces Oral History Project, http://researchdata.uwe.ac.uk/104/179/roh-oh-kri-si-edit.pdf, p. 7 (accessed 5 November 2019).
92 H. Ellert, *The Rhodesian Front War: Counter-Insurgency and Guerrilla Warfare, 1962–1980* (Gweru: Mambo Press, 1989), pp. 25–26.
93 Godwin, *Mukiwa*, pp. 207–214.
94 David Lemon, interviewed as part of the Rhodesian Forces Oral History Project, http://researchdata.uwe.ac.uk/104/224/roh-oh-lem-da1-appr.pdf, p. 33 (accessed 5 November 2019).
95 'Condemned! – The Tight Fisted Rhodesians Who Couldn't Care Less About the Boys on the Border', *Illustrated Life Rhodesia*, 12 October 1978, pp. 18–9.
96 Caute, *Death of White Rhodesia*, p. 214.
97 Geraint Jones, interviewed as part of the Rhodesian Forces Oral History Project, http://researchdata.uwe.ac.uk/104/133/roh-oh-jon-ge1-appr.pdf, p. 15 (accessed 5 November 2019).
98 A. A. Black 'Letters: Call up More Africans', *Rhodesia Herald*, 30 April 1977, p. 8.
99 'Disgust at Employers' Attitude', *Rhodesia Herald*, 10 December 1977, p. 8.
100 'Problem Over Jobs Foreseen', *Rhodesia Business Herald*, 16 March 1978, p. 1.
101 Mike Boardman, interviewed as part of the Rhodesian Forces Oral History Project, http://researchdata.uwe.ac.uk/104/178/roh-oh-boa-mi-appr.pdf, p. 24 (accessed 5 November 2019).
102 Godwin and Hancock, *Rhodesians Never Die*, p. 161.
103 M. W. Murphee (ed.), *Education, Race and Employment in Rhodesia, Association of Round Tables in Central Africa and the Centre for Inter-Racial Studies* (Salisbury: University of Rhodesia, 1975), quoted in Stoneman, *Skilled Labour and Future Needs*, p. 12.
104 Caute, *Death of White Rhodesia*, pp. 303–304 (original emphasis).

105 Simon Krige, interviewed as part of the Rhodesian Forces Oral History Project, http://researchdata.uwe.ac.uk/104/179/roh-oh-kri-si-edit.pdf, p. 7 (accessed 5 November 2019).
106 Ibid.
107 Nyamfukudza, The Non-Believer's Journey, p. 34.
108 Tanya Lyons, Guns and Guerilla Girls: Women in the Zimbabwean National Liberation Struggle (Trenton: Africa World Press, 2004), pp. 128–136; Mike Kesby, 'Arenas for Control, Terrains of Gender Contestation: Guerilla Struggle and Counter-Insurgency Warfare in Zimbabwe 1972–1980', JSAS, 22:4 (1996), pp. 561–584.
109 Rhodesia Herald, 19 December 1977, p. 8.
110 'Women – Rhodesia's Unsung Heroines', Rhodesia Herald, 13 January 1978, p. 8.
111 'Women to Serve in Army and Air Force', Rhodesia Herald, 28 June 1975, p. 1.
112 Alison Ruffell, interviewed as part of the Rhodesian Forces Oral History Project, http://researchdata.uwe.ac.uk/104/119/roh-oh-ruf-al-appr.pdf, p. 8 (accessed 5 November 2019).
113 Lyons, Guns and Guerilla Girls, p. 132.
114 'New Beat for Women Reservists', Rhodesia Herald, 28 March 1978, p. 7.
115 Mr and Mrs Medway, interviewed as part of the Rhodesian Forces Oral History Project, http://researchdata.uwe.ac.uk/104/225/roh-oh-med-st-appr.pdf, p. 12 (accessed 5 November 2019).
116 'No Other Life: A Tribute to the Women of Rhodesia', www.youtube.com/watch?v=yACnZz6vtk8 (accessed 28 July 2019); Godwin and Hancock, Rhodesians Never Die, pp. 41, 285.
117 Law, Gendering the Settler State, p. 108.
118 Doris Richard-Smith, 'Let's Cancel all Office Parties', Rhodesia Herald, 6 December 1977, p. 10.
119 Doris Lessing, The Grass Is Singing (London: Heinemann 1973); Godwin, Mukiwa, p. 243.
120 The mother of Daphne Anderson also had a painful and isolating marriage. See Anderson, Toe-Rags, chap. 1.
121 Caute, Death of White Rhodesia, p. 36.
122 Southern Rhodesian Report of the Commission of Enquiry into the Inequalities or Disabilities as Between Men and Women (Salisbury, Rhodesia: Government Printers, 1956), pp. 10–14.
123 See Mhike, 'Sexual Delinquency'. Oral evidence suggests that this practice continued into the 1960s.
124 'Are They Doomed to a Life of Loneliness?', Illustrated Life Rhodesia, 2 October 1974, pp. 11–12.
125 Viv Bradley, 'Singular Problems', Rhodesia Herald, 29 April 1977, p. 10.
126 Interview with Moss.
127 'Heather Silk', Rhodesia Herald, 22 October 1975, p. 8.
128 Interview with Sharon Smith, Chris May and Jackie Wright, white women aged between sixty and ninety, Essex, November 2016.
129 Romola Valmai Sherwell, The Guinea Fowl Girl (Armidale, NSW: Fastnet Books, 2012), p. 113.
130 Interview with Moss.
131 Parkyn, Roses Under the Miombo Trees, p. 4.
132 Ibid., p. 21.
133 'PTC Women Workers' Sickness Problem', Rhodesia Herald, 8 August 1974, p. 7.
134 'Women Must Not Suffer Job Discrimination', Rhodesia Herald, 23 May 1978, p. 6.
135 'Start Lecture Courses for Women', Rhodesia Herald, 30 May 1978, p. 8.
136 'Reaping Rewards of the Emancipation Struggle', Rhodesia Herald, 22 October 1975, p. 5.
137 Sotto Voce, 'Lady Clerks', RRR, February 1976, p. 15 (emphasis added).
138 'Bulawayo No. 2 Branch Notes', RRR, October 1973.

139 *RRR*, April 1974, p. 13.

140 'Umtali No. 4 Branch Notes', *RRR*, March 1974, p. 12.

141 'Unified Conditions of Employment', *RRR*, April 1978, p. 11.

142 'Membership Fees: Females', *RRR*, October 1980, p. 5.

143 Sotto Voce, 'Lady Clerks', *RRR*, February 1976, p. 15.

144 Brian Holleran, 'Railways' Proposals for Lady Employees!', *RRR* October 1976, p. 9; 'Clerical Identification Survey', *RRR*, December 1977, p. 9.

145 Headquarters of the Zimbabwe Amalgamated Railwaymen's Union Bulawayo, *Minutes of the 1973 RRWU Conference* (Bulawayo: RRWU, 1973), p. 6.

146 Godwin and Hancock, *Rhodesians Never Die*, p. 32.

147 Solange Bertrand, 'Wife's Morning Looks can Boost or Bomb', *RRM*, p. 44.

148 'Bulawayo No. 2 Branch Notes', *RRR*, May 1974, p. 12.

149 Fairfax, 'Letters to the Editor', *RRR*, February 1969, p. 13.

150 M. W. Beaton, 'No Racial Restriction in Training', *Rhodesia Herald*, 10 May 1974, p. 14.

151 *Debates of the Legislative Assembly* (Southern Rhodesia: Government Printer, 1973), pp. 1669–1770.

152 'Umtali Branch No. 4', *RRR*, March 1963, p. 32.

153 Headquarters of the Zimbabwe Amalgamated Railwaymen's Union Bulawayo, *Minutes of the 1963 RRWU Conference* (Bulawayo: RRWU, 1963), p. 45.

154 'Songs of the Working Man', *RRR*, September 1962, p. 16.

155 See 'Rhodesian Trade Union History', *RRR*, June 1974, pp. 4–6.

156 Eildon, 'Bulawayo Branch No. 2', *RRR*, December 1968, p. 13.

157 Van Eeden, *Crime of Being White*, pp. 54, 58.

158 Clem Tholet, *With His Hands*, www.youtube.com/watch?v=DVLS8ny0HUU (accessed 27 July 2019).

159 'It Took Determination, Hard Work, Resilience', *Rhodesia Herald*, 16 May 1974, p. 8.

160 *Locomotive Express*, August 1972, pp. 6–8.

161 'President's Notes', *RRR*, November 1974, p. 5.

162 *Debates of the Legislative Assembly* (Southern Rhodesia: Government Printer, 1971), p. 1984.

163 See Duncan Clarke, *The Distribution of Income and Wealth in Rhodesia* (Gweru: Mambo Press, 1977).

164 *Debates of the Legislative Assembly*, 1973, pp. 1669–1770, 1783–1788, 1890.

165 *Debates of the Legislative Assembly*, 1971, pp. 1984, 1899, 2002.

166 Eildon, 'Bulawayo Branch No. 2', *RRR*, December 1968, p. 13.

167 *Debates of the Legislative Assembly*, 1971, pp. 2048, 2061.

168 *Ibid.*, pp. 2028–2029, 2057.

169 ICOMM: *Rhodesian Front Principles and Policies*, 1962, p. 2.

170 Ministry of Labour and Social Welfare, *Governments Policy on Labour* (Salisbury, Rhodesia: Government Printers, 1971), pp. 6–7.

171 *Debates of the Legislative Assembly* (Southern Rhodesia: Government Printer, 1965), pp. 614–615.

172 'Big Tonnages of Goods Pile up From Rail Strike', *Rhodesia Herald*, 6 August 1964, p. 1.

173 'Emergency Action Threat by NR Government Ends Rail Strike', *Rhodesia Herald*, 19 August 1964, p. 1.

174 'AEU Bans Overtime in S. Rhodesia', *Rhodesia Herald*, 5 August 1964, p. 1.

175 'Work to Rule Has No Effect', *Rhodesia Herald*, 18 August 1964, p. 1.

176 Eildon, 'Livingstone Branch Notes', *RRR*, December 1964, p. 15.

177 Godwin and Hancock, *Rhodesians Never Die*, p. 58.

178 'Editorial', *RRR*, June 1967, p. 1.

179 *The AEU of Rhodesia and the Rights of A Free Trade Union* (Bulawayo: Mardon Printers, 1967), pp. 29–30. In 1967 the AEU boasted a paid membership of over 5,000 and claimed to represent the interests of over 24,000 employees in Rhodesia under industrial conciliation laws who worked primarily across the Rhodesia Railways, engineering and motor manufacturing industries, the Rhodesian Iron and Steel Company and the Bulawayo Municipality.

180 Godwin and Hancock, *Rhodesians Never Die*, p. 24.
181 Headquarters of the Zimbabwe Amalgamated Railwaymen's Union Bulawayo, *Minutes of the 1970 RRWU Conference* (Bulawayo: RRWU, 1970), p. 19.
182 Godwin and Hancock, *Rhodesians Never Die*, p. 23.
183 Davies, *Race Relations in Rhodesia*, p. 420.
184 'Salisbury No.1 Branch Notes', *RRR*, October 1974, p. 13.
185 Davies, *Race Relations in Rhodesia*, p. 422.
186 'Valedictory Message from Jim Kinley, Ex-President of the RRWU', *RRR*, October 1973, pp. 3–4 (original emphasis).
187 See Sue Onslow (ed.), *Cold War in Southern Africa: White Power, Black Liberation* (Abingdon: Routedge, 2009).
188 NAZ: GEN-P/REP Republican Alliance, Principles and Policies.
189 In the election the Republican Alliance received the following percentage of the vote in these districts: Bellevue, 10.5; Belvedere, 6.2; Bulawayo North, 5.5; Bulawayo South, 8.6; Gwelo, 12; Jameson, 14.9; Mabelreign, 7.3; Queen's Park, 8.3; Raylton, 4.4; Salisbury Central, 16.9; Salisbury City, 5.3; Selukwe, 10; Umtali West, 2.5; Waterfalls, 11.2.
190 Godwin and Hancock, *Rhodesians Never Die*, p. 324.
191 Davies, *Race Relations in Rhodesia*, p. 424.
192 Hills, *Rebel People*, p. 66.
193 'Attack on Rail Talks', *Bulawayo Chronicle*, 6 November 1972. See also Laura Bear, *Lines of the Nation*, p. 64.
194 Chris Mears, *Goodbye Rhodesia* (Eastborne: Antony Rowe, 2005), p. 135.
195 'Kafue Branch Notes', *RRR*, June 1965, p. 15.
196 'Concern Over Future of Trade Unionism in Northern Rhodesia', *RRR*, September 1962, p. 4.
197 'Wankie Colliery Strike from Monday', *Granite Review*, May 1964, pp. 2–5. See also Phimister and Tembo, 'A Zambian Town'.
198 Will Jackson and Harry Firth-Jones, 'No End to the Trouble: Decolonisation Anxieties and the Evacuation of White Settlers from Kenya, 1963–4', in *States of Anxiety: Affect, Power and Social Lives in Africa*, ed. Andrea Grant and Yolana Pringle (Athens: Ohio University Press, 2020, in press).
199 Danielle Dunbar and Sandra Swart, '"No Less a Foe Than Satan Himself": The Devil, Transition and Moral Panic in White South Africa, 1989–1993', *JSAS*, 38:3 (2012), pp. 601–621; Nicky Falkof, *Satanism and Family Murder in Late Apartheid South Africa: Imagining the end of Whiteness* (Basingstoke: Palgrave Macmillan, 2015).
200 Examples of this propaganda include *The Massacre of Innocents* (Rhodesian Government: Ministry of Information, 1978).
201 'They Jeered as Yhey Strung him Up', *Illustrated Life Rhodesia*, 17 March 1976, pp. 8–9. There is plenty of evidence regarding whites soldiers' use of torture, including sexual violence, as part of counterinsurgency campaigns in Kenya and Rhodesia, see Caute, *Death of White Rhodesia*, p. 139; Ellert, *The Rhodesian Front*; Caroline Elkins, *Britain's Gulag: The Brutal end of Empire in Kenya* (London: Pimlico, 2005).
202 Oral evidence collected in June 2019 suggests that these stories of castration of white men, particularly in independent African states, were not infrequent among white men in Rhodesia.
203 See Mike Kesby, 'Arenas for Control, Terrains of Gender Contestation: Guerrilla Struggle and Counter-Insurgency Warfare in Zimbabwe 1972–1980', *JSAS*, 22:4 (1996), pp. 561–584; Morrell, 'Of Boys and Men'.
204 Jane Parpart, 'Militarized Masculinities, Heroes and Gender Inequality during and after the Nationalist Struggle in Zimbabwe', *NORMA*, 10:3 (2015), pp. 312–325.

205 Jane Parpart, 'Masculinity/ies, Gender and Violence in the Struggle for Zimbabwe', in *Rethinking the Man Question: Sex, Gender and Violence in International Relations*, ed. Jane Parpart and Marysia Zalewski (London: Zed Books, 2008), p. 187.
206 *Songs That Won the Liberation War*, compiled by Alec Pongweni (Harare: College Press, 1982), pp. 11–15.
207 Hills, *Rebel People*, p. 242.
208 Dick Gledhill, *One Commando* (Castletown: RLI Pubishing, 1997), pp. 3, 5, 141.
209 *Ibid.*, pp. 181, 196.
210 *Ibid.*, p. 125.
211 Parpart, 'Masculinity/ies, Gender and Violence', p. 190.
212 Marc Epprecht, 'Black Skin, "Cowboy" Masculinity: A Genealogy of Homophobia in the African Nationalist Movement in Zimbabwe to 1983', *Culture, Health & Sexuality*, 7:3 (2005), pp. 257–258.
213 Moorcroft and McLaughlin, *The Rhodesian War*, p. 130.
214 Caute, *Death of White Rhodesia*, p. 54.
215 Keith Nell, *Viscount Down* (South Africa: Keith Nell, 2011), p. 170.
216 *Ibid.*, p. 280.
217 See, for example, Keegan, 'Gender, Degeneration and Sexual Danger'.
218 Godwin and Hancock, *Rhodesians Never Die*, pp. 41, 285; Gledhill, *One Commando*, p. 76.
219 Jacqueline Rose, 'I Am a Knife', *London Review of Books*, 40:4 (2018), pp. 3–11; Hannah Arendt, *On Violence* (London: Harvest, 1970).
220 In the last seven months of 1972, 10 per cent of RALE members were lost to wastage. *Locomotive Express*, January 1973, p. 7.
221 Caute, *Death of White Rhodesia*, p. 154.
222 'Employing Expatriates Uneconomic – Rickards', *Business Herald*, 25 May 1978, p. 1.
223 Godwin and Hancock, *Rhodesians Never Die*, p. 179.
224 'Wage Restraint Has Helped Minister', *Rhodesia Herald*, 15 March 1978, p. 1; 'Prices and Wages', *Rhodesia Herald*, 18 March 1978, p. 6.
225 'From the General Secretary's Desk', *RRR*, April 1977, p. 2 (original emphasis).
226 'Assistant General Secretary Addresses the Association of Lecturers in Further Education', *RRR*, April 1977, p. 5.
227 Caute, *Death of White Rhodesia*, p. 266.
228 'Gabellah Gives Assurance to Whites', *Rhodesia Herald*, 30 May 1978, p. 1; 'Don't Rush to Bridge the Wage Gap', *Rhodesia Herald*, 18 May 1978, p. 2.
229 West, *White Tribes*, p. 47
230 Parpart, 'Masculinity/ies, Gender and Violence', p. 195.
231 'Getting on with It', *Rhodesia Herald*, 7 January 1978, p. 4; 'Lack of Schools Upsets Lochinvar', *Rhodesia Herald*, 7 January 1978, p. 1; 'Rail Families Moving Out of Lochinvar', *Rhodesia Herald*, 12 January 1978, p. 9.
232 'Great Expectations', *Illustrated Life Rhodesia*, 12 October 1978, pp. 12–13.
233 Godwin and Hancock, *Rhodesians Never Die*, p. 200.
234 Caute, *Death of White Rhodesia*, pp. 225–227.
235 'Disheartened, 'Exodus Due to Policies of Employers', *Rhodesia Herald*, 28 January 1978, p. 6.
236 'Guarantees on European Employment', *Rhodesia Herald*, 6 January 1978, p. 10.
237 'Pensions: RF Battle All But Lost', *Rhodesia Herald*, 6 October 1979, p. 1.
238 'Railmen Are Worried About Pension Payments Externally', *Business Herald*, 18 May 1978, p. 1.
239 Clarke, *Distribution of Income and Wealth*.
240 Caute, *Death of White Rhodesia*, p. 439.
241 *Ibid.*, p. 441.
242 *Ibid.*, pp. 430–431.
243 Evans, 'Wretched of the Empire', p. 176.

244 D. Tevera, and J. Crush, *The New Brain Drain from Zimbabwe*, Migration Policy Series, No. 29 (Cape Town: SAMP, 2013).
245 Alois Mlambo, 'A History of Zimbabwean Migration to 1990', in *Zimbabwe's Exodus: Crisis, Migration, Survival*, ed. Jonathan Crush and Daniel Tevera (Cape Town: SAMP, 2010), p. 63.
246 Jonathan Crush and Daniel Tevera, 'Exiting Zimbabwe', in *Zimbabwe's Exodus*, p. 5; Zimbabwe Census, 2012, p. 22, https://web.archive.org/web/20140901192722/www.zimstat.co.zw/dmdocuments/Census/CensusResults2012/National_Report.pdf (accessed 12 September 2017).

CONCLUSION

Underpinned by the idiosyncratic development of racial capitalism in the territory, Rhodesia established a reputation quite distinct from the aristocratic excesses associated with the white highlands of Kenya or the poor whiteism and Afrikaner nationalism that characterised white South Africa. The Rhodesian state attempted to cultivate an image of the settler colony as the British imperial destination for the aspirant and respectable working man and adventurous, yet subservient and family-orientated woman. During settler rule the image of hardy European farmers imposing promethean mastery over the African environment and transforming supposedly unused land into productive agricultural assets was used to obscure broader settler anxieties about white rule and the inequalities that underpinned European agricultural success. White agriculture formed an important and powerful block in the settler colonial structure; land apportionment and state intervention in white and African farming was hugely important in shaping how the colony developed, the hardships Africans endured and the contentious inequalities that remain today. Land continues to take centre stage on issues of colonial redress and has been successfully instrumentalised by ZANU PF to consolidate its power. Yet, for the most part, Europeans who migrated to Rhodesia settled in urban areas. Many were wage labourers who attempted to secure work with high status and skill or find a position that consisted of the supervision of African workers. The presence of these white workers, their struggles over the racialised division of labour, urban space and influence over the state was essential to the specific historical trajectory of Rhodesian settler colonialism.

White workers saw themselves as the propelling force behind Rhodesia. They depicted themselves as builders of empire whose labour enabled the spread of 'white civilisation'. The RNA commemorated the first trained nurses in Rhodesia by arguing that 'this intrepid band of girls were the real pioneers in geographical, political and economic history'.[1] According to RALE, when George Stephenson drove the first locomotive he had not only brought forth a 'new means of public transport, but he had also brought to birth a new race of men'.[2] This brand of imperial whiteness was rooted in working-class experience. It was made in factories, mining towns and railway communities and profoundly shaped by the transnational movement of workers across empire. Its existence among a considerable layer of settlers had deep implications for the broader racialisation of African society as well as what it meant to be white in Rhodesia.

In writing this book I have tried to show that Marxism is neither inherently deterministic nor is it unable to provide a sophisticated analysis of culture, gender or race.[3] Marxism provides a useful tool in understanding colonial rule precisely because it allows for a conception of race and class as mutually constitutive and inseparable from the historical development of capitalism. Race is not exogenous to class relations but is deeply embedded within capitalist and colonial social structures.[4] Race, as various scholars have shown, is a historically specific ideology that emerged in seventeenth-century capitalist social property relations to justify slavery and colonialism.[5] The capitalist mode of production creates constant differentiation among capitalists and workers; competition and mechanisation produce different profits, wages and labour processes across industries. Race and other ascriptive ideologies naturalise the inequalities produced by this differentiation. Unemployment and the existence of layers of workers surviving on low-skilled, low-wage work becomes explained through reference to innate racial characteristics of particular groups – such as laziness or indolence – rather than a consequence of capitalist accumulation.[6] Ideologies of human difference map race and class together. The undeserving poor and the underclass are in essence *fundamentally racial* categories, just as racial others have overwhelmingly formed the bulk of the most brutally exploited, dispossessed and marginalised classes in the modern world.[7]

Moreover, capitalism produced and reinforced novel forms of social control just as it encouraged the popularisation of new narrow definitions of work. While 'work' can refer to a variety of subsistence and market-orientated activities, as industrial society developed work was increasingly defined as gainful employment that took place outside of the home in exchange for a wage. By the twentieth century other forms of labour, including housework and subsistence agriculture, had fallen outside of the popular definition of 'work'.[8] In Rhodesia, white male workers used this restricted definition of work *specifically as wage labour* to construct their racial and gendered identities and denigrate other types of work performed largely by women and Africans. Racial and gender hierarchies that underpinned the settler colonial structure were replicated in the organisation of the workplace. Settlers laid claim to particular identities by constructing and performing 'white' work, which was contrasted with the work (or its perceived absence) of racialised and gendered others.

Under capitalism, workers are also pitted against one another on the labour market as sellers of their labour power in ways that reproduce and strengthen race. Workers are encouraged to organise on the basis of existing ties (whether gender, race, nationality, skill) to defend themselves against weaker sections of the working class.[9] White British men variously rallied against Africans, non-British whites and women as cheaper sources of labour who threatened to replace or undercut them. Struggles over work were organised on the basis of ascriptive social identities. White workers reinforced, contested and reinterpreted ideologies of race – as well as those of nationality and gender – as they struggled over the boundaries and conditions of 'white male work'.

Work was transformative; it was an arena in which race, class and gender identities were forged, claimed and performed. Yet white work was always a deep source of ambivalence. On the one hand, the very notion of 'white work' offered a means of differentiation from Africans and a source of pride, respectability and racial identity. On the other hand, the struggles over the boundaries of white work meant recognising that many Europeans did not have an innate higher productivity, ability or workmanship than Africans; it signalled that some Europeans could not secure white work without colour bars or protective measures from the state. Lower-class immigrants provoked particular concern over their ability or willingness to act in ways that supported ideologies of racial difference. But elite settlers also feared that lower-class whites were *too racist* in ways that threatened the stability of racial hierarchies. Anxieties also sprung from concern over the presence of racially ambivalent social groups among white workers, whether the physical proximity to non-British whites or doubts over the racial status of some workers who self-identified as white.

The wages of whiteness were double-edged; white skin could be a source of pride and status but also one of shame and dislocation. This humiliation was only deepened by the existence and actions of middle-class Africans and African trade unions who challenged white workers' claims to superiority. Despite white affluence and a racialised occupational structure, not all whites secured unfettered wealth and neither did all white workers attain skilled or supervisory positions in the workplace. As white men increasingly failed to secure a monopoly over skilled work as the century progressed, it is evident that once jobs became 'black', even if employers were willing to hire whites in the position, the respectability and therefore the desirability of the work had been compromised.

Confusion about what constituted white or male work was compounded by imperial flows of labour that both informed and disrupted white workers' ideologies and identities. White workers' identities were shaped by the inevitable tensions resulting from earlier settlers' sense of Britishness being challenged by newcomers, but also by competing ideas over the appropriate role of trade unions and the 'correct' political allegiances of white workers. In the early twentieth century the trade union bureaucracy was considered to be comprised of the most radical and politically engaged section of white workers in contrast to a supposedly apathetic rank and file that lacked political education and in many cases respectability. Yet this was not necessarily accurate across the entire settler period. As the century wore on trade union bureaucracies were regarded as increasingly conservative and a barrier to militant action by sections of white workers.

Particularly from the Second World War white men and women increasingly failed to control the organisation of labour and the types of work in which they were involved. Fears over African incursion were often articulated through the physical and representational contest over space, which included attempts to erase Africans from the pavement, the workplace, the city and the suburbs, as well as social clubs, railway platforms and carriages, hospitals and schools. White workers' desires for African elimination from the labour process was hampered by capital's reliance on cheap African labour in the region, a lack of whites to fulfil all available positions, and their own desires to be waited upon by black domestic servants. Despite periodic attempts to invest menial manual labour with respect and dignity and appeals to create a large class of working-class whites, this remained a collective fantasy.

The attitudes of male-dominated trade unions towards white women's entrance into the labour force were informed by a degree of pragmatism; white women were preferable to Africans and defending the colour bar was more important than maintaining a strict gendered division of labour. White women's employment was tolerated as a necessary measure if it was thought to prevent white families from becoming destitute. In other instances white women's employment was justified through emphasising it as a temporary or extraordinary measure. When white workers' organisations did agitate around women, it reinforced notions of white women's vulnerability, which was contrasted with African men and employers. In turn white male workers constructed a white masculinity that located men as providers and defenders of women from the ravages of capitalism. Yet white women were not passive bearers of gender and racial ideologies. As workers in their own right, but also as wives, mothers, daughters and divorcees, white women were central to white communities and social reproduction. Their status and idealisation as mothers of the race and nation relied upon their acquiescence; upon their acting in ways that reaffirmed existing gender norms. Anxieties and panics emerged when these norms were threatened or transgressed and reflected broader attempts to enforce particular racial and gender hierarchies and, from the 1970s onwards, growing pessimism over the future of white male power.

This book has sought to provide some historical antecedents for current conceptualisations of white victimhood and anxieties around white poverty. In modern Zimbabwe precarious and lower-class whites both readily denounce their *larney* counterparts and attempt to differentiate themselves from the very small number of impoverished whites. Language that links poverty to sexual and racial health continues to be utilised to explain racial degeneration and white destitution. One white man I spoke to in 2015 explained that the handful of white homeless persons in Bulawayo had probably 'always been shagging the blacks'. Other familiar figures of white vulnerability have retained their centrality to the ways in which white identity is represented, particularly the elderly and infirm. These whites are hailed as a failure of postcolonial government, and specifically land upheavals of the early 2000s. In 2009 the British *Telegraph* lamented that

> Fred Noble, a 78-year-old Scot, will return to Fife this weekend, 51 years after he and his wife departed with £100 for what was then Britain's Crown Colony of Southern Rhodesia. He worked for Rhodesia Railways, retiring on a pension with medical aid 13 years ago ... About 1,500 other Zimbabwean pensioners have no foreign citizenship, no family and no means of escape.[10]

These narratives draw heavily upon images of the white 'aristocrats of labour' who 'built civilisation' and made Rhodesia's economy thrive, but who now lie abandoned in a failed pariah state. Such narratives usually divorce contemporary Zimbabwe from its longer history of brutal settler colonialism and privileges the suffering of whites over the mass of black Zimbabweans who have always disproportionately suffered the terror inflicted by the settler and independent state.

Danelle van Zyl-Hermann has highlighted that in South Africa, white working-class discourses of victimisation that were prevalent during the later years of apartheid have found resonance among a wider layer of whites as democratisation removed their 'political *baaskaap*'.[11] Likewise, in his examination of the rise of racism, nationalism, xeno-phobia and neo-fascism, particularly in the decade since the global cap-italist crisis of 2007–08, Paul Gilroy has noted that 'the invocations to whiteness now circulating in Europe are freighted with notions of victimage and vulnerability'.[12] In these narratives immigration, multi-culturalism, affirmative action or basic equality are variously framed as the cause of white distress; from Afriforum and the AWB's fallacious overestimates of white poverty and white squatter camps across South Africa, to former English Defence League leader Tommy Robinson's claims to be standing up for a white working class and protecting vulner-able white women and children, to Donald Trump's self-stylisation as a champion of maligned white blue-collar workers in the United States.

Appeals to reverse racism, a besieged white minority and white impoverishment are often rooted in previous articulations of white identity and power. Yet the effectiveness of racialised class appeals requires the active distortion of histories of oppression and inequality and obfuscation of the role of capitalist social relations in creating and reproducing this differentiation. In attempting to counter such distortions this book has emphasised the active participation of white workers in the ongoing and contested production of race and the insep-arability of race, class, nationalism and capitalism. In doing so it has shown that class division did not erode the potency of racial ideolo-gies, but neither did processes of 'othering' create uncompromised cross-class unity. White workers were *unequal* partners in the white nationalist project; they required constant disciplining. Their conflicts, confrontations and compromises with Africans, the settler elite and international and domestic capital played no small part in shaping the construction and demise of Rhodesian settler colonialism.

Notes

1   '70th Anniversary of the First Rhodesian Trained Nurse', *RNN*, 5:2 (June 1972), p. 7.
2   *Locomotive Express*, 15 October 1971, p. 1
3   Criticism of Marxism gained increasing traction within the context of the fall of the Soviet Union and the rise of postmodern critiques of grand narrative his-tory. For overviews, see Ellen Meiksins Wood, *The Retreat from Class* (London; New York: Verso, 1998); Alex Callinicos, 'Whither Marxism?', *Economic and Political Weekly*, 31:4 (1996), pp. 9–17; Bryan Palmer, *Descent into Discourse: The Reification of Language and the Writing of Social History* (Philadelphia, PA: Temple University Press, 1990).
4   Adolph Reed Jr., 'Marx, Race and Neoliberalism', *New Labour Forum*, 22:1 (2013), pp. 49–57.
5   Eric Williams, *Capitalism and Slavery* (London: Deutsch, 1964); Allen, *Invention*; Karen E. Fields and Barbara J. Fields, *Racecraft: The Soul of Inequality in American Life* (New York; London: Verso, 2012).

CONCLUSION

6 Capitalism produces a 'reserve army of labour' who become racialised. The reserve army of labour here refers to a 'relatively redundant population' who are surplus to the needs of capitalist accumulation being not directly involved in the valorisation of capital. For more on the reserve army of labour, see Karl Marx, *Capital: Volume 1* (London: Penguin Books, 1976), pp. 781–794. For an explanation of how this reserve army becomes racialised, see Charles Post, 'Comments on Roediger's *Class, Race and Marxism*', *Salvage*, 25 October 2017, http://salvage.zone/online-exclusive/comments-on-roedigers-class-race-and-marxism (accessed 20 September 2018).

7 Kenan Malik, *The Meaning of Race: Race, History and Culture in Western Society* (Basingstoke: Macmillan, 1996); John Welshman *Underclass: A History of the Excluded, 1880–2000* (London: Hambledon Continuum, 2006).

8 Andrea Komlosy, *Work: The Last 1000 Years* (London: Verso, 2018), p. 3.

9 The centrality of race to capitalist accumulation is highly contested among Marxists. See David Roediger, *Class, Race and Marxism* (London: Verso, 2017). The best formulations of the relationship of race to capitalist social relations are to be found in Adolph Reed Jr, 'Unravelling the Relation of Race and Class in American politics', *Political Power and Social Theory*, 15 (2002), pp. 265–274; and Charles Post, 'Comments on Roediger's *Class, Race and Marxism*', *Salvage*, 25 October 2017, https://salvage.zone/online-exclusive/comments-on-roedigers-class-race-and-marxism (accessed 27 March 2020).

10 Peta Thornycroft, 'Zimbabwe's Destitute Britons to be Repatriated', *Telegraph*, 28 May 2008, www.telegraph.co.uk/news/worldnews/africaandindianocean/zimbabwe/5394171/Zimbabwes-destitute-Britons-to-be-repatriated.html (accessed 12 September 2018).

11 Danelle van Zyl-Hermann, 'Baas or Klaas? Afrikaner Working-Class Responses to Transformation in South Africa, ca. 1977–2002', *International Labour and Working-Class History*, 86 (2014), pp. 142–158.

12 Paul Gilroy, Holberg Lecture, University of Bergen, 4 June 2019, www.newframe.com/long-read-refusing-race-and-salvaging-the-human/?fbclid=IwAR1fZhvVHs_dklFQdk5pp7MQdf3TFW7pSMO2pduEg6Pe5Ggf3ZNWoR9gFe8 (accessed 17 July 2019).

SELECTED BIBLIOGRAPHY

This bibliography is by no means a complete record of all the works and sources I have consulted. It serves as a convenience for the reader who wishes to pursue further study of the subjects discussed herein.

Primary sources

United Kingdom

The British Library
Institute of Commonwealth Studies
LSE Library
National Archives of the United Kingdom

Zimbabwe

Bulawayo Railway Museum Archives
National Library of Zimbabwe
University of Zimbabwe special collections
Zimbabwe Amalgamated Railwaymen's Union Headquarters, Bulawayo
Zimbabwean National Archives
Zimbabwean Parliamentary Library

South Africa

National Archives of South Africa, Pretoria

Secondary sources

Alexander, Peter, 'Coal, Control and Class Experience in South Africa's Rand Revolt of 1922', *Comparative Studies of South Asia, Africa and the Middle East*, XIX, 1 (1999), pp. 31–45.

Allen, Theodore, *The Invention of the White Race* (London: Verso, 1994).

Barnes, Teresa, *'We Women Worked So Hard': Gender, Urbanisation, and Social Reproduction in Colonial Harare, Zimbabwe, 1930–1956* (Portsmouth, NH: Heinemann, 1999).

Boersema, Jacob and Rory Pilossof, 'Not All Whites Are Farmers: Urban Whites and White Privilege in Post-Colonial Zimbabwe', *Africa*, 87:4 (2017), pp. 702–719.

Caute, David, *Under the Skin: The Death of White Rhodesia* (London: Penguin, 1983).

Godwin, Peter, *Mukiwa: A White Boy in Africa* (London: Picador, 2007).

Godwin, Peter and Ian Hancock, *Rhodesians Never Die: The Impact of War and Political Change on White Rhodesia, 1970–1980* (Harare: Baobab Books, 1995).

Hyslop, Jonathan, 'The Imperial Working Class Makes Itself "White": White Labourism in Britain, Australia, and South Africa Before the First World War', *Journal of Historical Sociology*, 12:4 (1999), pp. 398–421.

Jackson, Will, *Madness and Marginality: The Lives of Kenya's White Insane* (Manchester: Manchester University Press, 2013).

Jeater, Diana, 'No Place for a Woman: Gwelo Town, Southern Rhodesia, 1894–1920', *JSAS*, 26:1 (2000), pp. 29–42.

Kennedy, Dane, *Islands of White: Settler Society and Culture in Kenya and Southern Rhodesia, 1890–1939* (Durham, NC: Duke University Press, 1987).

Kriger, Norma, 'The Zimbabwean War of Liberation: Struggles within the Struggle', *JSAS*, 14:2 (1988), pp. 304–322.

Krikler, Jeremy, *White Rising: The 1922 Insurrection and Racial Killing in South Africa* (Manchester: Manchester University Press, 2005).

Kufakurinani, Ushehwedu, *Elasticity in Domesticity: White Women in Rhodesian Zimbabwe, 1890–1979* (Leiden: Brill: 2018).

Law, Kate, *Gendering the Settler State: White Women, Race, Liberalism and Empire in Rhodesia, 1950–1980* (New York: Routledge, 2016).

Lee, Christopher, *Unreasonable Histories: Nativism, Multiracial Lives, and the Genealogical Imagination in British Africa* (Durham, NC: Duke University Press, 2014).

Lessing, Doris, *Going Home* (London: M. Joseph, 1957).

The Grass Is Singing (London: Heinemann 1973).

Lowry, Donal, 'Rhodesia 1890–1980: The "Lost Dominion"', in *Settlers and Expatriates: Britons Over the Seas*, ed. Robert Bickers (Oxford: Oxford University Press, 2010), pp. 112–149.

Lunn, Jon, *Capital and Labour on the Rhodesian Railway System, 1888–1947* (Basingstoke: Macmillan in Association with St Antony's College, 1997).

McCulloch, Jock, *Black Peril, White Virtue: Sexual Crime in Southern Rhodesia, 1902–1935* (Indiana: Bloomington, 2000).

Masakure, Clement, 'On the Frontline of Caring: A History of African Nurses in Colonial and Postcolonial Zimbabwe, 1940s–1996' (unpublished doctoral thesis, University of Minnesota, 2012).

Mhike, Ivo, 'Intersections of Sexual Delinquency and Sub-Normality: White Female Juvenile Delinquency in Southern Rhodesia, 1930s–c.1950', *Settler Colonial Studies*, 8:4 (2017), pp. 1–19.

Mlambo, Alois, *A History of Zimbabwe* (New York: Cambridge University Press, 2014).

'"Some Are More White Than Others": Racial Chauvinism as a Factor in Rhodesian Immigration Policy, 1890 to 1963', *Zambezia*, 27:2 (2000), pp. 139–160.

Money, Duncan, 'The World of European Labour on the Northern Rhodesian Copperbelt, 1940–1945', *International Review of Social History*, 60:2 (2015), pp. 225–255.

SELECTED BIBLIOGRAPHY

Morrell, Robert (ed.), *White But Poor: Essays on the History of Poor Whites in Southern Africa, 1880–1940* (Pretoria: UNISA, 1992).

Nyamunda, Tinashe, '"More a Cause than a Country": Historiography, UDI and the Crisis of Decolonisation in Rhodesia', *JSAS*, 42:5 (2016), pp. 1005–1019.

Parpart, Jane, 'Militarized Masculinities, Heroes and Gender Inequality during and after the Nationalist Struggle in Zimbabwe', *NORMA*, 10:3 (2015), pp. 312–325.

Phimister, Ian, *An Economic and Social History of Zimbabwe, 1890–1948: Capital Accumulation and Class Struggle* (London: Longman, 1988).
'White Miners in Historical Perspective: Southern Rhodesia, 1890–1953', *JSAS*, 3:2 (1977), pp. 187–206.

Posel, Deborah, 'Whiteness and Power in the South African Civil Service: Paradoxes of the Apartheid State', *JSAS*, 25:1 (1999), pp. 99–119.

Raftopoulos, Brian, 'Nationalism and Labour in Salisbury 1953–1965', *JSAS*, 21:1 (1995), pp. 79–93.

Raftopoulos, Brian and Alois Mlambo (eds) *Becoming Zimbabwe: A History from the Pre-Colonial Period to 2008* (Harare: Weaver Press, 2009).

Raftopoulos, Brian and Ian Phimister, *Keep on Knocking: A History of the Labour Movement in Zimbabwe* (Zimbabwe: Baobab Books, 1997).

Ranger, Terence, *Bulawayo Burning: The Social History of a Southern African City, 1893–1960* (Oxford: James Currey, 2010).

Roediger, David, *The Wages of Whiteness: Race and the Making of the American Working Class* (London: Verso, 2007).

Roos, Neil, 'South African History and Subaltern Historiography: Ideas for a Radical History of White Folk', *International Review of Social History*, 61:1 (2016), pp. 117–150.

Rosenwein, Barbara, 'Worrying About Emotions in History', *American Historical Review*, 107:3 (2002), pp. 821–845.

Shadle, Brett, *The Souls of White Folk: White Settlers in Kenya, 1900s–1920s* (Manchester: Manchester University Press, 2015).

Shutt, Allison K., '"The Natives Are Getting Out of Hand": Legislating Manners, Insolence and Contemptuous Behaviour in Southern Rhodesia, c.1910–1963', *JSAS*, 33:3 (2007), pp. 653–672.

Stoler, Ann Laura, *Carnal Knowledge and Imperial Power: Race and the Intimate in Colonial Rule* (Berkeley: University of California Press, 2010).

Summers, Carol, *From Civilization to Segregation: Social Ideals and Social Control in Southern Rhodesia, 1890–1934* (Athens: Ohio University Press, 1994).

van Onselen, Charles, *Chibaro: African Mine Labour in Southern Rhodesia, 1900–1933* (London: Pluto Press, 1976).

van Zyl-Hermann, Danelle, 'Baas or Klaas? Afrikaner Working-Class Responses to Transformation in South Africa, ca. 1977–2002', *International Labour and Working-Class History*, 86 (2014), pp. 142–158.

SELECTED BIBLIOGRAPHY

Veracini, Lorenzo, *Settler Colonialism: A Theoretical Overview* (Basingstoke: Palgrave Macmillan, 2010).

Vickery, Kenneth P., 'The Rhodesia Railway Strike of 1945, Part One: A Narrative Account', *JSAS*, 24:3 (1998), pp. 545–560.

West, Michael, *The Rise of an African Middle Class: Colonial Zimbabwe, 1898–1965* (Bloomington: Indiana University Press, 2002).

INDEX

Ingram Content Group UK Ltd.
Milton Keynes UK
UKHW021257260623
424058UK00025B/208